AF361483

DIPLOMACY AND DISREGARD

STUDIES IN HUNGARIAN HISTORY

László Borhi, editor

DIPLOMACY AND DISREGARD

The Hungarian Revolution and the United Nations, 1956–1963

András Nagy

Translated by David Robert Evans

INDIANA UNIVERSITY PRESS

This book is a publication of

Indiana University Press
Herman B Wells Library
1320 East 10th Street
Bloomington, Indiana 47405 USA

iupress.org

Translation funded by the László Tetmajer Fund of the
Hungarian Studies Program, Department of Central Eurasian
Studies, Indiana University Bloomington.

For customers in the European Union with safety or GPSR concerns,
please contact Mare Nostrum Group B.V., Mauritskade 21D, 1091 GC
Amsterdam, The Netherlands. Email: gpsr@mare-nostrum.co.uk

First printing 2026

Cataloging information is available from the Library of Congress.

ISBN 978-0-253-07027-2 (hdbk.)
ISBN 978-0-253-07028-9 (pbk.)
ISBN 978-0-253-07030-2 (ebook)

CONTENTS

PREFACE

The events of 1956 in Hungary represented a turning point not only in the Cold War but also for the international institutions, including the United Nations, that were established precisely to manage and limit—if not abolish—global tensions. The thirteen days of the 1956 Hungarian Revolution, with all the hopes, expectations, and tragedy of the country's ultimate suppression, made history—not just during those bright thirteen days but also during the seemingly never-ending decades that would follow them. This was the case not only in Eastern Europe or on the old continent; the events provided a useful lesson for those working on resolving conflict, managing colliding interests, and establishing international cooperation—not to mention those suffering the effects of conflict or disunity.

The events described in this book do not adhere only to the narrative of the 1956 Revolution, although they do build on it; instead, they begin on November 4, 1956, the dawn of the Revolution's suppression. This date represents one of the most dramatic turning points of the Cold War, when it became evident to both the left and right that the erosion of the communist system had begun and was irreversible, even as the empire built on this system was becoming stronger. This book surveys this process not in terms of the internal dynamics of the Soviet bloc but rather through the lens of the spheres of interest that were being redefined at the global level through the UN, the community of nations as re-created just years previously, whose founding principles would be overwritten in de facto, if not de jure, terms by the fate of and world response to the 1956 Revolution. This drama was in essence a continuation of the tragedy of how the Revolution was quelled. Although it has received less attention, it is of no less significance.

I began my study of these events more than a quarter century ago; halfway into this period, I presented my research in my book on Povl Bang-Jensen, in which I reconstructed the fate of the Danish diplomat, one of the key actors in the "Hungarian question" (as UN terminology referred to the 1956 Revolution and its suppression). Bang-Jensen, through not only his actions but also his life and tragic death, revealed contradictions that held significance for not just one fate but many—not least that of the global body itself. At that time, the UN Archives' holdings on the Hungarian Revolution had not been fully opened; by now, they are much more accessible. During my research, I was unable to study the enormous documents collection of Klára Héderváry, one of Bang-Jensen's closest colleagues, which details the process of the UN investigation. Since then, however, I have gained access to this collection. Previously, it was not possible to research the Hungarian secret service documents, which would enable one to construct an entirely new, distinctly inauspicious narrative—regarding not just the UN but, inter alia, the foreign policy of the Revolution or the history of Hungarian emigration, which played such an important role. Earlier, I had no access to one of the most comprehensive document collections, which is in Australia (where the Rapporteur of the UN committee investigating the Hungarian question was from); in large part, this has also become available. Back then, the documents of the Hungarian foreign ministry and the Ministry of the Interior were not available in their entirety. Gaining access to these allowed me to create a highly precise record of the sequence of events and possible scenarios, including those involving the UN actually acting according to its founding principles.

The list of archives and collections of historical documents is a long one. I studied the personal notes in the manuscript archive of Secretary-General of the United Nations Dag Hammarskjöld, I read the documents in the possession of the Bang-Jensen family, and I acquired the notes of the two journalists researching the fate of the Danish diplomat right after his death.[1] Responses to my queries—some of which were rejected—came from diverse places important to this research, like Thailand, New Zealand, and Sri Lanka.[2] These sources are important because this story is indeed a global one.

This book is the summation of many lines of inquiry. It attempts to reconstruct the sequence of events from a variety of perspectives at once, events that no longer tell the "Hungarian" story but rather represent a contribution to the lives of all who, in an increasingly globalizing world, place their trust in international cooperation and solidarity and in the institutions and values that underpin them. We do this even if we have little reason for it. Or is that precisely when trust matters most?

Notes

1. DeWitt Copp and Marshall Peck were collecting material for their book *Betrayal at the UN* immediately after Bang-Jensen's death.

2. The first UN special envoy to deal with the Hungarian question was a Thai diplomat, then a New Zealand diplomat, while one member of the UN Special Committee on the Problem of Hungary was from Ceylon (today Sri Lanka).

ACKNOWLEDGMENTS

D uring my research, I have received an extraordinary amount of assistance from academics, specialists, friends, and institutions. The support I received from Per Bang-Jensen, the son of Danish diplomat Povl Bang-Jensen, has been greatly appreciated. It took the highly dedicated efforts and striking perseverance of Katalin Bogyay, Hungarian Ambassador to the UN, to open up the previously classified documents in the UN Archives; I am very grateful to her for her help. I was able to use the collection of former UN officer Klára Héderváry thanks to the Blinken Open Society Archives in Budapest. My research was supported by the Hungarian 1956 Memorial Committee; while writing my book, I was a senior research fellow of the Institute of Advanced Studies in Kőszeg, Hungary. My investigation has from the outset been assisted by Zsolt Németh, former deputy foreign minister of Hungary, then president of the Foreign Affairs Committee of the Hungarian Parliament.

I would like to express my gratitude to all the experts in this field who have been a constant source of support for my work: László Borhi's attentive interest and perceptive suggestions have been crucial throughout the whole process.

It was exactly when I planned to finalize my manuscript that I received the—since then reclassified—documents from the United States that helped build a picture of the work of the FBI (or lack thereof) relating to Bang-Jensen's case and to the further effect of the 1956 Revolution. I am grateful for the intervention of those at the Hungarian embassy in Washington, DC, without which, almost certainly, I would still be waiting for my request to be considered.

The English translation that forms this present volume was made possible by a grant from the Tetmajer Project of the Department of Central Eurasian Studies at Indiana University.

DIPLOMACY AND DISREGARD

INTRODUCTION

The Historiography of the International Context
of the 1956 Hungarian Revolution

Throughout my research and the process of writing this book, I was able to build on the scholarly achievements of many historians who, from the time the Hungarian Revolution was suppressed, investigated, documented, and researched its international context. Scholars focusing on the founding, organization, and workings of the United Nations and historians of the Cold War proved dependable sources. Historical research concerning the important actors and groups during the time the Hungarian question—the events during and after the 1956 Revolution—was on the UN's agenda (1956–62) also formed the basis of my work. I often had to reach back to earlier times to fully understand what happened after October 1956 and why it happened the way it did. Without the massive amount of historical evidence and analysis provided by scholars working in these fields for several decades, I could not even think of embarking in the direction I did. I am deeply indebted to them.

My research was primarily based on documents previously inaccessible to scholars, and it was both a privilege and responsibility to read and process these for the first time. I learned a great deal from colleagues who were pioneers of the systematic historical research concerning the international context of the Revolution and who presented their results in the larger narrative of the great power struggle between the US and the USSR that determined the atmosphere of the Cold War era. I also based my work on historical studies focusing on related issues, like the role of developing countries after the process of decolonization or the reformist movements inside the post-Stalinist power structure.

I grew up in communist Hungary, where the events that began on October 23, 1956, were officially stigmatized as an anticommunist counterrevolution that the Soviet "comrades" had to suppress, yet in our family, the memory of the Revolution was alive (I was given the middle name of Imre in honor of Imre Nagy, reformist politician and leader of the Revolution). The secret literature of the Revolution—leaflets, newspapers, books—was kept carefully hidden in the shelves of our family library, and my first encounters with the writings of Béla Király, György Heltai, Miklós Molnár, and several others captivated my attention at an early age. These same texts were important to my scholarly research on the international context of the 1956 Hungarian Revolution and my investigation into the tragic history of Danish diplomat Povl Bang-Jensen.

The memories and testimonies of those who remained in Hungary after 1956—such as György Litván, Miklós Vásárhelyi, Árpád Göncz, and many more—were first narrated confidentially to friends after these men served prison terms. Later, the Soros Foundation sponsored a series of interviews with participants in the Revolution who had left Hungary after the Revolution was defeated. This oral history collection provided important details that I later used for my research.

In 1989, an explosion of suppressed memories of 1956 created a new environment for historical scholarship. After the political changes that led to the Wall coming down and democracy being reestablished in Hungary, the memory of the 1956 Revolution became the point of reference for the new political leadership. The events of the Revolution, slandered by the communist propaganda of previous years, were reclaimed in light of recollections and documents that had been banned for thirty-three years. These memories now overwhelmed public spaces. Previously inaccessible documents from the files of organizations such as the Hungarian Socialist Workers' Party leadership and state security services, among others, were published and made available to researchers. In 1992, Russian president Boris Yeltsin handed over to Hungarian president Árpád Göncz crucial documents from formerly classified Soviet archives that provided a dramatic behind-the-scenes narrative of the events. Files from the KGB and Soviet Army commanders were also of extreme importance concerning the history of the Revolution and its aftermath.[1]

Publications of documents annotated and analyzed by scholars greatly assisted my research regarding the foreign policy of those countries that determined the fate of the Hungarian Revolution on the global scene. Files and documents from the British Foreign Office, the French Ministry of Foreign Affairs, and the US Department of State were extremely important, as was access to the archives of India and the former Yugoslavia—both countries were involved in Hungarian foreign (sometimes even internal) politics after 1956.[2] The documents held by several countries dealing with the "Hungarian question" at the UN were unpublished—including Denmark, Ceylon (Sri Lanka), Australia, Tunisia, and Uruguay. Each of these countries had been represented by a member of the UN Special Committee on the Problem of Hungary, and I needed to request access to conduct research and consult documents from their archives. After the report of the Special Committee was published in 1957, the "Hungarian question" at the UN was designated to the Special Representatives nominated by the UN General Assembly. New Zealand and Thailand provided two such Special Representatives. I relied on archival documents of these Special Representatives made available by historians who had previously conducted research on their records. I am grateful to these scholars for sharing those documents and their results, which were highly relevant to my work.[3]

The foreign policy of the 1956 Revolution has been analyzed at various times by György Litván, Charles Gati, and Johanna Granville.[4] The role of the UN in these events was elaborated first by Béla Király[5] and then by Csaba Békés, who, with Gusztáv D. Kecskés, published several relevant UN documents, including a chronology of events, a bibliography, and a biography of participants. Kecskés later focused on the activity of the International Committee of the Red Cross. The IRC had strong links to the UN, and the two organizations worked together to solve the humanitarian crisis both inside Hungary and outside its borders, assisting the refugees who left the country after the Revolution was suppressed.[6]

Great power dynamics were the primary determinant of the international context of the 1956 Hungarian Revolution; therefore, in addition to considering Moscow's agenda, the responses of Washington had to be analyzed and interpreted. László Borhi's thorough and systematic research revealed many aspects of US policymaking before, during, and after the Revolution that eventually led to secret negotiations between Hungary and the US. In 1962 these negotiations finally led to the removal of the

Hungarian question from the UN agenda in exchange for granting partial amnesty to the imprisoned revolutionaries.[7] Magdolna Baráth's research on Soviet-Hungarian relations and her publications concerning the Hungarian diplomatic corps were also fundamental to my research.[8] Mark Kramer's reconstruction of the Cold War atmosphere was helpful, as were publications that included analysis and documents of major importance focusing on the Cold War.[9]

My research also relied on monographs on those who played key roles in the events leading to the Hungarian Revolution, notably János M. Rainer's book *Imre Nagy*[10] and biographies of Dag Hammarskjöld, Ralph Bunche, Henry Cabot Lodge, and others. I also consulted the memoirs of significant personalities such as Soviet diplomat Arkady Shevchenko, the highest-ranking personality who defected to the West in 1978 after being the Under-Secretary-General of the UN, and Charles Bohlen, an American diplomat and expert on the Soviet Union who served as ambassador in Moscow from 1953 through 1957.[11] All of these works served as guides and often as methodological manuals for my research as I attempted to understand and interpret everything that happened—and did not happen—with respect to Hungary during and after 1956, in the UN and elsewhere.

The Composition of the Book

The narrative of this book follows a chronological order, focusing on the UN's responses to the events unfolding in Hungary from the outbreak of the Revolution through the course of its suppression and finally to the terror and revenge that followed. While I do not provide a detailed account of the historical moments of October–November 1956, I elaborate on their resonance in the international community during the Cold War, focusing on the practical and rhetorical responses given by the UN. Based on my archival research, I discuss behind-the-scenes compromises and both secret and open negotiations, and I try to describe the atmosphere of the time by reconstructing a few dramatic, previously unknown case studies.

The book begins by presenting the expectations Hungarians had of the United Nations after Hungary became a member in 1955—expectations that contributed to the political fermentation leading to the Revolution. However, the events of October 23, 1956, and the first Soviet invasion on October 24 of that year were beyond the UN's authority, as they had been characterized by the ruling Hungarian politicians as the "internal affairs" of the country. Few people knew that this characterization was the condition Moscow set as a basis for a compromise with the political leaders in Budapest. However, once the second and final Soviet invasion was underway, Prime Minister Imre Nagy turned to the UN, first to guarantee and then to at least acknowledge Hungary's neutrality. But Nagy was too late, in part due to the masterfully executed sabotage in the UN by the Hungarian communist secret services (which were influential throughout the process of Hungary joining the UN) and in part due to the indifference toward and ignorance about Hungary by the most influential member states, who were preoccupied handling the concurrent Suez Crisis (Israel's attack on Egypt, followed with military support from French and British forces).

In the following chapters, I discuss the UN's attempts to find a political solution according to its Charter and how those attempts repeatedly failed, as neither Hammarskjöld nor neutral observers were allowed to visit Hungary. This prohibition was dictated by Hungarian authorities as instructed by their Soviet masters; thus, all UN resolutions were ignored. However, the approaching humanitarian crises created by the Soviet invasion's devastating consequences were successfully addressed by the great amount of relief collected by the UN and supplied to Hungary by the International Committee of the Red Cross. That the UN was the real donor had to remain anonymous because it was considered an enemy of the communists, who presented it as interfering in the internal affairs of the people's democracy. The demand for a political solution remained on the UN's agenda for several years, but the UN's options as determined by its Charter were limited and even as set not properly exploited. The representatives of the Soviet-installed Hungarian government could and did remain in the UN, even when their mandate was suspended in February 1957 and leaders of the Revolution faced legal challenges in their efforts to serve and represent their homeland.

The UN was successful in solving the refugee crisis resulting from nearly two hundred thousand Hungarians leaving the country, but once again, the cooperation of the Red Cross was crucial to creating, organizing, and running the refugee camps. The brutal consolidation of power in Hungary was systematically reported to New York, but easing the repression and terror seemed to be beyond the UN's capacity. The Secretary-General and the Secretariat attempted to address the most important issues in postrevolutionary Hungary nearly a dozen times and in multiple different ways, but the General Assembly's resolutions were disregarded by Budapest and Moscow. The Hungarian government rejected any initiatives to, as they put it, "interfere in the internal affairs of the country," as they defined any attempts at UN intervention, recalling their characterization of the early Imre Nagy government. The UN's only political achievement with respect to Hungary was the formation and activity of the Special Committee on the Problem of Hungary and its report on the Revolution, which focused on its causes and consequences. The many internal contradictions in the Special Committee's work and its report demonstrated the UN's unwillingness to deal seriously with the Hungarian problem and even suggested that some crucial actions had been sabotaged. For example, the Secretariat of the UN effectively refrained from calling an emergency session after the report was issued; thus, a discussion of the Hungarian situation in the General Assembly was scheduled for the fall session, nearly a year after the events took place. Information from Hungary concerning the economic crisis and the terroristic vengefulness of communist leader János Kádár's regime regularly arrived at the UN but only rarely reached the members of the Special Committee. Due to administrative maneuvering, the supplemental reports requested by the UN resolutions were never written. At the same time, "UN spies," as the communist propaganda referred to a handful of persons in Hungary submitting information to the UN, were identified, arrested, and executed as a means of instilling fear and demonstrating the consequences of reaching out to the international community.

Previously inaccessible archival evidence has proven to researchers that the top authorities of the UN, the Secretary-General and his deputies, were reluctant to meet the demands of the General Assembly resolutions concerning Hungary and deliberately and cunningly avoided taking appropriate action, even though they had been properly informed of the dramatic situation as it occurred. At the same time, the Hungarian secret services, reorganized after the Revolution and infiltrating refugee communities as well as the UN, obtained sensitive information, undermined the credibility of the UN report on the Hungarian question, and intimidated those willing to submit information to the organization. The most poignant consequence of the UN's mishandling of the Hungarian situation is the tragic story of Danish diplomat Povl Bang-Jensen, the Deputy Secretary of the Special Committee, who had earned the trust of the Hungarians. Bang-Jensen came to see obstacles behind the UN's activity that seemed to confirm earlier warnings of a disillusioned Eastern bloc diplomat who had alerted him that security problems might be coming from the highest levels of the UN. His conflicts with UN leadership led to his removal from the Special Committee in what some saw as a warning to discourage other UN employees from criticizing the system. He was later found dead on Long Island, and it is still unknown whether he was killed or committed suicide.

In addition to the story of Bang-Jensen's fight for truth, there is the account of the secret trial of the leaders of the Revolution and the execution of Imre Nagy and his "criminal gang," as the Soviet-installed Hungarian politicians characterized some of the members of the legitimate government established during the Revolution. The UN had been fully briefed on alarming information about the proceedings against the Hungarian revolutionaries, who had been promised they would not be harmed, yet the news about their execution caused a total shock in New York. There was little the organization could do, but even this little—a second report—was more a recounting of excuses for the UN's inaction than a serious analysis of what happened and why.

This book explores the inability of the UN Special Representatives to effectively address the "Problem of Hungary." When no hope remained that the UN Charter would be observed by the Hungarian authorities, secret negotiations started between the United States and Hungary about a possible solution. These negotiations resulted in a political bargain proposing "amnesty for mandate": the Hungarian government granting amnesty for those who had participated in the Hungarian Revolution would grant Hungary a mandate to fully participate as a UN member state. In practice, this led to Hungary regaining full rights in the UN but failing to observe any resolution, while those who had suffered behind bars for many years in Hungary were pardoned for crimes they did not commit. The whole process of Hungary's "rehabilitation" concluded with an official visit of Secretary-General U Thant to Hungary in 1963, a first ever visit of a Secretary-General of the UN to Hungary. U Thant was received by the highest leadership in a landmark event that seemed to close a difficult chapter and opened a new one, yet in reality it was a perfect example of mutual hypocrisy, demagoguery, and staged meetings with "the people" of Hungary, who finally lost their hopes in the principles the UN was built on. The visit started a new chapter in the history of both Hungary and the UN without properly closing previous chapters that were full of contradictions.

Notes

1. Gál, *"Jelcin–dosszié."*

2. Haraszti-Taylor, *Hungarian Revolution of 1956*; Litván (1994); Borhi, "Az Egyesült Államok"; Békés (2000); Hajdú, *Magyar-jugoszláv kapcsolatok 1956*; Bethlenfalvy, *India és a magyar forradalom 1956*.

3. Lidegaard, *Defiant Diplomacy*; Joldersma, *Ceylon and the United Nations*; Nagy (1996).

4. Litván, *The Hungarian Revolution*; Gati (2006); Granville (1997).

5. Király, *A magyar kérdés az ENSZ-ben*.

6. Békés, *Az 1956-os magyar forradalom*; Békés and Kecskés, *A forradalom és a magyar kérdés az ENSZ-ben*; Kecskés, "Humanitárius segítségnyújtás globális méretekben."

7. Borhi, "Rollback, Liberation, Containment or Inaction?"; Borhi, *A vasfüggöny mögött*; Borhi, *Magyarország a hidegháborúban*.

8. Baráth (2002); Baráth and Gecsényi, *Főkonzulok, követek és nagykövetek*.

9. Kramer, "The Soviet Union and the 1956 Crises." The short-lived *Cold War International History Project Bulletin*, edited by C. Ostermann, is also a valuable resource. Further relevant articles can be found in the *Journal of Cold War Studies*, edited by M. Kramer.

10. Rainer, *Nagy Imre. Politikai életrajz.*

11. Berggren, *Dag Hammarskjöld*; Urquhart (1998); Nichter (2020); Shevchenko, *Breaking with Moscow*; Bohlen, *Witness to History*.

1

THE 1956 REVOLUTION
AND ITS PROSPECTS

Hungary at the UN's Door, Within and Without

The 1956 Hungarian Revolution shook the Soviet empire and set in motion a historical chain of events. Although the uprising was unexpected, it actually resulted from a prolonged period of political fermentation that began with Joseph Stalin's death in 1953. Despite various setbacks, by 1956, the events seemed irreversible, not least because Hungarian communist leaders (as observed time and again, and with concern by their Soviet overseers) were unable to satisfactorily address the demands for change and growing discontent first expressed by members of the intelligentsia—many of them former believers in communism—and then permeating society as a whole. Those who participated in and profited from the upheaval became allies of factory workers who were punished by a constant obligation to increase output, of peasants who were stripped of their last crops, and of former members of the bourgeoisie who were humiliated and distrusted. The all-embracing political system subsumed every aspect of life and society and became an unbearable burden on the country.

On October 23, 1956, a student protest gave voice to repressed Hungarians, demanding basic freedoms and criticizing the transgressions of the Stalinist system. The demonstrators marched to the parliament building, where those assembled demanded to hear communist politician and former prime minister Imre Nagy speak. Nagy had been set aside by the Hungarian Stalinist leader, but from the summer of 1956 onward had become a symbol of reform and the center of the anti-Stalinist political movement. The demonstrators wanted to hear him and wanted him to hear their demands. An initially peaceful protest and political rally was followed by armed skirmishes, and the growing crowd toppled a prominent statue of Stalin. Representatives of the protest movement became determined to read out their demands on Hungarian state radio and made their way to the radio station. It was from the radio building that the Hungarian state security service, the ÁVH (Államvédelmi Hatóság), charged with protecting the building, fired into the crowd.[1] A few hours later Soviet tanks rolled in, martial law was announced, and the leaders of the Hungarian Communist Party denounced what they called the counterrevolution.

But once set in motion, the events were unstoppable. The confused party and government leaders did not wish to suppress the Revolution by force, nor, at this stage, did Moscow demand such a move. In the following days, revolutionary councils were established in factories and other workplaces, parties were formed, and newspapers were published without censorship. It seemed that the communist authorities would bend to the demands of the revolutionaries. A Soviet delegation arrived in Budapest, after which fighting eased and then ended. Imre Nagy assumed leadership and expanded his government to include those who had previously been sidelined.

Hope strengthened and pervaded the whole country. The foundations of a new system were about to be laid. Based on the reports of the Soviet politicians returning to Moscow, the Kremlin's leaders had decided to allow "fraternal countries," a euphemism for the satellite countries under Moscow's domination, greater room to maneuver. The official announcement of this decision was published in *Pravda*, the Soviet party newspaper. On the same day, however, the Politburo—following heated debate—defied the announcement, demanding that the Hungarian Revolution be violently suppressed.

Assuming that the USSR would be focused on Hungary, the United Kingdom and France decided to escalate to armed conflict to resolve the Suez Crisis. But Moscow, expecting the escalation in the Middle East, feared total war, as Egypt was supported by the USSR and the attackers were close allies of the United States. Under these circumstances, the Soviets felt they could hardly afford to let strategically positioned Hungary go free. This proved a miscalculation of US support for the armed conflict; nevertheless, during the last days of the Revolution, just as Hungarians' hopes were beginning to rise, the Soviet Army prepared to mercilessly put down the uprising.

The conflict and changes in Hungary were already in the headlines and on the UN Security Council's agenda for October 28, but the situation was anything but transparent. Therefore, the Western powers did not submit a proposal for a resolution, and Hungary's representative—following the instructions of the government in Budapest, which held out hope for a peaceful solution—referred to the events of the previous few days as a domestic matter.

When Operation Whirlwind, the military campaign led by Marshal Konyev to suppress the Hungarian uprising, began on November 4, 1956, the revolutionaries had no chance, at least not militarily. Yet many thought that the United Nations, as an institution of international conflict resolution, would prevent one of its member states from using armed force to stifle political changes brewing in another member state. This illusion was fed in part by both Hungary's pride and joy after the inclusion in the UN the previous year and the UN's ability to establish peace in Suez at the same moment in history. On November 7, 1956, while the Hungarian Revolution was still being fought, the UN General Assembly voted to establish a UN Emergency Force to serve as peacekeepers on the border between Israel and Egypt. In the case of the Suez Crisis, the UN's resolutions were abided by quickly and decisively due to the mutual consent of the two great powers, the Soviet Union and the US.

The General Assembly took no meaningful action on Hungary, however. The faith Hungarians had placed in the implementation of international law was crucial: The Paris Peace Treaties that formally ended World War II had referred to the key role of the UN. A reference to the UN Charter also appeared in the Soviet-Hungarian Treaty of Friendship, Cooperation, and Mutual Assistance, signed in 1948, and further developed and expanded into the Warsaw Pact of 1955 that was later used to "legitimate" the intervention in Hungary in 1956. Yet Hungary's full membership in the United Nations ten years after its establishment was cause for optimism. The UN was about the union of nations, the principles of which were recorded in its Charter, rather than an alliance of peoples as the League of Nations used to be. It was also about solidarity, which meant that despite losing the war, Hungary still received UN aid even prior to being a member. Prime Minister Ferenc Nagy in 1946 asked the UN Secretary-General to continue this support for the sake of its nascent democracy.

After World War II, Hungary repeatedly asked to be admitted to the United Nations, only to be answered with Cold War logic—first, outright rejection (1947), then with a proviso that it change its social system in order to join (1948). Leaders of Western countries could hardly have thought that the Hungarian communists would hand over power to democratically elected popular representatives or that freedom of the press or assembly would be introduced as part of putting human rights on the agenda. Naivete was even less evident on the communist side: the nomination of Andrey Vishinsky, the chief prosecutor of Stalinist show trials, as Soviet representative to the UN was a travesty of the UN's basic principles, and thanks to the ideological divisiveness of the Korean War, communist propaganda painted the UN as a subsidiary of the United States.

Hungarian foreign policy prioritized involvement in the work of the UN's specialized organizations even when it seemed clear the country's membership was out of the question; to this end, the foreign ministry in Budapest made a financial contribution. The check was signed by Károly Szarka, who would play a key role in later events and who, before traveling to New York in 1953, was informed of the subversive activities of communist secret services working under diplomatic cover at Western legations and missions. The director of the station (effectively a Hungarian communist intelligence center under diplomatic cover) operating at the legation in Washington, DC, requested that Szarka "undertake tasks on our behalf,"[2] principally by establishing contact with the UN. By this time, Hungarian representatives could sit as observers at UN sessions, but most of these so-called diplomats were employees of state security agencies. Recently declassified documents of the communist secret services reveal that, for the Hungarian leadership, the UN was not so much a diplomatic forum or a belated opportunity for Hungary's meaningful inclusion in the international community but rather a chance to gather intelligence and provide a diversion from—or even a springboard for—more ominous activities.[3]

As the United States was considered by many Hungarian politicians to be the archenemy of communism, one of the most important intelligence stations was the one operating in Washington, DC. The Hungarian secret service operation based there had a staff of eight (four operatives, a coded radio operator, a typist, and two drivers) who did not know each other's identities. Most of them had been trained in the Soviet Union and assumed their positions under various cover stories. Among the operatives in Washington were secret agents who would later play important roles in our story, among them Péter Várkonyi, later Hungarian foreign minister, and Gyula Eörsi, an expert on international law.

The Hungarian consulate operated in New York. In Washington the FBI was able to keep Hungarian staff under constant surveillance, but operations in New York were less transparent, and although "UN employees [were] not immune from arrest" (unlike secret service operatives enjoying diplomatic immunity), the police were not allowed to enter the UN building, and those working there "were able to establish wide-ranging, uncontrolled relationships."[4] When Hungary was given observer status at the UN in 1953, the secret service operatives reported back to Budapest that "we have all opportunities at our disposal" and, regarding the composition of the delegation, suggested that it should be the secret service, not the ministry, that should send the "foreign affairs staff."[5]

But this was only one side of the exploitation of the UN. In early 1954, István Tatár, an undercover agent for the ÁVH, visited the UN's protocol division to inquire about the opportunities afforded by Hungary's observer status. At that time, he also visited László Hámori, a Hungarian-born employee at the UN Secretariat, with "orders to ensnare him."[6] Hámori's uncle was living in Hungary, and his uncle's return to Budapest from forced deployment to the countryside as a potential class enemy was offered as a reward for Hámori's collaboration. The secret service agents gave Hámori the code name Bertalan, and because he had a Hungarian passport, he was included as part of the Hungarian quota in the UN. A Hungarian agent known as János Arany[7] tried to convince Hámori that an oath made to the people was more important than loyalty to the United Nations. The plan misfired, however. Hámori (Bertalan) was cautious and refused to negotiate with the ÁVH men. In doing so, he chose to abandon hope of ever seeing his only living family member again.

The Hungarian secret service also had its sights on a Hungarian-born woman who worked in the UN Gift Center. This accomplished young woman spoke six languages and was given the code name Csikós (Wrangler). She was thought to be very knowledgeable about security measures and the workings of what the Hungarians called the UN's "internal police" and was considered capable of establishing connections with both diplomats working at the UN and visitors from abroad.[8] She could potentially be extorted by Hungarian agents posing as diplomats who would try to negotiate her mother's emigration from Hungary. Csikós smelled a rat, however, and disappeared without a trace between her first and second visits from the ÁVH.

Czechoslovak comrades (as communists used to call one another) representing their country at the UN recommended that their Hungarian colleagues recall all employees of Hungarian extraction back home, proposing that whoever refused to collaborate with them should be stripped of their citizenship, and that anyone causing a disturbance should be prevented from leaving the country.[9] This was when the Hungarian secret service set its sights on Klára Héderváry, a talented and multilingual young woman who had previously lived in Belgium and then studied at Harvard and Columbia Universities. As the secret service agents wrote in their notes: "She emigrated at the time of the persecution of the Jews (in c. 1939)." This was information very few people were aware of concerning the woman calling herself Claire de Hedervary, who was aristocratic in manner and proud of her noble status and who never admitted her real identity.[10]

The Hungarian secret services strongly criticized the repeated failure of Hungary to gain membership in the United Nations in 1954: "The Foreign Ministry committed a serious error regarding the delegation. . . . Permanent residence in New York for the station would have made an entirely different line of work possible."[11] The error referred to was presumably the presence of diplomats in the delegation, who effectively took the place of secret service agents who wanted to be working under diplomatic cover in positions of decision making. However, the issue of Hungary's membership was not primarily one of diplomacy but rather of bargaining between the great powers.[12] This bargaining often came to nothing, so, in 1955, the year of Hungary's admission to the UN, the Hungarian secret service station included the following goal for the delegation: "using the performance of official duties as a cover, . . . to make regular visits to New York every two-three weeks in order to study the situation with agents and to choose a suitable meeting-point."[13] With Hungary's admission to the UN, there was no longer a need for such cover stories.

Even as late as in October 1955 and despite extensive diplomatic and secret service preparations, Hungary's admission to the United Nations was by no means certain, a fact protested by leaders of the Hungarian émigré community in the West. The particular choreography of mutual extortion between the great powers allowed the admission of certain countries to remain in doubt until the very last minute, even if the country in question was of particular importance to either the American or the Soviet side, for admission depended on the composition of the Assembly and the votes that could be won. At the historic moment when Hungary's admission seemed poised to take place, there was instead procrastination and a hiatus during which more bargaining behind closed doors occurred. At this stage, agent János Arany had had enough of the to-ing and fro-ing and went home to sleep. As a result, at the historic moment that Hungary joined the UN, there was not a single Hungarian in the Hall. The following day, the newspapers in Budapest gave over their headlines to the news of the foreign policy triumph, while the missing János Arany was obliged to provide a report accounting for his absence.[14]

Once all obstacles to the establishment of an intelligence station inside the United Nations had been cleared, a "large part" of the Washington station was moved "to the secretariat established alongside the Hungarian UN delegation."[15] The station was led by Imre Hollai, a major in the ÁVH who played a decisive role in the UN's failure to respond to calls for support during the 1956 Hungarian Revolution and later held an important position within the UN. Hollai was originally a mechanic, and he began his secret service work at the Stalinist interior ministry. In September 1955, he was made a major and swore an oath of secrecy that he would never break, not even in later years.[16]

The other leading ÁVH agent in the Hungarian UN delegation was Pál Rácz, who became acquainted with the various UN committees in the late 1940s when, as attaché to Geneva, he established contact with a number of European bodies. His career in state security began in 1950; by 1952, he was a top-secret agent with the state security service and "ran a network," meaning that other agents reported to him. He was sent to Washington in 1955 and then to New York, but in 1957, he was designated persona non grata in the United States and expelled from the country. His career in Hungary progressed rapidly, and by 1970, he was a major general; later, from 1980 through 1986, he was able to return to the US as part of the Hungarian UN delegation.[17]

In March 1956, Sándor Rajnai, a Soviet secret service officer and one of the leaders of the Hungarian Intelligence Agency, reported that "the intelligence officers under the cover of the UN have considerably greater room to maneuver"[18] than diplomats. As a result, the secret service station covering North America, which soon expanded to a staff of fourteen, was moved to New York. We read that during "the organization of the New York object," the report of the secret service agents suggests that "the most important organizational foundation for the station is to ensure the observation of the [UN] secretariat on a legal basis."[19] Admission to membership in the UN was thus a tool for secret service operations: there would soon be three or four operative staff members and a secret service employee in the rank of counselor working alongside the diplomats, serving as head of the secret service station. The other secret service operatives were required to have a diplomatic rank of at least second secretary. The driver, junior officers, counterintelligence officer, and radio operator guaranteed security, as did the maintenance staff and even the furnishings for the building, all of which had been chosen with great care. The members of the station kept an eye on each other to reduce the risk of discovery.

As all new member states could send employees to work for the various bodies of the United Nations, the "filling of the apparatus alongside the UN" was an obvious opportunity for the Hungarian secret service, which soon reported that "it is possible to get inside the UN Secretariat."[20] With the Secretariat being the nexus of the UN's affairs, ÁVH officers placed there were able to establish "wide-ranging" connections "that could not be kept in check" and were able to cooperate with "the station placed in the Permanent Delegation,"[21] even though, according to the UN Charter, international employees were independent from national delegations.

In January 1956, Secretary-General Dag Hammarskjöld invited the newly accepted members to lunch; the Hungarian flag, together with those of the other new member states, was raised on one of the flagpoles standing in front of the UN building in New York on March 9, 1956. That summer, UN Under-Secretary-General Andrew Cordier visited Budapest, conducting negotiations with a Hungary full of hope. As the formal act of accreditation, the Hungarian mandate was accepted at 11:30 a.m. on June 25.[22] The fall season of 1956 was the first at which the People's Republic of Hungary was present as a full member. No one expected that this new kid on the block would soon become the star of the show.

In September, Hammarskjöld received Péter Kós, who, as Hungarian ambassador in Washington, also undertook the country's UN representation. Accession to the UN meant that the international department of the foreign ministry in Budapest had to be restructured and technical and staff conditions had to be guaranteed. Kós reported on these conditions, not without concern, to Deputy Foreign Minister Endre Sík. They looked for an office in New York, but the Hungarian Mission had no table, no hatstand, and no chandelier and so could not host receptions, though a typewriter had been provided. At this time, the quarterly budget for the Hungarian secret service station was $3,223.

The Revolution as Seen from New York

Hungary's recent admission to the United Nations and the tangible way this affected the country's ability to maneuver in foreign policy must have raised Hungary's hopes and contributed to the ever-increasing political ferment in the summer of 1956. Henceforth, it was not only possible to read the UN Charter but, once it was ratified, it became part of the Hungarian legal system. Some of the brightening of Hungary's historical horizon at this time might also have been due to the withdrawal of Soviet troops from Austria in line with the state treaty of 1955, which allowed the country, formerly partially occupied by Moscow, to announce its eternal neutrality.

The political changes in Hungary caused considerable worry in the Kremlin, whose leading functionaries paid a visit to Hungary in the first half of 1956, followed by a military exercise that may have been a dress rehearsal for Soviet military intervention in the country.[23] The Hungarian UN delegation assembled at this time reflected the beginnings of political change in Hungary, and the plan was for reformers from Imre Nagy's circle to be sent to the UN. But in the end the US embassy would receive visa applications not from reformers from the circle of Imre Nagy like Géza Losonczy and Miklós Vásárhelyi, who later participated in the Revolution, but from the hardcore Stalinist leaders of the Ministry of Foreign Affairs, Imre Horváth and Endre Sík.

On October 23, 1956, the day the Revolution broke out in Hungary, the routines inside the glass tower of the UN Headquarters in Manhattan went on as usual. Hammarskjöld first met with his deputies and then, according to his diary, attended the plenary atom, which referred to the task of reducing the nuclear threat. This was followed by a cocktail and then a reception. In the evening, the New School of Social Research arranged a celebration of United Nations Day one day short of the eleventh anniversary of the organization's founding.

Many have reconstructed in detail what happened and what did not happen at the UN from this evening on. The initial news from Hungary was received with delight by the majority of the UN members but obtaining accurate information on the events of subsequent days proved challenging. The outbreak of the Revolution was unexpected, the representatives of the international press had not yet reached Budapest, and diplomatic missions did not always have a good understanding of events. The picture soon became clearer, however, and after the first Soviet invasion of Hungary, on

The badly damaged building of the communist daily paper *Szabad Nép* (Free people) during the Hungarian Revolution. Copyright: Fortepan #163273. Donated by Hajnal Gödér.

the night of October 23, news of the armed intervention reached UN Headquarters, although its legal justification and scope were not fully known.[24] Péter Kós tried to get more information from Budapest, while Moscow hurriedly sent envoys to the Hungarian capital to negotiate. Imre Nagy and Ernő Gerő together received Anastas Mikoyan and Mikhail Suslov, members of the Soviet presidium, and after these negotiations a deal of some sort did not appear entirely unlikely.

For Moscow, the prerequisite for any agreement with Nagy and Gerő was a promise there would be no intervention from the United Nations. Given the hope of acquiring independence and reviving democracy, this did not seem an impossible request. So came the telegram from Moscow to Budapest stipulating that the UN would not intervene. Rewritten, with limited amendments, this message was sent on to New York to Péter Kós, stating that the events in Hungary beginning on October 22 were a domestic matter for the People's Republic of Hungary over which the UN did not have jurisdiction. Kós read the telegram to the UN Security Council, thus finalizing the delivery of the order from Moscow, while in Budapest, the leaders of the Revolution still trusted they would come to an agreement with the Soviets. An agreement had seemed possible. But the opportunity for an independent Hungary would be gambled away, not by the dogmatists in Moscow, but rather by France and the United Kingdom and their military actions in Suez, which would soon lead to an armed confrontation in the Middle East.

The statement Kós read provoked enormous outrage from the revolutionaries in Hungary who did not know about the negotiations between the Hungarian and Soviet leaders.[25] It was hard to convince the public that a military attack from abroad could be considered a domestic matter while the planned agreement was not publicly known. Yet Kós's orders had been unambiguous, and he had implemented them in a professional fashion. The outrage over the statement soon turned into character assassinations of Kós: it was claimed that the Hungarian envoy to the UN also went by the name Konduktorov (which was true) and that he was a Soviet citizen (which was not true). In this heated atmosphere, both claims served to discredit the envoy, which was an easier course than having to admit that he had followed the instructions of the revolutionary government, as suggested by Moscow.

The UN Security Council was led by the Frenchman Bernard Cornut-Gentille when Péter Kós, as a guest, read out the statement of the Hungarian government. The statement inevitably engendered suspicion among UN member states as to how to interpret the events that had taken place in Hungary. In Hungary, the outrage continued to grow. Many perceived the statement as a betrayal, and Kós was immediately recalled from his posting in New York, though there was no official documentation concerning his accreditation being revoked. Kós returned to Hungary but only got as far as Prague, where a number of Stalinists were waiting in the political transit zone. Kós would accompany them to the United States after the Revolution was defeated.

In the meantime, there were serious controversies concerning the foreign policy of revolutionary Budapest caused in part by the decision of prime minister Imre Nagy to weed out Stalinists from the foreign ministry. Nagy himself took control of foreign policy and designated the parliament building as the place where foreign policy decisions were made. He soon appointed Imre Horváth and invited György Heltai to work with him on foreign affairs. As a result, the telegrams to the UN Secretary-General were sent directly from the Hungarian Parliament in Budapest, sidelining even the Hungarian UN delegation in New York. Nagy could not, of course, override the Hungarian UN delegation altogether, so after Kós was recalled, he mandated that deputy head of mission János Szabó represent Hungary. In doing so, he unintentionally sealed the fate of the 1956 Hungarian Revolution at the United Nations, as Szabó, under code name Bertalan Székely, was working for the Hungarian secret service.

When the Soviet intervention against the Hungarian Revolution was placed on the agenda of the UN Security Council, the Soviets immediately vetoed discussion of the matter, arguing that the Revolution was no more than a reactionary uprising supported by the United States. The French, meanwhile, considered that Soviet suppression of the uprising in Hungary not only contravened the UN Charter but also the Paris Peace Treaties and indeed even the Warsaw Pact, which had been presented as the legal foundation for the invasion.[26] The United Kingdom, on the other hand, questioned whether the use of Soviet military forces stationed in Hungary under a valid treaty and at the behest of the Hungarian government could be called an intervention at all.

In light of the Soviet veto at the UN Security Council and under the aegis of the UN's 1950 so-called Uniting for Peace initiative (General Assembly resolution 377[V]), the issue of the Hungarian Revolution found its way to the UN General Assembly, where no country had a right of veto. It remained difficult, however, to see the situation clearly from New York: there was no US ambassador to Budapest, and the telegraph machine at the French delegation was out of order. Therefore, the UK mission, with its excellent local reporting and operational telegraph machine, was one of the few sources of news.

Mikoyan and Suslov, the Soviet envoys returning home from Budapest, did not rule out a consolidation of the Revolution at this time, provided the Soviets would be partners rather than subjugators. As debates in the Kremlin intensified, Mikoyan threatened to commit suicide if the Soviets used force,[27] but the compromise achieved was hopeful and implementable, offering fraternal countries their sovereignty and more room to maneuver.

It is not easy to determine whether it was the Suez debacle, photographs of lynchings of members of the ÁVH on the streets of Budapest, or perhaps the struggle for power inside the Kremlin taking another turn that forced Moscow to take a step that would lead to tragedy. But what was still a domestic matter on October 31 would as of the following morning become an international question. It was not the internal course of the Revolution but rather external circumstances that forced Imre Nagy to change his position:

on the same day that Moscow's signaled tolerance of relative sovereignty for the satellite nations was announced in *Pravda*—a cause for significant optimism in Budapest and beyond—it became clear that it was time for blood and weapons rather than for equality and sovereignty in Hungary. This was obvious from the movements of Soviet troops: instead of withdrawing, they were beginning, or rather preparing for, an invasion.

Soviet ambassador Yuri Andropov was summoned to the Hungarian Parliament to explain himself. His response was rife with equivocation as well as lies of Byzantine proportions. As the situation became disturbingly clear, Imre Nagy played his foreign policy card, declaring Hungary to be neutral and claiming that it had withdrawn from the Warsaw Pact—both measures squared with the demands of the revolutionaries, of course. But at the time, this was also a desperate attempt to strengthen Hungary's negotiating position with massive internal support—though massive, too, were the forces being prepared and armed to defeat the Revolution.

At the debate on proposals for the government session held on November 1, only two ministers from Nagy's government, György Lukács and Zoltán Szántó, opposed the plan to leave the Warsaw Pact, and even they objected more to the form this would take than to the idea itself. The other members of the revolutionary government—including János Kádár, who would later be installed as premier by the Soviets—agreed with the decision. Péter Mód, at that time working in the Ministry of Foreign Affairs and heading its Revolutionary Council, was tasked with formulating a position statement. It is worth noting that Mód would later change his position; he would go on to represent the Kádár government at the UN, after which he would criticize his own statement for many years. Andropov, called back to the government session, continued to mislead and prevaricate; at this stage, Kádár was still in agreement with the revolutionary government. He voted in support of withdrawing from the Warsaw Pact, only to disappear sometime that afternoon and change allegiance.

The decision of the Hungarian government was telegraphed to New York not once but twice. First, they asked for a guarantee of neutrality from the great powers, then they asked only for recognition. There was little chance of either coming to pass: a guarantee was not on the table even in the case of Austria, and recognition of neutrality would come only after lengthy negotiations, not simply as the result of a government announcement. Neither did the telegrams refer to the UN Security Council, where the question was on the agenda, but rather to the UN General Assembly, which would only be convened on November 12. And even then, the telegrams recommended a standard rather than an urgent debate on the issue. Whether this was due to incompetence, sabotage, or hurriedness, we cannot know.[28]

The Stalinists and revolutionaries at the Hungarian foreign ministry summoned the leaders of the diplomatic missions to Hungary, so they could announce Hungary's "eternal neutrality" and, by rescinding the Warsaw Pact, eliminate the legal basis for Soviet intervention. In light of this government statement, Stalinists Imre Horváth and Endre Sík, who were heading to the UN General Assembly, were recalled. They awaited the historic changes in Prague, joining the other pro-Soviet politicians there who had escaped from Hungary to safety. Imre Horváth would later secretly fly from Prague to Moscow to participate in the forced persuasion of János Kádár—who had already been transported there—to change allegiance. The revolutionaries working in the foreign ministry compiled a list of diplomats to be recalled, including the ÁVH officers positioned at foreign missions. Their exposure of these officers as agents and not diplomats would later cause serious problems for the Kádár leadership, who wanted to once again use their skills when they regained power and continued the praxis of the Stalinist system.[29] The revolutionaries were aware that the pro-Soviets and Stalinists in the foreign ministry did not support their actions, so insurgents occupied the building and had to be removed by Béla Király, leader of the National Guard. Pamphlets appeared, claiming the UN was already debating "the Soviet intervention in our country's domestic affairs."[30] Not for a minute did the revolutionaries imagine that the greatest obstacle to a diplomatic solution would be in New York.

Imre Nagy nominated János Szabó to replace Kós by telegram—a distinctly unusual occurrence in the history of the United Nations. Then again, a revolution is in itself an unusual event. The UN Under-Secretary-General Dragoslav Protitch,[31] a Yugoslav who continued to play a key role in the events that unfolded, accepted Szabó's accreditation, and read the telegram at the 752nd session of the Security Council, at 5:00 p.m. on November 2, 1956.[32] Hammarskjöld acknowledged the receipt of Nagy's message and circulated Nagy's statement to the representatives of the member states as an official record of the Assembly.[33] Despite this, Szabó complained in his messages sent to Budapest that without accreditation, he was unable to take part in the Security Council's work and that he awaited further instructions.

János Szabó (*right*) at the General Assembly debate receiving instructions for sabotaging the Hungarian question. Copyright: UN Photo Archive #7725487.

"Stop needlessly repeating what has already been said," came the response, which required him to confirm that all of Nagy's previous statements represented the official position of the Hungarian government and instructed him to request that the Security Council recognize Hungary's neutrality. The message from revolutionary Budapest added that discussions were underway with representatives of the Soviet Union; when Szabó was given the floor at the decisive session of the Security Council, this was the only thing he mentioned.[34]

By this stage Soviet Army marshal Ivan Konev, in charge of the suppression of the Hungarian Revolution, had already given instructions to his officers. They filled the oil reserves, distributed munitions, and drafted the daily dispatches, which spoke of the "revival of fascism" in the heart of Europe. Of the officers, many had participated in the victory over fascism; that they would be attacking antifascists and communists was obscured by the official propaganda, according to which the Paris Treaties also obliged their signatories to obstruct the reemergence of fascism.[35]

Washington did not yet have a clear idea of the unfolding events. Any information received from the US legation in Budapest, which had no minister, was intermittent and confused. Tibor Zádor, the spokesman for the Hungarian legation in Washington, was characterized as being in a state of "surprise and disarray." Zádor was uninformed, with no information or instructions arriving from Budapest.[36] State Department employees tried to find out what was happening from the leaders of the Hungarian émigré community in the US, who, it was claimed, were "in constant contact with the leaders of the Hungarian uprising." Béla Varga, the last speaker of the freely elected Hungarian Parliament and a leading Hungarian émigré politician in the US, claimed that Imre Nagy was "the most insidious traitor in Hungarian history," and said the US should not be expected to do anything more than send coal in the winter.[37] Propaganda from the United States was now available throughout Hungary via Radio Free Europe, which had been jammed during the Stalinist era. Radio Free Europe became one of the most important sources of news in Hungary, however the US-sponsored and Munich-based radio station sided with Cardinal József Mindszenty, the conservative primate of Hungary imprisoned by the Stalinist authorities on trumped-up charges, who had been liberated during the Revolution. These Radio Free Europe broadcasts made clear the station's propaganda goals, which helped undermine Imre Nagy's authority and rouse anticommunist feeling, thereby shattering Hungarian national unity.

According to the otherwise well-informed British authorities, Imre Nagy's "puppet government" did not enjoy the support of the Hungarian people. All this was enough for US secretary of state John Foster Dulles to announce at the session of the Council of National Security that "it was impossible to do business with the present Hungarian government."[38] Radio Free Europe called the Hungarian prime minister a "traitor and a murderer of the nation," urged that the agreed-upon cease-fire be rejected, and considered the results of Imre Nagy's efforts to be no more than "bullets, persecution, Soviet troops, and terror," with only the state security thugs on the side of a "government with blood on its hands." When Imre Nagy extended his cabinet to include popular politicians, Radio Free Europe claimed that they "were better suited to the convicts' bench than to any ministerial post." Yet on October 31, they would report on "Hungary's rebirth" and the country's "leader sent by God." In addition, the US voice in Munich—the editors of Radio Free Europe—convinced the revolutionaries that there would be

Imre Nagy, leader of the 1956 Hungarian Revolution, addresses the crowd gathered in front of the parliament building. Copyright: Fortepan #141576. Photographed by Franz Fink.

armed support for the Hungarians in their fight for freedom. This promise was not merely a notion not subscribed to in Washington but one that had actively been outlawed there.[39]

If the information coming into Washington was confusing, New York was getting even more meager updates: though the Hungarian Revolution was put on the agenda, no kind of proposal for a resolution was submitted to the UN Security Council. Because of Imre Nagy's telegrams, the Council refused to recognize, let alone guarantee, Hungarian neutrality in the peak of the Cold War. Indeed, across the ocean, the very idea of neutrality was an anathema: How could anyone be neutral in the fight between good and evil?[40] And while UN envoy Henry Cabot Lodge emphasized the psychological and propaganda opportunities afforded by the Hungarian Revolution and talked of troop withdrawal, sovereignty, and negotiations, he tabled no motion for a vote, and the session was—at Yugoslav instigation—postponed to November 5.[41] Most importantly, the Suez Crisis became the focal point of attention, with the Israeli-British-French attack dramatically cooling relations among the Western allies. In addition, Washington voted with Moscow against its European friends in the very hours that the Soviet invasion of Hungary was being planned.

The Western allies were concerned that any joint resolution proposal could be used against the two Security Council member states (Britain and France) intervening in Egypt, so they hesitated even to submit one. Yet as early as October 26—before the Suez Crisis began—the allies' confidential correspondence suggested that a broader implementation of the principles the Hungarian situation recalled was a cause for concern. The instruction of Secretary of State Dulles was to delay dealing with the Hungarian issue until November 1 and to await the arrival of the official envoy. The US elections also influenced American politicians' willingness to get involved in the campaign. They preferred to be careful about foreign policy, and when Dulles gave his UN speech on November 1, he made no mention of the Hungarian Revolution. When news of the Soviet troop movements reached New York there was talk of establishing an observation group,[42] and by this stage the British ambassador in Budapest urged that the United Nations take action.[43] Over the first five crucial days, however, the organization would remain inactive.

This successful breeding of disarray was part of the Soviet strategy. At the Security Council, Soviet UN representative Arkady Sobolev questioned the authenticity of the messages coming from Budapest, and as János Szabó was unwilling to support their authenticity, Imre Nagy sent a message confirming that all his telegrams were authentic and legal.[44] While the UN Secretary-General was waiting for "clarification,"[45] Szabó was in no hurry to publish the messages. Then, when he was urged on by Budapest, he had problems with his own mandate. On November 4—the day of the second Soviet invasion—Szabó handed Hammarskjöld an informal note, stating that he had no mandate to participate in the special session and that he had received no information or instructions from Budapest.[46] He said only that negotiations were taking place between the Hungarian and Soviet sides. This was said as if they were approaching agreement in the spirit of the UN resolution, when in fact the Hungarian delegation, led by Defense Minister Pál Maléter, was just being arrested in Tököl, outside Budapest, by the general of Soviet state security.

Meeting of the Security Council discussing the Hungarian question, presided by Under-Secretary-General Dragoslav Protitch. Copyright: UN Photo Archive #128699.

While the US delegation had considered asking someone to come from Budapest to provide a firsthand account of events,[47] it was later recalled that János Szabó asked for Imre Nagy to send a "fascist" to read the statement of neutrality.[48] This precisely identifies Szabó's alliance: at this time, only the Soviets considered the Hungarian freedom struggle to be a fascist coup. Szabó had been a member of the UN delegation beginning in August 1956, his secret service work was not rated highly at Budapest headquarters, and he had no achievements to his name—or so they would later write of him. But the leaders of the Hungarian secret services were wrong, for, on the days that mattered, his ignominious efforts were indeed a "success": the sabotage and disruption caused by "Bertalan Székely" (Szabó) at the United Nations were much more damaging to the cause of the Revolution than Kós's reading of the official telegram could ever have been. Furthermore, because Imre Nagy had authorized him, there was no doubting Szabó's legitimacy, something that would prove to be important later.

According to documents of the Hungarian state security services, ÁVH agent Pál Rácz was Szabó's "handler." In the crucial days of the Revolution, Rácz established official contact with him, which is why Szabó refused to read Imre Nagy's declaration. In other words, Szabó got his instructions not from his superiors in the foreign ministry in Budapest but rather from Pál Rácz and Imre Hollai, and "although 'Székely' did not have certain knowledge of Comrade Hollai's position in Hungarian intelligence, he implemented the advice and instructions given, even at the most difficult times"[49]—as Szabó's bosses would later describe it. For at the time of the Revolution, "Comrades Hollai and Rácz were forced to retreat into the shadows. [. . .] Székely was left on his own, with no directions from headquarters."[50] Even if during the Revolution the ÁVH became disoriented and many undercover operatives had their agendas exposed, the secret police remained the real center of power and operated as such. For "in this period Comrade Hollai repeated[ly] visited the Soviet Permanent UN Mission, where the Soviet comrades gave him information on events back in Hungary and on expected developments."[51] The Soviet envoys to the UN in New York, in other words, knew more than Premier Kádár and his ministers knew; the former were receiving history lessons in Moscow, while the latter were in hiding from revolutionaries, many of them at the Soviet base in Tököl. As Hollai recalls, "We were always talking to [Szabó], and, as regards the Hungarian position, he carried out the instructions that we established together. [. . .] All he asked was that we did not leave him in the lurch, if something were to happen."[52] The Hungarian position, then, was created and became historically important through the consensus of the two ÁVH officers and the modest Szabó, as they followed the orders of the Soviet comrades.

Just six months later, in March 1957, Péter Mód and Imre Hollai described the situation to the UN Department of the foreign ministry in Budapest as "constant and quickly changing instructions" arriving from Budapest, while the "broken and limited contact"[53] with headquarters only heightened the confusion. "Alongside the declaration" of Imre Nagy, they recalled, "they sent an anti-Soviet speech. The Hungarian delegation was not willing to read this speech out, because it was entirely clear that, should it do so, this could easily lead to UN troops being sent to Hungary to fight against the Soviet Union."[54] Others involved also recall that it was only after this that the Kádár government was created; that is, the delegation did not execute the instructions received from the legitimate prime minister, just as Hollai did not obey the recall he received from the foreign ministry.[55] When Rácz and Hollai learned of the formation of the Kádár government, they knew that the UN Secretary-General had been informed, which thereby invalidated Imre Nagy's earlier messages. Szabó notified the UN of the formation of the new government and in so doing had the opportunity—an achievement even by Eastern European standards—to represent both the Revolution and the counterrevolution.

This aroused attention in the Assembly Hall: Karl Eskelund, the Danish delegate, requested information on the "gentleman's" accreditation, while Lodge, given the transfer of power from one Hungarian government to another, raised the question of legitimacy.[56] At this point, Ferenc Nagy, ex-prime minister of Hungary, now immigrated to the US, and Pál Auer, another Hungarian politician in exile and leading expert on foreign policy, wrote to the UN to ask to speak,[57] wishing to represent Hungary on the basis of their former authority. They did not receive a reply, but from then on, to avoid any disturbances, the building of the Hungarian UN Mission was put under police protection to guarantee that the diplomats were unharmed and able to move freely. Of course, this measure was seen by Kádár's propagandists as provocation and house arrest,[58] even though it actually signified the guardians of freedom vouching for the personal and legal security of those seeking to extinguish freedom.

Lost Chances for the Hungarian Case in the United Nations

Apart from the trauma of the crushed Revolution, the greatest outrage was the continuous presence of the oppressors at the United Nations, while the revolutionaries could hardly step inside—this even though one of their more significant and charismatic leaders, Anna Kéthly, would soon be arriving in New York.[59] In the last days of the Revolution, Kéthly had been in Vienna, participating in the Socialist International conference from November 1. Following the Soviet intervention, she twice attempted to return to Hungary without success. Kéthly realized that, as the only Hungarian politician in a "free territory," she had retained her room to maneuver. At this point, only the UN complex itself represented a suitable place to address the international organization, so in her telegram of November 4, Kéthly informed Hammarskjöld that she was on her way to New York to turn to the great community of nations for help before the meeting of the Security Council. But the Secretary-General's office only forwarded the

United Nations General Assembly discussing the Hungarian question, in the presence of Secretary-General Dag Hammarskjöld (*left*), President of the General Assembly Wan Waithayakon (*middle*), and Under-Secretary-General Andrew Cordier (*right*). Copyright: UN Photo Archive #7720220.

telegram with the following words: "Action to Cordier, Protitch."[60] Kéthly's arrival in the United States made headlines; in New York, she again offered her services to the UN Secretary-General. Despite her more cautious wording this time, she received no reply, so two days later, she informed Hammarskjöld that at 4:00 p.m., she would appear in his office in an official capacity to relate her firsthand experience of the Soviet intervention and the egregious contravention of the UN Charter.

Hammarskjöld again failed to reply, and Minister of State Kéthly's planned "appearance" came to nothing. In her telegram the following day, Kéthly objected to his silence; two days later, the Secretary-General finally found the time to express his regrets that it had been "impossible" to receive her, before directing her to Protitch, his deputy, as well as Constantin Stavropoulos, the chief legal counsel of the UN.[61]

In the meantime, the three ÁVH men—Imre Hollai, Pál Rácz, and János Szabó—continued to occupy the Hungarian delegation's seats, while the reactivated Stalinists boarded a plane in Prague. On the one hand, this was a scandal; on the other, it was the result of the accreditation telegraphed by Imre Nagy to Szabó ("Székely") rather than Kéthly. During this critical time period for Hungary, Hammarskjöld's diary was full to bursting with efforts focused on preventing the Suez Crisis from exploding at any moment. His failure to respond may also have been due in part to the fact that the reports summarizing the Hungarian question came from distinctly unusual and perhaps even suspicious sources. He learned, for example, that Anna Kéthly had left Hungary on October 30, which indicated that she could only have gotten firsthand evidence from before this date. Her ministerial appointment occurred in her absence; she would have gone to Budapest for her documents, but the border had already been closed because of Soviet military operations.[62] For her part, Kéthly only wished to play a part in government if she was given a mandate to do so in democratic elections, but this never came to pass.

In Kéthly's later recollections of this episode, Imre Nagy's famous telegrams referred to her as someone who could represent Hungary before the United Nations, but there is no evidence of this in the documents. According to her memory of events, "I was informed of my appointment" on November 2, but at this time, the council of ministers had still not come to a decision on the question of the UN delegation. The following day, Imre Nagy proposed that the "deputy foreign minister" should go to New York with Kéthly. The relevant government resolution was drawn up, but by November 4, the council of ministers was no longer able to pass it.[63]

Philosopher and political thinker István Bibó, who was at the government meeting, observed that "Hungary's sole legitimate representative abroad" was Minister of State Anna Kéthly, but for the UN, such a statement could hardly have been a valid "legal source." Bibó, well versed in the law, only "observed" this, which is not the same as having a mandate, and even less acceptable as an official UN appointment for the accreditation committee. As Kéthly remembers it, Hammarskjöld could not accept her nomination "in the absence of official formalities,"[64] and it would not only have been risky for the Secretary-General to make an exception to the UN's operating regulations; it would have been impossible: accreditation is not within the remit of the Secretary-General but rather in the hands of a committee that would continue to fiddle around on the question of the Hungarian mandate for another six years.

The thought of giving a platform to revolutionaries or representatives of people fighting for their independence struck dread into even those of the great powers that would otherwise respond favorably to Kéthly. This was true of the strongly anticommunist Republic of China in Taiwan, which did not want a UN platform provided to revolutionaries from mainland China.[65] It was also true of the United Kingdom because of Cyprus and of France, with Algeria in turmoil. There was no shortage of independence movements opposed to those Western democracies that objected to the suppression of the Hungarian Revolution, but these Western states preferred to associate with puppets, as the Kádár government was defined, rather than set a precedent of doing so with revolutionaries.

Although many demanded that such "puppets" be ousted from the United Nations,[66] the accreditation of Kéthly would have meant that the UN did not recognize the Kádár government, the legitimacy of which was derived from force—more precisely, military force and even more precisely, Soviet military force. The next logical step would thus have been to banish Moscow from the very United Nations that it had cofounded.[67] This idea never developed, primarily because the United States relied on the Soviet vote regarding the Suez Crisis in the process of creating the new, bipolar world order. The US did hesitate to recognize the Kádár government; the US minister arriving in Budapest did not present his credentials to the Revolutionary Worker-Peasant Government. Then again, the US had not been quick to recognize the Imre Nagy government either.

The US State Department leaders—the same ones who would later approach Anna Kéthly—refrained from referring to the minister of state of the revolutionary government as a "minister of state."[68] Washington did consider giving Kéthly a hearing at the UN, but this could not happen without pressuring the United Kingdom to agree, and Spain would not have allowed it in the end. That country was happy to give military assistance to Hungary but could not abide the United Nations providing a platform to revolutionaries.

Hammarskjöld later accepted a visit from Kéthly, who "claimed that he [Hammarskjöld] could not recognize my appointment without an official notification." During a visit to Scandinavia, former Hungarian minister of state Kéthly would add some "bitter comments" about this lack of notification.[69] Kéthly argued that even the Soviet Union had recognized Hungary's revolutionary government as the USSR started official negotiations with it. Later, on November 24, 1956, Kéthly appealed to the fact that Kádár was a prisoner of the Soviets and so was not responsible for his actions. She demanded that the members of the Imre Nagy government be released, but some of those members, like Kádár himself, were not only already free but also members of the new government. When Kéthly became better acquainted with UN procedures, she made individual appeals to the members of the Credentials Committee, which was composed of elected representatives of the member states who voted on the question of the mandate. However, they did not want to support Kéthly either.

All these reactions to the Hungarian uprising were based not merely on hostility or bureaucratic obstinacy but rather on caution. Initially this was because it was impossible to verify the reports coming out of Hungary both during the Revolution and as it was being quelled. On one occasion, a Security Council session was suspended pending the arrival of news from Budapest.[70] The telex connection broke off at the most dramatic possible moment as the Telegram Unit reported that there was "no communication with Budapest."[71] Disturbing news of the humanitarian drama caused by the crushing of the Revolution did make it through; as a result, the UN member states reached consensus as they voted on urgent aid for Hungary.[72] It is difficult to overstate the significance of the humanitarian work that began in the wake of these events. The "Main Committee for Refugee Affairs is doing its work," the Secretary-General said on November 7. At the same time, he promised to report on the actions taken in accordance with the resolutions brought at the UN Assembly,[73] expressing hope that the organization would treat not only the symptoms but also the causes—everything that had led to the humanitarian crisis. The report from the Secretary-General was delayed, however, as was an overview of the Hungarian political situation and any attempt to influence it as the UN Charter would have demanded.

On November 8, Hammarskjöld handed a note to the Hungarian UN delegation stating that, with the Assembly resolution of November 4, the UN condemned the armed intervention taking place in Hungary and requesting it be made possible for him to directly observe the circumstances in the country, whether in person or through his envoys, in order to report on them to the Assembly. He asked for permission both for the observers to enter Hungary and for the entry and free movement of UN colleagues who had been given the task of investigating the situation. He added that he expected a quick response to his message, just as the General Assembly expected a quick response from him. At the same time, the UN Secretariat produced a detailed list of potential observers.[74] According to the letter, Hammarskjöld was himself willing to travel to Hungary, even though his primary destination at this time was the Middle East, where bombs and parachutes were falling, and armies were marching against each other. On

November 10, there was still "no answer" from Budapest,[75] but the Secretary-General initiated a discussion about how to implement the resolutions. He sent his message to the Soviet representation at the UN and received a reply a few days later that everything happening in Hungary was a Hungarian internal affair. Budapest replied that they were "studying" the content of his message; they then concluded that the UN had no say in Hungarian domestic matters.[76] On November 13, the Secretary-General asked Hungarian deputy foreign minister István Sebes to reconsider his characterization of the events from October 23 onward as "internal affairs."[77] When this did not happen, Hammarskjöld—presumably to exert pressure—mentioned the prospect of aid as well as allowing observers into the country. His intentions were noble, but the result was calamitous: the Hungarian side was even more angry and refused to reconsider this characterization, a refusal that could have also referred to UN aid. The Secretary-General decided that the UN should reconsider the implementation of its resolutions and the instruments it could use to affect the flow of aid and hastily separated the issue of humanitarian assistance from political questions, lest anything put efforts to save lives at risk.

By this time, the Hungarian government had prepared its official position on the so-called counterrevolution,[78] which did nothing to ease the minds of those who were still hopeful for a peaceful solution concerning the Revolution whether in New York or Budapest. The acceleration of events can be precisely reconstructed from Hammarskjöld's diary: on October 24, he had lunch with Lodge and met with Mongi Slim, a UN Ambassador from Tunisia; on the following day, he notes "S.C." (presumably referring to the Security Council) followed by a question mark. From October 28 to October 31, Hammarskjöld writes about the Hungarian situation in his diary on a daily basis, followed by the word "Assembly" from November 1 forward.[79] On the afternoon of November 3, "S.C." appears again, and "Assembly" that evening. Early in the morning on November 4, a dramatic session of the Security Council took place, and was continued at 4:00 p.m. (10:00 p.m. Budapest time). These meetings resulted in a ten-to-one vote supporting United Nations Security Council resolution 120 and called for an immediate meeting of the General Assembly to consider the Hungarian question. By this time, Hungary was the only item mentioned in the Secretary-General's diary. The subject of the UN General Assembly session instead became the Suez Crisis, however. The following day, US Ambassador Cabot Lodge appeared in Hammarskjöld's office; the day after that, Soviet

Road crossing after the second Soviet invasion of November 4, 1956. Copyright: Fortepan #39833. Donated by Gyula Nagy.

Ambassador Arkady Sobolev did the same. The reception on November 7 for the thirty-ninth anniversary of the Great October Socialist Revolution was crossed out in the diary, while from November 8 to 12, the only entry referred to the Assembly. A speech to peacekeeping troops was marked for November 14, at which point the UN forces had already been organized, equipped, and sent to Suez.[80]

By this time, a different military force was already "pacifying" Hungary. On November 14, "Mr. Horváth," who served as Hungarian minister of foreign affairs both before and after the 1956 Revolution, visited Secretary-General Hammarskjöld.[81] But Hammarskjöld left on a trip to the Middle East immediately following this meeting, and until November 19, the Secretary-General's personal resolution of the Suez Crisis overwrote any other business he might have had.

One factor in the Secretary-General's lack of focus on Hungary could have been an analysis of the situation in Hungary received by Hammarskjöld on the evening of November 9, following on from previous reports. While the analysis did not discuss matters of substance, it did emphasize the efforts of the prewar Hungarian political forces to take control of the

Revolution, with the apparent intention of taking the edge off this extremely dramatic state of affairs. What the analysis failed to mention was a new and brutal contravention of the UN Charter: the deportation of Hungarian revolutionaries—and not only revolutionaries but simple people the Soviets randomly arrested—to the Soviet Union.[82] These reports were confirmed by a variety of independent sources. In a telegram, US delegate Lodge asked the UN to intervene, adding that if the Secretary-General did not act, the American UN Mission would go to the press. Hammarskjöld understood not only the extortion attempt but also how powerless he was. At this point, he told his deputy that this Hungary affair—of all affairs—was simply beyond his powers of endurance.[83]

The Secretary-General's reluctance to get involved may have been due to his areas of expertise: he was a passionate believer in international law and had originally been an expert on economic affairs. The notion of a violent uprising is perhaps rather hard to process from either of these perspectives, and if it could be understood, it would be unlikely to be seen in a positive light. However attached Hammarskjöld was to liberal democracy, he clearly did not see revolution as the way to achieve it. Instead, he might have preferred some form of evolutionary process that, in his view, could be irreversible. The romance of a revolution did not square with his refined tastes, broad and deep erudition, or transcendent nostalgia (even in the most turbulent of times, he established a meditation room at the UN).

There was another important element in this unfortunate constellation of influences: the question of when and how Hammarskjöld heard about the events in Hungary. He was not easily convinced by primary sources. A yellow note attached to a dossier full of desperate messages from the revolutionary forces said that "H[ammarskjöld] does not seem to show an interest in these."[84] It was the UN staff responsible for this area—the members of the Secretariat's Department of Political and Security Affairs, led by Protitch—who prepared summaries of the Hungarian developments for the Secretary-General, constantly and systematically collecting information and organizing and ranking the various messages and reports. Through this process, documentation might be no more than a brief commentary, for example, "Note on the Course of the Insurrection in Hungary"[85] or a "Review of Events, 23 October–20 November, 1956." There were also reports titled "Summary of Events" or simply "Note."[86] The newspapers, however, provided very thorough coverage—a number of foreign journalists were stationed in Budapest throughout the Revolution—and UN member states had their own independent sources of news, which found their way to UN delegations in New York through each country's foreign ministry.

It appears as if the summaries sent to Hammarskjöld were inspired by the Soviet position, for in the reports compiled by Protitch's department, those behind the events in Hungary were referred to as insurgents or rebels, and hardly ever as revolutionaries. No mention was made of the students' demands, the statue of Stalin being pulled down, the ÁVH shots fired next to the Hungarian radio building, or the mass murder committed on the square in front of the Hungarian Parliament. But these reports did include statements that the revolutionaries "continued to fire at Soviet patrols, despite a cease fire agreement," that there was mention of "counterrevolutionary elements," that the "fluctuating elements of a revolutionary situation defy precise portrayal," and that it was impossible to have a full view of the situation on account of the continuous changes.[87] The authors of one of these unsigned reports describe Imre Nagy—not a charismatic figure, but one rising to his task—simply as the "unhappy prime minister" who was attempting to reconcile incompatible demands. The term "revolutionary army" appeared in the report at the UN Headquarters in New York, but there was no such thing in Budapest.[88] In describing the reasons for and events of the Revolution and its aftermath, there were quotations from the Soviet-installed politicians János Kádár and Ferenc Münnich and others and from the Soviets themselves. In the nine-page report, deportations are accorded a mere four lines among the events that followed the suppression of the Revolution—four lines that include Moscow's denial of these deportations. The bias expressed in these unsigned reports surprised even those working at the UN Secretariat, as the underlined words, question marks, and notes on the copy of it indicate.[89] The conclusion of the analysis is telling: According to the report, even without Imre Nagy's resignation as prime minister the Presidential Council could dismiss him. By this act, an earlier barrier to the Soviet agenda in the constitutional procedure, the provision that Imre Nagy would have to resign to be removed, was remedied.[90] That is, a new prime minister arriving in a tank, as János Kádár did, was legitimate, even without the lawful resignation of the former prime minister, Imre Nagy.

The story of Dragoslav Protitch, the "émigré Yugoslav," is a curiosity in its own right—one that, according to conflicting rumors, involved anti-communism, kinship with the Croatian ultra-nationalist group the Ustaše, and loyalty to the Soviets. Protitch was in a delicate position as a result of his appointment as the United Nations Under-Secretary for Political and Security Council Affairs. As Trygve Lie, the first UN Secretary-General, explains in his book, just after his appointment he was advised that the "Big Five" had reached a secret agreement in London that the Soviets would appoint the Under-Secretary-General (then called the Assistant Secretary-General) for Political and Security Council Affairs. Lie writes that the decision should have been made by a recommendation from the Security Council and then a vote from the full General Assembly—the same procedure as when the Secretary-General is appointed. Not only was this not done for Protitch's appointment, but the Soviets continued to appoint under-secretaries-general from 1946 through 1987. As a result every person filling this position from 1946 to 1993 was a Soviet with the exception of Protitch, who served from 1955 to 1957. In June of 1957, Protitch was replaced by Anatoly Dobrynin, who served as Under-Secretary-General of the department until 1959. While this does not mean that Protitch was in the Soviet camp, it probably means that the Soviets would not have appointed him if they thought that his appointment would create problems for them. Protitch likely had little faith in the loyalty of his department's many Eastern bloc employees and must have been keenly aware that the days of his tenure, ultimately squeezed in between Soviet-appointed department heads, were numbered.

Although initially quite partisan, later reports from Protitch's department to the Secretary-General were slightly more cautious and seemed to attempt at least a semblance of objectivity by primarily publishing documents that included the source "R.B.," which stood for "radio broadcast." After November 4, once independent radio broadcasters in Hungary had gone silent, it was the first-rate translations of the triumphant reports of the Kádár regime's central propaganda machine that were placed on the Secretary-General's desk in quick succession.

News from Hungary did, of course, sometimes reach the United Nations from other sources, one of the most important being the surveys of the International Commission of Jurists, undertaken with great expertise and based on precise information. But these surveys reached the UN's leader only in a very filtered form, if at all.

The effect of the Hungarian Revolution's suppression spread beyond the shocked reactions of Western communist parties. The brutality of the Soviets during the conflict led to divisions and dramatically declining membership in communist parties, mainly in the West (where these parties were somewhat popular), and to desperation among the disarrayed peoples of

Soviet tank on the street of Budapest after the second invasion on November 4, 1956.
Copyright: Fortepan #149258. Donated by Gyula Nagy.

Eastern Europe. It was in November of 1956, once the Revolution had been crushed, that a few high-level, to this day unidentified, diplomats from the Eastern bloc working at the UN decided that the actions in Hungary and the inaction in New York could no longer be tolerated.[91] These diplomats were convinced, and had evidence, that the deadlock over the Hungarian question was no coincidence and was in fact the direct result of heavy Soviet influence on UN leadership. They knew they would be taking an enormous risk by publicizing these pronouncements, so they planned to release the information with great care. They did not turn to the officials of the United Nations or the United States—even indirectly—but instead to a Scandinavian, someone considered to be neutral but with high-level US connections. This was Povl Bang-Jensen, a Danish employee of the UN Secretariat who had worked for the Danish embassy in Washington during the war, had assisted the antifascist resistance in Denmark from that position, and who they rightly assumed had high-level US connections. These anonymous diplomats trusted Bang-Jensen, and when they passed their information to him asked only that he inform Washington at the highest level of the dire state of affairs in the United Nations. Bang-Jensen was advised to not write anything down and to not send information through official channels, as there it could encounter officials whose loyalties could be questioned. The diplomats' suspicions were that even the State Department and CIA had been infiltrated by Soviet operatives. Instead, Bang-Jensen was to inform the head of intelligence services or president directly. Because the diplomats knew there was no turning back from this point, they asked for asylum in return for providing this information.

Bang-Jensen was well aware of the obligation brought by the trust placed in him. He acted quickly and circumspectly, establishing contact with James Barco, who worked at the US delegation to the UN and who he suspected was in contact with US central intelligence.[92] He revealed no more than was absolutely necessary to protect his sources and asked Barco to write nothing down. Barco listened but did nothing for months. When he did finally take action, he wrote down everything and did all he should not have done.[93] The desperate and outspoken diplomats disappeared from New York. Whether it was in light of Barco's inaction or notes, or indeed entirely independent these factors, the diplomats were stationed elsewhere or sent to Siberia or the Lubyanka.

In light of all this, it is easy to understand how the UN's legal department saw nothing objectionable in the Hungarian delegation's accreditation, even though the official document did not have the exact date, only the month (November). The signatures, it is true, attested to legal continuity: István Dobi, the president of the Presidential Council of the Hungarian People's Republic, and István Kristóf, secretary of the council, signed the accreditation, just as they had signed previous documents. According to the official mandate, from November 1956, Hungary would be represented at the United Nations by Imre Horváth, Endre Sík, Imre Vajda, Imre Hollai, Pál Rácz, and János Szabó.[94]

What was acceptable to the UN leadership and its relevant committees was, beyond a certain point, unacceptable to the Hungarian delegation. On December 11, in the heat of the debate, the entire delegation, led by Imre Horváth, stood up and marched out of the Assembly Hall in disgust. Their sense of powerless rage and the sting of the series of humiliations they had experienced expressed itself as protest. Horváth's entourage announced that the Hungarian delegation would not participate in the work of the Assembly until the Hungarian question was debated in the spirit of the UN Charter. Even today, we still do not know whether Stalinist bureaucrat

Imre Horváth, minister of foreign affairs of Hungary, addressing the General Assembly.
Copyright: UN Photo Archive #128704.

and minister of foreign affairs Horváth and his entourage were following instructions of some kind[95] or whether the disgruntled protest was done merely to prevent the minister's blood pressure problems from worsening to the point where Horváth had a stroke in front of the community of nations—not much later, his health problems would force him to ask his deputy to deliver his speech to the Assembly.[96]

Storming out was the easy part—but what about getting back in? This question fell to Péter Mód[97] to answer. Mód arrived in New York in January 1957 with valid accreditation, only to become an emblematic figure in the later struggle. Not long before, he had led the revolutionaries in the Hungarian foreign ministry; now he became the foreign administrator of the Kádárist counterrevolution. His arrival made the headlines, and his letter of credence was accepted by Hammarskjöld in person. Protitch would eventually warm to him, though he first thought Mód was a refugee, which he could easily have been because of his role during the Revolution.[98] Mód was well educated, knew Europe, and had served time in jail. Now that the Hungarian delegation had left the Assembly Hall in rage, the corridors of power were his only place to maneuver. Both Budapest and Moscow pondered the manner of his return: it should be neither conspicuous nor sly, neither aggressive nor self-critical.

That the Hungarian delegation to the UN was "isolated and passive" could be sensed in Budapest from its reports, and negotiations with other satellites and their Soviet taskmasters did nothing to help.[99] Bulgaria and Poland argued for the Hungarian delegation to return to the Assembly Hall, while the Soviets—namely Deputy Minister Vasily Kuznetsov and UN envoy Arkady Sobolev—feared that this move would only encourage certain Western member states to have the Hungarian delegation removed. And, although the UN had not changed its position on the Hungarian question since the delegation had withdrawn, Mód was right to sense that "the longer we wait, the harder it will be to return."[100] In the end, his approach won the day. The delegation took its place successfully and without upheaval. This was thanks not just to Mód's tactics nor to the insulted Horváth returning to Hungary but also to UN procedure, which sought neither to sanction the delegation's continued withdrawal nor to render difficult its return. In addition, the relevant committee had neither rejected nor accepted the Hungarian delegation's mandate but simply suspended it. The Mission was able to use its offices and the UN's infrastructure and could speak in debates and submit documents with the UN letterhead; the suspended mandate merely affected its vote and eligibility. This proved to be a rather dreadful, disastrous precedent—not least because it was in stark contrast to the measures taken regarding the Suez Crisis. Yet this aggression did not lead to a world war; indeed, chances for world peace only improved, as former antagonists stood on the same side while the aggressor democracies were forced to veto the condemnatory resolution in the Security Council, only to be defeated at the Assembly. Following this, however, the former aggressors had to implement the UN resolutions, resolutions the Soviets and their Hungarian "comrades" never took seriously for an instant. It was as if there was a double standard at the UN: there was one rule for those who kept to the norms, and a rule that could be broken with impunity by the miscreants.

The United Nations had another success: the efficient and impressive UN military force, created out of nothing as the UN had no standing army and had to organize, equip, and transport the UN Emergency Force to Suez. The soldiers in blue helmets did not set out to fight but rather to guarantee a tense and armed peace. A condition of their deployment was that both belligerent parties accept the authority of the UN. In Budapest, it was hard to imagine this being put into effect, as there was no revolutionary army and Béla Király forbade the regular Hungarian Army from taking up arms in resistance. Later, the state security institutions recognized that the commander-in-chief of the National Guard considered this a "suicidal" move, one that could not come to pass, if only because the Hungarian-Soviet military negotiations, which continued until the last minute, seemed promising.[101]

As he retreated west from Budapest heading toward Nagykovácsi, Béla Király stopped at the residence of the US minister and asked about the UN army.[102] Meanwhile, political thinker István Bibó, in a proclamation written in the parliament building as it was already occupied by the Soviets, suggested the possibility of the "UN police" intervening if the Soviets refused to retreat from Hungary. That the revolutionaries "expected UN intervention in November" would later be recorded at the ÁVH,[103] just as the newspapers, in the headiest days of optimism, reported that the UN had "enough moral standing, and, if need be, enough power" to see to it that its resolutions were implemented.[104] György Szennik, fascist billboard painter turned ÁVH agent, who first gave the resistance fighters Red Cross aid and then assisted their "eradication" by giving precise reports on them to the Soviet Army, also knew that the insurgents were "hoping for assistance from the UN troops."[105]

Naturally, the United Nations was aware of all of this. Radio operators in Gothenburg picked up the Hungarians' calls for help, which passed through the Swedish foreign ministry to Hammarskjöld's desk. These messages called for parachutists to land in Transdanubia[106] to fight the Soviet troops. Many at the UN were aware of Bibó's proclamation sent abroad, as he had handed it in person to the embassies and legations he could access. His fellow minister Anna Kéthly also believed the UN's "police force" could return the lawful government to power;[107] she considered the situation in Egypt to be a precedent.[108] And the émigré Hungarian politicians offering to represent Hungary also requested the use of UN forces in the name of the "imprisoned" government to secure a cease-fire in the country.[109]

The UN did not even consider the possibility of employing armed forces, however. At most, the organization might have wanted observers to monitor Soviet troop withdrawal.[110] But the opposite occurred, and it seems the UN was in no mood to watch the invasion.

Even during the Soviet attack, Béla Király hoped the UN would at least help both sides to come to some kind of agreement. One of the key charges later leveled against Imre Nagy was that he turned to the UN, whose "intervention" could have started a global war. Even though Nagy never referred to weapons (nor did the UN have any), in the course of the investigation and then the trial, the prosecutors and their political masters invented the doctrine of military intervention and turned this into a charge of treason: the prime minister would have attacked his own country with foreign weapons.

Through all this, the communist politicians handled Secretary-General Hammarskjöld with kid gloves, making sure he would not be held personally responsible for the decisions of the institution he led. They did not want him to hear of him making a visit Hungary, however, and repeatedly rejected his feeblest attempts to do so.[111] In fact, the leaders of the UN never for a moment considered taking back by force what the Soviets had taken from Hungary by force. Even those American politicians who supported the Hungarian cause thought it would be "utterly irresponsible" to send the UN police to Hungary: they believed the insurgents should avoid taking on even more risk when the international community could offer nothing more than moral support.[112]

US president Dwight D. Eisenhower was concerned that if the Soviets thought their security buffer in Eastern Europe was vulnerable to collapse, they might feel obliged to resort to "extreme measures," in other words, to nuclear weapons and a world war.[113] It seemed wise not to take a chance on such eventualities—especially for one little European country. All troop movements in Western Europe were halted: NATO was unable to do exercises in these critical weeks, and no weapons were to enter even Austria, the only noncommunist-ruled neighbor of Hungary. Eisenhower sent communist leader Nikita Khrushchev a special message that the US would not look kindly on a breach of Austria's sovereignty. The Soviets were within their rights to move as far as Hungary, but no further. By mid-December, the powers in the West could see quite clearly what they had not seen for ten years: that uprisings in this region must not be encouraged, as there was little chance of any real support if this happened.[114] This represented a turning point in US Cold War policy. Previously, this policy had been one of containment and liberation, but no longer. The rhetoric broadcast by Radio Free Europe and other means to what some called the "captive nations" only belatedly followed this cynical but wise political decision, a delay that would cost many lives.

It is hard to draw clear conclusions about the events surrounding the ill-fated Hungarian Revolution and the UN, but there were several factors involved. First, a sabotage was executed inside the Hungarian Mission, which was not only infiltrated by secret agents but somehow dominated by that faction and independent of the Hungarian foreign ministry's instructions. Other factors were the lack of reliable information from Hungary, the misleading of Secretary-General Hammarskjöld by his closest colleagues, and the reluctance of the great powers to recognize Imre Nagy's government and its envoy Anna Kéthly in her official capacity. The Suez Crisis and the conflict among Western democracies were to be the final, fatal blow to all the expectations and hopes Hungarian revolutionaries had nurtured.

Notes

1. ÁVH is the abbreviation of the Hungarian Államvédelmi Hatóság, the state security authority or infamous communist political police.
2. Állambiztonsági Szolgálatok Történeti Levéltára (Historical Archive of the Hungarian State Security Services; hereinafter: ÁBTL) 3.2.6. OL-11/I.
3. This was highlighted by János Radványi, secret service agent, then foreign affairs officer, who was chargé d'affaires at the Hungarian legation in Washington from 1962 until 1967.
4. ÁBTL 3.2.6. OL-8-011/VIII.
5. Ibid. and ÁBTL 3.2.6. OL-11/I.
6. Tatár visited Rodzianko, director of the protocol division. ÁBTL 3.2.6. OL-011/II. László Hámori worked at the UN Secretariat from 1947 onward.
7. János Arany was a nineteenth-century genius of Hungarian verse whose name was used by intelligence agent Pál Rácz. A first lieutenant from 1952 to 1957, he was an undercover foreign affairs member of staff and later a major general. Many years later, he was the leader of the Hungarian delegation to the UN (1980–1986). ÁBTL 3.2.6. OL-8-011/VIII.
8. Ibid.
9. ÁBTL 3.2.5. O-8-079.
10. Claire de Hedervary (1920–2020) was born Klára Héderváry in Budapest. She left Hungary and moved to Belgium years before the persecution of Jews in Hungary. ÁBTL 3.2.6. OL-8-011/XII.
11. ÁBTL 3.2.6. OL-8-011/XII.
12. In 1954, Imre Nagy again requested Hungary's admission to the United Nations. Magyar Nemzeti Levéltár Hungarian National Archive (hereinafter MNL) XIX-J-1-j, box 55. Külügyminisztérium Ministry of Foreign Affairs (hereinafter KÜM)/26h.
13. February 23, 1955. ÁBTL 3.2.6. OL-011/V/B. The proposal contains the selection and testing of "two physical drop-off points" and two "marked positions."
14. See the newspaper *Szabad Nép*, December 16, 1955; ÁBTL 3.2.6. OL-011 V. B.

15. Lieutenant-colonel István Markotán, Captain Endre Torda, and Pál Rácz, an intelligence agent and a counterintelligence officer, all moved to New York.

16. Hollai Imre (1925–2017) was an intelligence officer under diplomatic "cover."

17. Pál Rácz's file: ÁBTL 2.8.1.-6528 and ÁBTL 3.2.5. O-8-79.

18. ÁBTL 3.2.6. OL-011/II.

19. ÁBTL 3.2.6. OL-08-011/VIII.

20. ÁBTL 3.2.6. OL-08-011/II.

21. ÁBTL 3.2.6. OL-08-011/VIII.

22. Swedish Royal Library (Kungliga Biblioteket), Dag Hammarskjöld Samling (hereinafter DHS) L 179:173.

23. During their visit, Mikhail Suslov and Anastas Mikoyan recommended that the party leadership be made younger, that the percentage of leaders of Jewish extraction be reduced, and that attacks be made on "antiparty groups."

24. Prime Minister András Hegedűs only signed the request for Soviet assistance some days later.

25. "The Treasonous UN Delegation Should Be Replaced at Once!" *Igazság*, October 30, 1956; "Kós Péter—Lev Konduktorov," *Magyar Nemzet*, October 31, 1956.

26. National Archives of Australia (hereinafter NAA), A 1209, 1957/5279.

27. Szereda and Rainer, *Döntés a Kremlben.*

28. On the two telegrams, see Békés, *Európából Európába.*

29. "The comrades sent from the ministry of the interior find themselves in a difficult position in the embassies. They have been almost completely exposed." MNL 288f., storage unit 32/1957/7 (documents of the Foreign Affairs Division of the Hungarian Socialist Workers' Party [MSZMP] Central Committee). On November 1, they ordered the diplomatic missions to send the intelligence operatives home at once. See Baráth and Gecsényi, *Főkonzulok, követek és nagykövetek,* 40–41.

30. Izsák, Szabó, and Szabó, *1956 plakátjai és röplapjai,* 70.

31. The FBI pointed out that, following the communist takeover in Yugoslavia (during the period of the Tito-Stalin friendship), Protitch remained in the Yugoslav foreign service. See the documents published by the FBI (on the basis of the Freedom of Information Act) in the Bang-Jensen Archive (hereinafter BJI, National Széchenyi Library, Manuscript Archive, Fond. 413), box 33.

32. The documents have survived among the so-called Cordier papers, placed in the archive of Columbia University by the outgoing Under-Secretary-General Andrew W. Cordier, Columbia University, Butler Library, Rare Books and Manuscript Collection (hereinafter ACP).

33. United Nations Archives and Records Management (hereinafter UNARM) S-0442-0138-06.

34. MNL XIX-J-1-j 81, box 4/j. See also Gál, *A "Jelcin–dosszié,"* 127.

35. Similar instructions were sent to Sobolev, Soviet envoy to the UN, by the Central Committee of the Soviet Communist Party. See Gál, *A "Jelcin–dosszié,"* 59.

36. Radványi (1995), 3–7.

37. See Béla Varga's statement from his press conference held on October 28. MNL XIX-J-1-j, box 55.

38. The British position is cited in Haraszti-Taylor, *Hungarian Revolution of 1956,* 112–17. At the same time, US chargé d'affaires Spencer Barnes asked that the

media should avoid making statements regarding Imre Nagy. Cited in McCargar, *A Szabad Európa Bizottság*, 275.

39. There was no question of US forces or even of UN peacekeepers. See the telegram from the State Department on November 4, 1956: National Archives and Records Administration (hereinafter NARA) 764.00/11-456.

40. For Lodge's statement on neutrality, see Finger, *Your Man at the UN*, 79.

41. NARA 764.00/10-2556. According to the UK representative to the UN, on November 3, 1956, Lodge had no authorization to submit a resolution proposal, given that the situation in Hungary was "too obscure." See Haraszti-Taylor, *Hungarian Revolution of 1956*, 164.

42. NARA 764.00/29-1056. It was presumably this that caused news to spread in Budapest that a UN committee was arriving in Hungary.

43. See Haraszti-Taylor, *Hungarian Revolution of 1956*, 451.

44. November 3, 1956. Imre Nagy's telegram to Hammarskjöld. UNARM S-0442-0138-06. See the document's archive of János Péter, MNL XIX-J-1-j, box 81.

45. See the US Department of State telegram of November 1, 1956. NARA 764.00/11-156.

46. DHS L 179:83.

47. See the October 29, 1956, telegram from the US Mission to the UN. NARA 764.00/10-2956.

48. ÁBTL K-1360/I.

49. Ibid.

50. See the 1961 report titled "On the Discharged Secret Operative with Code Name Bertalan Székely," in which Hollai's report is cited from the Hungarian foreign ministry on March 11, 1957. ÁBTL K-1360/I.

51. Ibid.

52. Ibid.

53. As early as November 23, 1956, Hollai wrote a note titled "Some questions relating to the Hungarian question." MNL XIX-1-24a, box 3 (New York).

54. Mód and Hollai reported to the members of the UN Department of the Hungarian foreign ministry on March 6, 1957. MNL XIX-J-24-a, box 1 (documents from the Hungarian High Consulate in New York). Szabó should have delivered the speech on neutrality at the special session of the UN Assembly (which was convened to discuss the Suez affair). MNL XIX-J-1-j 81, box 4/j.

55. Hollai was involved in the work of the Assembly when it voted on the Austrian proposal for aid. MNL XIX-J-24-a, box 1.

56. On November 2, 1956, the Department of State in Washington asked the same of its head of legation in Budapest. In response to this US interest, Károly Szarka gave a dilatory response on November 3. NARA 764.00/11.356.

57. Pál Auer was one of the key figures in the Hungarian émigré community. Together with Ferenc Nagy, on November 3, he drew the attention of the United Nations to the impending Soviet invasion. UNARM S-0442-0138-06.

58. MNL XIX-J-1-j, box 209. See also Sík, *Bem rakparti évek*.

59. Anna Kéthly was a social democrat who had spent time in prison and was invited by Imre Nagy to join his government.

60. UNARM S-0442-0139-06.

61. Ibid.

62. Ibid.; Kéthly, *Száműzve, de le nem győzve*, 14.

63. György Heltai was going to go to the UN. See MNL MSZMP documents, 290f.

64. Ibid., 56.

65. Until 1971 China was represented by the Kuomintang.

66. Australia's position suggested there was consensus that "Mr. Horváth" was a Soviet puppet and that it was time to remove him from the Assembly. NAA A 1209 1957/5279.

67. To member states, this was self-evident. As UK representative Pierson Dixon put it, the act of the Soviet Union had "shaken the foundations of the UN." NAA A 1209 1957/5279.

68. NARA 764.00/11-2656.

69. The Swedish *Dagens Nyheter* wrote about this on November 21, 1956. On the copy of this article there is a handwritten note from Hammarskjöld instructing that it be attached to the Hungarian documents. ACP Box 184.

70. The suspension was enacted when Szabó unofficially informed the Security Council that a new government had been formed. The Security Council did not pass a resolution. Radványi (1972), 15.

71. ACP, box 184.

72. "Humanitarian Assistance to the Hungarian People." UNARM S-0445-0195-12550-1.

73. Some UN documents date the first activity of an observation group from November 4: "Group of Three on Hungary, November 4, 1956–December 12, 1956." For the full documentation on this, see: ACP, box 184. Hammarskjöld sent a copy of the note to Budapest. The group, made up of three lawyers, began its work on November 16, 1956; on November 23, 1956, the Secretary-General asked the Hungarian authorities to allow them into the country. NARA 764.00/11-1156. See the 18 January 1958 chronology of the Hungarian foreign ministry. MNL XIX-J-1-j, box 56. UNARM S-0009-0002-09.

74. DHS L 179:83.

75. Ibid.

76. From Foreign Minister István Sebes on 10 November. DHS L 179:83.

77. UNARM S-0442-0138-06.

78. István Sebes forwarded this to New York on 19 November. UNARM S-0442-0138-06.

79. "S.C." = Security Council; "G.A." = General Assembly. DHS L 179:173.

80. At a press conference on May 21, 1959, Hammarskjöld said: "I don't think that the Assembly or any of its members asked me at the same time to pay attention to everything that was happening in Budapest." UNARM S-0442-0138.

81. DHS L 179:173.

82. According to Soviet documents, four to five thousand detainees landed in Soviet prisons, including ex-communists and students. Sixty-eight were minors, of whom nine were young girls. Eight detectives from the KGB dealt with those held in custody. Szereda and Sztikalin (1993), 155–57.

83. Lodge had previously informed Cordier that Hungarians were being deported. The Under-Secretary-General suggested they turn to the Hungarian

government, which was qualified to respond; the latter simply denied the claim. NARA 764.00/11-1456. Hammarskjöld was unimpressed by the ultimatum, saying the UN could do little to assist the Hungarians while acknowledging that it might endanger his position. After a certain point, he refused to be pressured on the matter. UNARM DAG 1.1.1.1.3, box 15. During the investigation of the UN Special Committee, it became clear that the application of international pressure played a role in stopping the deportations. *Report of the Special Committee on the Problem of Hungary. General Assembly Official Records: 11th Session Supplement No. 18. (A/3592)*, 126.

84. UNARM DAG 1.1.1.3.

85. UNARM S-0188-0006-00003 (Protitch files).

86. UNARM S-0445-0196-12884-Part A 2UC.

87. Ibid. The reports state that Imre Nagy was not on top of events, was not suitable for establishing realistic policy, that the events were not transparent, and that the regime was not stable. According to these reports, the uprising started when Mátyás Rákosi, the de facto communist leader of Hungary prior to the Revolution, introduced reforms, but he was deposed, allowing pre-1948 political forces to gain the upper hand. Imre Nagy did not respect the new line taken by Soviet leadership, which is why he rescinded the Warsaw Pact. The country was ruled by nationalism, and in the armed clashes, the state police, together with loyal members of the party, was defending the system. UNARM S-0445-0196-12884-Part A 3UC.

88. "Hungarian Revolutionary Army." UNARM S-0445-0196-12884-Part A 3UC.

89. UNARM S-0445-0196-12884-Part A 3UC.

90. Ibid. On December 10, 1956, according to the "Note on the Course of the Insurrection," the summoning of the Soviet Army took place on the basis of a Hungarian government resolution. There was no opportunity for the "niceties of constitutional procedure" while order was being restored, but the Presidential Council recognized the government on November 9, so this legal deficiency was resolved. UNARM DAG 1.1.1.3 Protitch files.

91. According to confidential sources, this took place on November 25, 1956, so it is conceivable that they broke ranks not just because the Revolution had been crushed but also because Imre Nagy had been kidnapped: as he left the Yugoslav embassy in Budapest, Nagy was arrested by the KGB. See *The Bang-Jensen Case*, 27–37. See also Mrs. Bang-Jensen's witness statement before the committee of the UN Senate, BJI, box 31.

92. According to a CIA document, he was the intelligence liaison within the US Mission to the UN. BJI, box 33. For the memoirs of the embittered diplomat, see James Barco, "Recollections of Dag Hammarskjöld and the United Nations," Oral History Research Office, Columbia University, 1964. For a reconstruction of this, see Copp and Peck, *Betrayal at the UN*; and the Senate Report (1961). See also Robert Morris's witness statement before the Senate committee, BJI, and *The Bang-Jensen Case*, 40–42. He later wrote about this in Morris, *Self Destruct*.

93. See the results of the investigation of the US Senate. *The Bang-Jensen Case*.

94. UNARM S-0446-0105-0004-00001 UC. See Hollai's report from 11 November. MOL XIX-J-1-k. 69. 4j.

95. Sík blurted out to László Hámori, the Hungarian-born member of the UN Committee, that the Hungarian delegation was being pressured not only by the

Soviets but also from "within." Horváth was a Stalinist, Rácz a police officer, and the others were not primarily diplomats. The US Mission reported as follows: NARA 310.5/12-656.

96. Sík, *Bem rakparti évek*, 164. Imre Horváth died soon afterward.

97. Péter Mód was Hungary's Ambassador to the UN from 1957 to 1961.

98. Mód's report, 23 January 1957. MNL XIX-J-1-j, box 209.

99. Diplomats from countries in the socialist bloc regularly met at "friendly" embassies to compare notes. MNL XIX-1-24-a.

100. MNL XIX-J-24-a, box 1.

101. Béla Király, commander-in-chief of the National Guard in 1956. His orders were relayed to the ÁVH by his adjutant, who used the cover name "Virág" (Flower). ÁBTL 1.6.90-6/1/1957.

102. But he was only able to talk to the gardener. See the interview with Király in Swartz, *A New Look at the 1956 Revolution*, 547.

103. Ministry of the Interior meeting, MNL XIX-B-1-j, box 1. Later, the executions of István Batonai and László Batonai were based on them waiting for word from the UN troops that they would finally fight the Soviet invaders together—now considered to be an act of treason. See Hegedűs, *1956 Kézikönyve I. kötet*. By this time, the ÁVH had officially been disbanded, but the personnel of the political police were more or less the same. See Radványi (1972), 58.

104. *Magyar Függetlenség*, November 2, 1956. p. 1.

105. ÁBTL 3.1.1. BT-602/1. We will see more of "Szeles" Szennik's story later.

106. 4 November 1956. Stockholm. UNARM S-0442-0138-06.

107. ACP, box 184. In Hungary, Kéthly was accused of "urging an openly armed intervention" that politicians would "push through as an UN measure." MNL XIX-J-41-a. The UN obviously did not have a "police force."

108. UNARM S-0890-0008-0001-00001 UC.

109. According to the message from Ferenc Nagy and Pál Auer. UNARM S-0442-0138-06.

110. UNARM S-0890-0008-0001-0001 UC.

111. Rahman, *Magyarország, 1959–1959*. Foreign Minister Horváth's advice to Hammarskjöld was that if he postponed the Assembly's debate on the Hungarian question, they might consider inviting him to Budapest. (See the letter from Imre Horváth dated 27 November 1956.) NARA S-0442-0138. As a result, the Secretary-General rejected the US request to raise the question of the Hungarian UN mandate, as this might obstruct his visit to Hungary. NARA 320.5764/12-556.

112. The Australian diplomatic service also noted the US position. NAA A 1209 1957/5279. The police learned that workers of various kinds would have used strikes to force the visit of the UN Secretary-General. Kajári, *Rendőrségi napi jelentések*, 2:49.

113. Radványi (1972), 11.

114. NAA A 1209 1957/5279.

2

THE CRISIS IN HUNGARY AND ATTEMPTS FOR RESOLUTION

The Initial Political Shock at the UN

Shocked by the Soviet invasion, the UN Assembly called an emergency session, where it passed the resolution that Hungary should allow UN observers to enter the country and guarantee their freedom of passage. This resolution was telegraphed to the government in Budapest. The selection of these observers as well as a planned committee of investigation was already underway. To help them better prepare themselves, the UN Secretariat compiled a dossier of information, for which it approached the representative of the Hungarian government at the UN. In line with the existing instructions of the cabinet led by Imre Nagy, this delegate was deputy head of mission János Szabó, as he had the valid accreditation.[1]

Given the UN resolution, there was doubt over how Secretary-General Dag Hammarskjöld could satisfy his obligation to observe, report, and recommend, as indicated by a memorandum; he was, after all, compelled by the UN Assembly to resolve the situation.[2] Hammarskjöld could see that the authenticity of his mandate as Secretary-General depended on whether he could implement UN resolutions, so, in an aide-mémoire of November 8, he surveyed the steps that had to be taken. Yet the chosen form of the memorandum made it perfectly clear that he could only make a "Note Verbale," an official document of the steps he had to and wanted to take but that he was unable to achieve in practice.

Two days later, on November 10, the Secretary-General noted with regret that he had still not received a reply to his urgent proposal to implement the resolution of the November 4 Assembly. He noted this in an aide-mémoire to the Soviet representative to the UN. At a press conference on November 12, Hammarskjöld spoke of two groups: one would conduct a general investigation in Hungary, and the other would make direct observations on location. His words seemed to suggest that serious preparations were underway, but the documentation reveals that UN Under-Secretary-General Dragoslav Protitch merely put together a list of names of potential nominees, enclosing the list of states with diplomatic representation in Budapest.[3]

Despite what was said at the press conference, Hammarskjöld had a sense that observers would hardly be able to enter Hungary and that there was little chance of cooperation from the side of the Hungarian authorities. Furthermore, any kind of local presence would mean establishing direct contact with the János Kádár government, which appeared troublesome as it was imposed by the Soviets after the Revolution was suppressed. The Secretary-General considered a group of observers made up of representatives in Budapest of "strictly neutral states,"[4] but it would have been difficult to reconcile this with the diplomatic status of these missions, representing the relevant countries that may not include observation of events on spot. When British ambassador Leslie Fry proposed something similar, the Hungarian authorities considered it an attempt to overthrow the system.

In UN terminology, the phrase "Hungarian authorities" was used to refer to the usurpatory, Soviet-installed Kádár government, a government that was not only challenging to view as legitimate but also difficult to contact. On November 12, Hungary became "disconnected" from international communications,[5] and the situation in New York was no less difficult. The UN Secretariat could not understand why observers were not allowed in Hungary if there were no deportations, if the Soviets were not shooting anyone, and if the situation was returning to normal. Communist politician Imre Horváth and his colleagues were challenged in New York representing Hungary at the UN by the less-than-transparent government measures, and they faced a shortage of funds, so the Soviet comrades helped out their devotees with a sum of $15,000.[6]

If neither the UN peacekeepers, the so-called blue helmets, a committee of investigation, nor a committee of observers were allowed to enter the territory of Hungary, Western politicians would align themselves with the supporters of the Revolution in the hopes that the Secretary-General would visit the country to mediate. Among the UN documents,[7] a note on November 14 surveyed the conditions necessary for a visit by the

Secretary-General, which also led to the question of humanitarian aid.[8] Other documents include dates that relate to Hammarskjöld's visit, which suggests some sort of coordination. News that Hammarskjöld was heading to Budapest repeatedly spread among the delegations. The conditions for the Secretary-General's visit were confirmed by legal experts and listed the privileges and exemptions enjoyed by the United Nations on the basis of those arrangements to which Hungary, like other member states, was a signatory. This legal reasoning was no doubt prepared at the Secretary-General's request: he wanted to see his room to maneuver in writing before he departed. The response of the legal experts was that, from a legal point of view, Hungary was obliged to accept all UN representatives and, therefore, by extension, the UN's leader. Thus visas were to be granted at the first possible opportunity, and travel arrangements were to be guaranteed for the UN's representative.[9] But in the end, Hammarskjöld did not make the trip to Hungary. Confidential sources claim that he did not even seriously consider going to Hungary; if this is true, the statements and "process of negotiation" seem distinctly cynical.[10]

Three years after these events, Hammarskjöld would look back on his plan to visit Budapest and see quite clearly that during those first days of November, the situation in Hungary was still in flux and Hammarskjöld's presence could have made a difference. Yet from New York at that time the situation was not precisely clear and there was not yet a specific demand for his visit from Budapest. No one thought he should leave New York during the dramatic moments of the Suez Crisis.[11] Furthermore, a trip to Budapest would have thrown him into the legal quagmire of the Revolution, whereas the situation in Suez was both legally and politically unambiguous.[12]

A later account of the crises surrounding Hammarskjöld's planned trip accurately described his frustration, intensified by his "being groomed as a scapegoat" for how the whole affair unfolded in Hungary. This description revealed the UN's complete impotence when, together with its Charter and majority opinion, it was confronted with the resolute deviousness of one of its member states.[13] For the Soviets, the Suez affair was a godsend, as it exacerbated animosity toward imperialists and hindered potential cooperation among the Western democracies. Meanwhile, former colonies were reluctant to vote with their erstwhile colonialist masters, who had since become champions of liberty.

A later record described the Hungarian situation during and after the Revolution as a complete failure. Hammarskjöld's hesitation and "slowness"[14] could have been responsible, although events might have taken the same course during a feverish hurry as opposed to the pointless meditation and unproductive waiting. Hammarskjöld could not go so far as to admit his guilt, however, as that would have affected his mandate, showing that he was incapable of keeping abreast of events he was charged with managing. The "production of a bundle of papers" on Hungary could hardly be considered a success, and it seems that at a critical time this was the most that the UN leader was able to achieve.[15] However, the UN's reticence to act on behalf of Hungary was not merely a matter concerning Hammarskjöld but rather the UN itself—its prestige, the trust invested in it, and how this trust resounded among Europe's repressed Eastern half. Or had the Assembly made a mistake when it had obligated Hammarskjöld to undertake impossible tasks? It is worthwhile to ask if any member state suggested that sanctions be imposed on Hungary or, more importantly, on the Soviet Union. This question is documented quite precisely: none did. For years, the community of nations merely went through the motions regarding the scandal, but no proposals were put forth to take effective or even seemingly effective steps. The Secretary-General could not entertain such notions, so he accepted that he might be made a scapegoat. He also accepted that Hungary's ghost would haunt him as long as he lived.[16]

Hungarian social democratic politician Anna Kéthly claimed in a statement that Hammarskjöld's visit to Budapest could have prevented the bloodbath caused by the Soviet Army's invasion, but she made this claim more out of despair than from an awareness of the facts of the case.[17] When the invasion did come to pass, the Secretary-General repeatedly made plans to travel to Hungary; on one occasion, the Assembly even ordered a break so that he might make arrangements for his trip.[18] In certain moments it was as if even the Hungarian government and its Soviet taskmasters might not object to such a visit, not least because this would have been a de facto recognition of the regime.[19] The visit was planned for December 5–6, 1956, and the UK Ambassador to the UN noted after his meeting with the Secretary-General that Hammarskjöld had "murmured something [. . .] about 9th December."[20] On December 4, the Secretary-General sent a telegram to the Hungarian foreign minister about his visit, requesting a reply within three days—a reply he did not receive. Nor did he receive a response from the Soviets, to whom he sent the same telegram.[21]

The hypocrisy of the United Nations is writ large in the telegram sent from New York to Geneva on December 11 regarding the potential dates for Hammarskjöld's visit, which referred to "Friday when it became apparent that no one was going to Budapest from the UN."[22] Under-Secretary-General Philippe de Seynes nevertheless secretly left for Budapest, not to make preparations for Hammarskjöld's visit, but rather to conduct negotiations with the Hungarian authorities about the supply of aid.[23] By early January, there was still only talk of the Secretary-General's journey being "postponed" and of his "mission" as being a possibility.[24] This was until János Kádár ruled out in an interview any possibility of the visit—presumably to the Swedish diplomat's not-inconsiderable relief.[25] At the same time, the Hungarian secret service (ÁVH) gained access to the coded messages of the French embassy, which allowed it to follow in detail the secret exchange of telegrams between Paris and Budapest concerning the Secretary-General's visit and to read the French reports acquired from New York. According to the ÁVH's somewhat inexpert interpretation of the French text, Hammarskjöld "would receive the gratification of prestige," while sources close to the Secretary-General claimed that he "is not even attempting to make the best of the opportunity to come to Hungary."[26] According to the French, the UN's forceful influence could "end foreign interventions and deportations," and the Secretary-General's procrastination was damaging to "the prestige of the UN" and "consigns into oblivion the resolutions regarding Hungary."[27]

But why would Hammarskjöld have deliberately sought out trouble? Just as the US had let him know the extent of his room to maneuver in Guatemala in 1954, so the Soviet Union was telling him now. We now know that Hammarskjöld would sometimes weep in solitude and express feelings of despair in the company of his loyal bodyguard; he even occasionally considered suicide, captivated by the idea of becoming some kind of self-sacrificing, mystical martyr.[28] As he had no wife or children, rumors of his homosexuality became the subject of gossip, but, aside from guesswork, there was no proof that this was true. But were these rumors his Achilles heel, through which he became vulnerable to blackmail from those who held sway over him? And could this vulnerability be the very reason they had wanted him as Secretary-General? Hammarskjöld seemed to enjoy his single status and had a rich intellectual life. Perhaps this is what allowed him to suffer the endless mud, blood, and suffering that was thrown his way.[29]

In his reports as Secretary-General, Hammarskjöld recalled the 1956 events in Hungary and the Suez and proudly noted that the former situation did not lead to war. Perhaps these two historic conflicts were entwined with each other through their outcomes: success in troubleshooting where consent of great powers was achieved, as in Suez, and the UN's failure to intervene on behalf of Hungary. Those who were left in the lurch could experience for themselves the essence of a joke that was doing the rounds in Budapest: There were only two ways to help Hungary. The first was simple: the Lord would descend from Heaven and resolve the crisis. The second was much more difficult: the United Nations would help. But this would require a miracle.

Attempts to Help Hungary: The Humanitarian Aid

The crisis in Hungary was complex to the degree that no easy solution could have been imaginable, much less feasible. But the UN tried to do what was possible to avoid a humanitarian catastrophe once the political one seemed to be unavoidable, though this course probably ultimately resulted in more victims than Soviet weapons and Kádár's executioners had taken. The mode of this aid was exactly in line with Hammarskjöld's heroic pragmatism. He did not mind the shame, condemnations, or scapegoating if that was the price to pay for the powdered milk, medicine, coal, and other aid necessary for survival reaching Hungary from the UN, but all these operations had to remain secret. If the UN's role in delivering this aid had been made public, the political saber-rattling would have undone this crucial humanitarian operation.

That Hammarskjöld was keenly aware of all the contradictions and consequences inherent in the situation created by the Soviet intervention in Hungary is recorded in his memoirs, which include confidential sources not intended for public consumption. The Secretary-General was also aware of the stark contrast between his efficiency in dealing with the Suez Crisis and his utter paralysis concerning the Hungarian question. As stated in an unsigned memorandum: "H[ammarksjöld] himself of course having offered and attempted to do what he could, realized as did all the governments concerned that there was nothing to be done except to take whatever humanitarian measures seemed to be possible . . . a bitter and frustrating conclusion from which he almost certainly suffered more than from the irresponsible criticism which he received."[30] Aid from the UN was also determined by its Assembly's resolutions and reached with full consensus.[31] The Soviets did not want to prevent the UN from feeding the people and rebuilding all that they had so deliberately destroyed.

But the resolution concerning aid to Hungary was not easy to implement, and it proved to be terribly urgent. Where would aid come from, who would take it to Hungary, and under what guise would they distribute it? And what needed to be distributed, and to whom? And if those who had usurped power called the UN the enemy, would they allow the aid to reach the needy, even if it had been brought at the request of UN resolutions?

One aid agency was present at the Revolution even before the UN resolutions were brought. The International Committee of the Red Cross provided professional and apolitical help with considerable self-sacrifice. The first request for aid from Budapest to Geneva came on October 27, just four days after the Revolution broke out: on that day, the first aid worker set out for Vienna and then Budapest, and the following day, a Swissair plane transported six hundred units of blood plasma to the Hungarian capital along with two aid workers, one of whom, René Bovey, remained at the scene.[32] Despite the rush, the contents of the deliveries were in line with a list that had been agreed on over the telephone, as Geneva was able to communicate with Budapest on numerous occasions.[33] Aid was delivered regularly, and the airlift was in operation until the days before the Soviet invasion. The airport in Budapest was only closed on November 2, as a preparation for the march into Hungary. When aid shipments could no longer be transported by air,[34] they were transported to the country in convoys, but for a period after November 4, even this was not possible.

Unlike the UN, the International Committee of the Red Cross was not hindered in its work by the ambiguous legality of its mandate;[35] the Revolution and invasion could be considered neither a war or a natural disaster. In addition to presence of mind, the Red Cross also had local knowledge: in the spring of 1956, the League of Red Cross Societies sent more than three and a half million aid parcels to those affected by the Danube flooding and assisted in the distribution of the aid.[36] This was extremely significant because communist politicians were suspicious of, if not outright hostile toward, the International Committee of the Red Cross. At an international conference in 1952, the Soviet envoy angrily criticized the aid agency, charging it with "crimes against humanity,"[37] and the lack of action during the Holocaust was hard to explain for many nations.

Joseph Stalin's death led to an easing of the Soviet position: in 1954, Moscow ratified the Geneva Conventions of 1949, which provided the legal foundation for the work of the aid agency, and the Parliament in Budapest followed the Soviets' lead. Later, in 1956, a genuine connection was

Red Cross vehicles carrying relief supplies and waiting to enter Hungary. Copyright: International Red Cross Photo Library #V-P-HU-N-00022-01.

established between the International Committee of the Red Cross and the Hungarian Red Cross Society, as the provision of assistance for those affected by the flood required significant organization and cooperation.[38] It was a major advantage for the International Committee of the Red Cross during and after the Revolution that they already had experience in Hungary, unlike other relief agencies. And, during the Revolution, it was the Hungarian Red Cross Society in Budapest that made the request for aid to Red Cross headquarters in Geneva—and from its newly elected leaders, no less: during his brief period in office, Imre Nagy was able to dismiss the Stalinist clique running the Red Cross Society in Hungary. But the pace of events placed a limit on humanitarian activity, which is how, after the Revolution was quelled, a group of five doctors took over the direction of humanitarian action in Hungary.

The International Committee of the Red Cross not only supplied aid, it also called on the opposing parties in the conflict to observe the Geneva Conventions, which enforced the protection of prisoners of war, the ban on taking hostages, the obligation to treat the wounded, and other requirements. Through radio broadcasts, the International Committee of the Red Cross reminded the population and combatants of these obligations; they also sent memoranda to Moscow and Budapest.[39] It was thanks to these efforts that International Committee of the Red Cross envoy H. G. Beckh was able to visit ÁVH officers who were detained—or rather protected from public wrath—by the Transdanubian Revolutionary Council and to meet Attila Szigethy, the leader of the council. There could be no question of anyone visiting the revolutionaries imprisoned by the ÁVH officers, even though the International Committee of the Red Cross repeatedly requested the opportunity to do so and to offer assistance and receive information about their captivity. It was only after the Revolution was suppressed and the prisons were packed with revolutionaries that the ICRC was able to send a few aid packages to the infamous Gyűjtőfogház (Central Detention Facility) in Budapest. It would be another eight years before a representative of the organization in Geneva was able to visit one of the Hungarian penal institutions.[40]

When the International Committee of the Red Cross repeated its appeal for support on November 4, Hungary's airports and border were closed, and most broadcast channels had gone quiet.[41] The Geneva Conventions continued to be contravened—fifteen trucks waited at the border, beyond which gunfire could be heard. One week after the invasion, the shipment was permitted to enter Hungary.[42]

The staff at UN headquarters in Geneva hurriedly reported these events to New York, where, on the morning of November 10, they again agreed aid should be provided to Hungary, and that it was clear to them that only the International Committee of the Red Cross was in a position to deliver it.[43] On November 12 came the news that the Hungarian government would be happy to accept the shipment. At that time, the aid providers had no details as to the shipment's volume and composition, but the possible resumption of aid delivery was news of great importance.[44] In New York, Imre Horváth quickly drew up an off-the-cuff list of Hungary's particular needs, while another more precise and detailed list was sent from Budapest by Hungarian deputy foreign minister István Sebes. So these efforts to provide crucial information about humanitarian needs were made by none other than members of the Kádár government.[45]

This situation presented a difficult legal dilemma, yet someone had to provide lists of requirements and visas for aid workers. That could hardly be Imre Nagy, who at the time was being surrounded by Soviet tanks at the Yugoslav embassy in Budapest, which had provided temporary asylum for him and for his close associates. Uncertainty over who was in charge hindered delivery of the newly launched aid shipments: aid workers entering Hungary, who requested a Soviet officer grant a temporary cease-fire while the convoys passed, reported they did not know who or where the leadership was and so had no one to negotiate with.[46] They were backed by the consensus that had been established regarding the supply of aid and provisions for refugees, and to which, according to the UN's press release, the Soviet and Hungarian authorities had given their "complete cooperation."[47] The news from New York regarding cooperation was confirmed by Major General Kuzma Grebennik, commander of Soviet forces in Budapest, who promised "every assistance" for the swift and undisturbed delivery of the aid shipments.[48]

All these moves were a tribute to the partnership between Hungary and the Soviet Union, but they also established a difficult condition: that the question of aid be completely separated from any political solution. Any kind of quid pro quo would risk the success of the humanitarian operation. As recorded in a memo in New York from the UN section in charge, the provision of aid should be "independent of any political mission."[49] This was in line with what Adrian Pelt, the UN official dealing with aid to Hungary, had written to Hammarskjöld from Geneva, cautioning that doing otherwise would make an exceptionally delicate situation even more difficult.[50] So in no less paradoxical fashion the UN officer hoped that the "UN will not, repeat, will not make any public gesture in connection with this situation."[51] Therefore, all this ambiguity regarding the UN's role in delivering aid was not merely the necessary consequence of the heightened tensions in the situation—turning a blind eye to brutality, broken promises, and other misdeeds to ease the burden of the victims—but actually a direct demand from the most important aid agency—in fact, the only aid agency—able to gain access to the country.[52] On November 10, Léopold Boissier, president of the International Committee of the Red Cross, was reluctant to put the organization at the UN's behest, as he felt this would endanger its "strictest neutrality." He only agreed when he considered this to no longer be a threat.[53]

For the Hungarian Stalinists, of course, none of this selfless generosity and strict neutrality was credible, or at least none of it was likely, and they capitalized on the International Committee of the Red Cross aid supplies in both direct and indirect ways, continually slandering and threatening the agency itself. Deputy Foreign Minister Endre Sík flew from Budapest to

Vienna on a Red Cross plane so he might fly to New York from there. As he remembers it, "Apparently it was bringing medicine [. . .] but we know by now that Red Cross planes were also transporting weapons and Hungarian counter-revolutionaries."[54] Such slanderous claims went from being simple lies to part of the propaganda and then into jurisdiction; at a trial, it was even said that there were three rows of hand grenades hidden in the butter brought by Red Cross officials, which were then to be transferred to Corvin Circle, a bastion of the Revolution.[55]

The other misdemeanor committed by the Red Cross from the communist perspective was its insistence on adhering to the Geneva Conventions, specifically regarding the collection of data on deportations. Because of this, the political police objected to and investigated Erzsébet Döller, a resident of Soroksár on the outskirts of Budapest, telling a Red Cross employee on a taped recording that "she was supposedly deported," as the police lieutenant who signed the document had put it.[56] This was documentary evidence for the Red Cross, which wanted to ensure that the Geneva Conventions were adhered to, but it was even more useful ammunition for the oppressors of the Revolution seeking revenge.

Another episode illustrates the oppressive contradictions in providing aid—the story of György Szennik.[57] Szennik was a loyal fascist propagandist turned diligent communist agent, whose language skills, driver's license, and Viennese connections allowed him to join the distribution of the International Committee of the Red Cross aid, as its work was assisted by Hungarian volunteers on the ground. From early November 1956, Szennik transported aid to Budapest; in line with the Red Cross guidelines, he distributed it to everyone, that is, both revolutionaries (who persevered, he claimed, because they were "hoping for help from UN troops") and the population at large.[58] With his knowledge of the area and brilliant drawing skills, "during his journeys to the provinces, he recorded what he had seen of the hiding-places of some counter-revolutionary groups in both words and drawings, on the basis of which the Soviet comrades were able to eliminate these groups."[59] He reported on the movements of the so-called counterrevolutionaries many times a day, uncovered their centers of operations, gave them provisions, then assisted in their liquidation.

Part of the background to this story is that, as a young man, Szennik had used his talent as an artist to create fascist propaganda: his posters were well known and popular. He also assisted in the deportation of Jews and

Lieutenant General Szilárd Bakay;[60] by this time, he wore an SS uniform to avoid the jurisdiction of the Hungarian authorities. After the war, the young artist, distinctive because he had lost an eye, was recognized, arrested, interrogated, and charged. In jail, he turned his coat after considerable torment: he first painted ÁVH officers, then was co-opted as a mole who, according to the state security documents, "worked on" his former comrades with some success.[61] Contemporary records disclose that he overperformed in his role as a "qualified agent" (as he was characterized); the leader of the operative group was happy with his work, though his obsequious diligence would attract the negative attention of his fellow inmates.

The day after the Revolution broke out, Szennik asked the leaders of the disintegrating ÁVH for their instructions, which, for the time being, were to find a place among the revolutionary institutions.[62] He worked his way into the administrative apparatus of the Parliament, tried to establish connections at the foreign ministry and with the Széna Square insurgents, and set up the Hungarian October Friendship Alliance. He was initially trusted because of his time in jail. Later, his help with supplying aid would play an important role, allowing him to use the prestige and contacts he had gained to help see "a number of leading counter-revolutionary individuals and groups wishing to emigrate" after the Soviet invasion.[63] On one occasion, the Soviets arrested him, and he was taken with other aid workers to the city of Székesfehérvár, where they confiscated his camera. He begged the Hungarian authorities to return it to him, to no avail. When he was allowed to leave, his convoy drove into crossfire, during which the Austrian Red Cross Society volunteer sitting next to him was seriously injured. Szennik survived the attack unscathed. Tracing the routes of the aid convoys, he reported that the workers' councils organizing the resistance were using the aid to build the strike reserves. Thanks to this information, resistance leaders Sándor Bali and Sándor Rácz were taken into custody "on the basis of his [i.e., Szennik's] active participation."[64] Because of his broad network of contacts, Szennik received reports that he continued to pass on to the political police: these reports included details about those about to emigrate, methods used to cross the border, the fees involved, and the network of those helping refugees to escape. The secret service leaders were worried that their agent would come under suspicion, and so recommended Szennik be "taken into conspiratorial custody,"[65] which was followed by a house search. The conspiracy was such a success that Szennik himself did not know what had happened to him. He was beaten at the police station, but he remained unmasked. He was trusted by his fellow prisoners, so he was able to "smuggle out letters from his fellow inmates, and pay visits to all their relatives,"[66] thus allowing him to continue his betrayals. Szennik's career moved from strength to strength: following his arrest, he was transferred, that is, prepared for work in the West, which would provide even more opportunities for him.

The significance of the aid program was not diminished by such atrocious contradictions, nor by the number of aid packages that ended up in the hands of the political police or among buyers on the black market. The International Committee of the Red Cross tried to estimate the scale of the loss: it accounted for around 2,700 deaths and 20,000 injured, a large number of residential buildings destroyed, and a multitude of hospitals partially or completely demolished. There was no milk, eggs, sugar, coffee, or tea in the shops. There was a shortage of antibiotics, insulin, bandages, and hospital appliances. According to the Red Cross's calculations, there were a quarter of a million people in need in Budapest alone, including children, pregnant women, the elderly, and the disabled, who were unable to stand in line even if there was anything to stand in line for.[67]

The UN Secretary-General began implementing the Assembly's resolution on aid as early as November 5, and accordingly he awaited the Hungarian delegation's list of the most urgently needed items. It was made clear that this did not constitute recognition of the Kádár government,[68] only an acknowledgment that its members were best able to determine what was needed. The UN leadership was considering, as yet only in hypothetical terms, whether UN aid workers would have to consult with "local" Hungarian representatives.[69] On November 10, almost a week after the Soviet invasion had begun, the aid requirements were still not clear, yet the following day, the documents mentioned that immediate steps would be taken "with the cooperation of the Hungarian delegation."[70] Hungarian doctors requested equipment, food, and clothes, so the UN had to acquire these and organize their transport to Hungary.[71] Endre Sík, who was in New York to continue negotiations, prepared a list, one that was as off the cuff as it was unfit for its purpose.[72] Hammarskjöld nevertheless announced that he was pleased that the Hungarian government was cooperating with UN institutions on solving humanitarian problems, and on November 13, he mentioned that the Hungarian authorities should consider the measures of the other UN resolutions.[73] He made no such suggestion ever again, as Hungarian authorities threatened to stop aid operations once they became connected to political questions.

By this time, the list of aid items required for survival was already being drawn up in Budapest: its source was presumably the same group of Hungarian Red Cross Society doctors who had previously joined the aid program. They were in contact with the headquarters in Geneva and temporarily accepted by the current Hungarian leaders. The list telegraphed from Budapest was long and no less striking, to the extent that it presented a picture of destruction, injuries, and a worsening humanitarian crisis. There was a shortage of an extensive array of medicines, expertly specified, as well as the basic equipment needed for the treatment of injuries, "particularly morphine," and coal, gasoline, sowing seed, and a dozen other items necessary for basic existence. The Hungarian government not only expressed its gratitude for this assistance, it even agreed that the UN could inspect how the aid was being used on the ground and that negotiations could be held—whatever this meant.[74] It probably meant very little, as nothing in the way of substantial (political) dialogue was to take place, either then or later.

Hammarskjöld entrusted the coordination of the aid supplies to his experienced and efficient colleague Philippe de Seynes. De Seynes announced that the list of aid requirements was complete, but transportation of all this aid was beyond the UN's ability.[75] The Secretary-General added a handwritten note to the effect that the hope of the aid being sent under the aegis of the UN should be retained regardless of the position of the Hungarian government toward the UN, but he also understood de Seynes's qualms that the UN alone would be unable to create and operate the entire apparatus that would be required to transport the aid to Hungary to store and distribute it.[76] Meanwhile, Pelt informed Hammarskjöld and his deputy from Geneva that, led by experienced managers, the infrastructure of aid provision had been established in Vienna and was now in operation.[77] Similarly, at the same time that the UN General Assembly resolutions were executed, though not explained, the International Committee of the Red Cross had realized the logistics of collecting, storing, transporting, distributing, recording, and financing aid, which was subject, given the extraordinary circumstances, to a great many conditions. This system encountered challenges, such as the contracted delivery company unexpectedly going bankrupt, difficulties with getting visas, and suddenly needing to employ

Under-Secretary-General Philippe de Seynes, in charge of aid to Hungary after the Revolution, secret visitor of Kádár in early 1957. Copyright: UN Photo Archive #7741672.

and train dozens of new Swiss staff and transport them to Hungary.[78] At the International Committee of the Red Cross's request, first a dozen, then many hundreds arrived from the national Red Cross Societies, but in the field, it was Hungarians who had to deliver the aid packages. These are the people with whom the UN should have cooperated, but the strict neutrality of the International Committee of the Red Cross was not compatible with the arrival of the UN, which passed resolutions condemning the invasion just at this time.[79]

The Secretary-General did not see things differently than the UN resolution, and he certainly did not see them from Budapest. Still, a UN aid coordination office was established in New York, and on November 13, 1956, a bank account was opened to collect the funds for assisting Hungary. Urgent donations were addressed to the United Nations, sometimes to Hammarskjöld directly, but it was his deputy who oversaw them. De Seynes soon took on more employees to form a team that would direct the entire operation from across the Atlantic (but through Geneva and Vienna) to deal simultaneously with the aid program in Hungary and the refugee issue in Austria and Yugoslavia.

Only the International Committee of the Red Cross operated on the ground in Hungary. This was not done under the auspices of the United Nations, but it enacted the UN's aid program as its exclusive partner.[80] The legal foundation for this was resolution 339 of the UN General Assembly, passed on November 9, 1956, and the contract between the two organizations was based on this resolution.[81] The International Committee of the Red Cross made it clear that in the course of its work, it would take into account no consideration other than the order of priority of needs,[82] that is, that the organization would help anyone with no other considerations or types of selection.

In the first days after the Revolution, no one knew what exactly was needed in Hungary. For example, a large amount of powdered milk arrived from Rijeka, Yugoslavia, and medicine from Switzerland.[83] The scale, priority, and nature of Hungary's needs did begin to become clear, however. The concrete decisions on these matters were made in Vienna, where on November 16, the representatives of the Hungarian Red Cross Society met the leaders of the international agency. Here five doctors signed the cooperation agreement with operational director Roger Gallopin, and Hungarian ambassador to Vienna Frigyes Puja countersigned on behalf of the Hungarian government on the same day.[84] The signed agreement was hastily telegraphed to New York. The signees also described the recommended mode of distributing the aid, which was entrusted to Swiss aid workers,[85] and informed the Secretary-General that Hungary had no more than three weeks' food reserves remaining, meaning that the warehouses would be empty by early December.[86]

New York was informed by Geneva of just what a "hard winter" Hungary could expect after the Director of the United Nations International Children's Emergency Fund (UNICEF; now the United Nations Children's Fund) succeeded in consulting directly with representatives of the

Hungarian government.[87] Meanwhile, the representative of the Hungarian Red Cross Society traveled to Switzerland to report in person to the agency's headquarters on what there was to know of the situation in Hungary.[88]

Meanwhile, extremely detailed summaries were prepared in both New York and Geneva on the operation, including the scale and composition of the aid program. Constant negotiations were taking place between the International Committee of the Red Cross and the United Nations. Aid workers at the scene were happy to determine that—at least relative to the size of the operation—theft of aid items was relatively low and that only a small number of the items appeared on the black market. The latter appeared inevitable, if only because a part of the shipments was sold commercially so that the income could go into a bank account to be spent on other forms of aid.[89]

Meanwhile, in Hungary, the aid effort was not felt as strongly as the people had hoped. The resources at the UN's disposal were dispiritingly modest relative to the country's needs and could only provide enough tangible assistance to around 2 percent of the population in need of it.[90] The significance of this was explained to Myer Cohen, the UN official in charge of aid to Hungary, by Pierre Obez, the UN officer in Geneva and contact person between Geneva and New York, who cited hearsay that in Hungary in 1956, some 2 percent of the population was actually communist, and 98 percent was neutral or, in his words, downright anticommunist. When the 2 percent looked to the Soviet Union for help, as Obez said, "we know what happened." But when the 98 percent turned to the West and the United Nations for assistance, they were given merely empty words and unimplemented resolutions.[91] In one letter written to the UN Secretary-General, Pelt, who played a crucial role in the aid operation, stated that the devastating situation in Hungary "hit Western Europe emotionally to a degree much greater than it is generally understood outside Europe."[92] And if even after this the West was unable to help, they were effectively shoving the Hungarians into the toxic grip of the Eastern powers. De Seynes wrote to the UN's US delegation that the aid to Hungary meant that the UN's resolutions were not just flowery words.[93]

The United Nations could be no more than a silent partner, however. As to how it could be more than this, the Secretary-General requested a legal opinion.[94] He sensed the importance of the UN's part in the aid operation actually being under the UN's aegis, but there was concern that this could lead to the expansion of political disputes into the humanitarian operation.

Yet the US insisted that it be marked as the exclusive sender of the (very considerable) aid it sent, without mentioning even the International Committee of the Red Cross, despite its central role in the aid's distribution.[95] For the United States, this meant receiving political return on its humanitarian investment, but this was too much for the Hungarian authorities.

The planning and implementation of aid was also strongly hindered by the UN leadership receiving, as late as January, a report on the "political and economic chaos" in Hungary—both were consequences of a general strike, among other factors. The food shortages were worsened by the abolition of the obligatory appropriation of agricultural quotas, leaving cities and industrial centers without food.

The first estimations proposed enormous sums required just to guarantee the most basic of conditions for people to survive. It soon became clear that the restoration of the economy would require many further millions, not just because of the Revolution and the Soviet attack but also because of the damage previously wrought by Stalinist economic policy.[96] According to Under-Secretary-General de Seynes, more than $30 million would be required before the next harvest in July 1957.[97] The staff of the humanitarian system then translated these requirements into everyday needs and tasks: since the Revolution, 120,000 mothers and children were in need of milk; 150,000 schoolchildren needed at least one plate of hot food a day; 10,000 aid parcels had to be distributed every day to avert a humanitarian crisis, and so on.[98] Windows had to be replaced and buses and trains needed to be run their routes, all of which required coal and gasoline.[99]

János Kádár, recognizing the direness of the situation, announced that the country would accept aid with no political strings attached.[100] All that remained was to figure out the logistics of getting these aid items to Hungary by water, road, or rail. The organization and logistics for the supply chain started in New York, passed the goods through Geneva and Vienna, and finally delivered them to the industrial island of Csepel in southern Budapest. Csepel was home to the main aid distribution warehouse, where seventy-five Hungarian laborers processed the shipments and yet more workers helped them reach their destinations. The Csepel distribution team were in day-to-day contact with the International Committee of the Red Cross's temporary headquarters in Vienna, where more warehouses were at the disposal of the aid effort; this is also where staff from international organizations were received and where requests for aid were collated and passed on. At the Budapest end of the chain, Willy Meyer led the operation, attempting to judge the constantly changing needs and staying in contact with the Hungarian Ministry for Food as much as he was able.

The *stricte impartialité* observed by the Swiss[101] was at once a moral instruction and an essentially impractical dogma that gave those receiving the aid food for thought and even provoked outrage, failing as it did to discriminate between victims and their oppressors. Another source of disagreement was the fact that part of the aid went to those outside Hungary, that is, to the refugees. Many in Hungary no longer considered those receiving refuge elsewhere to be in genuine need. Meanwhile, the portion of the aid that did get to Hungary was, as seen from outside the country, inevitably falling into the hands of the restoration of neo-Stalinism; in other words, it was supporting exactly that system the Revolution had been targeted against. Hungarian politicians not only viewed the aid with suspicion, but cast adverse aspersions on the International Committee of the Red Cross, calling it a front for the destructive wishes of Western imperialism, a spying organization, and a continuation of the "counterrevolution" through different means.[102] While the more militant members of the revolutionary émigré community attempted to block the aid from reaching Hungary altogether, Anna Kéthly suggested that it be sent directly to Imre Nagy's government.[103]

Reflecting on the reservations of the US, the UK, the Netherlands, and Belgium, which would have sent aid to the Hungarians by bypassing the Kádár regime, de Seynes wrote to the UN headquarters in Geneva in early January 1957,[104] stating that such views were "gently unrealistic." The UN operation was also criticized by members of the US Congress, who claimed it was assisting those who were repressing the rebellious Hungarians; furthermore, US law forbade support for communist states, even in the form of commercial loans.[105] On January 19, 1957, US congressman David Crook commented bitterly on the UN Secretary-General's report on the Hungarian aid program—including as it did $20 million of US taxpayers' money—and confirmed that the United States wanted to help the people of Hungary but did not wish to contribute to the maintenance of the system against which they had risen up. For this regime had struggled with economic collapse well before the Revolution broke out; one factor in the Revolution might have been the low standard of living that was one of the consequences of arrogant economic dilettantism.[106]

Those working at the United Nations were well aware that the aid sent to Hungary served to ease the consequences not only of the Revolution and the intervention but also of inept Stalinist economic policy. Might the UN operation serve as a precedent for the disillusioned citizens of the other socialist states, who shared a similar fate but were unable to or did not dare to revolt? How could the UN convince doubters—including its key donors—that they were wrong about the pressing issues concerning aid distribution when in fact they were largely right? There was no remaining option except to cite UN General Assembly resolutions that urged the provision of aid.

Yet alongside rational concerns and pragmatic arguments, there was a striking phenomenon: the tangible, startling apathy that followed the first pleas for assistance and accompanied the rhetorical expressions of extraordinary sympathy. On November 15, the Secretary-General called on the member states to provide aid; the responses were disappointing in their content and even less impressive in their size.[107] With wise foresight, the staff at the UN Secretariat did not place the rejection messages among the documents presented to the Assembly;[108] henceforth, they turned not to the delegates of member states but rather to the general public and citizens of the member states. The means for this was an exceptionally well thought out and comprehensive press campaign that marshaled the power of public opinion to exert pressure on reluctant governments and to call on all parts of society to support the Hungarians' cause. This publicity campaign filled many thick folders in the UN Archives, precisely detailing how many different channels the UN used to meet its mandate, even when its member states did not appear ready to do so.[109]

On November 28, 1956, the UN's Department of Public Information (DPI), effectively the UN's press office, comprised of the organizations that surveyed the ever more dramatic circumstances in Hungary and the progress of the refugee crisis and determined the most important conditions necessary for the aid program to be initiated and implemented, set about influencing the public mood with exceptional thoroughness, organization, and focus. At this time, the most important means of swaying public opinion was the printed press, so journalists were flooded with moving news stories and detailed information, journalists whom they continued to contact even after headlines about the Hungarian Revolution had been squeezed from the front pages. They would suggest what films and programs the BBC could use to support the joint operation and show how photographs and personal accounts could help generate a lasting impression. These efforts were broken down almost daily into further specific tasks during telex conferences held between New York, Geneva, and Vienna.[110]

Along with newspaper stories, the role of film was also crucial. In terms of its direct impact, it may have been even more powerful. A film crew soon set about preparing a film titled *OUT*, which dealt with Hungarian refugees—it was not possible to film within Hungary, at least not for filmmakers from Western democracies. The press office of the United Nations followed every step of the process, from the editing, through sound dubbing, to distribution, to ensure that the film would have the power to mobilize support that had been expressed as a priority by the UN's relevant division on January 10, 1957.[111] The release of the film and its distribution strategy brought to a mass audience a celluloid drama that portrayed, through the eyes of a Hungarian refugee, how and why people escaped Hungary and what was waiting for them on the outside after they did so.

As part of this campaign, members of the UN's press department instructed their colleagues working in the crisis zone on what and how they needed to document to provide UN cinema news with sufficient and suitably powerful information to maintain public interest. This meant that the UN press department was able to supply journalists with fresh new stories on a regular basis.[112] Shooting film material was not allowed in refugee camps, and emotional footage suggesting dependency and despair had to be used with caution, not only because of the right to privacy of those depicted but also for reasons of storytelling: people are most effectively moved to action not by misery but by the sight of real hope tasted and then lost.

The relevant archival documents show that the UN campaign also helped the international press keep the Hungarian question at the forefront of global attention for so many months, as was regularly related in the progress reports of the relevant division. Finally, the international caravan of sympathy did set off on its journey, and with considerable cargo.[113] Having reviewed and again clarified the legal foundation for the supply of aid[114] and having determined that the UN's mandate was even more clear-cut than that of the Red Cross, the UN at last began to receive offers of aid in response to its requests for it, and from just about every member state. In light of previous failures, Dag Hammarskjöld addressed each state in turn. Commitments made were summarized, country by country, listing the promised funds or items, their value, and the expected time of transfer or delivery, and noting also just how much promised aid became a reality in the months that followed versus what remained only empty words.[115]

To see the situation as it was, and to gain an exact picture of the needs that had not been satisfied, it would have been important to know what and how much was arriving to Hungary from "friendly" countries. From the moment the Revolution was suppressed, the elimination of the consequences of the destruction brought by the "counter-revolution" was on the agenda, as communist propaganda defined the Hungarian uprising, and aid was sent to the Hungarian population for the healing of wounds caused by the military "assistance." The UN Secretariat only had estimates of all this assistance at its disposal,[116] as UN employees rarely had access to exact data. The detailed daily survey of the Hungarian press had a questionable reputation, as there was no way to check the propagandist source material. According to the UN's calculations, every socialist state played its part in supporting Hungary. In early 1957, Hammarskjöld and his staff arrived at an aid budget of $6–$7 million;[117] later, the "rough total" of commitments made would come to $420 million.[118] Communist bloc solidarity would thus be ten times the humanitarian support provided by the US, although this included long-term loans granted for reconstruction and economic development. In other words, the bloody drama of tightening political bonds would be complemented by the lasting grip of economic interdependence.

The effect of the campaign begun and still successfully maintained by the United Nations could be felt in the exceptionally energetic and multifaceted activity of those nongovernmental organizations, religious associations, humanitarian foundations, private individuals, and diverse social groups and institutions that all quickly and intensely joined the aid effort. The UN kept a long list of donor organizations and groups that ran to a number of pages: it was no small task to record, identify, and group them to determine the nature of their activity and to place them in the context of the aid effort as a whole. The coordination of the various aid efforts was from the outset one of the most important though difficult tasks. For example, the documents give the same space to the mention of a parcel of clothes sent by a Margaret B. White in Nebraska as to the thousand wool blankets and half-million dollars of aid offered by the Cooperative for American Remittances to Europe (CARE).[119] The trade unions were also present in the form of their "world alliance," a spontaneous creation and one not dominated by the Soviets and that did not intend its donations for the "the vanguard of the workers' movement"—as the Communist Party leadership liked to refer to itself—but rather for those the "vanguard" had defeated and those fleeing it. Representatives of religious organizations such as the

Quakers, the YMCA, and Pax Romana massed on the Austrian side of the Hungarian border, as did the Ford, Rockefeller, and other eminent private foundations. The international alliance of university students supported the students among the refugees, and staff from child welfare foundations were also present.[120] In the interests of coordination and cooperation, the UN commissioned Charles A. Hogan as the UN official in charge of cooperation between agencies to remain in contact with the NGOs, religious associations, and other institutions; that this was not merely a formal or pragmatic measure is proven by the fact that a number of those organizations and institutions were given consultation status in the Economic and Social Council of the UN.[121] Their role was exceptional in that, alongside the UN's broad-based organizational efforts, the civic groups, churches, and private foundations could assist particular parts of society, address specific problems, or respond to unexpected needs.

Paradoxically, cooperation between the UN Secretariat and the UN's specialist bodies developed less smoothly. Food and Agriculture Organization (FAO) representatives arrived in Hungary soon after the Revolution, and the documents show that a Hungarian delegation visited the FAO's headquarters in Rome, Italy, in January 1957.[122] The United Nations Educational, Scientific and Cultural Organization (UNESCO) was quick to promise urgent educational assistance to Hungarian schools and delivered on this promise some months later, at a cost of hundreds of thousands of dollars.[123] UNICEF was involved in the management of the crisis from the start, with its director spending four days in Budapest in March 1957, attempting to relieve the difficulties faced by mothers and children to the tune of $700,000.[124] The documents suggest that these operations were independent of the UN's overall aid program; on more than one occasion, the Secretary-General learned of these events only after the fact, which caused problems and misunderstandings, among them being the UN as chief coordinator failing to live up to its mandate, which also had serious consequences.

Inevitably, an operation of this extraordinary size and made up of so many components would generate contradictions, to which both those affected and the press would respond. One repeated objection was that aid selflessly given by the West would be purloined by the authorities, thereby undermining the whole point of the exercise. *Life* magazine detailed such malpractices in its report from Hungary, in which it concluded that a good part of the aid was ending up on the black market or in police warehouses.

The irreparable damage caused by this article was sharply felt in Geneva and New York, as it cast a shadow over the whole aid operation.[125] We will never know whether the source of this news was really the well-informed British embassy or instead the Indian chargé d'affaires (who claimed that only as much of the aid reached beyond party leaders to working people as was needed to bribe them)—and perhaps it does not matter.[126] It was Maurice Paté, a UN officer working in Geneva, who had to answer to the international and US outrage, confirming that in Hungary, the International Committee of the Red Cross operated entirely independently and free of external influence and that he had himself been witness to this when he met laborers on the scene.[127] The principles of the International Committee of the Red Cross meant that communists deserved assistance just as much anticommunists did, and secret servicemen as much as revolutionaries. Who was given aid was determined only by need, not political conviction or revolutionary or counterrevolutionary involvement. Of course, the political elite had better access to goods, but these were not necessarily the aid supplies distributed by the International Committee of the Red Cross and more likely assistance from the East, where the newly established militia and the cadres loyal to the usurpers of power enjoyed priority treatment.

Part of the aid did indeed enter the commercial system. Alongside the items distributed for free, some were also sold, with the revenue placed in a Red Cross bank account opened in Hungary. This was used to finance their operations, and to purchase items that were invaluable but not listed among the aid donations in order to distribute them for free. It was evident that the black market was not the same as this official system of selling aid items, but was it really possible to prevent the streetwise Hungarian population from illegally selling part of the aid that was not needed or saving toward a planned emigration, given how expensive the human traffickers were?

The damage that proved most irreversible was caused by another group both favored by and critical of the aid operation: the propagandists of the Kádár regime. They were highly suspicious of the Western humanitarian project from the beginning. In their minds, the Red Cross was no more than a meeting place for "right-wing aristocrats."[128] The ex-ÁVH officers managed to find labels in the aid packages, distributed with such care and neutrality by the apolitical organization, that read "Kill the communists!" or "Kill the Russians!"—which, given that not even the UN insignia was allowed to appear on the packages, seems highly unlikely. We cannot know whether there really were such labels, or if so, whether they were mere provocations or real attempts to alter events, but the waves of the scandal rippled as far as the *New York Times* and to the Secretary-General.[129]

With time, it became increasingly difficult to obtain Hungarian visas for the drivers of the aid convoys and those accompanying them.[130] Just as the aid effort became more successful (because the danger of humanitarian catastrophe had passed), the authorities attempted to compromise those who had played a part in keeping it alive, before discrediting and expelling them. On April 15, 1957, the *New York Times* reported that the Hungarian authorities had closed the border to the convoys, which for Hungarians had become the symbol of the West's attention and support.[131] This alone would have been reason enough for the Hungarian authorities to be removed, while the hardline members of the Hungarian Communist Party leadership had from the outset accused the International Committee of the Red Cross of supporting the counterrevolutionaries, helping to sustain the strikers, and keeping the spirit of the resistance alive.[132] A later report tells of outright accusations of the organization's "illegal intelligence activities" and its cooperation with "absconders" and "internal reactionaries."[133] The Hungarian leaders of the Hungarian Red Cross Society were replaced in May and then taken into custody in July. In addition to ideological charges, some criminal charges were also invented: accepting gifts counted as corruption, and commercial activity involving aid supplies that was tantamount to racketeering.[134] Only one of them, a doctor, had actual charges pressed against him, and the International Committee of the Red Cross covered the cost of his defense. The organization did not want to bid a hasty retreat from the place of the greatest aid operation since World War II, especially not as a result of trumped-up criminal charges. One reason for this was that, with its leaders removed, the Hungarian Red Cross had returned to the circumstances before October 1956, when those running the organization were loyal to Moscow, not Geneva.[135] The laborer given a jail sentence was thus the last victim of the humanitarian operation; some of the previous victims had died for the cause. Volunteers had lost their lives to Soviet gunfire, but the Hungarian allies of the Soviet invaders also abused doctors and nurses for treating the insurgents, in some cases causing their deaths.[136]

By this time, the new harvest was ripe, and the stormy and bloody post-revolution consolidation process stabilized industrial output to some degree, while the people's economy slowly recovered with assistance from the East. This helped Kádár's propagandists crown their previous ingratitude and shamelessness by placing the UN aid effort fully in the firing line. In the course of so-called "operation potato,"[137] the Hungarian authorities alleged that the tens of tons of seed potatoes that had come as an aid shipment from the Netherlands were infected with disease, and in all probably deliberately so. They announced that the Western imperialists had, under the guise of providing aid, sought to undermine Hungarian agriculture. This charge was not plucked entirely from thin air, but it was duplicitous; both the United Nations and its specialist agricultural bodies left no stone unturned in seeking the truth. The objections raised by the Hungarian authorities, the various statements, expert opinions, telex conferences, and correspondences filled a multitude of dossiers. They kept an archive of the minutes of the meetings with Hungarian officials, documents, and laboratory results, a number of which reached Hammarskjöld's desk,[138] as did the final verdict, the outcome of an irreproachable investigation undertaken by a Danish expert, which showed that the potatoes in fact bore no capitalist infection of any kind. But by this stage, the donors had had enough of the institutionalized libel that they encountered in lieu of appreciation. They were fully aware that this was no mere technical or administrative mistake but rather simple ill will,[139] something that was a thousand times more dangerous than any potato infection.

Perhaps these events help to explain why Hammarskjöld never prepared a separate report on the aid operation to Hungary, even if the volume, organization, and significance of that aid were without parallel. Instead, the topic became merely a part of the UN Secretary-General's yearly report.[140] In July 1957, he expressed his gratitude in person to the leaders and staff of the International Committee of the Red Cross at its headquarters in Geneva.[141] The agency's report was included among the UN's documents, providing the most comprehensive and precise survey of the successful, selfless, and hugely significant aid operation in Hungary.[142] According to the report, between October 1956 and June 1957, the cost of the aid distributed was $17 million. The list of donors and donations was also published, with appendixes detailing every record, agreement, and request that documented the legal basis for the aid program and the details of its technical implementation. The beneficiaries of the operation numbered more than one million, and every detail of the prolonged and unhappy drama was evident: milk, bandages, chocolate, coal, ambulances, medicines, dry pasta, and, alongside everything else, seventeen automobiles with which the undertaking could be continued—or, rather, could have been continued.

In summarizing the UN's efforts during the critical time after the Hungarian Revolution, it becomes clear that there were both successes and failures. From the beginning, a political solution seemed hard to achieve and later proved to be impossible; neither the visit of the Secretary-General nor attempts to mediate between the revolutionaries and their oppressors were feasible. Meanwhile, the resolutions of the UN General Assembly remained unobserved by those to whom they referred. The only significant contribution the UN could provide was generous and continuous humanitarian assistance for the Hungarian people, an action unprecedented after World War II. Yet this aid from the UN, considered an enemy by the Hungarian communist authorities, remained intentionally unnoticed. This was a deliberate strategy by the UN for fear that the communist authorities would hinder the vitally important flow of aid that millions benefited from if it had taken broad credit for the action.

Notes

1. November 6, 1956. Columbia University, Butler Library, Rare Books and Manuscript Collection (hereinafter ACP), box 182. At this time, Anna Kéthly did not even have a valid passport. NARA 764.00/10-1157.

2. November 6, 1956. ACP, box 182.

3. UNARM S-0009-0002-09. The list of November 8, 1956, included a list of names and specializations of the visiting scholars. ACP, box 184.

4. Indonesia and Palestine were mentioned as precedents. ACP, box 182.

5. UNARM S-0442-0138-06.

6. MNL XIX-J-1-k, box 55.

7. UNARM S-0009-0002-09. A visit by Cordier is mentioned in one document. UNARM DAG 1.1.1.3. All this can be reconstructed from the documents of the Hungarian Socialist Workers' Party (MSZMP). MNL MSZMP documents, 228.f 5/2. See also MNL 288.f 32/1962.

8. See the message from Under-Secretary-General Philippe de Seynes. DHS L 179:83. Indian politician Krishna Menon later met Soviet premier Nikolay Bulganin in Moscow; as a result, on December 11, 1956, the US Ambassador wrote that Hammarskjöld might travel to Budapest. NARA 764.00/12-1156. Following this, the Secretary-General announced that he would visit Budapest for three days beginning on December 16. DHS L 179:83. The Australian Mission to the UN had announced as early as November 30 that the Secretary-General was traveling to Hungary. NAA A 1209 1957/5279. In similar fashion, Lodge's suggestion would have mandated Hammarskjöld to make a statement to the Assembly. Olgyay, *Hungarian Revolution and the United Nations*, 79–81.

9. The memorandum of the legal division on December 6, 1956. UNARM S-0445-0195-12852-2UC.

10. See the UK Ambassador's telegram of January 8, 1957. ("The Indian first secretary has disclosed that de Seynes told him that the United Nations Secretary-General never wished to come here in December, and readily accepted the Hungarian Foreign Minister's reasons why the visit should be deferred.") British Foreign Office (hereinafter FO) 371/128666.

11. UNARM S-0009-0002-09. The same was later mentioned in a source close to Hammarskjöld. UNARM S-0975-0030-0001-00001 UC.

12. Hammarskjöld listed the solution to the crisis among his previous successes: "Suez will be my third child [. . .] with the help of God, be able to teach it to walk." Berggren, *Dag Hammarskjöld*, 2.

13. UNARM S-1078-0064-0002-00001 UC.

14. Ibid. Australia was of the opinion that the Secretary-General was "acting too slowly." NAA A 1209 1957/5279.

15. Australia recorded this opinion on December 18, 1956. NAA A 1209 1957/5283.

16. UNARM S-1078-0064-0002-00001 UC.

17. November 21, 1957. *Dages Nyheter.*

18. This was cited by both Hollai and Mód. MNL XIX-J-24-a, box 1.

19. NAA A 1209 1957/5283. See Rahman, *Magyarország, 1959–1959.* In his telegram sent on December 5, 1956, to the US secretary of state, Béla Varga claimed that the Secretary-General's journey would be "completely useless and even harmful." NARA 764.00/12-556. Jagan Nath Khosla, Indian ambassador to Prague, later visited Budapest; in his presence, Kádár argued that a visit from the Secretary-General would have weakened his position. When the news spread in Tatabánya that Hammarskjöld would visit Hungary, eighty thousand people prepared to head to the border. Kajári, *Rendőrségi napi jelentések*, and MNL MSZMP documents, 228.f 5/2.

20. ACP, box 184, and NAA A 1209 1957/5279.

21. ACP, box 184.

22. UNARM S-0445-0198-13174 UC.

23. Philippe de Seynes (1910–2003), UN Under-Secretary-General, responsible for the humanitarian aspects of the Hungarian question.

24. UNARM S-0445-0196-12852-1UC.

25. ACP, box 182. The "exclusive" interview of January 16, 1957, was conducted by Herman Ray.

26. "Informational Report on the Journey of Hammarskjöld to Hungary and on the UN's Committee of Five." ÁBTL BM II/2 (The UN committee dealing with the Hungarian question was referred to as the Committee of Five, as it was made up of five diplomats.)

27. Ibid. The United Nations published a statement in the last days of 1956, listing the UN's resolutions and the attempts to resolve the situation from October 28 to December 31. Protitch files, UNARM DAG 1.1.1.3.

28. Berggren, *Dag Hammarskjöld*, 4.

29. Hammarskjöld translated poetry during Security Council sessions. Berggren, *Dag Hammarskjöld*, 2. According to his diary, he met Martin Buber, Niels Bohr, and other eminent intellectuals. DHS L 179:172 and L 179:173.

30. UNARM S-0009-0002-09.

31. UN resolution 1129, General Assembly, Session XI, November 1956.

32. ACP, box 182.

33. UNARM S-0445-0199-13409-9 UC October 27–29, "Summary of Relief Announced to Geneva as on October 30, 1956 midnight."

34. Ibid.

35. On the dilemmas regarding the legal status of the "conflict" in Hungary, see Cardia, *Magyar október*, 197.

36. UNARM S-0445-0200-13409-2 UC.

37. The foundation for the Soviet criticism, above and beyond the "bourgeois" nature of the Red Cross, came from the role it played in the Second World War: in this view, the agency failed to adequately protect and assist either prisoners of war or those detained in concentration camps. See Kecskés, "Humanitárius segítségnyújtás globális méretekben."

38. Cardia, *Magyar október*, 22–32. See the report by the Red Cross: "Report on the Relief Action in Hungary. October 1956–June 1957. Geneva, October 1957." UNARM 0445-0199-13409-4UC.

39. This had already taken place on November 2, 1956. UNARM 0445-0199-13409-4UC.

40. Cardia, *Magyar október*, 49–51.

41. UNARM 0445-0199-13409-4 UC ("All communications were cut off").

42. UNARM 0445-0199-13409-4 UC and ACP, box 182.

43. UNARM S-0445-0197-12888 UC.

44. UNARM S-0445-0198-13186-1 UC "Hungarian Note Verbale [. . .] welcomes assistance." November 10, 1956. DHS L 179:83.

45. The Secretary-General met Imre Horváth on November 14 to discuss this. UNARM DAG 1.1.1.3.

46. Cardia, *Magyar október*, 48.

47. DHS L 179:83.

48. Kuzma Jevdokivomich Grebennik (1900–1974), guard major general, in 1956–57 commander of the city of Budapest. UNARM S-0445-0196-12884-Part A-1 UC.

49. UNARM S-0445-0197-12888 UC.

50. Ibid.

51. ACP, box 182, and DHS L 179:83.

52. UNARM S-0445-0197-12888 UC.

53. UNARM S-0445-0199-13407-6UC.

54. Sík, *Bem rakparti évek*, 150.

55. Markó, *A pesti Rambo*, 1; and Radványi (1972), 37.

56. MNL XIX-J-1-k, box 56.

57. György Szennik made his mark as a painter, then joined the far-right movements; his propaganda billboards were even known in the Third Reich.

58. ÁBTL 3.1.1. BT-602/2.

59. ÁBTL 3.1.1. BT-602/2, "Szeles."

60. Szilárd Bakay elaborated on the military aspects of the attempt to leave the Axis in 1944, as well as investigating the possibilities of armed resistance to Germany.

61. ÁBTL 3.1.1. BT-602/1, "Szeles."

62. ÁBTL 3.1.1. BT-602/1.

63. Ibid.

64. Following the Soviet invasion, there was a general strike in Hungary that lasted for weeks. ÁBTL 3.1.1. BT-602/1.

65. Ibid.

66. ÁBTL 3.1.1. BT-602/1.

67. Cardia, *Magyar október*, 60.

68. ACP, box 184.

69. Ibid.

70. On November 10, 1956, Pelt wrote about this to Hammarskjöld and de Seynes. DHS L 179:83.

71. DHS L 179:83, November 11, 1956.

72. November 16, 1956. UNARM S-0445-0196-12852-2 UC.

73. November 13, 1956. ACP, box 182.

74. Ibid.

75. UNARM S-0445-0199-13411 UC.

76. Ibid.

77. DHS L 179:83.

78. At the height of the aid effort, 126 vehicles were assisting the Red Cross operation in Hungary. Cardia, *Magyar október*, 58–59. UNARM S-0445-0200-13409-2 UC.

79. Considerable documentation has survived on the concerns of the International Committee of the Red Cross. UNARM S-0445-0199-13411 UC.

80. Cardia, *Magyar október*, 58.

81. Ibid., 171.

82. Ibid., 58.

83. ACP, box 182.

84. Cardia, *Magyar október*, 56–57. Frigyes Puja, ambassador to Vienna from 1955 to 1959.

85. UNARM S-0445-0199-13409-4 UC.

86. November 17, 1956. UNARM S-0445-0197-13165-11 UC.

87. The UN body for children's welfare, the United Nations Children's Fund. ACP, box 182.

88. December 20–21, 1956. Cardia, *Magyar október*, 242.

89. Ibid., 61.

90. UNARM S-0445-0198-13174 UC. December 7, 1956.

91. UNARM S-0445-0198-13174 UC.

92. January 29, 1957. UNARM S-0445-0196-12884 Part B 3 UC.

93. December 13, 1956. UNARM S-0445-0199-13289 UC.

94. UNARM S-0445-0199-13278-2UC. December 6, 1956. Schachter, head of the legal department. UNARM S-0445-0197-13165-10UC.

95. UNARM S-0445-0197-13056-1UC. This was agreed on January 4, 1957, at the State Department.

96. All this was quite evident well before the Revolution. On October 12, 1956, Yuri Andropov reported to Moscow that the economic situation in Hungary was continuously worsening but that the party leaders "were not dealing with the people's economy." Szereda and Sztikalin, *Hiányzó lapok 1956* (1993), 89–90.

97. January 14, 1957. UNARM S-0445-0196-12884-PART B UC.

98. UN UNARM S-0445-0196-12884-PART B 1 UC and Cardia, *Magyar október*, 60–61.

99. UNARM S-0445-0197-12888 UC.

100. UNARM S-0890-0008-0001-00001 UC.

101. Cardia, *Magyar október*, 58.

102. See the state security documents cited by Gusztáv D. Kecskés. Kecskés, "Humanitárius segítségnyújtás globális méretekben."

103. UNARM S-0890-0008-0001-00001 UC.

104. UNARM S-0445-0196-12884-PART B 2 UC.

105. UNARM S-0445-0199-13407-2 UC (January 7, 1957). State Department: US "would extend no loans or economic aid to the Hungarian puppet government headed by Kadar." UNARM S-0890-0008-0001-00001 UC.

106. UNARM S-0445-0196-12884-PART B 1 UC.

107. UNARM S-0445-0198-13185 2 UC.

108. UNARM S-0445-0199-13407-1 UC. "There are a number of negative replies on our files which are not included in this draft [General Assembly] document."

109. UNARM S-0445-0195-Part B-1 UC. "UN Publicity Campaign for the Promotion of Humanitarian Assistance to the Hungarian People."

110. UNARM S-0445-0195-12843-1 UC. December 19, 1956. "Lead for Hungarian Newscast."

111. UNARM S-0445-0195-12843-1 UC. "Suggested Points for Final Appeal of the Film OUT."

112. UNARM S-0445-0195-12843-2 UC.

113. UNARM S-0445-0199-13411 UC.

114. See Schreiber's letter on the legal implications of the Assembly resolution. UNARM S-0445-0197-13165-9 UC.

115. UNARM S-0445-0194-12539-1,2. "Humanitarian Assistance to the Hungarian People. Appeals and Offers of Assistance. Daily Report on Relief—Assistance Provided and Received."

116. UNARM S-0442-0140-0003-00001. "Unconfirmed Reports of Forthcoming Relief Supplies to Hungary," and "Estimation of Donations from Eastern Countries."

117. In their report of January 10, 1957, Ewing, Sinard, and de Seynes presented a total aid figure. Soviet government: 38 million rubles; city of Moscow: 10.8 million rubles; China: 30 million rubles; Mongolia: 900,000 rubles; North Korea: 401,000 rubles; Vietnam: 3 million rubles; Czechoslovakia: 30 million crowns; GDR: 22 million marks; Poland: 100 million zlotys. UNARM S-0445-0196-12884–Part B 3 UC. "Report on Present Economic Situation in Hungary." In 1956, the purchasing power of $100 was roughly equivalent to $951 in 2020.

118. "Long time credits [. . .] very rough total" of $420 million. UNARM S-0445-0196-12884–Part B 3 UC.

119. "Humanitarian Assistance" UNARM S-0445-0195-12819 UC. Here we can also find a list of financial contributions: private individuals sent checks; for example, some nurses sent twenty-five dollars. UNARM S-0445-0200-13409-2UC. According to his letter of January 21, 1957, a CARE representative wished to be present at the distribution of its aid shipments, but as he was not permitted to do so, the International Committee of the Red Cross distributed the blankets. Meanwhile, their food

packages could not be passed on because of the label that read "Gift from the US People." MNL XIX-J-1-k, box 94.

120. UNARM S-0445-0195-12558-1 and S-0445-0195-Part B 1 UC. "Humanitarian Assistance, NGOs," and "List of Organizations Working in Austria."

121. UNARM S-0445-0195-Part B 1 UC.

122. The urgency was justified by preparations for the planting in the spring, as Wahlen acknowledged their journey in a letter dated January 11, 1957. UNARM S-0445-0196-12852-1 UC. According to his telegram of January 23, 1957: "Following agreed with Hungarian group visiting Rome [. . .] method of distributing seeds." UNARM S-0445-0197-12892-1 UC.

123. March 15, 1957. "Emergency Educational Assistance." UNARM S-0445-0195-12550-1.

124. Paté wrote to Hammarskjöld about this on March 13, 1957. UNARM S-0445-0196-12852-1UC.

125. UNARM S-0445-01965-2840 UC.

126. NAA A 1209 1957/5283. According to Australian documents, "The UK Legation in Budapest received numerous and reliable reports that Red Cross supplies have been given to well known communists and sold to people." Rahman, *Magyarország, 1959–1959*, 2.

127. Paté's letter of November 17, 1956, to Ellsworth Bunker, president of the US Red Cross. UNARM S-0445-0197-13056-11 UC.

128. ÁBTL 3.2.5. O-8-125/1. "Other International Organizations." This is a highly illuminating survey of the Western aid bodies.

129. See the article in the *New York Times* and Cohen's letter of March 7, 1957, to the Secretary-General. DHS L 179:84.

130. The Red Cross published a press release on this on March 28, 1957. UNARM S-0445-0197-13165-7 UC. At the high point of the aid operation, 150 Swiss laborers were working on assisting the Hungarians.

131. *New York Times*, April 15, 1957. "Hungary Hinders Red Cross Relief." UNARM S-0445-0199-13408-2 UC.

132. See the memorandum of April 15, 1957. MNL XIX-J-1-o.

133. MNL XIX-J-1-k, box 55.

134. UNARM S-0445-0197-12888 UC. "Arrest of Directors of the Hungarian Red Cross." See Cardia, *Magyar október*, 75–76.

135. Ibid., 62–63.

136. Ibid., 76.

137. The expression was used in the UN documents to describe the operation (April 17–29, 1957). UNARM S-0445-0197-13165-1UC-6UC.

138. All of these survived among Hammarskjöld's documents. DHS L 179:84.

139. UNARM S-0445-0197-13165-6UC.

140. "Report of the Secretary General to the General Assembly." UNARM S-0445-0199-13408-1UC. According to the documents, heated debate accompanied the way the report was ultimately presented.

141. Cardia, *Magyar október*, 21.

142. UNARM S-0445-0199-13409-4 UC.

3

RESPONSES TO THE HUNGARIAN
CRISIS BY THE UN

The Secret Missions of the UN to Hungary

From the days of the Hungarian Revolution onward, the International Committee of the Red Cross operated the distribution of aid to the region with strict neutrality and exemplary organization. Within two months of the Soviet invasion, the United Nations had sent two delegations to the Hungarian capital to discuss the possibility of providing aid, both in total secret and against a backdrop of intense political saber-rattling.

The first aid mission was initiated and implemented not by United Nations Headquarters in New York but by the UN Food and Agriculture Organization (FAO) in Rome. The FAO leadership was presumably aware that, despite an exaggerated emphasis on heavy industry after World War II, land was Hungary's key resource and the humanitarian crisis could not be resolved with industrial goods. If the aid shipments could help address the immediate catastrophe, in the longer term, it would be Hungary's agricultural output that must guarantee survival. So, just six weeks after the Soviet invasion, a delegation of two experts in agriculture, Dr. Friedrich Traugott Wahlen and Pierre Sinard, along with Willy Meyer from the Red Cross, were sent from Rome via Geneva, Bern, Zürich, and Vienna, to Hungary.[1] In Vienna, the experts inspected the International Committee of the Red Cross warehouses, its fleet of cars and trucks, and its distribution center.[2] It is not known what legal right they had to make this inspection or who arranged a subsequent meeting in Győr, Hungary, where they held discussions with their Hungarian partners and surveyed the most urgent needs before returning to Rome. Over the course of this secret mission, the delegates avoided all publicity and scrupulously kept the UN's humanitarian and political resolutions separate.[3] Although the minutes do include a reference to making political contact, in the end, at the telegraphed request of the director, this was avoided.

The point of this trip was to restart agricultural production and the food industry in Hungary. This was surely in line with the International Committee of the Red Cross's strategy,[4] but the conditions for that to happen were far from being met. Agricultural operations were encumbered not only by the destruction wrought by the fighting and unusually early onset of winter, but the disintegration of the cooperatives, which brought about new, challenging circumstances, in part because of unclear property rights concerning animals and machinery.[5] The lack of feed also became alarming. This critical situation could be resolved only by the premature slaughter of livestock, but that sacrificed later breeding potential and the long-term supply of meat. Yet the intense activity of the slaughterhouses did lessen the food shortage and thereby aid consolidation.

The FAO officers' report revealed the conditions of Hungarian agriculture, making it possible to plan aid and allow agriculture and food processing industries to return to capacity. Yet it did not provide a full view of the Hungarian economy, just as it failed to provide a thorough investigation of the critical circumstances leading to shortages. It seems strange, therefore, that the report emphatically stated that there was no need for further delegations to visit Hungary,[6] just as the visit of the UN Under-Secretary-General Philippe de Seynes was being prepared in New York. The word "Why?" handwritten on the report succinctly expresses the incomprehension caused by the secrecy of the FAO visit, its narrow agricultural remit, its avoidance of political connections, and its brevity.

Two days after the FAO report was finalized, the detailed plan for the visit to Hungary of de Seynes, the UN Under-Secretary-General responsible for aid, was also complete. The delegation would be small to "preserve secrecy" and the goal of the visit was to survey the situation. The visit would involve consultations but not discussions. The details were finalized in New York with the Hungarian delegation to the UN, which agreed that it would be a fact-finding mission and kept out of the public eye, as de Seynes would remember after news of the visit broke.[7]

The Director-General of the FAO informed the UN leadership that the FAO was "vitally involved" in the handling of the Hungarian crisis[8] and did not want to send Dr. Wahlen, who had recently returned from the first FAO delegation to Hungary, back to Budapest. Their involvement should not, Binay Ranjan Sen, Director-General of FAO, added, affect de Seynes's secret consultations.

De Seynes and his colleagues prepared thoroughly for the trip. Along with László Hámori, the UN officer in charge of Hungary, Hungarian-born economist Rudolf Nötel also assisted; their briefings dispensed with the one-sidedness of the previous information that had reached UN Secretary-General Dag Hammarskjöld. Hámori outlined the political situation, its background, and the particularities of the present state of affairs, and provided an annotated list of Hungarian politicians and economic experts, including Prime Minister János Kádár, whom de Seynes would likely meet in Budapest.[9] As further background information, he included a list of the members of government under both Nagy and Kádár, as well as a copy of Hungary's constitution, the country's most important statistics, statements made by its government, the sequence of events of the Revolution, and, finally, some information about Hungary's churches and political parties.[10] This document drew attention to the fact that the Hungarian Red Cross Society had been under the influence of the government, adding that the role of the workers' councils formed during the Revolution continued to be significant, for most of them had been reorganized in the wake of the bloody consolidation under Soviet control.

Among the documents intended for the Under-Secretary-General was the memorandum of the UN Economic Committee relating to Hungary;[11] Nötel later revisited the highly critical state of affairs, emphasizing the urgent need for aid.[12] In his estimation, stocks of food and other critical supplies would have run out by October 23 and had not been replenished since, unless the aid promised by the Soviet Union and other socialist countries had arrived and eased the shortages.[13]

Kádár had already attended to the issue of food supplies "together with the commanders of the Soviet troops," after marshal of the Soviet Army and minister of defense Georgy Zhukov's report had mentioned that there was widespread hunger among the Hungarian population.[14] Based on the resolution of the leadership of the Central Committee of the Soviet Communist Party, the Council of Ministers of the Soviet Union decided on November 5 on the details of the "fraternal assistance to be given to Hungarian workers," which placed the acquisition of certain goods and their delivery to Hungary under the auspices of the ministries. The volume was every bit as significant as the speed; the Civilian Aviation Directorate was involved in the coordination of transporting medicines so that Soviet insulin, penicillin, and morphine could reach those who needed it as soon as possible.

Transportation, heating, and the restarting of industry all demanded coal and petroleum. Nötel's study states that Nagylengyel, the center of Hungarian oil production, was flooded, and promised shipments from Poland and Czechoslovakia to make up for the shortfall were not forthcoming. A three-week general strike brought a shortfall of one and a half million tons of coal. Coal power stations ran out of their reserves on October 31 in Budapest and mid-November in the rest of the country. Nötel put the number of damaged buildings at forty thousand, and though reconstruction had begun, buildings were hardly habitable with no heat.[15] He noted that there was no heating in a number of hospitals, a situation only worsened by damage to roofs and windows; he compared the extent of the devastation to that experienced in 1945 during the heavy fighting of the Second World War that destroyed a great part of Budapest.

Among the reasons for the decline in Hungarian coal production was the mass emigration of coal workers: calculations suggested some thirty to fifty thousand men were missing from the mines. Neither were there enough workers to undertake maintenance; a number of mine shafts collapsed, while others were inundated with water.[16] Wages were paid even during the strike, however, so the country could not balance its books, and without coal, there was no heating, trains, or electricity.

The Hungarian authorities were quick to state that Rudolf Nötel "has published untrue data on the People's Republic of Hungary,"[17] even though the Hungarian-born economist had played a key role in economic aid to the country. For the political police, the ex-ÁVH, however, even this was a source of suspicion; they investigated Nötel, robbed him of his Hungarian citizenship, and later positioned secret service agents close to him. The trusting Nötel had also allowed some of them into his circle of friends.

Throughout the trip, de Seynes referred to his visit as a "technical" one. Even if news of his journey would emerge afterward, while he was in Hungary he was able to avoid all publicity,[18] lest the Hungarian public learn that Hammarskjöld's deputy was in the city for meetings, especially as those meetings were exclusively with Kádár and other Soviet-backed politicians.

De Seynes arrived in Budapest from Vienna on January 4, 1957, accompanied by two of his colleagues, and in an International Committee of the Red Cross automobile.[19] The Hungarian side organized everything in the capital: the accommodations, consultations, and a "recce" of aid being distributed. The Under-Secretary-General expressed his "perfect satisfaction" with how the whole machinery worked, including the administration conducted in difficult circumstances.

The UN Under-Secretary-General received a detailed list of the most urgent needs; this would later be added to by Hungarian economic policy leaders. Agricultural needs were important, as were more general problems that threatened the fundamentals of the Hungarian economy, such as shortages of goods, including food, and high rates of unemployment and inflation.[20]

The most acute problem was the food situation. The reorganization of agriculture meant that it was impossible to estimate the amounts of goods coming in. There was a surplus of meat as a result of the forced slaughter, but eggs were slow to reach the towns and becoming more expensive. Confectionery disappeared from stores completely (and at Christmastime, too), but there was enough bread and milk in the larger cities, so there was no need for a ration ticket system, and prices did not rise too quickly. Transportation was hindered by the lack of coal and the huge number of damaged vehicles, however.

De Seynes would later make a strong distinction between aid and reconstruction, emphasizing that his trip had been dedicated to the former. Yet his meetings with Hungary's economic and political leaders were indeed about restarting the economy, for it was only a working economy that could supply the domestic market and produce for export. The Hungarian authorities were on board with this idea, and the delegation was received by Kádár himself. They were taken from the Erkel Theater's matinee performance of *Carmen* for talks that lasted as long as the fourth act.[21] It is not known whether de Seynes mentioned this in his report because he wished to evoke the atmosphere of the city rising from its ruins or to note a memorable operatic performance—just as it is not known why a whole morning of a brief three-day visit had been dedicated to Bizet.

The trip to Hungary did not remain a secret for long. Perhaps the press learned of it via Mohamed Ataur Rahman, the Indian chargé d'affaires, who was known to share rumors from time to time, or from some other UN source, but it was an event, if not quite a sensation, whose newsworthiness was only increased by the fact that it was supposed to be kept secret. It seems the Western public was surprised by the delegation's discussions with the usurpers of power in Hungary.[22] Being professionals, however, the UN team members had prepared a press statement in advance in case news of their visit went public.[23] Myer Cohen, Executive Director for Relief to the Hungarian People, had already telegraphed de Seynes on January 5, to say that in response to stories in the New York media, the UN would immediately put out a press release on the trip.[24] On January 7, de Seynes received instructions to talk to the press, but not about the essence of the issue; he did as requested, tactically and not a little cynically, based on an outline that Vernon Duckworth-Barker, the information officer, had telegraphed to him.[25] This stated that the Hungarian side had not set any conditions except that (1) there should be no prior publicity and (2) that the delegation would not deal with political issues and so would have nothing to do with the resolutions passed by the UN Assembly on the reception of observers in Hungary or the visit of the Secretary-General. The delegation was interested in finding facts and hoping to get a glimpse of the Hungarian economy as a whole, but its members did not elaborate on any specific proposals.

A good illustration of the bad faith of the Hungarian negotiators was that many of them considered the visit an intelligence operation, and while they held the palm of one hand open, they shook the fist of the other.[26] This was despite de Seynes's efforts both at the press conference and in his report to the Secretary-General to avoid any reference to Budapest's war-torn condition or the number of Soviet troops to be seen on its streets. Neither did de Seynes talk to the revolutionaries, still free at the time, nor to representatives of the workers' councils or people on the street.[27] The Hungarian Ambassador to the UN added that de Seynes had spoken highly of Comrade Kádár, but this was not substantiated by any other source.[28]

The UN Secretariat published a report of the visit, calling the delegation a UN-FAO mission;[29] that is, the specialized body became an independent partner, and the document was also slightly pre-dated. In his report of January 17, Hammarskjöld referred to this document as one that was part of the humanitarian operation to help the Hungarian people in line with the resolution of the Special Assembly.[30] Cohen and the UN officer in charge of economic and social affairs Ralph Townley's meeting with Hungarian deputy foreign minister Endre Sík suggested that the government in Budapest was happy with the visit,[31] although Sík's comrades in Budapest thought it "did not bring the hoped result." Indeed, the UN experts had been undertaking illegal intelligence activities, had produced opposition propaganda, and had supported dissidents and reactionaries in Hungary as well.[32]

The report was extremely cautious and contained no proposal of any kind, nor did it mention reconstruction, only the easing of the humanitarian catastrophe.[33] This did not prevent penetrating Western objections from being raised in terms no less strong than the communist criticisms, which verged on libel. The British, Dutch, and US Ambassadors to the United Nations were all alarmed that UN leaders had depended on the administrative capacities of the Kádár regime,[34] but this was not entirely true. Kádár's government was in no position to guarantee the movements of the delegation; only the Soviets were capable of this. The "disturbing reactions from delegations" reached not only de Seynes but also the Secretary-General: one US senator claimed the FAO had directly supported the communists.[35] It was hard to deny that the communists had enjoyed the largest part of the support, and that the greatest sponsor of that support was none other than the anticommunist United States.

There was no meeting scheduled with de Seynes in Hammarskjöld's diary before the visit to Budapest, but a number are noted as having taken place after the fact.[36] The FAO leadership was quick to telegraph New York about the mission, celebrating the spirit of cooperation and the important experience gained in the course of the journey.[37] The truth was rather more contradictory: On January 21, Cohen stated that it was vital from then on to define roles precisely and that the UN leadership must continue to insist that the FAO agree on the steps it took with the UN and hand over all information to the officers working on the Hungarian issue. However, it seems that this did not happen. Later, Cohen would be even more critical in his opinion that there should be further coordination among the UN, the FAO, and the International Committee of the Red Cross.[38] This raises the question of what types of coordination did exist between them. First, they had the idea of sending a UN officer to Budapest to mediate. Then Cohen traveled to Geneva at the end of January for discussions with the president of the International Committee of the Red Cross.[39] At this stage, the aid effort had been in place in Hungary for almost three months, so it was high time for this meeting.

The UN Attempts to Find a Political Solution

As the aid operation progressed, it became increasingly obvious that further resolutions of the UN Assembly were being explicitly contravened with no consequences. This was particularly significant because the UN Charter primarily contained legal and political principles, not humanitarian ones, and the UN was only able to deal with the consequences, not the essence, of the Hungarian Revolution. At the outset of the crisis, it seemed quite plausible that the UN would be able to play a role in Hungary, as the UN statement of November 12, 1956, mentioned two groups: observers and an investigating committee.[40] The UN leadership had held discussions with legal experts Oscar Gundersen from Norway, Arthur Lall from India, and Alberto Lleras from Colombia, who were already preparing for the journey. The documents tell us this seems so definite an opportunity that Arthur Lall had even accepted an advance on his per diem expenses in Hungary: a total of $750 to cover the period from November 16 to December 16.[41] In other words, UN representatives would have arrived on the scene within two weeks of the invasion in order to investigate the situation in Hungary over the course of an entire month. Lall was recommended to the Secretary-General by Krishna Menon, the Indian ambassador accredited in Moscow, and it is worth noting that Lall had previously described the Hungarian Revolution as a CIA putsch,[42] though it may also have been a contributing factor that India did not consider the agreement of the Hungarian government a condition for inclusion in the committee.[43]

On November 7, the UN Secretary-General sent a telegram to Emil Sandström, president of the Swedish Red Cross Society, who, as a well-recognized international jurist, had successfully mediated in severe conflicts and had already been included in UN committees on Palestine. Hammarskjöld also invited Phil Jessup from the US, whose knowledge and experience of international law was second to none. Hammarskjöld would also have been keen to see a high-profile diplomat from Asia on the committee. The UN's haste to send observers to Hungary is evident from its management of the documents. Hammarskjöld approached Galo Plaza, former president of the Republic of Ecuador, who accepted the commission out of a sense of moral obligation, only to return his mandate because the Hungarian government had not changed its stance that the Revolution was an internal affair of the country.[44] Samar Sen, another Indian, was also mentioned, as was Colombian minister and representative of the Organization of American States Alberto Lleras. Lleras was honored by the request and became the driver of the nascent committee, if only for a brief time.[45]

Finally, on November 16, 1956, a group was formed, comprising Lleras, Lall, and Gundersen. According to Hammarskjöld's diary, he had a meeting with them at 5:00 p.m. on November 28, even though at this stage they had not yet been approved by the Hungarian government to enter Hungary, despite repeated reminders sent by the Secretary-General.[46] Behind the scenes, the decision had presumably not yet been made in Budapest—or rather in Moscow, where decisions were made that time—but the rejection would not be slow in coming.[47] The committee continued its work while it waited, which for the time being consisted of studying various documents and making repeated attempts to be allowed into Hungary. Later, they would settle on just visiting neighboring countries, of which only Austria would have accepted them in defiance of Soviet disapproval. The committee quickly determined that the Assembly's condemnatory resolution was entirely appropriate and that Soviet intervention posed a threat to weaker nations and international peace. It was in this light that they studied the peace treaty, transcripts of radio broadcasts, and the news that reached them of deportations.[48]

Given the hardening Soviet-Hungarian position and the narrowing room to maneuver, however, the committee questioned whether it was worth continuing.[49] They first decided to suspend their activities, and then the members of the group returned their mandates. The documents reveal that they informed Hammarskjöld of this on December 11, after which came Lleras's letter of resignation, followed by the official resignation of the investigating committee as a whole.[50] Under-Secretary-General Dragoslav Protitch's documents referred to the committee's activity from November 4 to December 12, suggesting that the preparatory work lasted for five weeks. The committee members justified their resignations by saying that they had been mandated not to write history but to make history, so if their investigation were restricted to the study of documents that were widely available, then there was no point or significance to their efforts.[51]

This defeat was as revealing as it was alarming, but it remained obscured. Hammarskjöld repeated his request to Yugoslavia, Austria, and Romania to accept observers. Then, on December 10, he spoke to Dutch delegates to the UN about the observation of the situation in Hungary,[52] but nothing came of this. The prolonged inaction of the three-man committee did not go unnoticed by a number of delegations, however. It was clear to many that Hammarskjöld's tasks in the Middle East had taken him to the verge of a nervous breakdown, leaving him with neither the energy nor the attention the Hungarian question demanded. At this stage, he had planned no serious operation nor any kind of sanction.[53] Though it was again suggested by some member states that a group of observers made up of accredited diplomats be established in Budapest,[54] the real observational work fell to the Hungarian secret police, who followed the diplomats' movements and learned of their plans. The operation of the group was rendered impossible by the foreign ministries of the relevant countries, as they considered it incompatible with diplomatic status and did not want to sacrifice their diplomatic missions in Hungary. They considered that Budapest would have reacted strongly to the release of any information.

These same foreign ministries received precise and detailed reports on events in Hungary. They knew what had happened during the Revolution and after the Soviet invasion, but there could be no question of gathering this information into a joint report. All these documents would only be passed on to the United Nations later, when the UN Special Committee on the Problem of Hungary was formed, and even then only at the request of the Secretary-General. Certain embassies were in an awkward position, of course. Socialist bloc countries were clearly unable to take on any such task, while the Yugoslavian mission had become compromised after offering asylum to Imre Nagy and his associates. The Poles, whose loyalties would sometimes falter, had given their backing to the invasion, while the other socialist countries had been even more explicitly supportive. The embassies of the "imperialist countries," as communist propaganda described Western democracies, were tacitly suspected, if not explicitly accused, of being the active initiators of the so-called counterrevolution and of actively supporting those opposed to the regime. India may have been, and indeed was, some kind of exception to this. The leading voice of the developing nations was important to Kádár and his comrades—not least because of the country's vote at the UN—while the revolutionaries hoped that India could mediate between the downtrodden Hungarian people and Moscow. When, in the name of the last government coalition, cabinet member István Bibó prepared a consensual memorandum to assist political progress, he used Indian mediation to send it to Sir Senerat Gunewardene (Ratnakirti Senerat Serasinghe Gunewardene or R. S. S. Gunewardene), the Special Committee member from Ceylon, and from there on to Soviet premier Nikolay Bulganin, who received it through Indian chargé d'affaires Mohamed Ataur Rahman. Both intermediaries would then become witnesses—and corpus delicti—at the criminal trials of Bibó and his associate Árpád Göncz.[55] Rahman continued to pretend that the Hungarian issue was important to him and took steps both to inform his government about the Hungarian situation and to further the case of allowing UN observers. But he did not really believe in the cause of the Hungarian revolutionaries and was reticent in his relations with those who represented them, noting that their recommendations about the resolution of the situation were all rather similar, that they failed to present them properly, and that the whole enterprise seemed hopeless as well as unacceptable.[56]

India received news reports with interruptions. Indian chargé d'affaires Rahman sent telegrams from Vienna, which meant that the information contained therein—including news of Imre Nagy's growing anxiety about Soviet troop movements—arrived after a significant delay. Instructions from New Delhi likewise arrived either late or not at all; Prime Minister Jawaharlal Nehru did not seem to know what was happening.

Nehru's ambiguous stand concerning the Hungarian Revolution can in part be explained by his Kashmiri background: on the issue of whom the disputed territory of his homeland belonged to, the Soviets backed India, which accorded with Nehru's leanings, while the US stood alongside Pakistan. Nehru's alignment with the Soviets on a partition that joined Kashmir with India seemed to sometimes override both his moral compass and his personal feelings with respect to the Hungarian Revolution, even if the latter were affected not just by the political situation but also by a Hungarian family member.[57] Nehru's visit to the US in December 1956 was an important moment for both countries, but it did not change his stance concerning Hungary. Another explanation for the halfhearted Indian stance was that Chargé d'affaires Rahman in Budapest observed the various episodes and figures in the Revolution with no small amount of distaste, expressing animosity toward Anna Kéthly, Zoltán Tildy, and even Cardinal József Mindszenty, not to mention members of the former aristocracy. Although Rahman reported conscientiously on the fighting and deportations (sometimes even exaggerating both),[58] he did not extend his sympathies to the revolutionaries, not even after the Soviet invasion. He claimed they were just hanging around waiting to be arrested.[59]

Rahman did not have a good opinion of the "puppet government" either; he thought its members were not telling the truth and unable to get their stories straight.[60] Their incoherent falsehoods were striking even to this novice diplomat. Nevertheless, India did the most in the interests of the UN becoming involved in resolving the Hungarian crisis, first discussing the work of observers, and then sending the eminent Indian ambassador Jagan Nath Khosla as Nehru's private envoy from Prague to Budapest. Kádár received the Indian diplomat, and with the desperate sincerity he exhibited in his first months in office explained that a visit from the UN Secretary-General would lead to a campaign against his fragile government, meaning that the Soviets would soon depose him.[61] Everyone knew that the Stalinists in Moscow, hungry for revenge, were ready to attack and that their support among the fraternal countries was not insignificant. Khosla argued that money would be forthcoming from the UN, that Kádár would be able to forestall the deterioration of the situation and win time to consolidate his new government and political cause, and that the very arrival of an official UN delegation would represent a full recognition of the new Hungarian government.[62] Kádár remained resolute.

It is a sign of India's determination that, following Khosla's failure, K. P. S. (Krishna) Menon, a friend of the Soviets and India's ambassador to Moscow, arrived in Budapest, giving hope to the vanquished that he might squeeze out some concessions for the revolutionaries.[63] Leaflets appeared on Menon's arrival in Budapest in the hope that foreign intervention could assist in the peaceful consolidation of the new government. As Menon was escorted through the city, his driver was determined to pass by streets that had been devastated in the Revolution and he also managed to drive right into a women's demonstration.[64] The destruction and unrest had a considerable effect on Menon. He met with Sándor Rácz, the leader of the workers' councils, and they visited factories that were at a standstill because of the strike and listened to the despairing workers.[65] After he returned to Moscow, Menon raised the issue of an urgent solution to the Hungarian situation directly with Foreign Minister Dmitri Shepilov; while at the UN, he recommended that Hammarskjöld travel not to Budapest but rather to Moscow, as this is where he would be able to resolve the Hungarian question.[66] This advocacy was too much for the Soviets, who officially informed New Delhi that if its ambassador did not halt his improper interventions in Hungarian domestic affairs, they would request his immediate recall.[67] That they had the power to do so was clear, for it was just at this time that New Delhi asked Marshal Zhukov, Soviet minister of defense, to oversee the long-overdue modernization of the Indian military, while the visit of Nikolay Bulganin and Nikita Khrushchev opened a new chapter in the history of Indian-Soviet friendship.

The Hungarian problem was hardly a matter of indifference to India's neighbor China, as Nehru would tell József Kővágó, the mayor of Budapest during the Revolution, some years later. Chinese premier Zhou Enlai made repeated visits to New Delhi during and because of the crisis, and he and Nehru spoke for hours about Hungary.[68] At this time, many people looked to China as an alternative model for the construction of socialism and as a place from which hope and even support might be forthcoming. In the spring of 1956, Mao Zedong, president of the People's Republic of China, announced the short-lived Hundred Flowers Campaign, which encouraged the proposals of a diversity of models and methods for building a socialist state. On November 2, the pro-revolutionary weekly paper *Irodalmi Újság* (Literary news) was referring to India and China when it wrote that both the West and the East were "on our side."[69] On the day before the article was published, Imre Nagy and his foreign policy advisor György Heltai conducted a two-hour discussion with Ambassador Ho Te-Ching, who showed support for their initiatives. Little could they know that in the meantime, Khrushchev had come to an agreement on a military solution to the Hungarian question with a Chinese party delegation holding talks in Moscow, or that a good number of the ex-Stalinist dictator Mátyás Rákosi's henchmen had asked for and were granted asylum at the Chinese embassy in Budapest.[70] It was only after the invasion of Hungary that it became clear that Beijing would have dealt with the insurgents more brutally than the Soviets did: among other proposed actions, they recommended one hundred times as many executions to eradicate the kernel of the movement as Kádár's executioners committed.

The Situation of the Hungarian Refugees Assisted by the UN

There was one aspect of the Hungarian problem that the United Nations did manage to resolve, and it did so in an exemplary fashion that would be tangible to hundreds of thousands of people. This was the Hungarian refugee drama. It was in no small part thanks to the UN that it did not become even more of a tragedy than it did.

According to UN reports, the first groups of refugees started arriving in Austria from Hungary on October 27, 1956, but the majority of these people returned to Hungary after "order was restored,"[71] which seems to suggest that it was compromised communists and terrified ÁVH officers who had escaped over the border, thinking that the inimical West was safer for them than their homeland. Others from this group went eastward; the UN did not mention them, just as it did not mention the former Stalinists who went directly from the Soviet base in Tököl to Moscow. Many from

Eastern Hungary left for the Ukrainian Soviet Socialist Republic, while the ÁVH leaders in Szeged and their families were given asylum in Yugoslavia, carefully separated from the other refugees.[72]

Disillusioned revolutionaries arrived in Austria, and other Hungarians crossed the opened border out of a sense of adventure, a fear of the Revolution potentially being reversed, or a terror of reviving antisemitism.[73] A week after the Revolution broke out, the refugees' numbers had multiplied,[74] but the Austrians did not turn anyone back, take anyone into custody, or check anyone's background. Others were not so casual. The Americans turned to their preferred expert on these matters: an agreeable and permissive beauty who served the footballers, tough guys, and ÁVH men at a popular local joint in Vienna called the Rozmaring Café. US military counterintelligence tasked this operative with uncovering Soviet intelligence agents. The documents pertaining to this key operative have survived among the papers of Hungarian intelligence, revealing that those involved knew of the role she played.[75] The ÁVH station in Vienna was one of the largest and most active in the West, and agents were constantly being resettled from Budapest to Vienna. One of these was Miklós Szabó, whom the secret police referred to using the code name "Kerekes" and who won the trust of Anna Kéthly and Béla Király. Szabó would go on to become the negotiating partner for the UN High Commission for Refugees (UNHCR).

The number of ÁVH officers and other agents leaving Hungary was overshadowed by the flood of refugees, who from November onward put the endurance of the UN and its partner organizations to the test. For the League of Red Cross Societies, this was the greatest refugee crisis in its history,[76] one the UN described as "fateful," especially because the UNHCR had only recently been created. But the main protagonist was Austria, where, as of 1956, there were already 150,000 earlier refugees who had not yet found homes, 30,000 of whom still lived in refugee camps.[77] Unexpectedly faced with the crowds flooding across its eastern border, this small country found that its financial resources were stretched to the limit. Some thirty to forty thousand people arrived between October 28 and November 18, 1956, then on average an additional two thousand each day, but there were days when many more arrived on Austria's doorstep.[78]

On November 19, the UN officer in Geneva, Pierre Obez, reported to de Seynes that by his calculations, as many as sixty thousand refugees might arrive in Austria from Hungary in the next six months. Assuming that providing for one refugee for one day cost only $1, an estimate of what

Refugees after the Soviet invasion trying to cross the Austrian
border on a broken bridge. Copyright: NARA #1579685103.

this would cost came to a total of $23 million.[79] On November 20, a UN
aid worker named Maurice Paté traveled from Geneva to Vienna. Once at
the scene, Paté no longer felt capable of trying to estimate the numbers of
refugees, and daily reports showed his caution to be justified.[80] UN reports
provided more exact data for the arrival and movements of refugees, and it
soon became clear that the numbers would surpass all existing estimates.[81]

Apart from the size and intensity of the flood of refugees, there was
another key factor at play: the condition of the people. In the most dramatic
moments of the Revolution, Soviet troops had opened fire on the fugitives,
injuring many of them.[82] Even in Austria, many wondered what would happen if the Soviets were to cross their border and return to the stations they
had held when the country was occupied by the four great powers. But this
did not override the principle of solidarity: everyone could come, and come
they did. The Austrians did take the precaution of not handing over military barracks to accommodate refugees, as it was preferable for soldiers to
be stationed in them.

Meanwhile the refugees continued to arrive, in freezing temperatures,
in clothes repeatedly soaked by trampling across marshlands; exhausted,
hungry, and desperate for medical attention; with children and older relatives and with many having lost contact with their relatives during the

grueling journey.[83] It is clear from the documents how the imperative to help was tantamount, but it could never be enough. It was too early to raise the question of what the norms of aid should be: registration was complicated and coordination was difficult—humanity trumped rationality. Mobile kitchens were stationed at the border, and volunteers awaited the refugees with tea and blankets. Groups of doctors and interpreters were employed, and transport vehicles were made available nearby so the arriving Hungarians could be accepted on a continuous basis.

Alongside the League of Red Cross Societies, the Austrian government, and the UNHCR, the Intergovernmental Committee for European Migration (ICEM)[84] also became involved in providing aid for refugees. This agency had the most experience, even if it did not have a budget to match that of the other agencies. The participation of the United Nations brought a certain amount of transparency, although its leaders did not want everything to be transparent for the Soviets. The news reached the UN of dramatic episodes in which Soviet-aligned Hungarian soldiers used machine guns to force a group of twenty people back from Austrian territory; on other occasions, the fugitives were arrested and beaten or imprisoned as a means of intimidation.[85] Two-thirds of those arriving were male, three-fifths between the ages of eighteen and thirty-five.[86] Overall their health was very good, as the World Health Organization and the International Committee of the Red Cross noted. They were emotionally devastated, however, and understandably upset; the reports predicted personal conflict and displays of aggression, and they were right.[87] Some arrived with tuberculosis, and some with psychological disorders.[88]

It soon became clear to the International Committee of the Red Cross that part of the aid intended for Hungary would have to be redistributed to the refugees. It also understood that the fate of the Hungarians leaving their homeland would be a real test of humanity's conscience.[89] But, at least at the beginning, the task of ensuring that the stateless would not also be homeless seemed an insurmountable one. Although the Austrian government authorized the use of abandoned buildings by the refugees—including the infamous Habsburg barracks at Traiskirchen—these had to urgently be made habitable. Many buildings had been used by previous occupying forces, and they were in a decrepit state; a quarter of them had refugees already living in them.[90] As a result, the International Committee of the Red Cross was also entrusted with the task of establishing refugee camps across Austria, so the accommodations along the border were suitable to house newly arriving refugees. Thanks to the UN's contribution, prefab houses arrived in Austria, but temporary accommodations also had to be set up in guest houses, schools, sanatoriums, and numerous other places. One member of the League of Red Cross Societies of a given country was responsible for each individual refugee camp: Finland, the United Kingdom, Canada, Sweden, and more than a dozen other countries, under the unified direction of the league. Documents reveal that the pressure was greatest in March 1957, when fifty thousand people arrived from a wide variety of social classes and parts of Hungary, with differing needs and mentalities—all in need of housing and food. Later, it would prove important, while they were waiting to travel on further or to settle, to provide the refugees with employment and activities to keep them busy. Some began to work at nearby factories or in the fields, some of the women looked after the children in the refugee camps, and in time the administration and maintenance of the camps was undertaken by the residents, who thereby earned extra benefits such as additional cigarettes, food vouchers, and occasionally money.[91] By the summer of 1957, it had proven possible to help 180,000 people to continue their journey or settle in Austria, which was an extraordinary achievement.

Another important task for the International Committee of the Red Cross was to reunite families. Many had been broken up in the course of setting off on their journey, either because of struggles trying to cross the border or perhaps even once in this new and unfamiliar world in which they found themselves. Finding and identifying family members was no easy task, as refugees often arrived in Austria with no papers and did not speak any foreign languages. In principle, the reunification of families should have been achieved in the country first offering refuge, but in practice this was not so easy, in part because the refugees had to be sent on urgently to make space for new arrivals, and in part because there was no guarantee that refugees would end up in the places they were sent to. The large number of children arriving presented particular difficulties. Sometimes they arrived on their own, some ran away from their families, and others were sent by their families with a tag attached to their person with a written request that the child be passed on to an acquaintance, relative, or a particular organization.

All this was exacerbated by the fact that keeping records of the refugees was extremely difficult, and, in the first stages, almost impossible. On November 13, 1956, the UNHCR and the organizations working along the border held a meeting after seeing that the Austrian authorities were unable to deal with the initial task of registration.[92] On November 20, a steering committee met in Geneva to discuss the Hungarian refugees, but its members seemed unsure whether all the organizations affected were present, as the situation was dire not in Switzerland but along the Austrian-Hungarian border. Later, they debated on a telex conference to discuss how an intensive yet also spontaneous process could be, if not coordinated, then at least followed. A specialized body of the UN reconvened on January 17, 1957, and determined that a systematic operation for receiving refugees was the most pressing need, suggesting that since October 1956—that is, for almost three months—such an organized effort had not yet come into being.[93] The documents from the meeting tell us that the key players—the Austrian government, the UNHCR, and the League of Red Cross Societies—came to an agreement at the end of February on the schedule for the reception and provision of Hungarian refugees and their registration and further travel, breaking down the areas of obligation, allocating tasks and budgets to individual organizations, and coordinating their efforts.[94] The lion's share of responsibilities again fell to the League of Red Cross Societies, which took on the maintenance and operation of a number of refugee camps; the UN's specialized agency could at best check up on these, provide financial support, and monitor how the money was used. Almost fifty thousand people lived in these forty refugee camps for some period, and it was only the continuous process of moving refugees on that kept the camps from becoming overloaded. Sometimes camp residents became impatient, and if there was no way forward, then the only option seemed to be returning home. The siren songs of the Kádár propaganda machine had also started to sound, offering amnesty to all those returning to Hungary—but without mentioning the details of the constantly changing conditions applied to this amnesty.

By January 15, 1957, Péter Mód, representative to the UN, was circulating among member states and as an official UN document the decree of the Presidential Council, addressed to the UNHCR, according to which anyone returning to Hungary before March 31 would receive amnesty. The document stated that no case could be brought against refugees relating to their illegal border crossing or for any of the armed events that took place from October onward; indeed, to assist repatriation, the homes and personal belongings of refugees would be protected.[95]

At the same time, the Hungarian government's Repatriation Committee began its operations in Austria, where full-blooded ÁVH officers intended to seduce some fugitives, as they called the refugees, to return home.

But those entrusted with escorting people back to Hungary were immediately offended when representatives of the Austrian Ministry of the Interior and the UNHCR accompanied them on their visit to the refugee camps, even though the authorities only took this action because they feared for the Hungarian officials' safety.[96] It is worth noting that in the Hungarian foreign ministry's documents, the term *refugee* was replaced with the word *absconders*,[97] and it was made clear to the administrative apparatus that the amnesty only applied "to the fact of abscondment"[98] and not to "counter-revolutionary" activities. The Stalinist Ministry of the Interior apparatus narrowed this path even further: according to the information of the Chief Division for Political Investigation, "enemy intelligence bodies exploit the opportunity to return to Hungary without fear of criminal charges and send some of their agents to Hungary via this route." This meant that those returning to Hungary under amnesty would be kept under Ministry of the Interior observation—many under house arrest—while others had their identity documents confiscated as well as everything else they had brought home with them—even the oranges they had purchased in Vienna. As for those who had returned to Hungary earlier, perhaps as illegally as they had left it, they would be investigated retroactively, for the second illegal border crossing only worsened the first crime, and so the majority "had to be processed."[99]

The trauma experienced by refugees before leaving Hungary was no less an ordeal than the problems they faced in unfamiliar environments, at the mercy of others and uncertain of their future. Horror stories spread among the refugees, telling of exploitation at the hands of the West, girls being forced into prostitution and being exposed to various prejudices, whether against Hungarians or those coming from communist countries. Some countries did little to dispel these fears: disappointed Hungarians were returning en masse from Turkey, Ireland, and the Dominican Republic, to name but a few. Of the 21,000 Hungarians who immigrated to the United Kingdom, 1,300 returned home, while 6,000 headed over the Atlantic Ocean—British mining communities were not welcoming of cheap labor from Hungary. At Hungarian consulates, disillusioned "absconders" were encouraged to return home with no warning that the property of those departing to unknown places had been confiscated and that their reward might be in the form of call-up papers for the Hungarian Army.

The political police traced the paths of "enemies of the People's Republic" abroad as well as at home, with the apparatus of Hungarian embassies serving this function alongside intelligence stations; the World Federation of Hungarians was also used as a cover for this activity. Records of refugees filled six thick volumes under the auspices of the Ministry of the Interior[100] with statistics that gave a picture of the social situation, profession, age, and former residence of the "absconders" based on detailed (and secret) data.

In the wake of the Revolution, one of the priorities for Hungarian intelligence and the secret police was the suddenly expanded émigré community, a community they had previously worked their way into and now flooded with incoming refugees. Although during the Revolution the Hungarian secret service network had fallen apart a little, its work was given new impetus by the newly reorganized secret service agencies, the newly established management of intelligence groups, and the redefined priorities of both groups. In April 1957, Hungarian politician Károly Szarka asked for detailed reports from the twelve most important embassies on the political orientation and activities of dissidents on their radar, as well as their relations with earlier émigrés.[101] Prior to 1956, the Hungarian exile community had included a number of Arrow Cross (Hungarian Nazi) members, fascists, and compromised politicians who were suddenly reactivated by the events of the Revolution, while the new group of émigrés included communists, social democrats, and left-wingers. The short two weeks of the Revolution and the resistance movement that followed unified groups of very diverse persuasions, which then separated, and—as happens so often after defeat—came into conflict with one another.

The Hungarian secret services had a great deal of information on the new wave of emigrants, for many of them had done time as political prisoners. The documentation of these prisoners and the "confessions" extracted through torture—together with information about their friends and other prisoners—were now fully at the disposal of the secret services, providing ready ammunition for rocking the émigré community at its core.

The refugee question became one of the battle fronts in the Cold War: beyond the benefits that Hungarian refugees brought to Western countries with their knowledge, talent, and diligence, the breadth of confidential information that could be either openly or surreptitiously obtained was invaluable to the intelligence services of the countries to which they immigrated. The United States was one of the most attractive destinations for Hungarian refugees, as well as being the most generous supporter of aid to Hungary.[102] At Camp Kilmer, the Armed Services Prisoner Intelligence Committee established the Historical and Statistical Survey Team, which undertook what they called "evaluations" of the refugees who had recently reached the free world and were waiting to continue their journey. Its Sociological and Technical Research Unit worked for twelve to fourteen hours a day, with a staff of two hundred, sixty of whom were deployed (to use a military term) at any one time. Among the 32,000 Hungarian refugees in the US, the research unit conducted hearings with 3,200 of the 6,000 refugees selected for interviews. Of these, 1,500 intelligence reports were compiled, with many hundreds of documents attached.[103] The intelligence officers performed their task strictly undercover, lest it be discovered that the leading country of the free world was doing things that perhaps only the Hungarian secret services would have believed it capable of.

While Hungarian refugees were assisting the United States Secret Service, whether knowingly or unknowingly, diplomats from Eastern bloc countries claimed they had evidence of Soviet infiltration of the CIA, the US Department of State, and the offices of the Secretary-General of the UN. Danish diplomat Povl Bang-Jensen was contacted and promised crucial evidence of these communist infiltrations while these informants were in New York, but they left suddenly, and he never met with them again. Before they disappeared, the diplomats had urged Bang-Jensen to get in touch with James Barco, who worked at the US delegation to the UN. Barco first refused to disclose whether he had had delicate information forwarded to him, but later, against Bang-Jensen's instructions, wrote a report on what Bang-Jensen had told him. Some sources suggest Barco even knew the names of the diplomats who had shared information about the Soviet espionage.[104] Quite apart from being a breach of trust, Barco's report produced no tangible results. Many months passed after the concerned diplomats had first established contact (in November 1956), with no consequences then or later. At least nothing transpired in New York or Washington; whether anything happened in Moscow, we may never know. All this only came to light in Washington in an investigation initiated many years later, at which point Barco swore under oath that Bang-Jensen had never told him anything about Soviet bloc defectors.[105] The United States Secret Service followed the investigation, but there was no public-facing evidence that an investigation was forthcoming on their part, just as there was no attempt to confirm or deny the dangerous information that the UN Secretariat might be under Soviet control. The Secret Service merely examined Bang-Jensen's index card to check his background and then did the same thing at the request of the State Department in Washington.[106]

For the communist propaganda machine, there was another way to exploit the refugee crisis: the stories of its children. Many young people set out into the world in the fall of 1956 and then, in the early winter, found themselves adrift in a strange environment, with no family or other help. Many of them had run away from home, care institutions, or dormitories, and it was not possible to give a precise figure as to their number.[107] The Hungarian authorities immediately took up their cause both at the UN and with the International Committee of the Red Cross,[108] as they attached particular importance to the status of children: international treaties obliged recipient countries to send minors back to their home country. Meanwhile, in Geneva and New York, there was concern about the vacillating nature of the announced amnesty and the inconsistencies between the news emerging from Hungary and that from the official government line. Of particular concern were the contradictions from Budapest, which announced a "one-way street" for the unification of families: the only route was for repatriation (that is, being sent home), and there was no reciprocity, much less any mention of human rights.

Yet Hungarian government propaganda was tireless, and its efforts met with some success. In January 1957, the Canadian women's movement turned over a letter to the UN Secretary-General, passing on a desperate message from mothers in Hungary: "Send our young folks home."[109] On reaching his station, Péter Mód wrote a memorandum on the issue of child refugees, publishing numerous pleading letters from Hungarian parents asking for the return of their sons and daughters who had drifted to the West, been "seduced" by it, or simply escaped to it.[110] The majority of the letters were probably genuine; many of them were in the original form and included the name, address, and other details. Sometimes the theme of Kádárist propaganda surfaced through the parents' words; there was a sense that the letter had been written under duress, but even here the personal concern nevertheless comes through. Many minors were later sent back to Hungary. While still in the West, the older ones were thoroughly questioned about their motivations, even if they were going home of their own accord: Was it really their own decision, or was it the result of duress or extortion?[111]

In every case, the International Committee of the Red Cross sought to establish contact with the parents.[112] Legally, its hands were tied—there was no room for deliberation in the case of a child. Nevertheless, it was questionable whether it would be doing the right thing if it followed the law.

The Hungarian authorities repeatedly objected to the obstruction of repatriation; they were now the ones who spoke of threats, intimidation, extortion, and false promises. The propagandists circulated stories about child labor, prostitution, human trafficking, and fantasies about various forms of coercion—imaginings that were on occasion backed up by shocking and disturbing real-life examples.

The UNHCR and the International Committee of the Red Cross made a number of attempts to reunite families in the West: fleeing parents sometimes left their children behind in the hope that international law would ensure they would be able to follow them. The Kádár regime did not show any willingness to let the children leave, however, and when the aid agencies turned to the UN Secretary-General on their behalf, the laconic response was merely that he was not in a position to act in an official capacity.[113]

The UN International Children's Emergency Fund (UNICEF), the UN's specialized agency on children's issues, became deeply involved in the aid program. In March 1957, its representative arrived in Budapest with $700,000 worth of aid; from there, he traveled to Prague, to Warsaw, and then on to Moscow as part of a mission to what he called "contributing" countries. That these Soviet-aligned countries welcomed the UNICEF representative suggests they considered it possible to help refugee children via the UN, while granting other kinds of aid generated by fraternal countries. But there is no mention of the issue of reuniting families in their documents.

Hungarian government propagandists were happy to cast aspersions, and while tracing the fates of the refugees, they found, exaggerated, and presented as typical episodes that illustrated how hard life was for them. While these stories served the interests of neo-Stalinist propaganda about the West, it also stoked fear and disgust regarding the fate of Hungarian émigrés. When the propagandists attempted to substantiate their allegations, however, this generated diplomatic notes and legal cases; their rhetoric of libel generally did not come out of the confrontation well when it met with reality.

Of course, there are many truly tragic stories to tell about the fates of Hungarians entirely at the mercy of others, not understanding the language, having no contacts, working in the mines or on scorching plantations or production lines, with many of them falling afoul of trickery, manipulation, and downright villainy.[114] But these tragedies were far outnumbered by the splendid examples of solidarity and assistance that made the story of the resettlement of the Hungarian 1956 refugees such a success; neither before, during, nor after World War II had refugees experienced similar degrees of empathy and keenness to help. Hungarian Ambassador to the UN Péter Mód divulged a list of painful refugee stories to the United Nations, but he met with misfortune when the authorities in the countries accused with exploiting refugees immediately investigated the allegations and published their findings. The Austrian Ambassador to the UN refuted Mód's claims and provided over six pages of evidence for their baselessness before adding how odd it was that the same Hungarian authorities who were ignoring the UN's resolutions on Hungary should be bringing their grievances to the UN. Even more strange, he added, was that the Hungarian government did have not a word of thanks to give Austria for providing safety and provisions for 170,000 of their compatriots.[115] The British, mentioned in a different dossier, also investigated the claims and found them to be groundless, and Her Majesty's government was "surprised" that it was the Hungarian authorities, who were constantly contravening human rights, who were so keen to see these rights observed in other countries.[116]

While the refugees traveled on to their recipient countries, the UN organized the huge volume of personal stories of refugees into categories and tables and converted them into data. When the enormous effort to accommodate the refugees was translated into numbers, they revealed its unprecedented success: in ten weeks, one hundred thousand Hungarians had been welcomed into Austria and then successfully moved on to twenty-eight other countries. The logistics of this situation were more difficult than they appeared from these data: not all countries wanted to take just anyone from anywhere, and the refugees, of course, wanted to establish and achieve their own priorities.[117] The costs involved were enormous, and this sometimes became a decisive factor in determining the refugees' fate.[118] Yet it was already clear that the crisis would come to an end and be replaced by other crises, including the resolution of the political issues still dividing Hungary and the UN member nations.

The Unanswered Questions of Legitimacy

It was as if time itself was left feebly to provide the answer to the question of legitimacy; as weeks went by people became accustomed to the unacceptable. Not even the Soviets questioned the legitimacy of the Imre Nagy government, and they began to engage in official talks with it, and there was a "crisis resolution" plan prepared in Moscow to address the issue. As Yugoslav secretary of state Dobrivoje Vidić put it many months later regarding the agreement between Yugoslav leader Josip Broz Tito and Khrushchev, "They tried to make it easier to liquidate the Imre Nagy government."[119]

On November 19, Western diplomats recognized that it was "unnecessary and premature to recognize the Kádár government,"[120] as the UN had done de facto by allowing Hungarian communist politician Imre Horváth, in New York as a representative of the Kádár administration, to speak. The British ambassador in Budapest reported that Hungarians were "especially disgusted" by this strange form of legitimacy, and he let his superiors know that Horváth did not speak for anyone apart from himself, a handful of Stalinists, and, of course, Moscow.[121] In January, the Labour Party in Britain had already recommended that Kéthly be recognized, not Kádár,[122] just as leaders of the State Department were wondering whether to retract the UN mandate of the Hungarian puppet delegation, accepting every risk this brought with it. Not only would this action break off diplomatic relations, it would make the work of supplying aid more difficult or even impossible. And it would be the captive Hungarian people who would suffer the consequences of this rift, so they gave up on the plan, hoping it would be easier to influence Hungary if it were inside the UN than if it were outside it.[123]

That Anna Kéthly would present little threat to the law-breaking Hungarian regime was the work not just of the United Nations but also of Kéthly herself. For she announced in Vienna that there was a danger of counterrevolution in Hungary,[124] citing as evidence the work of antifascist and anticommunist Cardinal Mindszenty, whom the US would end up protecting at their embassy. She was immediately followed in her alarmist rhetoric by longtime Stalinist politician Ernő Gerő. Gerő adopted the fearmongering terminology Kádár applied to the counterrevolution and joined Moscow and its Hungarian puppets in stigmatizing the events from October 23 to November 4 as "the white terror." Kéthly also made her participation in the government dependent on the Soviet troops leaving Hungary, yet by this stage, she wished to represent her country in New York precisely because of the Soviet invasion. Furthermore, the Soviet intervention in Hungary made it impossible for her to acquire a direct government mandate, a fact the UN was unable to ignore.[125]

As of November 5, 1956, it was still possible to make a proposal on implementing the UN Assembly's resolutions on aid in such a way that the UN did not have to recognize the Kádár government. Although the UN did add that should they recognize it, the UN was likely to become the most important source of information on assistance to the Hungarian people and their case for severing the contingency between recognition and aid had been made.[126] When the moral boycott of Kádár and his associates expanded and the insulted Stalinists left the Hall, UN leaders maintained contact with the delegation. They could justify this because no country had broken off diplomatic relations with Hungary following its legitimate government being overthrown by armed force—and although there was a certain reluctance on the part of Western opinion leaders, who made or at least intended to make strong gestures, they soon managed to get back to business.

The notion that everything that had happened was "a form of recognition of the Kádár government" had emerged in the Hungarian foreign ministry, where denials of Kéthly's valid mandate were avidly collected.[127] One last option remained for the international community's sense of what was right: the retraction of the Hungarian UN mandate, something that was hard to do without calling into question the legitimacy of the Hungarian government, as it was based on legal succession to the previous and legitimate government.[128] In the end, the only expression of international disdain would be a half-baked legal solution—the suspension of the UN mandate on February 6, 1957—as the investigation into the Kádár regime's legitimacy could only extend to a check on the letter of credence, which was validated by the same Presidential Council that had operated continuously from 1953. And the suspension of the mandate did little to restrict the rights of the Hungarian delegation in any case.

At its first hearing, on November 9, 1956, the UN committee investigating the Hungarian mandate did not pass any resolution, and although the US Ambassador to the UN recommended that the usurpers have their right of representation removed, this did not become an official proposal.[129] Meanwhile, they had considered the implications of divesting the Hungarians of their UN Mission; in this, not only moral arguments played a role but also the desire to avoid setting an uncomfortable precedent for future usurpers in case those might be in the Western Hemisphere.[130]

After the hearing, Kéthly wrote in person to every member of the Credentials Committee, copying the letters to Hammarskjöld. The Secretary-General acknowledged receipt of the letters while being very cautious to avoid addressing Kéthly as a minister of state—for this is how she described herself, saying that she represented Hungary's "true government,"[131] and the United Nations had entered into contact with what can only have been considered a false one.

Meanwhile, the UN's condemnation, however restrained, annoyed the authorities in Budapest. Rightly seeing the United States behind the humiliation of discussing their mandate and questioning their legitimacy, they hurried to request the recall of the US minister in Budapest, who had dragged his feet in presenting his letter of credence to the new government.[132] The suspension of the UN mandate was not a permanent rejection of the Kádár government, however; the real decision was expected at the spring session of the UN's accreditation committee, at which the Hungarian mandate would have been raised together with the accreditation of other member states.[133]

Péter Mód did present his credentials, and his prestige as a delegate vis-à-vis that of the previous Hungarian representative was distinctly boosted by the role he played in the French Resistance, followed by his prolonged time in jail under Rákosi's Stalinist rule—whatever his role had previously been in establishing that rule. Mód's turncoat strategy during the 1956 Revolution had proved to be a great success: he was elected secretary of the Hungarian Socialist Workers' Party, a body made up of 230 employees of the foreign ministry.[134] To great press attention, Mód handed over his letter of credence to Hammarskjöld, of whom Mód reported—seemingly without irony—that he "wanted to be an apolitical secretary-general."[135] Later, Hammarskjöld replied to Mód—and thereby to Budapest and Moscow—that he had been "pressured" on the Hungarian question and that he would therefore "return" his mandate to the Assembly and "would not accept any further mandate relating to the Hungarian question."

While the Hungarian government worked for the next six years to remove the stigma of the suspended mandate, Deputy Foreign Minister Endre Sík later wrote, with possible exaggeration, that it was a "half-hearted resolution" that "was of no real-life significance": the Hungarian delegation was able to be present at sessions, to vote, and to make use of the entire UN infrastructure, including its podium.[136] But as few of Hungary's old friends remained and its isolation, beyond the fraternal countries, seemed complete, the Turtle Bay building, as the New York UN skyscraper was often called, suddenly appeared more like a battleground. Sík described how he and his fellow Hungarian diplomats received an education in "the art of combat," on "what for me is an as yet unchartered front of the class struggle."[137] The battle was underway—against no less an enemy than the UN Charter itself.

Zhou Enlai, on a visit to Budapest, said that there was nothing the UN could do and that even if it were to exclude Hungary—which, as the logical next step, he and his Hungarian host, Kádár, were assuming it would—he reassured Kádár that they would be together on the outside.[138] Meanwhile, the "dutiful voting machine of imperialism"—as Sík called the UN—excluded not Hungary but Kéthly from the opportunity of representation, preventing her from responding to Péter Mód's attack in the same form (a publicized official UN document).[139] Thus she could not bring to the attention of the member states that the Kádár government had made no mention of the Imre Nagy cabinet resigning and so could not lay a claim to legal succession. Nor could the Soviet intervention be considered an act of either the legitimate cabinet or the illegitimate one: the timing of it excluded both possibilities. As a result, the intervention was unlawful and a violation of the UN Charter.[140] Kéthly saw Nagy's statement as the guarantee of legal continuity; the statement was the basis for the foundation of the Revolutionary Council of Strasbourg. László Hámori informed the UN leadership of all this—but to no avail.[141]

Even in this seemingly ambiguous situation, some more distinct gestures were made. For example, in the second half of January 1957, Prince Wan Waithayakon, President of the UN Assembly, gave a dinner for the leaders of the socialist bloc delegations, at which Mód was present. Only a month later, the UN leadership requested the Hungarian delegation to pay its membership fees,[142] making it clear that, as far as the UN administration was concerned, the delegation from Hungary were full members. In early February, meanwhile, the Kádár government had already sent a Hungarian delegate to the UN European Office in the person of János Szita, referred to in Imre Horváth's letter to the Secretary-General as a councillor.

While the "apolitical" Secretary-General did not appear at the October Revolution anniversary reception of the Soviet Mission on November 7, 1956, he did meet Horváth on December 13;[143] then, on January 28, 1957, he visited the Soviet Mission. Although the important points of the Hungarian question were noted in his diary, he was toasting the usurpers in February and was present at the reception at the Hungarian Mission on April 4 to celebrate the anniversary of the Soviet Army's liberation of Hungary. While Hammarskjöld remained on speaking terms with the Hungarian émigrés, between mid-June and mid-September—summer or not—he met with Mód no fewer than three times.

The Cruel "Consolidation" in Hungary and Its Resonances

The UN leadership had plenty of information at its disposal on how the reign of terror in Hungary was flourishing and how it took its victims— first in an impromptu fashion, with raw brutality, then systematically and dressed in a cloak of legal process. In the weeks after the Soviet invasion, news of firing squads, arrests, summary executions, the terror of the militias in "quilted jackets," and many other episodes of reprisal reached New York.[144] The scrambling intensity of the reprisals was sometimes too much even for those in Hungary bent on revenge: the Hungarian Ministry of the Interior's summary of April 1957 found many of the arrests and imprisonments to be unjustified and condemned the "rule of the fist"; that is, the systematic and sometimes sadistic abuse of those detained. On more than one occasion, these actions cost the victims their lives. "They also beat a number of detainees to death in Szolnok county," details the report, the "also" being significant. The document says it was "common knowledge" that people loyal to the "people's democracy" were also mistreated.[145]

Within the UN, however, such information found its way not into the "Hungarian file" but rather put before the relevant UN committee as "violations of human rights." That is, the information was put into the global context of contraventions of laws, of which there were quite a few.[146] Importantly, the protection of sources was already an issue. The readers of such messages were asked to be especially circumspect to protect the interests of the senders, telling of the brutal methods of the Soviet occupation and then of its more relaxed grip, though this was accompanied by mass arrests, especially during the disbandment of the workers' councils.[147]

The reversal of the deportations had been evidence enough that attracting the attention of the United Nations could save lives or at least help make lives more livable. For a time, the invading Soviets indiscriminately put those considered to be "counter revolutionaries" onto freight trains.[148] From the outset, the Soviets and their Hungarian collaborators denied committing any serious crimes that contravened the UN Charter or international law and presented the Hungarians as being pleasantly surprised by their fraternal assistance; they further justified their actions by citing

Members of the Special Committee on the Problem of Hungary. Copyright: UN Photo Archive #7725521.

the inadequate conditions in Hungarian jails. The first news of those being deported to the Soviet Union was quick to arrive at the UN—from railroad workers, on the slips of paper thrown out of carriages, and from escaped prisoners—and forwarded to embassies, Western newspapers, and International Committee of the Red Cross workers. The issue was so serious that those at the highest level quickly became aware of it. Although Hammarskjöld did not act on it, the very existence of the chain of communication was enough for trains crammed with prisoners to make their way back to Hungary.[149]

As Kádár and his minister of interior, Ferenc Münnich, tried to remedy the situation,[150] a number of ex-ÁVH officers residing in the Soviet Union were involved in the interrogation of prisoners. For example, during the Revolution, forty of these ÁVH men and their families had escaped to Uzhhorod, just over the border in the Ukrainian Soviet Socialist Republic, in four or five Pobeda cars and a truck. With their expertise, these professionals joined the Soviet state security officers in their work at the local jail; there are several official records of their work there.[151] After the Soviet invasion of Hungary, the members of this team returned to their original posts. Although the ÁVH had officially been disbanded, its members were not demobilized or sent into retirement but were given new tasks. Previously, many of the ÁVH leaders had been criticized by the greatest perpetrator of them all, Rákosi himself, but the disbandment of the body was a decision made by the Revolution, one that Kádár did not overturn. Of the multitude of sadistic torturers who had worked in the interrogation rooms, the investigation into the ÁVH found merely a handful of them guilty: of 4,986 accused of human rights violations, only 15 were held accountable; the other 4,971 were found to be innocent and allowed to continue their good work.[152]

The Soviet invasion meant that tormentors who had been hiding in fear could now have their revenge on the revolutionaries; their enthusiasm for this was only intensified by the pent-up dread of their victims. The battles within the Communist Party can be traced through its attempts to rehabilitate the institution of terror. In April 1957, the guiding principles of the Hungarian Socialist Workers' Party (MSZMP) in April 1957 expressly emphasized that "the resilience of the ÁVH, standing by the people's regime to the end, was particularly heroic," a position that was echoed in many foreign ministry documents.[153] An important part of the consolidation of the regime built on terror was that, alongside the reorganized political police, the newly activated detectives worked with such enormous energy that they reactivated or newly conscripted dozens of secret agents. In the meantime, the so-called workers' guard battalions (paramilitary volunteer units to fight "counter-revolution") were established: by March 1957, there were thirty-eight of these operating in the provinces, and the Communist Party leadership planned to create another seventy workers' guard divisions, which would be supported by a grant of three million Czech crowns by Rudolf Barák, Czechoslovak minister of the interior.

The intensity of the reprisals was increased not only by the ex-ÁVH officers recapturing their leading position in the newly established political police but also by the fragility of the situation: a lingering general strike, a "dual power structure" due to the workers' councils, and countless episodes of passive resistance. All of this was accompanied by the constant reevaluation of the Revolution in Budapest, which was followed in detail by the UN. On November 12, 1956, in a telegram to Hammarskjöld, Deputy Foreign Minister István Sebes was still writing that the crowds marching on October 23 had expressed a number of democratic and patriotic demands that the Revolutionary Worker-Peasant Government "took on board as its own." His message also mentioned the possibility of refugees returning to Hungary without fear of punishment and the withdrawal of Soviet troops—though he was already citing the fourth paragraph of the Paris Treaties; that is, referring to the "appearance of organized fascist elements," who, together with common criminals, were gradually taking over control of events. These elements had murdered "hundreds" of progressively minded individual and their families and planned for further bloodshed; it was the government's obligation, with Soviet assistance, to stand up to them.[154] In his statement in December, Kádár blamed the policies of Rákosi for leading to these events; by the following year, he had changed his tune and mentioned not only fascists but also imperialists and their henchmen, who were unable to accept the people's democracy and the successes it had achieved.[155]

Meanwhile, at the UN Secretariat, from time to time they would produce a summary of "recent events in Hungary" that would be passed on to the UN's leaders, then put at the disposal of the Special Committee created in January. The interest of those who prepared these summaries covered not just the manifestations of terror but also the political demands of the workers' councils, the arrests, and the growing Soviet influence in the Hungarian economy.[156]

The United Nations received news not only of the executions as they began, but also of the tireless work of the executioners' legal lackeys at the prosecutor's office and the criticisms that the mass killings had not gone far enough. The UN followed these events with both great alarm and deafening silence that could no longer be ignored by the representatives of certain member states. The Italian UN Ambassador noted that the Secretary-General was fiddling with studies, investigations, and reports while the Hungarian population continued to be massacred.[157]

Only the International Committee of the Red Cross attempted to intervene; after all, Article 3 of the Geneva Convention, of which Hungary was a signatory, includes precise prescriptions on the rights of those in custody. As precedent, it cited the permission granted by Béla Kun[158] on April 28, 1919, for International Committee of the Red Cross officials to visit 48 political prisoners and 131 hostages in the Central Detention Facility in Budapest.[159] The International Committee of the Red Cross also cited the examples of Morocco, Algeria, Greece, and Cyprus, although the leaders in Geneva were, of course, sensitive to the distinction between political prisoners and prisoners of war. As a result, they recommended their workers in Hungary not to take an "overly rigid legal position," but on November 15, they made the case for the rights of the political prisoners, for them to

be able to be in contact with their families, and for their strict treatment
to be eased. They would then warn the Hungarian and Soviet authorities
about these recommendations on December 10,[160] although Hungarian Red
Cross Society employees in Hungary urged restraint from the Geneva headquarters, lest its demands endanger the success of the aid operation. The
humanitarian agency did not back down, however, and kept the matter on
its agenda. Although the "counterrevolutionaries" did not enjoy any kind of
international legal support, as the circumstances of their incarceration were
a Hungarian domestic matter, the attention was nevertheless significant.
The International Committee of the Red Cross wanted to send aid packages
to the prisoners; however, this was possible only a full two years later, and
even then, the Red Cross was not allowed to oversee their distribution. To
its repeated requests made in 1960, the International Committee of the Red
Cross would not receive a reply until four years later; it was not until 1964
that it could finally get an answer to the question it had first put eight years
earlier as to whether Hungary was complying with Article 3.[161]

In light of all that has been researched and revealed to this time, we
can conclude that the UN was unable to live up to its mandate even after
the Revolution, the political crises, and the questions about the legitimacy
of the usurpers of power. Several attempts were made to solve the Hungarian problem, but these resulted only in the suspension of the Hungarian
UN delegation's mandate. The UN's assistance was successful in easing the
humanitarian crises created by the mass exodus of Hungarians into Austria
and elsewhere, yet it was the International Committee of the Red Cross that
played the lead in this activity. The UN's efforts were highly significant in
helping the nearly two hundred thousand refugees to find their new homeland. The reestablished order of Kádár and the resulting systematic revenge
that ensued was reported to the UN, but it was nearly impossible to provide
help to those in trouble.

Notes

1. Wahlen was the head of the agricultural department of the UN. Pierre Sinard
was director of the agricultural division of the European Economic Committee.

2. Ibid.

3. Ibid. As revealed in the exchange of messages between Boissier and Obez.

4. UNARM S-0445-0196-12884-Part A 3 UC. "[Red Cross] . . . extremely pleased
at the proposal of action for the rehabilitation of food production."

5. According to the report, the agricultural cooperatives were on the brink of
collapse. UNARM S-0445-0196-12884-Part A 2 UC.

6. Ibid.

7. Columbia University, Butler Library, Rare Books and Manuscript Collection (hereinafter ACP), box 182. According to the press conference on January 18, 1957: "abortive attempt to go to Budapest by the SYG [secretary-general] preceded by my projected preparatory visit which never took place [. . .] I therefore undertook conversations here with the Hungarian delegation and we agreed on a fact-finding mission to Budapest. [. . .] no advance publicity."

8. UNARM S-0445-0196-12884-Part A 2 UC.

9. Alongside Kádár's, there was a list of twenty additional names. UNARM S-0445-0196-12884-Part B 4 UC.

10. "Background Information." "Note on the Course of Insurrection in Hungary." "Political Developments of Hungary 1945–1956." UNARM S-0445-0196-12884-Part A 1 UC.

11. See Memo, November 12, 1956. UNARM S-0445-0196-12884-Part B 4 UC.

12. Ibid.

13. UNARM S-0445-0196-12884-Part B 4 UC.

14. November 10, 1956. Gál, *A "Jelcin-dosszié,"* 103.

15. Among others, he cited the article of December 28, 1956, in *Népszabadság.* UNARM S-0445-0196-12884-Part B 4 UC.

16. UNARM S-0445-0196-12884-Part B 2 UC.

17. ÁBTL 3.2.5. O-8-125/1.

18. UNARM S-0927-0002-0009-00001 UC.

19. ACP, box 182.

20. Ibid. The needs listed were 10,000 tons of seed, machinery, artificial fertilizer, and 150,000 tons of grain. It notes that assistance was expected from the Soviet Union and China, but the extent of this help is not known. DHS L 179:83.

21. ACP, box 182.

22. UNARM S-0445-0196-12884-1 UC.

23. January 4, 1957. Cohen to Pelt: "If the story breaks through." ACP, box 182.

24. UNARM S-0445-0196-Part A 2 UC.

25. UNARM S-0445-0196-12884-Part B 6 UC, -Part A 2 UC.

26. MNL XIX-J-1-k, box 19.

27. ACP, box 182.

28. MNL XIX-J-1-j, box 208. The public in Hungary learned of the visit in the January 9, 1957, edition of *Népszabadság*: "What was the UN deputy secretary-general discussing in Budapest? [. . .] De Seynes was only interested in Hungary from a humanitarian perspective."

29. UNARM S-0445-0196-12884-1 UC.

30. UNARM S-0445-0196-12884-Part B 5 UC. "Report by the Secretary General: Question considered by the second emergency special session of the GA from November 4 to 10, 1956. Humanitarian activities to assist Hungarian people."

31. January 21, 1957. UNARM S-0445-0196-12884-Part B 2 UC.

32. MNL XIX-J-1-k, box 55. Thus they had been prepared to "reject the attempt to intervene, dressed up as an aid operation." MOL XIX-J-1-j, box 39. At the same time, Károly Szarka requested $30 million as "urgent aid" and "reconstruction aid." MOL XIX-J-1-k, box 19.

33. UNARM S-0445-0196-12884-Part B 4 UC.

34. ACP, box 182.

35. UNARM S-0445-0196-12884-Part B 1 UC.

36. DHS L 179:173.

37. UNARM S-0445-0196-12884-Part A 1 UC.

38. UNARM S-0445-0196-12884-Part B 1 UC. "Some orderly method of procedure needs to be worked out between UN, FAO and IRC. At present no coordinated action in this respect exists."

39. UNARM S-0445-0196-12884-Part B 1 UC. Boissier later made visits to Vienna, then Budapest. See Kecskés, "Humanitárius segítségnyújtás globális méretekben."

40. NARA 310.5/12-1056.

41. ACP, box 183.

42. NARA 310.5/11-656.

43. ACP, box 183.

44. November 30, 1956. DHS L 179:83.

45. Ibid.

46. DHS L 179:83. On November 28, 1956, Hammarskjöld asked Horváth for "immediate clarification of the position of your government."

47. November 30, 1956. DHS L 179:83.

48. According to a summary without date or signature. ACP, box 184.

49. There were other problems, according to the Colombian delegate: "Lall would raise all kinds of difficulties and Gundersen would be very legalistic." NARA 310.5/12-1056.

50. DHS L 179:83. December 12, 1956. Gundersen, Lall, and Lleras: "Note for the SYG" ACP, box 184. December 14. "Statement by A. Lleras of Colombia concerning the Suspension of the Commission of Investigation Appointed by the SYG." DHS L 179:83. The Secretary-General did not immediately make the resignation public. Cordier replied to the inquiring US representative to the UN that they had only verbally returned their mandates, even though Lodge had already received a copy of Lleras's letter of resignation from him. NARA 61164/12-1456.

51. ACP, box 184.

52. DHS L 179:83.

53. NAA A 1209 1957/5283.

54. Ibid. The chief Australian delegate reported on this from London on January 2, 1957.

55. Indian chargé d'affaires Rahman handed Bibó's memorandum to Senerat Gunewardene; it was in the drinks crate transported to the British embassy, where Árpád Göncz handed it to László Regéczy-Nagy. The document went from the embassy to Vienna, and from there via secret agents back to Budapest, where it became one of the items of evidence of Bibó's "active spy connections." See Regéczy-Nagy László interview. 1956 Institute, Oral History Archive (hereinafter OHA) no. 187. Also ÁBTL V-150352, III, 1157–66.

56. Ibid., 5.

57. The Hungarian-born Magdolna Friedmann married the Indian prime minister's cousin.

58. On November 11, he reported on twenty thousand deaths and eighty thousand injuries, then on November 18, he sent a report on the deportations. Bethlenfalvy, *India és a magyar forradalom 1956*, 1–2.

59. Rahman, *Magyarország, 1959–1959*, 2.

60. Bethlenfalvy, *India és a magyar forradalom 1956*, 1; and Rahman, *Magyarország, 1959–1959*, 3.

61. Rahman, *Magyarország, 1959–1959*, 1–3.

62. Ibid., 3.

63. Ibid.

64. Ibid. The driver, Tibor Kozmovszky, had previously been an ÁVH agent and would later be given tasks by the Hungarian secret service agencies.

65. Ibid., 4. At the Grand Hotel on Budapest's Margaret Island, he also met a few leaders of the Revolution, such as Gábor Magos. See Gábor Magos and Judit Gimes interview. OHA no. 531.

66. UNARM S-0890-0008-0001-00001 UC.

67. Ibid.

68. József Kővágó met Nehru in 1959. MNL P 2245, box 1.

69. Radványi (1972), 22.

70. Ibid.

71. UNARM S-0445-0200-13409-2 UC.

72. See Ambassador Lajos Cséby's greetings to Brilej from September 1957. MNL XIX-J-1-j (Yugoslavia) 11, box 4/j.

73. Antisemitic atrocities occurred at the time of the Revolution, but they did not become a significant factor in the political situation. Standeiszky (2007).

74. The International Committee of the Red Cross report states that more refugees arrived from October 30, 1956, onward. UNARM S-0445-0199-13408-4UC.

75. ÁBTL MT 493/1.

76. See "Hungarian Refugee Relief. Report of the Relief Measures for Hungarian Refugees Undertaken by the [Red Cross] League and Member National Societies in Austria, Yugoslavia and Countries of Transit and Resettlement, October 1956–September 1957." Geneva, 1957. UNARM S-0445-0200-13409-2 UC.

77. UNARM S-0445-0198-13185 1 UC. November 20, 1956. "Interim Report by the SYG on refugees from Hungary."

78. UNARM S-0445-0198-13185 2 UC.

79. DHS L 179:83.

80. UNARM S-0445-0198-13205 UC.

81. UNARM S-0445-0199-13411 UC.

82. ACP, box 182.

83. Ibid., and UNARM S-0445-0198-13185-2 UC. November 17, 1956. "Great increase in influx of refugees in the last 24 hours. [. . .] 3000 more without accommodation [. . .] Temperature minus 10 degrees centigrade. Clothing newly arrived refugees drenched through crossing matches." On the document, handwritten: "This is going to be very serious"

84. The ICEM, which worked outside the framework of the UN, was founded by the US and its allies to transport refugees from countries where they were too many in number (Federal Republic of Germany, Austria, Italy, Greece). Kecskés, "Humanitárius segítségnyújtás globális méretekben," 145-70.

85. January 20, 1957. UNARM S-0890-0008-0001-00001 UC.

86. UNARM S-0445-0200-13409-2 UC.

87. UNARM S-0445-0198-13185-2UC. Some of these were sparked by provocations, but the combined psychological burden of the memory of fleeing and of an uncertain future, not to mention the ordeal of life in refugee camps, was considerable.

88. October 30, 1957. According to the survey, there were 150 with tuberculosis and 600 with socialization issues. UNARM S-0445-0198-13185-2UC.

89. UNARM S-0445-0200-13409-2 UC 244. By this stage, only 70 US cents a day was available to provide for one refugee. February 7, 1957. UNARM S-0445-0199 13407-2 UC.

90. UNARM S-0445-0200-13409-2 UC.

91. Ibid.

92. UNARM-0445-0199-13185-2 UC. "UNHCR Co-ordinating Subcommittee on the Question of Refugees from Hungary."

93. UNARM S-0445-0198-13414-1 UC. January 17, 1957. "Systematic operation [. . .] needed." The UNREF published "The Problem of Hungarian Refugees in Austria" as a document of the UN Assembly, which surveyed the key tasks in hand: from coordination, through future operations, to the questions of housing, provisions, and further travel. The contributions of the various countries were noted and the longer-term needs listed, including the schooling of the children and the granting of smaller loans so that refugees could start a new life abroad. Only after this did they turn to the "difficult cases."

94. UNARM S-0445-0199-13245-1 UC. February 28, 1957. "Agreement on Assistance to Hungarian Refugees in Austria." There had, of course, been previous discussions and agreements. See: Kecskés, "Humanitárius segítségnyújtás globális méretekben."

95. UNARM S-0445-0138 and MNL XIX-J-1-k, box 56.

96. MNL XIX-J-1-j (Austria), box 30.

97. MNL XIX-J-1-k, box 94.

98. MNL XIX-J-20-a.

99. MNL XIX-B-1-a2, box 30.

100. MNL XIX-J-1-j, box 83, 5/1/004477.

101. They observed with interest the tensions between the members of the old and those of the new émigré communities, and between professionals and physical laborers. MNL XIX-J-1-j, box 116, 20/f.

102. With the increase in quotas, more than 30,000 refugees found their way to the United States.

103. Kecskés, "Humanitárius segítségnyújtás globális méretekben." See the telegram from the US Department of State on November 21, 1956. NARA 764.00/11.2156.

104. See the report by "SAC" (Secret Agent in Charge) sent to J. Edgar Hoover, director of the FBI, on January 13, 1960: "has learned from FBI that the names of these Iron Curtain diplomats were included in 3 written reports circulated at the State Department and among the US delegation at the UN." Bang-Jensen Archive (hereinafter BJI), box 33.

105. On May 7, Allen Dulles, director of the CIA, received a copy of Barco's memorandum of March 7, 1957. Dulles stated to a Senate committee on May 8, 1961, that "one of the questions that has never been resolved in the Bang-Jensen case involved

his alleged knowledge of the identities of certain Eastern bloc officials who desired to defect after the Hungarian revolt." BJI, box 33. According to a memo dated August 21, 1961: "[Barco] has denied under oath that Bang-Jensen mentioned anything about [defectors] to him." BJI, box 33.

106. March 20, 1957. FBI: "Check Bang-Jensen Files." On June 3, 1957, the State Department asked the FBI about "Bang-Jensen's credibility." BJI, box 33.

107. "Unaccompanied Children in the West." May 22, 1957. UNARM S-0445-0198-13185-1 UC.

108. MNL XIX-J-1-j (Austria), box 30, and Cardia, *Magyar október, vörös zászló és vörös kereszt között*, 82.

109. UNARM S-0445-0199-13274-1 UC.

110. UNARM S-0445-0199-13278-1 UC.

111. UNREF fourth session. UNARM S-0445-0199-13407-1 UC. "Standing Programme Sub-Committee Section V. Hungarian Refugees in Austria."

112. Cardia, *Magyar október, vörös zászló és vörös kereszt között*, 82.

113. UNARM S-0445-0199-13274-1 UC.

114. Of these, many have survived among Klára Héderváry's papers, National Széchenyi Library (hereinafter OSZK) Manuscript Archive, Fond 523. Claire de Hedervary Papers. In this collection, organized according to subject, the relevant documents are to be found in subject 10.

115. January 26, 1957. UNARM S-0445-0199-13274-1 UC.

116. From Dixon to the Secretary-General, January 22, 1957. UNARM S-0445-0199-13274-1 UC.

117. UNARM S-0445-0199-13414-2 UC and S-0445-0200-13409-2 UC.

118. "Notes on Statistics on Refugees from Hungary, Influx and Resettlement." The cost of travel was 74.90 USD within Europe, and 125 USD across the ocean.

119. MNL XIX-J-29-0.

120. The Australian foreign ministry papers cite Fry. NAA A 1209 1957/5282.

121. NAA A 1209 1957/5282.

122. The party made this decision on January 21, 1957: see the report from London of the Hungarian ambassador. MNL XIX-J-1-j (United Kingdom), box 14. 286. UN documents include the proposal of British members of Parliament to break off diplomatic relations. ACP, box 182.

123. UNARM S-0890-0008-0001-00001 UC.

124. MNL XIX-J-1-k, box 56.

125. Kéthly, *Száműzve, de le nem győzve*, 1.

126. ACP, box 182. "The Situation in Hungary Proposals to Implement Par. 7 and 8 of the Resolution A/3286."

127. As stated on February 12, 1957, in Budapest, "outside states" recognized the current government; that is, they looked at the Hungarian Revolutionary Workers' and Peasants' Government as the legitimate administration. In Budapest, they retrieved the documents relating to Kéthly's nomination, adding that this act of the Nagy government did not appear in the official Hungarian government record, *Magyar Közlöny* (Official Gazette). April 17, 1957. Summary of the mandate question. MNL XIX-J-36.

128. Sir Hartley Shawcross, an expert on international law, told the UN Special Committee that while the Kádár government was not legitimate, neither was that

of Imre Nagy; indeed, the latter would hardly have sworn an oath to the constitution written in 1949. Kéthly could claim succession, but so, too, could Kádár, who had been a member of the same government. British Foreign Office (hereinafter FO) 371/128677.

129. DHS L 179:83. Lodge recommended on December 10 that the mandate be rejected. NAA A 1209 1957/5279.

130. Australia reported on the Western position on February 24, 1957. NAA A 1209 1957/5279. Kéthly's speech at the Assembly was not even supported by the Ambassadors from the United Kingdom, Australia, the Netherlands, or New Zealand because of the "unwelcome precedent." See the telegram from the US Mission to the UN on December 22, 1956: NARA 310.5/12-2256.

131. DHS L 179:83.

132. Radványi (1972), 33.

133. DHS L 179:83.

134. The Hungarian Socialist Workers' Party (MSZMP) was created in 1956. Its founding members included Imre Nagy and János Kádár. MNL 288 f. Storage unit 32/1958/11. Documents of the MSZMP Central Committee, Foreign Affairs Division.

135. MNL XIX-J-1-j, box 209.

136. Sík, *Bem rakparti évek*, 169.

137. Ibid., 137. Sík describes how, during Hungary's political isolation, the United Nations was the only place they could meet foreign diplomats.

138. MNL XIX-J-1-j.

139. ACP, box 184.

140. Ibid.

141. DHS L 179:83. "Background Note on the Hungarian Revolution."

142. MNL XIX-1-24b. The question of when the Hungarian delegation would return to the Assembly Hall was considered crucial. Kuznetsov was concerned that this could raise the question of the mandate. See Mód's report of January 26, 1957. MNL XIX-J-1-j, box 230, and MNL XIX-1-24a (papers of the Hungarian consulate in New York).

143. DHS L 179:173.

144. The paramilitary units cooperating with the Soviets were referred to as *pufaj-kások* ("quilted jackets").

145. Summary written by the Hungarian Ministry of the Interior, April 10, 1957. The document mentions ninety-six unjustified arrests—some were kept in jail for an entire week. MNL XIX-B-1-y, box 1.

146. UNARM S-0445-0199-13247-1 UC. Instructions in January 1957: "Any outstanding communication relating specifically to violations of human rights in Hungary should be summarized and included in the confidential list of communications to be submitted to the Committee of Human Rights."

147. UNARM S-0445-0199-13247-1 UC. UNARM S-0890-0008-0001-00001 UC.

148. Váradi, "1956-os deportálások a Szovjetunióba."

149. János Linczmajer, in his fourth year at high school, made a witness statement on the deportations in front of the UN Special Committee (see para. 729 of the report). Váradi, "1956-os deportálások a Szovjetunióba," 42.

150. On November 14, 1956, Ivan Serov and Andropov stated that Kádár and Münnich "do not approve of this Soviet way of doing things." Gál, *A "Jelcin–dosszié,"* 32.

151. Váradi, "1956-os deportálások a Szovjetunióba," 41.

152. Markó, *A pesti Rambo.*

153. MNL 288. Storage unit 32/1959/2.

154. DHS L 179:83.

155. See Radványi (1972), 61. At this stage, Kádár referred even to Imre Nagy in more cautious terms than would later be the case.

156. UNARM 0445-0196-12884-Part A 2 UC. December 31, 1956. "The Recent Developments in Hungary." In addition to aid, Moscow contributed to the rebuilding of the Hungarian economy, and with it, an enhancement of Hungary's dependence, with a $50 million loan. Gál, A *"Jelcin–dosszié,"* 144.

157. Cited in Urquhart, *Hammarskjold,* 236.

158. Leader of the Hungarian Soviet Republic or "commune" in 1919.

159. Cardia, *Magyar október, vörös zászló és vörös kereszt között,* 132.

160. Ibid., 69, 189, 195.

161. Ibid., 104.

4

THE ATTEMPTS OF THE UN TO SOLVE THE HUNGARIAN CRISIS

Is There a Political Solution?

In January 1957, the UN General Assembly tried for the eleventh time to find some kind of political solution to the Hungarian problem, having passed one resolution after another in desperate attempts to address the situation after the Soviet invasion in Hungary.[1] By contrast, on the humanitarian front, the UN had been operating successfully.

Dag Hammarskjöld was unable to personally mediate during the most dramatic days after the Revolution, nor could UN observers be sent to Hungary. The UN General Assembly established an investigatory committee, the UN Special Committee on the Problem of Hungary, often known simply as the Committee of Five, but this committee did not begin its work until January of 1957. Thus to many Hungarians it seemed that the United Nations Organization (UNO) had "completely given up on a solution to the Hungarian question."[2] In the words of one Hungarian refugee, the only possible role for the UN was to become "a sort of complaints department,"[3] but it was unfortunately not one equipped to deal with the complaints it received.

By establishing the Special Committee on the Problem of Hungary to investigate the Hungarian question, Hammarskjöld was effectively admitting that his efforts had failed.[4] In early 1957, he returned the mandate the UN General Assembly had entrusted him with—the resolution of November 12, 1956—and thereby relinquished his responsibility. Setting up the Committee had originated as a US idea during the Revolution in October

123

1956,[5] but this initiative had by then been taken off the agenda. The subject was returned to the agenda in January 1957, and the United States discussed it with its allies. The United States wished to remain in the background and waited for a European country to make its proposals. It imbued the Committee more with political than legal clout, and its representativeness would be guaranteed by the member states involved in it: one from each continent. The Committee would investigate what happened in Hungary in October and November of 1956 and what led up to it—if possible in situ, and if not, then in the member states to which many Hungarians had fled. Hammarskjöld approved of this method, even though he was originally of the opinion that legally valid evidence needed to be collected through comprehensive and organized interviews with witnesses, including some who remained in Hungary. Developments, meanwhile, had to be continuously followed—this would have serious significance later on.

An initiative of this kind had been suggested on December 8, 1956, with the creation of a five-member body that could have reported to the Assembly; why this plan failed to materialize in December 1956 is not known.[6] By the time the Assembly resolution established the Special Committee, the background negotiations had already taken place and the majority of member states agreed with the initiative, but the Soviet-imposed Hungarian government considered it contrary to the UN Charter: according to them, the events in Hungary from October to November of 1956 should be considered internal affairs of the country. They immediately objected to the establishment of the Special Committee,[7] but the Committee nevertheless held its inaugural session on January 17, 1957. Alsing Andersen from Denmark was elected Chair, Sir Keith Charles Owen Shann (who preferred to be known as Mick Shann) from Australia was the body's Rapporteur, Mongi Slim from Tunisia represented Africa, Sir Senerat Gunewardene (Ratnakirti Senerat Serasinghe Gunewardene or R.S.S. Gunewardene) of Ceylon spoke for Asia, and Enrique Fabregat of Uruguay for the Americas. The administrative tasks associated with the selection of the Special Committee members, its operation, and the organization of its investigation fell to the United Nations Secretariat's Department of Political and Security Council Affairs, a chief department of the Secretariat, which had previously played a contradictory role in the (mis)information in its reports provided to the Secretary-General. The Department was run by Yugoslav diplomat Dragoslav Protitch, whose predecessor and successor were Soviet; a later US

Senate investigation would euphemistically describe Protitch's character as being not entirely full of integrity.[8]

Three of the Special Committee members (Slim of Tunisia, Gunewardene of Ceylon, and Fabregat of Uruguay) were ambassadors to Washington in addition to being their countries' Ambassadors to the UN. Some also participated in the work of other UN committees, which made it difficult for the Special Committee to maintain continuous activity. As to whether this was deliberate or simply a consequence of the political weight of the Committee is unclear, just as it is not known whether the selection of the diplomats involved factors other than their expertise and being representative of their countries and parts of the world. Andersen, the Danish social democrat politician who was elected Chair of the Committee, had been the Danish minister of defense prior to and during the German invasion; he had been sent to the UN to be out of the way. After the war, Andersen's failures to adequately prepare Denmark's military for the war were investigated by the Danish Parliament, which concluded that no action against Andersen was warranted. Although Andersen was not held to account, the findings of the investigation nevertheless remained a blot on his record, for in his role as minister, he had condemned the antifascist resistance within Denmark.[9] As Chair, Andersen was the face of the Special Committee, so when the Hungarian foreign ministry—in cooperation with the secret services—was tasked with discrediting it, they had an easy job of it. Its members announced that a "fascist" Nazi collaborator from Denmark would be defending the "fascist" Hungarian counterrevolutionaries, as the Hungarian communist propaganda referred to the Revolution. The authorities in Budapest also made use of an article by a propagandist named Jon Galster—whom they presented as Danish historian and who was in fact not a scholar—who accused his compatriot Andersen of being a traitor to his country.[10] The United Kingdom's UN Mission reported that the UN Secretary-General did not consider Andersen to be either principled or intelligent; it is not clear why he thought him suitable for the role of Chair of the Committee.[11]

The Australian diplomat, Shann, was the youngest Committee member, with excellent British connections and close ties to Under-Secretary-General Andrew Cordier. Enrique Fabregat, the Uruguayan diplomat, was known as a rhetorical champion of human rights.[12] Gunewardene received his degree at a British university and, during his mission, was in close contact with Hungarian diplomats.[13] He regularly received information in the form of propaganda provided by the Hungarian foreign ministry and would ask about key points in the investigation based on background materials passed to him from Budapest, using the information to try to justify the view of the Soviet-imposed Hungarian government. He knew, for example, that Anna Kéthly had not taken her oath of office as minister; he knew of the atrocities committed by insurgents and the problems associated with the election of József Kővágó, mayor of Budapest; and he was keen to prove that it had been a legitimate government that had called in the Soviets.[14] As the Committee was preparing their report, Gunewardene threatened to submit a minority opinion, then, before the report could be signed, he hurriedly traveled home, thereby running the risk of invalidating it. The Soviet secret service was also able to gain access to the codebook of the Ceylonese Mission to the UN and thus read the secret messages exchanged.[15] The Soviets also used bribery, dressed up as economic aid, to successfully gain even greater influence over Ceylon. Soviet deputy foreign minister Vasily Kuznetsov held many hours of talks with Gunewardene to dissuade him from participating in the Committee, yet the Ceylonese politician was the only member to be given a visa to visit Hungary in 1962. The fifth Committee member, Mongi Slim, was the only politician on the Committee of real stature: Slim would go on to be elected President of the UN Assembly. Slim's perspective on the Hungarian question was greatly influenced by the wars of independence from France in his homeland and neighboring Algeria—the latter involved genocide, with the systematic and continuous contravention of human rights by the champions of liberty, equality, and fraternity.[16]

The Special Committee represented the first time an investigative committee of its kind had been created in the history of the United Nations. The Committee's task was to uncover and interpret the forces behind the events in Hungary and to present its findings in an authentic way, which required knowledge of the historical background, documents to be acquired, and data to be collected. This was the work of a historian but with political overtones. The report was to provide information for UN member states so they could decide on the next steps to take.

The establishment of the Special Committee suggested that the existing resolutions had not been adequately justified; this was every bit as concerning as the fact that the report, when complete, would lead to more UN resolutions that could also freely be ignored without fear of consequence.

The Secretary-General soon informed the Hungarian delegation that the Committee's work would take time, and he did not think it likely that he would be in a position to submit a report before the end of the eleventh General Assembly.[17]

The UN leadership nevertheless provided considerable apparatus to assist the Committee's work: specialists, translators, typists, and administrators all worked at the secretariat to support the Committee. These efforts were arranged and organized by the Secretariat of the United Nations, specifically by Secretary to the Special Committee on the Problem of Hungary William Jordan from Britain and Deputy Secretary to the Special Committee Povl Bang-Jensen from Denmark.[18] That Jordan and Bang-Jensen were assigned to work together must have raised some eyebrows, as the UN Secretariat was well aware of their personal animosity from previous work together.[19] But their expertise was greatly needed as the task was complex: to obtain, register, and process documents and to organize hearings in lieu of an investigation in situ. The latter required them to select locations and organize travel and find, invite, and interview the witnesses and record their testimonies. Finally, there was the task of writing the report that would summarize the Committee's findings, or, more precisely, the writing of further reports,[20] as the continued attention of the international community would guarantee that, if it could not influence the past, the Committee would at least be able to influence the present and the future.

The Hungarian government learned of the creation of the UN Special Committee before it was inaugurated[21] and registered its objection to it as a renewed attempt at blatant interference in Hungary's internal affairs—a type of action the UN Charter did not allow for. Yet the operation of the Committee was within the range of the Hungarian secret services, which learned of messages exchanged, plans, and news sources.[22] Beyond the assertive Hungarian rhetoric, the even more assertive use of threats would play a role in unsettling embassy staff to such a degree that it would risk bringing an end to the operation of Western diplomatic missions in Hungary.

The UN Special Committee was thus right in the crosshairs of the Hungarian foreign ministry and the Hungarian intelligence services as part of what Hungary's deputy foreign minister Endre Sík had called combat—and not purely in a metaphorical sense. Hungarian intelligence and counterintelligence saw the UN Special Committee as a means to revive the counterrevolution that they claimed had been initiated from abroad and that they alleged continued to operate a spy network to obtain state and military secrets; for the Soviet-backed Hungarian government, data collected on the Hungarian economy, Soviet troop movements, and every moment of the outbreak of the Revolution and its suppression were considered strictly confidential information. Anyone assisting in acquiring and passing on this information would be considered an agent, spy, or traitor. Such rhetorical bravura was accompanied by the real threat of criminal proceedings.[23]

According to his diary, Hammarskjöld first met UN Special Committee Chair Andersen on January 21, 1957. Many weeks had passed since Hammarskjöld considered a plan to establish the Committee, suggesting that the visit was not overly urgent for him.[24] The direction the Committee was to take was outlined in an operational plan that clarified the most important issues and established the objectives of the investigation, including a list of key tasks.[25] The members of the Committee set out the rules of its procedures, looked over the records of previous attempts to resolve the Hungarian question, and agreed on an interpretation of the UN General Assembly resolution that had created the Special Committee. This was no easy task, as the resolution merely mentioned the situation in Hungary, which at this point seemed a painfully general formulation.[26] At this stage, the question of observation on location was still on the agenda; indeed, it was considered a sine qua non of the Committee's work that they be able to put their feet on Hungarian soil.[27] Hammarskjöld officially requested Hungary to allow the UN Special Committee to enter the country and meet with Imre Nagy, the prime minister during the Revolution, now imprisoned, who himself had previously been a communist politician. The Secretary-General also asked for all relevant documentation from those affected, including the Revolutionary Worker-Peasant Government.[28]

Even at this stage, the Secretary-General hoped that the UN Special Committee could demonstrate the results of the investigations in a legally valid fashion, but the proposal did make mention of the fact that a precise legal approach was not absolutely necessary.[29] The UN Special Committee was given legal assistance throughout its operation, but—unlike a previous three-man committee composed of experts of international law—its members did not include a practicing lawyer or expert on international law. Interviews with witnesses were recommended alongside the study of documents as the method of investigation; the plans even included a questionnaire for prospective witnesses.[30] Through the Secretary-General, the Committee Chair established contact with Péter Mód, head of the Hungarian UN Mission. The Secretary-General asked Mód to ensure that UN Special Committee members could travel to Hungary and, once there, move freely so that, in line with the UN Assembly resolution, they could gather the necessary information and witness statements for their work.[31] Mód's response was a clear and categorical no—and not just a simple no but a brash rejection couched in communist paranoia. As Mód reported to communist Hungary, "The reaction acting in the name of the UN seeks to provide permanent protection for the spy network operating in Hungary and its neighboring countries." In the English version of the communiqué, Mód added that the methods employed by the Committee were akin to those of intelligence agencies and other institutions of subversion.[32] As the chances of local observation work declined, it became ever more clear that those witnesses who had fled Hungary—revolutionaries, freedom fighters, those who prepared, participated in, and assisted the events of the Revolution—might be the only sources of information informing the Special Committee and its report.[33] The Committee was, of course, aware of the risks inherent in this method and planned to hold closed sessions lest the witnesses—or their loved ones still in Hungary or those mentioned in their testimonies—be placed in danger.[34] This would later become significant.

In the meantime, it also became clear that the government in Hungary had not only spread fear of revenge in Hungary but had, with its broken promises, general atmosphere of threat, neo-Stalinist methods, and slanderous rhetoric, set an irreversible process in motion. The United Nations in New York was aware of this—they had received desperate messages asking for help from Hungarians who had not been able to leave, as it would soon be too late. The completion of the report could have been that help, and the deadline for its creation was put at mid-February so that it might be submitted to the Assembly that passed resolutions on the Hungarian question.[35] Of course, this caused a real race against time. Hungarian diplomats were expecting the completion of the UN Special Committee's work and a position to be taken by the Assembly, with all its consequences (from the communist Hungarian perspective, assumed to be bad), to come in mid-February. However, the deadline began to get pushed back, with later plans mentioning the end of March. Meanwhile, the session of the Assembly was extended, so there remained hope that the report could find its way onto the agenda.[36] And when the Assembly did call a halt to its operation, there was the possibility of it being reconvened, should the situations in Hungary or Suez demand it.[37]

But the report was not finished by the end of March either. The deadline was moved to April, then May.[38] In light of these delays it can hardly have been an accident that the document was only presented to the member states at the end of June, when the Assembly was long over, the summer holidays were beginning, and the delegates were heading home. The seemingly deliberate nature of the timing is suggested by how Under-Secretary-General Andrew Cordier convinced Prince Wan Waithayakon, President of the Assembly, to not call a special session to debate the report but rather to time the discussion of the Hungarian question during the ordinary session in the fall. As a result, János Kádár and his comrades won almost an entire year to consolidate power in the system of terror in Hungary without international attention—and they were very aware that time was on their side.

Whether Cordier had a special agenda for delaying the presentation of the report, we may never know. People remember Hammarskjöld's right-hand man as a "pleasant and effective American."[39] He was among those who had overseen the birth of the UN; he came out of nowhere and was hired by Alger Hiss, who was the Secretary-General for the organizing conference for the UN held in San Francisco from April to June of 1945. Hiss would later be accused of spying for the Soviets during his career in the US State Department.[40] When Péter Mód arrived in New York in January of 1957, Cordier gave him "a very warm welcome," mentioned Under-Secretary for Economic and Social Affairs Philippe de Seynes's pleasant impressions of Budapest, and suggested that the Hungarian delegation should rejoin the Assembly as soon as possible.[41]

An enormous amount of documentation had already been assembled for the Special Committee by the staff of its secretariat, although some of the summaries from Protitch's department[42] seem to reflect Soviet points of view. Imre Nagy's position during the events in October was described as "precarious"; he was seen less as a revolutionary leader and more as a politician drifting with the flow of events.[43] But there was mention of the Soviet invasion, Nagy's abduction, Kádár's puppet regime, and the deportations. These chronicles, intended only for internal use, were marked as secret, but from mid-January 1957, they were handed over to the Special Committee.

The UN's librarians prepared a reading list for the benefit of the Committee, which included the Paris Peace Treaties after World War II, the Hungarian Constitution, and the Warsaw Pact; to these were added works of history, sociological and statistical handbooks, and a short survey of the events in Hungarian politics from 1945 to 1956.[44] More important articles from Hungarian newspapers and transcripts of radio broadcasts from the archive of Radio Free Europe were requested through the US delegation to the UN. This workaround was to avoid putting the UN in direct contact with a CIA-funded affiliate.

Finally, the Committee was presented with the reports of diplomatic missions, which the Secretary-General had officially requested from the UN delegations of member states with diplomatic accreditation in Budapest,[45] something not even the respective foreign ministries could object to. The Secretary of the Special Committee, William Jordan, was troubled by this, however, and in a letter to Protitch, he distanced himself from the initiative[46] even though there could be no legal or diplomatic objections to it, and, indeed, it concerned one of the most important sources, namely, the direct experiences of foreign witnesses.

The most accurate and thorough narrative was that of the British embassy, not only because of Ambassador Leslie Fry's experience and wisdom but also because of the varied connections the British had established in Hungary dating back to the period before World War II. Along with the thirty-nine-page document, the British embassy sent London a photocopy of just about every newspaper and journal published at the time of the Revolution, and their reports followed the events to the end of January 1957. These reports and actions suggest the opinion that the role of the United Nations was not merely to remember the better days but also to acknowledge and uncover the scandalous dark period that followed.[47]

Other embassy reports that reached the Special Committee also contained interesting new details. Italy provided a precise chronology and a highly compelling analysis of events: In Rome, the Italians were already watching the Soviet troop movements on November 2 and, though Imre Nagy had spoken cautiously regarding the Warsaw Pact on October 31, there was no trace of his comments the following day. Prime Minister Nagy wanted to place Hungary under the protection of the UN because he knew all too well what danger his government was in and that there was no one else to defend it—so wrote the Italians in their report, which extended to the first two months of 1957 and presented the consequences of all that had happened in the interim.[48] The French quoted their countryman and political philosopher Alexis de Tocqueville in their introduction, thereby placing the fresh and bloody events in both a historical and theoretical context.

The French report turned to the illegitimate nature of the Kádár regime, the clearest evidence for which was that it was not possible to inaugurate it in the Hungarian Parliament, as for two months it had been under the guard of Soviet soldiers. The French also provided a comprehensive list of the atrocities perpetrated over the course of the Soviet invasion, including reports of looting, deportations, and acts of cruelty; neither were they unaware of the rise of the ÁVH.[49] The Netherlands sent the Secretary-General an impressive "position statement" on the Soviet invasion,[50] and the Danes shared the report of Ole Lippmann, Danish politician and hero of the antifascist resistance during the war. Lippmann was a firsthand witness to the invasion, as he had arrived in Budapest with his medical equipment during the Revolution. Other embassies also sent information about the events in Hungary, confirming and further enhancing what had already been received.

The secretariat of the Special Committee circulated all this material to the members of the Committee, produced a "who's who" of the persons mentioned, checked and clarified ambiguous points in the information received, and established order among the names and terms used. The secretariat continued to document information as it was received and made accessible the minutes of the Committee's meetings on questions of operation and protocol and on points of consensus that had emerged.[51]

The Hungarian government's position did not officially reach the Special Committee, however. The Hungarian government did not consider the Committee's operation to be legitimate, so it did not engage in any contact with it. The Committee wished to investigate this attitude and the reasons behind Budapest's refusal to participate, so the Kádárist "narrative" found its way to the Committee through Hungarian press reviews and official party and government pronouncements. All this was publicized in the UN's Hungarian-language radio broadcasts—the citizens of countries affected by proceedings at the UN were always informed of the debates in their mother tongues.[52]

However, the international context during the Committee's investigation was not necessarily favorable for the task at hand. The dictators coming to power in South America were reluctant to enter into debates on human rights, much less to arrange elections under UN auspices. For the countries of developing nations, the Hungarian question was overshadowed by the crisis in the Suez, where the Soviet Union's prime minister, Nikolay Bulganin, was threatening even Paris and London with nuclear attack. On

October 4, 1957, the Soviets launched *Sputnik* into orbit, highlighting the superiority of Soviet space technology. Indeed, since 1959, Nikita Khrushchev's gift of a life-size model of *Sputnik* has hung over the lobby of UN Headquarters.[53]

The Activity of the Special Committee on the Problem of Hungary

The Special Committee prepared thoroughly for its investigation, and the secretariat staff put at its disposal operated with dynamism. As administrator, Jordan organized its operations in an exemplary fashion, and Bang-Jensen handled the tasks entrusted to him with expertise and zest. A number of Hungarian-born employees provided the Committee with background information, accompanied by important explanations of Hungarian history, culture, and mindsets. It was only after receiving these preparations that the Committee began hearing the testimony of witnesses.

The key figures in this process were, after all, those who had taken part in the events in Hungary in October and November of 1956, who recounted everything that had happened, the events that had led up to the Revolution, and the consequences of those events. The Committee only accepted reports based on firsthand personal experiences and ensured that they were representative in both social and geographical terms.[54] Yet it could only choose witnesses from among refugees, which inevitably distorted the Committee's lens. It is not known whether the picture of events would have been more authentic if the Committee had been allowed to enter a Hungary that had by then been "pacified" half to death, if its members had been able to interview the Stalinists, or if the judges involved in the post-Stalinist revenge had provided legal explanations for their decisions. Those involved with the investigation were aware that they were seeing the story they sought to uncover from a single perspective, and although there was no doubting the veracity of the reconstruction, Kádárist propaganda was able to exploit this asymmetry in the sources.

As such, the method by which the report was drawn up, that is, a reconstruction of events based on witness statements, became a tool for communist propaganda and terror. To discredit it, the Hungarian communist authorities identified the witnesses and undermined their credibility, as this might cause the foundations of the report to crumble. The majority of witnesses wanted to remain anonymous—to protect themselves and the safety of their loved ones still in Hungary and to prevent their former fellow combatants being identified from witnesses' testimonies. For at this time, preparations were already underway in Budapest for systematic reprisals and the criminalization of recounting the history of the Revolution; the witnesses' testimony could have been used by the investigating authorities as evidence. An anonymous witness statement was an unusual product of procedural law, one that the ill-intentioned communist justice system characterized as the legitimization of lying. The Hungarian communists would rely heavily on this characterization later in the proceedings.

In determining the methods of the Committee, its members planned to hold closed sessions, with just three witnesses giving evidence in public. The public testimony was planned to be a press event, with only prominent, charismatic, and well-prepared politicians having their say: Anna Kéthly, minister of state; Béla Király, commander-in-chief of the Hungarian National Guard; and József Kővágó, mayor of Budapest. In spite of the UN's efforts to focus on the Hungarian situation as the General Assembly's resolution requested, there were a number of odd irregularities in the proceedings: these key witnesses were not given a platform at the UN Assembly, they were not allowed to speak in an official capacity as representatives of the united emigrant body created in Strasbourg, the organization of the press event was accidentally or possibly deliberately mishandled, and only a smaller side room was allocated to the hearing. And yet none of these factors diminished the significance of their appearance, nor did the Soviet-Hungarian protest against those they termed three "chief criminals" being given a voice. According to the logic of Hungarian propaganda, they were recidivists. Béla Király was labeled a "war criminal," even though the documentation of his rehabilitation in August 1956 mentioned that this previous charge "has not been proven. His case is a typically political case [. . .] The testimonies are strained. Severe physical and moral coercion was used against him during the proceedings."[55] None of this mattered. They used confessions Anna Kéthly had made in jail when the "traitor to the workers" remorsefully admitted her crimes.[56] (Kéthly had been arrested both before World War II as a leader of the workers' movement and after the communist takeover, as a critic of totalitarianism.) The press was given access to ÁVH documents, as was standard procedure when character assassination was needed. Kéthly's cruel self-criticism given in prison was thus provided to a communist journalist and, in light of her later service in Imre Nagy's government as minister, a biting article was written about Kéthly's change of character.[57] József Kővágó's rehabilitation by the Hungarian justice system

Public witnesses of the Special Committee on the Problem of Hungary, József Kővágó (*left*), Anna Kéthly (*middle*), and Béla Király (*right*). Copyright: UN Photo Archive #123294.

was prevented by his political role in emigration policies; while the charges against others condemned in his case were dropped, those against Kővágó were not.[58] Thus the Special Committee's star witnesses were presented as "criminals" who had provided testimony on their own crimes, something no court would accept as valid evidence.

A number of attacks on the credibility of these witnesses pointed to the Kádár regime not considering its legal argument to be sufficient—that Kéthly had not officially been sworn in as minister; that the law abolishing the function of mayor remained unchanged, so Kővágó had not been a legitimate mayor of Budapest; and that Király had spent most of the Revolution lying in the hospital. Members of the Kádár regime acquired copies of some of the witnesses' testimonies, and even though the names of the witnesses themselves had been redacted, secret service officials had underlined the names of persons mentioned in their testimonies in red, justifying the witnesses' fears that those they had referred to in their testimonies would be subject to investigation.

In the end, Budapest did not follow up on any of their allegations against these witnesses or their associates, though it could have. There was little need to do so. Even Kéthly's supporters considered her statement to be overly long and slightly confusing. Kővágó was considered to be powerful but ordinary, and Király was primarily focused on military issues. All three testimonies appeared more like declarations than exposés on Soviet actions during the conflict or proposals for how to formulate a proposal to the UN for handling the "Problem of Hungary."

This did not stop the Hungarian secret services from monitoring the three politicians' contacts both in Hungary and abroad to prevent them from receiving information from "criminal accessories," as the Hungarian government viewed sources of information from ex-revolutionaries in Hungary. The government knew the three had a role in selecting the rest of the witnesses to appear before the UN, and among the ÁVH's goals were sowing discord amid the émigré community, discrediting its key leaders, and undermining their authority in the eyes of both the UN and the Hungarian refugee community. They set in motion a whisper campaign sowing propaganda against Béla Király and using their agents in the US to accuse the National Guard commander-in-chief of betraying the Revolution of 1956. The accusations against Király argued that he had "let military leadership slip through his fingers" and that he had deliberately undermined the success of the Revolution. The rumors alleged that he had known of the Soviet attack but not prepared for it—indeed, that he had prevented the Hungarian Army from responding by, among other things, forbidding the air force to mount a defense.[59] In Budapest, the secret service had thorough knowledge of Király's decisions and their motivations, as, both during the Revolution and after it, many of the commander-in-chief's close associates were its agents. They informed Budapest of Király's "financial affairs" and his love affairs, which, they claimed, also involved men. At this time in Hungary, allegations of homosexuality were considered criminal charges, so these rumors represented dangerous libel in military circles. These agents also worked to undermine the Hungarian Freedom Fighters Association that Király had established and later ran, and they focused on turning another preeminent Hungarian émigré politician and soldier, Lajos Veres Dálnoki, against Király.[60]

The Hungarian secret service also organized a campaign to discredit József Kővágó. Looking for an opportunity for extortion, they prepared a study of the circumstances of his mother-in-law, who still lived in Budapest, and they mapped his contacts and relationships in Hungary. They also re-leased the records of their interrogations of Kővágó from before the Revolu-tion in which he confessed to everything they charged him with: sabotage, spying, armed conspiracy, and anything else that came into the interroga-tors' heads.[61] Documents pertaining to his previous period as mayor (1945–47) emerged, which were used to construct corruption charges, and they tried to interfere with Kővágó's public appearances abroad.[62]

During this period, the frustrated Hungarian UN diplomats felt that Kéthly and her associates "were ruling the roost";[63] they were naturally of much greater interest than the Stalinists who stormed out of the Assembly in disgust and sulked in their offices. Even if Kéthly had not been given the floor in the Assembly in early November or late January, it was claimed she had "urged an openly armed intervention" against her homeland[64]—by the very people who had come to power through an openly armed interven-tion. The ÁVH achieved considerable success in trapping Kéthly in its web: soon, a good number of her acquaintances and sources were actually secret agents and photocopies of her letters were on the desks of state security of-ficers. The ÁVH had identified her pseudonyms, knew the floor plan of her Brussels apartment, and were aware of her travel plans, speeches, and even her medical history—and they were not reluctant to use this information to their advantage.[65]

The public hearings brought renewed public attention to the Hungar-ian question. The Soviets urged their Hungarian comrades to visit the UN Headquarters often and to hold press conferences. They also threatened Hammarskjöld: the Soviet Union was "deeply critical" of the interviews held with the three main "culprits," and claimed there had never been a precedent for anything like this in the UN's history.[66] Yet the Special Com-mittee also heard from hundreds of other witnesses, and its secretariat asked the public witnesses, émigré organizations, and foreign ministries of countries with large Hungarian refugee communities for their recom-mendations. The names did start coming, accompanied by the individuals' ages, professions, and addresses or contact information, in effect revealing who could give the Committee information about what.[67]

The hearings took place behind closed doors, and the majority of wit-nesses made this a pre-condition for providing testimony. György Heltai, who had worked in foreign affairs during the Revolution, specifically asked for the interviews to be kept secret;[68] the Chairman of the Committee gave his word on this before each witness statement was taken. Faith in the

United Nations had wavered significantly to the extent that some considered its Secretary-General a security risk in and of himself.[69] Given this guarantee of confidentiality, however, the witnesses offered to give their evidence, sensing the importance of the affair, trying to forget their disappointment in the UN, and thinking that what they had to say was significant. Yet they did not wish to risk their lives—still less the security of their loved ones—for the sake of a UN report. At this stage of the Cold War, there were still kidnappings, and refugees disappeared from refugee camps or were lost in transit. Political assassinations were carried out abroad, and in Hungary, some laws could make family members culpable for crimes committed by their relatives abroad.[70]

Following the public hearings, the Special Committee called further witnesses in New York, including a politician, an actress, students, workers, engineers, Red Cross workers, and animal breeders, to name but a few.[71] The majority of them had been through a CIA check at Camp Kilmer, many had been questioned by sociologists from Columbia University,[72] and a few had made statements to the US Senate. Nevertheless, the UN investigation into the events surrounding the suppression of the Hungarian Revolution was by far the most important forum, and many agreed to contribute further testimony. During the preselection process, which was primarily carried out by Bang-Jensen, with Klára Héderváry acting as interpreter, witnesses were told which of their recollections would be of most interest to the Committee and repetitions were edited out—witnesses were encouraged to touch on problems, events, and connections that other witnesses had not yet mentioned. According to communist propaganda, this amounted to influencing and even directly instructing witnesses. Because it was also Bang-Jensen's task to cover the per diems and travel expenses of the witnesses, those besmirching him claimed this amounted to "ordering" the witnesses and or even the "purchase" of their statements.

During the hearings, in addition to the Committee members, there were also members of staff present from the secretariat, alongside the interpreters and stenographers. The statements, questions, and answers were all recorded on tape; translated into English, French, and Spanish; and then typed up as verbatim transcripts. The power of the witnesses' words, the vividness of their experiences, and their passion and pathos moved the Committee members, though their individual interpretations of the events increased the possibility of misunderstanding.[73] Some elaborated declarations, others read out prepared texts, and many had to take breaks in their testimony due to nervousness and the painful memories they were evoking.[74] Few of the witnesses spoke English, and the interpreters were often stumped by new Hungarian abbreviations, bureaucratic terminology, and ideological neologisms. In New York, fourteen people were willing to give their names to the Special Committee, although the open hearings had concluded and they were testifying behind closed doors. The remaining twenty-two also testified secretly, but they insisted on anonymity as well—even the five members of the Committee would not have access to their names. The testimonies of the anonymous witnesses were later assigned a letter of the alphabet by Bang-Jensen to prevent someone from giving a statement twice. This was also the way to identify witnesses during the process of settling travel expenses and per diems. Povl Bang-Jensen kept the list of witnesses on his person—a sign of the Hungarian witnesses' trust in him.[75]

At this time, the Special Committee's trip to Europe was being prepared. At the end of January, the UN Secretary-General sent a message to the representatives of every member state, asking them to submit all the documents at their disposal related to the Hungarian question to the Committee and to suggest possible witnesses who could describe events with authenticity and based on their personal experience. Responses and lists of names were forthcoming, sometimes tagged with subjects: witnesses who could describe the fighting, the deportations, the workers' councils, and so on.[76] The US Mission to the UN not only passed names on to the Special Committee but also provided access to testimony given before the Senate[77] and to transcripts of radio broadcasts. The British, in addition to newspapers from the time of the Revolution, also sent the official documents they had collected, and the Australians sent the interviews they had held with the Hungarian refugees they had welcomed. Trade unions, émigré groups, and churches also provided lists of names and associated details.[78]

The Committee's secretariat worked on the selection of various European locations for the hearings, looking for suitable buildings, rooms, and equipment. They also organized visas, train tickets, and accommodations. Travel arrangements were made for the Committee members and the secretariat, as more than fifty UN personnel were to set off for Europe. The Special Committee was to begin its work in Geneva, for the UN headquarters there was not only able to provide infrastructure and ancillary staff but also seemed suitable as a base from which to travel back and forth. The Swiss government hesitated about formally hosting the Special Committee. As there was no official rejection, the UN continued to make its plans even in the absence of official consent. Switzerland also offered no witnesses, even though it had accepted a large number of Hungarian refugees. The Special Committee accepted the invitation of the government in Rome; the invitation from Paris was late, so this location for hearings was abandoned; and the Committee planned a visit to London, partly because of Ambassador Fry's extensive reports and partly because the contributions of the Hungarian émigrés there appeared promising.

Less successful, however, were the negotiations with Vienna, where the greatest number of Hungarian refugees had arrived, but whose circumstances were the most awkward. The Austrian foreign ministry first rejected the UN's request, citing its neutrality—a neutrality the violation of which was regularly raised by Moscow. The presence of the Soviets, whose troops had left Austria in 1955, was a very recent memory, and Hungarian Soviet propaganda regularly accused Austria of allowing the armed passage of "Horthyist fascist gangs" through its territory in 1956 and of encouraging subversive activity against neighboring Hungary. All of these allegations paid scant regard to the facts, even those that the Soviets had witnessed with their own eyes.[79] To question Austria's independence could have had catastrophic consequences, and Hungarian ambassador to Vienna Frigyes Puja wanted to uncover "what they were up to under the guise of neutrality." He reported back to Budapest on the continuous decline in Austro-Hungarian relations, a decline to which he continued to make a very considerable contribution.[80] As a result, the Austrian government had good cause to be extremely careful when considering the Special Committee's request, yet, as a UN member just since 1955—one that received significant assistance—it had little room to maneuver. So Austria stated that it would allow only a symbolic UN visit that did not involve seeing the refugee camps, with no witness interviews and minimal publicity. The Secretary-General's response was that, under these conditions, he saw no reason for a visit to Vienna.[81]

In the end, Vienna succumbed to UN pressure and allowed the visit to take place, although they requested that the visit not take place in mid-March: March 15, the anniversary of the 1848 revolution and war of independence of Hungary from Austria, was a potential trigger for a clandestine movement to incite an uprising. The Austrians promised to assist the Special Committee as much as they could, while at the same time trying to explain to the Soviets that Austria "could not allow itself not to let in the Committee" and promising that Vienna would "severely restrict its activities: no press conference, no statement, no camp visits." These statements came from Hungarian ambassador to Austria Puja's report on what he learned from the Soviet embassy, the source for which was Austrian deputy foreign minister Bruno Kreisky.[82] The compromise was made: the UN Committee could enter Austria, but the Austrian government made no list of witnesses, and the only people interviewed were those whom the secretariat of the Special Committee had sought out in advance. It is difficult to know how much of this was the product of the diplomatic fanfare of an Austrian foreign policy whose hands were tied, and how much a product of genuine doubts about the Committee, as noted in the press. To those at the Hungarian foreign ministry, it seemed that Austria, in an effort not to endanger the aid it received, "immediately agreed to let the Committee enter the country and do its work," which was, of course, a blatant lie— the Committee was confronted in Vienna with the greatest of difficulties thanks to its halfhearted welcome and the lack of advance preparation.[83] Furthermore, the Austrian government did little to maintain the security and privacy of the Committee's work, as its hearings were held not outside the city but rather in "one of the small palaces [in Vienna that] was furnished for them." This was according to one of the organizers, who was at the same time impressed that the Committee had arrived "with serious technical equipment," because "all interviews will be recorded on magnetic tape,"[84] a novelty at the time.

The Special Committee hearings held in New York helped refine the methods of the Special Committee, and lessons from the proceedings were debated, evaluated, and processed.[85] Although the Committee members had guidelines for the operation of UN investigative committees at their disposal[86] that emphasized the importance of witness anonymity, thoughts on the criteria for selecting witnesses, and guidelines on the use of language, their experiences elsewhere led to a new operative plan being elaborated in New York. Even this revised plan was regularly overwritten by day-to-day realities: many witnesses insisted on reading out prepared statements, while others would not respond to questions, only recounting what they thought important. There were also many claims that could not be checked or that were exaggerated. All these difficulties were overshadowed by the contradictions inherent to the workings of the investigative committee: Gunewardene's cross-examination was not always well-intentioned,[87] and he often embarrassed or angered witnesses. At other times, Fabregat's speeches championing human rights held up the proceedings. Worse were the inconsistencies between versions of statements caused by the chain of translations and retranslations; some witnesses were so dissatisfied with the interpreter that they preferred to take over in their broken English rather than allow misunderstandings to continue. Given these concerns about accuracy, it is worth noting that witnesses were not given the transcripts of their statements, even when they asked for them. In a rare exception, after receiving permission from Special Committee Chair Andersen, Bang-Jensen gave Ödön Pongrátz, the military leader of Corvin Circle, a pocket of resistance after the Soviet invasion, the "verbatim record" of his testimony to confirm whether it properly reflected his views and recollections. This led Jordan to approach Protitch and ask him to put a stop to this rather intuitive method of checking the text. Jordan further asked that it should not occur even where the transcription of the testimony was obviously at odds with what had actually been said.

The Committee's operations were further complicated by confusion over whether its members formed an independent UN body or whether they represented their own member states and were to receive instructions from their respective governments.[88] This was an important distinction, and there was no better example of the dangers involved in not clarifying the position and authority of the Committee than when, after the enormous amount of work done to complete the report, Gunewardene flew home to Ceylon, where the government was influenced by Soviet demands, in an effort to avoid signing it. His refusal to sign the report would have meant the extensive efforts dedicated to creating the report would be rendered futile.

The documents that recorded the administrative, legal, and financial conditions of the investigation and made it possible for it to do its work also allow us to reconstruct in some detail just what a challenge it was for the UN apparatus to organize the hearings. The "administrative pre-requisites" of the trip to Europe were ready by late February, and these included English, French, and Spanish interpreters, as well as typists. The typists would often turn out to be the "bottleneck," and sometimes intervention would be required from the Under-Secretary-General to help them grapple with the enormous piles of material to be typed up.[89] The secretariat was also responsible for buying airline tickets, arranging accommodations, arranging for per diems, and renting the necessary items and equipment. There was as much need for interpreting apparatus as there was for typewriters, duplication machines, recording equipment, and storage space. The secretariat of the Special Committee had to think of everything, from coffee to ashtrays—in those days, smoking was allowed during the hearings, which could go on until the early hours. Also important were the security precautions, which were not given adequate attention, an oversight that would have fatal consequences.

The first meeting of the Special Committee in Europe was at the Palace of Nations in Geneva. From March 11 to 15, members of the Committee interviewed five of the most important witnesses. György Heltai ("Witness X") related his testimony for a full three days. He had been closest to Imre Nagy during the most dramatic days, and most of what happened with respect to foreign policy was his doing. Other interviewees were Olivér Benjámin, former police commander and social democrat politician, and Hartley Shawcross,[90] the force behind the International Commission of Jurists, who provided a legal analysis of the Hungarian question. He was assisted in this by Andrew Martin, who had been born András Neugrüschel in Hungary and then enjoyed a career in the United Kingdom under his Anglicized name. For many years, he followed and published on the events of the reprisals in Hungary. According to a Hungarian secret service report, Neugrüschel "travelled to Geneva in the company of Shawcross" to "influence" the UN Committee. It seems he succeeded in this, as the legal foundations of the report in progress were outstanding.[91]

The Committee flew from Geneva to Rome. This was justified as much by Rome being home to the Food and Agriculture Organization (FAO), a UN special agency, and its involvement in aid to Hungary as by the large number of Hungarian refugees that Italy had welcomed. The UN Secretariat requested assistance from the FAO to undertake its work but did not receive any. The documents suggest help was instead provided by the Italian government, which charged the UN for their services.[92] The Secretariat noted that the Italians were not willing to cover any costs, so the full \$2,438 needed to enable the work was covered by the UN budget.[93] The hearings were held at the Palazzo dei Congressi in the modern part, the so-called EUR (Esposizioni Universale Roma) district of the city, far from the historical center but more spacious and sheltered than a historic building would have been. Police protection was provided day and night, and the security of the transport and accompaniment of witnesses was guaranteed by Edgardo Sogno, a retired military officer and former partisan as well as an intelligence agent, politician with royalist feelings, diplomat, and one of those who helped establish NATO.[94]

In Rome, sixteen witnesses came before the Committee, most of them freedom fighters or members of the revolutionary councils. There were also doctors and politicians, with shocking stories, who revealed unexpected connections. It so happened that a colleague was standing in for Mongi Slim while Gunewardene asked about thefts, lootings, and atrocities allegedly committed by the revolutionaries. Fabregat recognized that they could expand their focus to include the current situation in Hungary, to the trials, arrests, and everything else the Special Committee was constantly receiving information about. Jordan, however, did not agree that their mandate empowered them to do this, and, in his letter to Protitch, mentioned that he would tell the Committee Chairman as much.[95]

The investigation's next port of call, Vienna, was beautiful, impoverished, and chaotic. The previously distant attitude of the government was eased by a protocol lunch that included cordial conversation, avoided the appearance of formality, and allowed minimal publicity. It was in Vienna that the Committee's task proved the most demanding, as this location had the highest number of witnesses, the least preparation, and the most heated atmosphere. This all affected the Committee's work, and the accumulation of administrative duties, the clashing of incompatible priorities, and the resulting tensions brought the work to a sudden halt. Jordan and Bang-Jensen disagreed on the scope of their respective remits, the ranking of urgent priorities, and the capacity of the overburdened Committee staff to translate, type, and process testimonies. Taking a forced break, the diplomats walked around the city. Their work had to continue, however. The typists increased their speed, and stopgap solutions were found to ease the interpreters' burden; the apparatus faltered but sprang back to life. The conflicts eased, but memories of them remained fresh. Jordan reported to his superiors the almost crippling difficulties facing the project and staff. Given these challenges, it was an enormous achievement that the hearings took place, the minutes were completed, and the documents and information needed for the report continued to mount.

The Special Committee held its hearings in the center of the city, in the Pálffy Palace at Wallnerstrasse 6/a, which was rented from the Austrian state for 1,500 schillings a day. The secretariat of the Committee rented furniture and office fittings, and the German company Siemens supplied machinery to aid in translations.[96] The Austrian State Archive was housed in the same building, and the Joint Committee on Repatriation also operated from rooms there. This meant that Hungarian diplomats—including many of the intelligence agents at the well-staffed Vienna station—frequently passed up and down the corridors during the proceedings. For the witnesses, this was as worrying as the proximity of the Hungarian embassy. The news spread among the witnesses that those entering the building were being photographed from cars outside or buildings across the street. Some turned around and did not enter, while others arrived to give evidence with their appearance deliberately altered. Because of these concerns, in Vienna, the great majority of witnesses—thirty-one out of thirty-three—insisted on anonymity.[97] Here it was not enough for Bang-Jensen, who kept the list of letters to stand in for names, to go through the alphabet twice—he had to run through it three times. The witnesses' suspicion was not unfounded: Miklós Szabó, who took part in selecting and instructing witnesses, was all along working for the Hungarian secret service, while Tamás Pásztor, a former prison agent who was assisting the Committee in its work, was known to many of the witnesses, which rather undermined their faith in the investigation and their personal safety.[98] During his brief stay in Vienna, Pásztor succeeded in seducing Jordan's secretary, Ita Glance. The romance turned into marriage, but—precisely because of his past life as a prison snitch—it would be years before he was given a US visa.[99] To this day, it is unknown if some of the witness transcripts were in fact passed on to the Soviets, if the building was indeed successfully bugged by the communist intelligence services, if photographs were taken, and if, because of all this, there were people kidnapped to be taken home, as was rumored among the refugees.

The Hungarian secret service—whose reputation had been shattered during the Revolution and by the disclosure of names of secret agents at delegations—had by this point retaken its position at the UN and in diplomatic posts around the world; indeed, it had achieved new heights. A draft on the "intelligence situation" stated that one deputy minister and two head of department positions were required within the foreign ministry so that thirty intelligence officers could be sent to their stations with diplomatic cover and ten with "service cover." It also wished to transfer the personnel work of the ministry to the intelligence division of the Ministry of the Interior.[100]

The Special Committee hearings continued in London, running from the end of March until early April at Carlton House Terrace, which was under constant protection. The UK government assigned three security guards for five days, and another guard for four days, the cost of which, like all the other costs incurred by the investigation, the United Kingdom covered. The witnesses interviewed in London were predominantly young, intelligent, and communist—a combination that the Committee had not yet encountered. A number of them spoke English well, and their life stories were often gripping. Some had lived in the United Kingdom previously and become communists there, only to be imprisoned on their return to Hungary; after their release, they joined the Revolution and drifted back into exile.[101]

The Foreign Office invited the Special Committee to a lunch, during which Fry was able to talk at length with Shann. This was reported by the Hungarian secret service, which had learned of the occasion. Budapest's central intelligence agency also knew that the Foreign Office was "undecided whether to relay to the Special Committee" the data it had on deportations because of questions over the "discretion" of the Committee's members.[102]

At the end of its European journey, the Committee spent almost two weeks in Geneva, where it held hearings with new witnesses and called back those who had additional important information to relate before setting to work on writing the report. A Hungarian "diplomat" accredited in Geneva reported to Budapest that the Special Committee "heard even more witnesses than the first time, in even more conspiratorial fashion."[103] The heightening of the security measures that the Hungarian agent had referred to as "conspiratorial" might have been the result of the Committee's experiences in Vienna and London. Evidence was given by doctors, university lecturers, and politicians as well as "Witness XXX," a close colleague of Imre Nagy, who, as the one hundred and eleventh witness, would bring the hearings to an end. The Committee began to collate the information, going through the tasks involved in compiling the report, and then composing it. This took place in mid-April, six months after the Revolution had occurred. At this stage, no one imagined that another two months would pass before the report was complete, and yet another three months before it would be debated—almost eleven months after the Revolution and related events to it had unfolded.

At a press conference on the Special Committee's work, UN information officer Vernon Duckworth-Barker gave the public some clues about the nature of the investigation going on behind closed doors. He emphasized the fact that the Committee had encountered an almost complete cross section of Hungarian society in the course of its investigations. Despite the dramatic moments reviewed here and elsewhere, he described the atmosphere of the investigation as relaxed. He said that although the hearings had ended, they might be continued at some point—this would later be of great consequence. In response to a question, he said that the report would include the official Hungarian-Soviet position. In response to another, he said that only some of the interpreters were UN employees, and that external contributors also worked for the Committee. In other words, the gaps in security had become gaping holes. He reported that the Committee had been very close to the Hungarian border.[104] It is conceivable that this happened during the Committee's hiatus in Vienna; more likely, the information officer just wanted to give the impression that although they had not been allowed to enter Hungary, they had gone as far as they could possibly go. There had never been a question of the Committee being allowed to enter Hungary: the Hungarian foreign ministry claimed that it would only "accept information from individuals of a counter-revolutionary disposition" because their goal was to induce a new counterrevolution, and a new attack was being planned on the legitimate order in Hungary "under the cover of the Committee of Five."[105]

The Historical Narrative of the Special Committee and Its Controversies

It is an open question whether the UN General Assembly had wanted the Committee to produce historical source work, but a well-founded resolution needed to be based on a knowledge of the facts and an exploration and analysis of the connections among those facts. At the end of January 1957, the Committee's Rapporteur looked over the possibilities before them and had good reason to see the preparation of the "report or reports" as an "exceptional problem." The use of the plural here was key, because in this the resolution emphasized the need for continuing observation of the Hungarian situation and attention to and analysis of its progress—the report had not merely summarized a past event.[106] In fact, what was put together in mid-February was titled "First Report,"[107] and represented an outline for of future plans rather than a static document to be submitted to the UN General Assembly as a basis for resolutions.

With the initial phase of the investigation complete, methodological dilemmas once again came to the fore. After all, the significance of the document to be submitted to the Assembly depended in no small part on the nature and credibility of the information gathered as well as the tone of the text: its reception would be determined not by the facts alone but by how they were discovered and presented. The secretariat played a crucial role in this process, for the report was written not by the five members of the Committee but by the staff of the secretariat assigned to it: these personnel wrote the text that the Committee members had to sign off on. Jordan and his superiors, Protitch and Cordier, must have considered Shann, the Rapporteur, to be susceptible to their point of view, but the loyalty of the actual authors of the text cannot have been in question; at least not within a certain limit. It would be this limit that Bang-Jensen would later overstep.

During the investigation, the secretariat had acquired what it referred to as "further resources," which, among various memoranda, statements, and UN reports, included data from the Hungarian Statistical Office and Péter Mód's rebuttals.[108] Thus did the material come to be put together, the longest and most important part of which was the almost two thousand pages of minutes of the testimony of the witnesses, not to mention the seventy hours of audio recordings—the latter had also picked up background conversations during the hearings that were not included in the minutes.

The responsibility of the historiographers in writing this history in the context of the time was a considerable one. Reprisals were continuing in Hungary, and requests for aid were being submitted to the UN, which led to further questions: Should the Committee consider current events to be part of their work, or should their story end with the eve of the Soviet invasion? What should be done about ongoing and bloody retributions? And could the fate of Imre Nagy, who had specifically turned to the UN for help, really be a matter of indifference to them?

Some members of the Committee took a cautious approach, and deliberated about what the Assembly, after ten failed attempts, had actually mandated them to do. Even Fabregat, the champion of human rights, and Gunewardene, and Slim, who were supportive of all struggles for freedom, feared that any kind of intervention into current events would go beyond the factual and prearranged scope of the investigation.[109] This of course encouraged a certain degree of tunnel vision. Meanwhile, information continued to flow into the secretariat from Hungary about retributions. The Committee members could read translations of György Marosán's bloodthirsty speech; they knew that the political purges would extend to all echelons of society, from the military to the cultural sphere; and they could see that the economic situation had become dramatically worse and that the new tax on peasants could easily turn this drama into a large-scale tragedy.[110] Legal retribution also gained momentum, which caused prosecutors and judges to resign, as if to signal that what was coming was even worse than the sometimes appalling and partisan practices they had previously put up with.[111]

That the Committee paid less attention to the changing present than to the closed and unchangeable past could have been the consequence of caution, legal protocol, or consensus among its members. It could also have been the product of sabotage, successful maneuvering, or perhaps communist extortion. The report was completed, however—in itself an enormous task—and it represented an extraordinary achievement: a presentation of sources, a historiography, a lively narrative, and a detailed diagnosis. It was among the best surveys of the 1956 Revolution, with contributions from numerous participants and contemporaries. Its material had clear limits, but its relevance was universal; it was affected by the fluctuations of the workings of the United Nations, but it benefitted from the body's prestige and global outreach.

The process of writing and editing was strictly overseen by Jordan, working under Shann and with the trust of his superiors. By early March, there were instructions as to the fundamental principles and key priorities of the report: it was not to serve primarily as a chronology; rather, everything that had happened in Hungary, problem area by problem area, would be surveyed with discussion of why and how it had occurred.[112] These problem areas were based on thoroughly considered and detailed knowledge of the material and covered every aspect of what led up to 1956 and its events and consequences. And even if complete consensus had not been reached in the course of the investigation, partial consensus was achieved when the individual chapters were finalized, step by step, or, more specifically, text version by text version. The members of the Special Committee sometimes expressed their views quite strongly, however, and forcefully stuck to their own positions, and it was not unusual for them to be critical of the operation of the Committee as a whole. After a certain point, Fabregat believed that their work had not only failed to meet expectations but also to live up to the Assembly's resolution, and Gunewardene had plans to write a lengthy minority opinion alongside the report. The tape recordings reveal that it took a good deal of diplomatic effort to keep the always polite but sometimes quite heated debate on the straight and narrow, even where it could not resolve its tensions. This would be the job of the text of the report, and it was not an easy one.

The devil was, as always, in the details, so it is easy to understand why there were many attempts to produce the best version of individual chapters before the final version of the text was completed. Jordan sent the outline drafts—which had been written by the secretariat, then repeatedly checked—to Shann, who approved the versions of the text that the Committee members received. By early April, one- to two-page summaries of the chapters had been produced in Geneva. Based on these, it was possible to work out where information was still missing, where work could properly be started, and where the mass of material had to be most dramatically narrowed down. Povl Bang-Jensen, Marc Schreiber, Vernon Duckworth-Barker, Michel Pullain, Christopher Messinesi, Klára Héderváry, and László Hámori prepared the first outlines, which they then shared among themselves. After edits, insertions, omissions, and corrections, there would sometimes be six or seven versions before a chapter achieved its final form. Jordan kept a detailed record of which chapter was currently with whom, who the primary and secondary readers of a chapter were, and which (often delayed, yet always alarmingly tight) deadline could be kept. He asked his colleagues to prioritize their work over their private or family lives. In early May, a more detailed content proposal and short summary saw the light of day; these determined the future division of labor.[113] Thus the Rapporteur worked from a text that had been thought through, checked, and corrected many times over, and he either used or discarded these changes. His most important collaborator in this was Jordan: they worked together very closely and established a close friendship. There were disagreements and obstacles in the race against time: Fabregat would have written more about human rights; Slim considered that there were violations of laws in other countries that were at least as bad as in Hungary; and Gunewardene later proudly stated that he had forced the Committee to leave out eighty pages on human rights.[114] Andersen, the Chair of the Committee, had to go home to Denmark because of impending elections and did not plan to return to New York before mid-May. The lion's share of the work fell to the secretariat and the Rapporteur.

The documents show that intense, collective, and meaningful work was being done, imbued with the pathos of the events in Hungary and an awareness of the United Nations' responsibilities. A chapter was included on the restrictions of political rights in Hungary after November 4, 1956,[115] and even the fifth version of the thirty-two-page exposition of Soviet-Hungarian positions was not yet considered final.[116] Jordan continued to report on a daily basis on the process of composing the report in numbered letters to Protitch in London, copied to Cordier, as he was awaiting instructions, which he duly got. In line with these, the secretariat "toned down . . . emotional" language, softened the "more pointed observations," and demanded that the text be formulated in "civilized" terms, which, according to his letters, presented "considerable difficulty,"[117] as the subject was, after all, the barbaric suppression of an uprising. To add to the issues of style, there were problems with both translation and the impossibility of checking sources. This is not to mention the misunderstandings, inaccuracies, omissions, and the witnesses' obvious exaggerations—toward the end, the problems just seemed to grow and grow.

It was at this point that Bang-Jensen realized that the mounting inaccuracies, omissions, and mistakes could undermine the credibility of the whole report and jeopardize the prestige of the Special Committee, the UN Assembly, the UN itself, and, ultimately, the clear and appropriate answer to the Hungarian question.[118] When these errors not only found their way into the text but remained there, despite Bang-Jensen's reminders, his suspicions mounted. The Rapporteur had no interest in the lists of inaccuracies that Bang-Jensen conscientiously put together. When Bang-Jensen wanted to make his case, knowing he was in the right, Shann rejected his contributions in a humiliating fashion and without even reading his appeal. Jordan was happy to cite their job descriptions, according to which Shann alone was responsible for the report. It is unclear whether Jordan made this statement as a bureaucrat or an accomplice. Bang-Jensen then turned to Andersen, who had run up against the same wall when he had attempted to help. And when on one occasion Bang-Jensen was overly zealous in his attempts to convince the Rapporteur about the importance of correcting mistakes and including omitted details, Shann claimed that Bang-Jensen's behavior had been improper and asked Jordan to keep him away from the project.[119]

That communist propaganda did not capitalize on the errors in the text says less about the report and more about the changes to Soviet-Hungarian strategy at the time. Several attempts were made to register some mistakes and inaccuracies, but as they did not recognize the Committee's legitimacy, the Hungarian politicians did not want to enter into any disputes with it. They did not want to present a defense or rebuttal; they wanted to attack, to avenge the so-called counterrevolution, and to uncover the "imperialist machinations" that had led to the associated disorder and bloodshed. Had they wanted to discredit the report with objections, there would have been plenty of opportunity, for the chapters were received by the respective Hungarian ministries, who read them, criticized them, and, in foreign ministry documents, registered the mistakes—beginning with the fact that the ÁVH was on one occasion confused with the ÁEK, the Hungarian Central State Inspectorate. But France noted its serious objections, for example, that the questions surrounding the legitimacy of Kádár's government were much more pressing than the report suggested. The United Kingdom drew attention to the flaws surrounding the operation of the Presidential Council; this was a key issue for the legitimacy of the government.[120] This is not to mention that the number of protesters was incorrect, that the revolutionary demands in the text were not the most important ones, or that there was no mention of the statue of Stalin being toppled or of the bloodbath on Budapest's Köztársaság (Republic) Square. There was also confusion over dates in the report, whether of the timing of the entry of Soviet forces or of measures that had been antedated in the official record. To all eyes that had seen and checked the report, it was deemed full of errors. How could this have happened?

Considering the political response the UN gave to the "Hungarian Problem," it seems that several failed attempts did not force the organization to abandon its efforts to investigate, but its opportunities to maneuver were and remained extremely limited. The only achievement that significantly addressed the issue was the creation of the UN Special Committee on the Problem of Hungary and the report it produced. However, difficulties, unresolved questions, and even activities that seemed to verge on willful sabotage plagued the handling of the "Hungarian Problem" from the very beginning and continued throughout the conflict and investigation. With the exception of Bang-Jensen, no one wanted or dared to address these questions.

Notes

1. UNARM S-0890-0008-0001-00001 UC.
2. Letter to József Kővágó dated January 19, 1957. MNL P 2245.
3. January 7, 1957. MNL P 2245.
4. Letter to József Kővágó dated January 19, 1957. MNL P 2245.
5. According to a telegram of October 25, 1956, there would be the "establishment of Committee to determine facts and report results of findings to Council." NARA 764.00/10-2556.
6. December 8, 1956. NAA A 1209 1957/5279 "Established committee on ways and means composed of five member states to study as a matter of urgency [. . .] First report by December 12."
7. Under Soviet influence, India, Indonesia, Burma, and Colombia refused to join. On January 10, 1957, *Pravda* referred to those collecting information on "the executioners hanging patriots" as the "enemies of peace."
8. A January 12, 1957, telegram from the US Mission to the UN claimed that Protitch had put the Committee together. NARA 320.5764/1-1257.
9. See the interview with Erling Bjøl, OSZK TIT.
10. February 1957. The "Andersen dossier," MNL XIX-J-13-a (Copenhagen). Jon Galster, *Jeg anklager Buhl og Alsing Andersen for højforraederi* (*I Accuse Bruhl and Alsing Andersen of Treachery,* publication of the author, 1954). Galster had previously been caught up in libel suits, and in Budapest, his writings were used anonymously.
11. See the telegrams sent from the UK Mission to the UN on December 17 and 30, 1957. FO 371/128689 "[Hammarskjöld] complained privately of Andersen's lack of political judgment and backbone [. . .] never a strong character."
12. Carbajal-Victora warned the US: "[Fabregat] [. . .] would make a poor and ineffective member." NARA 310.5/1-1257.
13. The employees of the Hungarian Mission to the UN reported from New York on February 26, 1958, on their discussions with Arthur Basnayake, First Secretary of Ceylon: "At the height of the Hungarian question he provided interesting information on a number of occasions [. . .] Gunewardene had a significant braking effect." MNL XIX-J-1-j, box 209. July 21, 1957.
14. All of this was reported on February 19, 1957, by Mód. MNL XIX-J-24a, box 1 (documents from the Hungarian consulate general in New York).
15. Vladimir Arzenevich Grusha, Soviet diplomat and intelligence officer, was given the codebook needed to decode the Mission's exchange of messages by Dhanapala Samarasekara, Ceylonese diplomat to the UN. NARA 611.64/4-857.
16. See the telegram from the US Mission to the UN on January 12, 1957. NARA 310.5/1-1257. On the visit: MNL Hungarian Socialist Workers' Party (MSZMP) documents 288.f.32/1962/10. Shann exposed the inner contradictions of the Committee. See the letter from D. H. Popper on March 13, 1957. "According to Shann, Andersen, the Danish chairman, is weak and not overly intelligent. Fabregat is long-winded, illogical and not effective. Slim and his assistants greatly impress Shann as highly capable and intelligent people [. . .] Gunewardene is the most difficult of the lot. He is frankly hostile to the purposes of the investigation, drags his feet wherever possible, asks irrelevant questions and could only with difficulty be persuaded to agree to the

Committee's interim report. [. . .] Shann further states that the Secretariat, from Hammarskjold on down, has been hostile to the Committee." NARA 764.00/3-1357.

17. Péter Mód's report of January 28, 1957. MNL XIX-J-1-j, box 208.

18. A separate chapter is devoted to him and his work.

19. Tensions would appear later on, too. See the information provided to the FBI by Feng-Yang Chai, who worked at the UN Secretariat: "Bang-Jensen had a collision with Jordan [. . .] personality clash." Bang-Jensen Archive (hereinafter BJI), box 33.

20. The mandate of the Special Committee included the publication of "supplemental reports": "report its findings to the present Assembly session and thereafter to UN members and the Assembly if in session." UNARM S-0890-0008-0001-00001 UC. The Australians wrote about this on January 10, 1957. "SYG believes [. . .] continued observation of developments." NAA A 1209 1957/5283.

21. MNL XIX-J-1-o.

22. From January 12, 1957, to nearly a year thereafter, the Hungarian secret service listened in on the French embassy in Budapest. ÁBTL "Informational Report on Hammarskjöld's Visit to Hungary and Reports Relating to the UN Committee of Five." The memorandum dated February 14, 1957, "on the work done by Western embassies in Budapest on behalf of the UN" includes the time, location, and subject of the meetings that took place since the start of December 1956. They knew that UK ambassador Fry and Swiss embassy employee Fauso Malacrida were collecting information on the deportations. MNL XIX-J-1-k, box 56.

23. The summary by the political police claimed that "the report was essentially prepared on the basis of information from imperialist intelligence agencies and agents." This meant that the "witnesses [. . .] were either existing or newly recruited imperialist agents whose identity was kept from the public." ÁBTL V-150352 III, p. 1288.

24. DHS L 179:173 and DHS L 179:83.

25. January 30, 1957. "Future Work of the Committee. Rules of Procedure." Columbia University, Butler Library, Rare Books and Manuscript Collection (hereinafter ACP), box 183. DHS L 179:83. February 6, 1957. "Draft Working Paper—Tentative Synopsis of Questions." DHS L 179:83.

26. CHP, subject area 1. "The resolution does not define in detail the subject of investigation and observation."

27. Ibid., and ACP, box 183.

28. On Hammarskjöld's request and the related debates, see MSZMP documents, MNL 288.f./32/ 1962.

29. CHP, subject area 1.

30. Ibid. "Method: Oral Hearing and Questionnaire."

31. January 25, 1957. Hammarskjöld's letter to Mód. MNL XIX-J-1-k, box 37. On March 19, 1957, Jordan wrote a letter on behalf of Andersen, which Mód rejected on March 25. MNL XIX-1-24a.

32. MNL XIX-J-1-j, box 81 (documents of János Péter).

33. UNARM S-0890-0008-0001-00001 UC.

34. ACP, box 183.

35. DHS L 179:83 "Report at the Present Session."

36. CHP, subject area 1.

37. See March 8, 1957. General Assembly resolutions (XI) 1119.

38. DHS L 179:83. "Complete its report not later than 20 April." On April 26, 1957, the April deadline was reported from Vienna to Budapest, then, later, the "latest news," that the report would only be completed in the summer and so only be debated at the autumn Assembly. MNL, box 13. XIX-J-36 (documents of the Hungarian embassy in Vienna).

39. Berggren, *Dag Hammarskjöld*, 1. The Secretary-General was lost without his deputy, who sometimes worked at night in his office, spending the rest of the night in a special apartment. Andrew Wellington Cordier was on the staff of the US Department of State before he joined the UN.

40. There is an enormous literature on Hiss's spy activity. Investigative journalists wrote of his colleague Cordier: "No record at State Department how he was hired, no record as State Department employee [. . .] suddenly UN founding conference, as 'technical expert' hired by Alger Hiss." Copp-Peck Notes, BJI, box 35.

41. See Mód's report on January 28, 1957. MNL XIX-J-1-j, box 208.

42. UNARM S-0188-0006-0006 and 0007. "Report 1/4/1957," "Recent Developments" and "1/18/1957," with the inscription "To SYG" and "Prepared for Special Committee."

43. The thirty-two-page document provides a survey of events up to November 23. ACP, box 184.

44. UNARM S-0252-0001-0018-00001. December 10, 1956. "Note on the Political Developments of Hungary 1945–1956."

45. NAA A 1209 1957/5282.

46. ACP, box 184. February 1957. "I did not myself agree that such a decision was taken."

47. The British summary reached the Secretary-General on March 15, 1957, via the UK Ambassador to the UN. UNARM S-0442-0139-06 and UNARM S-0442-039.

48. April 5, 1957. CHP, subject area 1.

49. Ibid. "[ÁVH] more flourishing than ever."

50. Ibid. "Statement of Events."

51. CHP, subject area 1. "Summary records [. . .] discussion on conduct and business." There are fifty-seven items in the first six weeks of the Committee's operation alone.

52. The Hungarian UN Mission stated its objection to the establishment of the Hungarian-language broadcasts. MNL XIX-J-24a, box 1.

53. *Sputnik* 1 was launched on October 4, 1957.

54. In the preselection process, professionals, manual laborers, peasants, students, soldiers, and party bureaucrats were all lined up for interviews, and the reconstruction of events involved witness statements from doctors, freedom fighters, soldiers, an ÁVH stenographer, a deputy foreign minister, and student girls.

55. ÁBTL 1525/1. Béla Király was a military leader before, during, and after WWII. He joined the Communist army and served it faithfully, yet he was charged with high treason. He was arrested on August 17, 1951, then sentenced to death for war crimes, conspiring against the state order, and spying. He was not executed; in the process of the rehabilitation of show trial, victims' charges against him were dropped in 1956. MNL XIX-J-20a.

56. ÁBTL 1919/1,2,3,4,5. In addition to secret reports from 1932, the dossiers include Anna Kéthly's confessions made under duress in the 1950s.

57. The secret service in Budapest later began an operation targeted against Kéthly, "in order to provide a counterweight to her possible appearance at the UN."

58. Kővágó's rehabilitation was prevented because he "had become the leader of the counterrevolutionary groups that had fled to the West." MNL XIX-E-1-v. Documents of the Hungarian Ministry of Justice.

59. MNL XIX-J-36, box 15.

60. Ibid.

61. ÁBTL 3.2.4. K-1469 Kővágó (birth name: Kuronya).

62. In the summer of 1957, and afterward, Kővágó paid visits to a number of countries, where he talked about the Revolution and met politicians; each such occasion earned the condemnation of the Hungarian foreign ministry.

63. MNL XIX-J-1-n (documents of Imre Horváth).

64. MNL XIX-J-41a.

65. BM II/3. ÁBTL K-1919.

66. MNL XIX-J-24a, box 1.

67. CHP, subject area 1.

68. ACP, box 182.

69. See Bang-Jensen's letter of June 6, 1957, to Hammarskjöld. Copp and Peck, *Betrayal at the UN*, 177–80.

70. This is what Béla Király referred to in his statement to the US Senate. *The Bang-Jensen Case.*

71. See the webpage of the Open Society Archives (hereinafter OSA): Héderváry Collection / Witness Statements.

72. Columbia University Research Project on Hungary. Some of the interviews are available on the OSA webpage.

73. Translation took place from Hungarian to English, then from English to French and Spanish. Klára Héderváry recollects, for example, that, on the subject of forced nationalization, the interpreter understood and translated the word "bordellos" (*bordélyok*) instead of "barbers" (*borbélyok*). (Klára Héderváry's verbal statement.)

74. Some arrived in sunglasses, with hats pulled over their heads and collars up. A number of the witnesses revealed the scars from their torture by the ÁVH. Some had to be cautioned, and others ran away rather than have to make a statement. See the interview with Klára Héderváry, OSZK TIT.

75. Sándor Taraszovics quotes the words as they spread among the witnesses: "You can trust the Dane." OSZK TIT.

76. See, for example, the letter from the French representative to the UN on March 11, 1957. ACP, box 184.

77. On March 1, 1957. ACP, box 184.

78. ACP, box 184.

79. At inspections carried out along the border, they proved even to the Soviet inspectors that there were no armed "gangs" on Austrian territory; also, to demonstrate Austria's neutrality, former prime minister Ferenc Nagy was turned away on arrival at Vienna's airport.

80. MNL XIX-J-36, box 13.

81. Hammarskjöld to Protitch on March 4, 1957. UNARM Protitch files DAG 1.1.1.3.

82. Puja's letter of March 24, 1957. MNL XIX-J-36, box 13.

83. Jordan wrote to Protitch and Cordier on March 25, 1957: "Difficulties in Vienna [. . .] the government did no preliminary work." ACP, box 184.

84. ÁVH agent Miklós Szabó was involved in the organization. Szabó, *Foglalkozásuk*, 236. According to the reports of Division II of the Chief Department of Political Investigation on March 11 and April 6, 1957, "the intelligence work of the UN Committee of Five against Hungary" was assisted by a "professional staff" of twenty-eight and "recorded" forty-seven verbatim records; some of these even reached Budapest in Hungarian translation (though this was secret material, not intended to reach Hungary), with typography identical to the original. BJI, box 35.

85. February 2, 1957. "Draft Working Paper on the Formulation of a Guide in the Examination of Witnesses." 63 pages. CHP, subject area 1.

86. January 14, 1957. Bela von Block: "Procedure Employed by the UN Subsidiary Organs in Taking Evidence." Ibid. CHP, subject area 1.

87. Gunewardene called Imre Nagy a "dictator" because the people's will had not played a role in his election, and so Kéthly was, so he claimed, at the behest of a dictator. He quoted Kéthly's press statements on "fascist forces" and the "white terror," and he knew that she had not been sworn in, while Kádár had. Kéthly (n.d.), 21, 31. Of Béla Király and József Kővágó, Gunewardene stated "before the Bulgarian and Finnish delegates" that "they are simply fascists." See Mód's telegram of February 19, 1957, MNL XIX-J-1-j, box 231.

88. The February 1957 "Interim Report of the Special Committee" raises this question. CHP, subject area 1.

89. ACP, box 184.

90. Hartley Shawcross had served as the chief prosecutor at the Nuremberg trials, and the first British delegate to the UN.

91. ÁBTL 3.2.5. O-8-002/4. The "Dover" object dossier. In its analysis covering every detail of the judicial process, the International Committee of Jurists investigated the laws and measures that served the reprisals and terror, which, in its view, did not satisfy the basic requirements of legality and were contrary to the international agreements signed by the People's Republic of Hungary. It handed its conclusions to the Special Committee on March 31, 1957: *The Hungarian Situation and the Rule of Law*. BJI, box 37.

92. ACP, box 184.

93. Ibid.

94. Talking to two UN witnesses, Jankovich and Oltványi, Sogno suggested they send weapons to the illegal resistance groups in Hungary. His idea was that another insurgency could spread to the other socialist bloc countries. See the telegram from the US embassy in Rome on January 20, 1957. NARA 764.00/1-2057.

95. From Jordan to Protitch on March 19, 1957. UNARM Protitch-files, DAG 1.1.1.3.

96. ACP, box 184.

97. The secret services mentioned forty-seven witnesses; according to Héderváry's documents, thirty-one of thirty-three were anonymous.

98. Tamás Pásztor's role is referred to in Szabó, *Foglalkozásuk, emigráns*, 237, and in the report by "Roger": ÁBTL 3.2.3. Mt 499/1. One article claims that "those giving evidence warned each other of the detail [. . .] that the Hungarian-speaking

UN employee in the ante-room was for years an informer for the communist secret police." "Letter to Bang-Jensen." *Nemzetőr*, August 1, 1958.

99. In a telegram of November 18, 1957, from the Interagency Defector Committee, the military attaché in Vienna opposed the granting of a visa "based on CIA information furnished by this office." NARA 764.00/11-1857.

100. This led to the staff being increased by fifty to sixty. Analysis shows that, of diplomats working in the West, 10 percent were agents of military intelligence and 27 percent domestic intelligence. Where there was a station, the proportion was higher. At the ministry, the proportion of secret service operatives was 70 percent. Baráth and Gecsényi, *Főkonzulok, követek és nagykövetek*, 42–47, 66.

101. Pál Ignotus and György Pálóczi-Horváth were among the witnesses in London that the British Foreign Office official had suggested as potentially the "best UN witnesses." The British questioned how reliable the evidence of the communists was, however. See "Hospitality of the United Nations Special Committee on Hungary," March 19, 1957. FO 371/128675. "UN Special Committee on Hungary," April 1, 1957.

102. ÁBTL "Informational Report on Hammarskjöld's Visit to Hungary."

103. MNL XIX-J-24a.

104. Ibid.

105. MNL XX-10-k.

106. January 21, 1957. "Draft Working Paper on the Organization of the Work of the Committee," CHP, subject area 1.

107. In this reading, the second report was the document produced by the Special Committee, while the third report was the one following the execution of Imre Nagy in 1958.

108. See, for example, February 18, 1957. "Additional sources for draft report, memos, statements." CHP, subject area 1.

109. Background conversations recorded on tape suggested this. CHP, subject area 1.

110. NAA A 1209 1957/5282. Telegrams were regularly received from the International Committee of Jurists. On March 5, 1957, for example, one was addressed to "secretary Jensen" in person. ACP, box 184.

111. NAA A 1209 1957/528. In the estimations of émigré leaders before one of the committees of the US Congress, forty to fifty thousand people had been deported. They knew of fifteen to twenty thousand fatal victims and estimated the number of the arrested, interned, and imprisoned revolutionaries to be similar. See *International Communism*, p. VIII. The Special Committee did not act on even these exaggerated numbers.

112. March 4, 1957. "Working Paper for Outline of Report" CHP, subject area 2. They agreed on the principles governing editing in Geneva and recorded these in the minutes on April 8, 1957. NARA 310.5764/4-1657. Jordan's memorandum on March 5, 1957: "Tentative Organization of the Draft." UNARM DAG 1.1.1.3. Protitch files.

113. May 5, 1957. "Chapter outlines [. . .] areas in which further information is needed [. . .] Suggested Content and Short Overview of Report by Jordan. Distribution of Work." CHP, subject area 2.

114. MNL MSZMP documents 288.f.32/1962/10. May 28, 1958, report by Tibor Zádor, Hungarian chargé d'affaires in Washington, on his conversation with Gunewardene. MNL XIX J-1-j, box 231.

115. Ten pages of suggested corrections were attached. Hámori edited chapter XIV: "Political Rights since 4 November." CHP, subject area 2.

116. See "Chapter III. The Uprising as Seen by the USSR and by the Government of Kadar." Fifth draft. CHP, subject area 2.

117. Jordan's letter of May 9, 1957: "Labour on my part, both in toning down the somewhat emotional language [. . .] taking the edge of the more pointed observations." UNARM DAG 1.1.1.3. Protitch files.

118. István Dobi's statement, revealing that the Soviets were called in before Kádár took his oath of office, was omitted, as was Kádár's protestation before Andropov. It also did not transpire where the Kádár government was established. Ivan Serov, who arrested Pál Maléter, was escorted not by "Soviet officers," as was claimed, but by NKVD operatives, and so on. (See the list from May 30, 1957: "Chapter VIII. Omissions [. . .] Factual Errors [. . .] Some Notes re Factual Errors in 2nd Draft Chapter II.") BJI, box 3. This will be covered in greater detail in chapter 7.

119. Copp and Peck, *Betrayal at the UN*, 153–57.

120. The objections of the French embassy were listened to and recorded by the Hungarian intelligence services. ÁBTL "Informational Report on Hammarskjöld's visit to Hungary."

5

CONTROVERSIES AND COMPROMISES INSIDE THE UN

The Report's Timing

Once the translators had been given the final text of the UN report of the Special Committee on the Problem of Hungary, they could begin their work. It is important to note that the minutes had already been translated several times because Tunisian diplomat Mongi Slim did not speak English and Uruguayan diplomat Enrique Fabregat insisted on reading them in Spanish. These extra steps multiplied the opportunities for misunderstandings, not to mention the time and cost involved.

It was in Budapest that the most thought had been given as to how the UN might act toward member states that had ignored UN resolutions and violated the UN Charter. Hungarian foreign policy leaders tasked their well-tested apparatus with preparing for any turn of events that could ensue during the deliberations on the Hungarian question, from public humiliation to exclusion and from sanctions to complete diplomatic isolation. In Budapest they assumed the UN would act according to its basic principles; the UN itself made no such assumption.

Péter Mód sent the UN's preliminary report from New York to Budapest on February 26, 1957, and paid close attention to developments, which sources show he was readily able to do. When the Committee left for Europe, this was reported to Budapest from Hungary's European embassies and intelligence stations; these sources also alerted Budapest when the text had been put together by the secretariat. It was with some trepidation that they informed Budapest that the report "would perhaps be discussed with the General Assembly as early as April," only to then cable with relief that the UN Secretariat would not approve the text until mid-May, ensuring that the report would not be published before the end of May.

By late April, the Hungarian foreign ministry had prepared arguments in the event that the report would be debated before the close of the UN's current session;[1] at this stage, its officials were still thinking in terms of refuting claims item by item. The Soviet Hungarians had at hand a number of these defenses, one of which was that the UN Special Committee was using the testimony of "escaped traitors," who had fled to the West, which is where they suggested the counterrevolution had been initiated. In particular, they targeted the head of the Committee: if Danish politician Alsing Andersen had at one time "sympathized with Nazis," then he would no doubt have been happy to see the revival of fascism in the heart of Europe.[2] They mentioned the burning of piles of books and the bloodbath at Köztársaság (Republic) Square in Budapest, and tried, using the example of the siege of Hungarian Radio, to deny that these had been spontaneous demonstrations. Point by point, these arguments contradicted each claim in the UN document, which had not yet been published and which foreign ministry officials in Budapest should have had no knowledge of.

It was at this time that Soviet envoy to the UN Arkady Sobolev discussed the Hungarian question with Dag Hammarskjöld;[3] as a result of this conversation, Budapest instructed Mód to establish contact with the Secretary-General. Mód delivered the Hungarian government's invitation for Hammarskjöld to visit Budapest, then repeated in a press release that the Secretary-General was welcome to come "at a time that suited him."[4] Andrew Cordier, Under-Secretary-General of the UN, responded to Principal Secretary of the Special Committee William Jordan that Hammarskjöld did not wish to comment on the invitation, but that it would not be wise for him to state any kind of position on the Hungarian question before the report was published.[5] At a press conference, the Secretary-General stated that there was no need to raise the issue at this time,[6] so it seems that Mód was correct in his understanding that Hammarskjöld had talked with his deputies about the debate on the report being delayed until the fall. The Secretary-General later informed the Hungarian delegation that he did not think it necessary for the report to be debated and that the General Assembly would not be convened for that purpose "unless the majority of member states request it."[7] This communication was particularly unusual because the task of convening the Assembly fell to the President of the Eleventh

General Assembly, Prince Wan Waithayakon, not to Hammarskjöld. Hammarskjöld also told the Hungarian UN envoy that, as far as he knew, order had been restored in Hungary, and the economic situation was constantly improving,[8] which revealed more about the source of the Secretary-General's information than the actual situation in Hungary.

Hammarskjöld expressed his gratitude for Hungary's invitation but sidestepped having to accept it, saying he had to focus on the Middle East, which he claimed was a far more serious problem than the media portrayed it to be.[9] The implication was also that the Hungarian question was less of a problem than many believed, as there was "order" in Hungary—just as there could have been order in Suez had the aggressors there been given free rein. Hammarskjöld was hoping to be reelected at the fall session. He had no chance if the Soviets or any of the other four nations vetoed his reappointment as Secretary-General.[10]

"For us, the postponement of the debate can only be advantageous,"[11] Mód reported. Time, and perhaps not only time, was on their side. In May, Jordan cabled Andersen, who, despite promising to do so, had not returned to New York on account of the elections in Denmark, and would only do so a week later. Meanwhile, Rapporteur Mick Shann had to travel to his ambassadorial posting in Manila and was impatient to complete his tasks in New York. At the end of May, almost a month after the hearings had ended and the report had been written, Jordan complained to his superiors that because of member absences they "had made disappointingly limited progress." In other words, following Andersen's return and despite Shann's urgency to finalize the report and conclude the discussion, others had priorities that trumped the Hungarian question.[12]

At this point, the race against time was interrupted by an awkward publicity drama: details of the report were leaked before it was officially published. The text was obtained by the International News Service and published by the *Journal-American* in two successive issues.[13] As noted with satisfaction by the Hungarian foreign ministry, this was "highly unpleasant for the secretariat."[14] Jordan hurried to tell his superiors that he and his colleagues were not responsible for the leak and to reassure them that their security system was excellent. The subject of the security system would come up later, but to this point there had been no mention of such a security system and indeed there is no official record of such a system.[15]

Georgi Arkadyev, the Soviet envoy to the UN who supplied information to Mód, was told by the Indian politician Krishna Menon that the representative from Ceylon was the weakest link on the Committee. The Hungarian foreign service believed that Fabregat had loaned the confidential document to a journalist, who, "naturally, copied it."[16] That details of the report were made public caused a sensation—a clear reflection of the global interest in its contents and anticipation of its publication. But it was only a rough draft of the UN document that was made available, as the final report had yet to be debated by the Special Committee. The Hungarian UN diplomats reported this to Budapest, adding with relief that a further delay was expected because the Secretariat was by no means rushing the completion of the task at all.[17]

On June 4, 1957, the Special Committee published a press release stating that the report would be finished by the following week,[18] at which time the Secretary-General would be present at the Special Committee's session. However, the envoy from Ceylon, Sir Senerat Gunewardene, had traveled to Colombo for consultations without signing the document, which caused considerable consternation and confusion. The publication date for the report had once again become "uncertain," and the outcome of all the collaborative efforts was unknown.[19]

Following a change of government in Ceylon in 1956 that included Marxist parties in the coalition, the Soviet Union had provided increased foreign aid to assist the Ceylonese economy, resulting in increased political influence in the country. Additionally, on March 5, 1957, the FBI had caught a member of the Ceylon delegation to the UN, Dhanapala Samarasekara, in the act of handing over the codebook for secret telegrams to Vladimir Grusha, a Soviet "diplomat"; this confirmed that the Soviets had been able to read the cables relating to the Hungarian question from that point forward. After this discovery, Samarasekara was suspended, but the UN continued to pay his salary. He later quietly left New York, but not before the Secretariat had organized a going-away party for him.

In the meantime, in June 1957, telegrams followed Special Committee member from Ceylon Gunewardene to Colombo, seeking to clarify whether his departure signified that he was refusing to sign the document.[20] Diplomatic pressure was considerable, as not even the United Nations was willing to risk the efforts of the Special Committee coming to nothing so quickly. Adding to the pressure from the Soviets,[21] prominent Indian politician Krishna Menon played a role, first trying to persuade Gunewardene not to sign the document and then recommending that the government of Ceylon distance itself from its envoy.[22] As it happened, the Ceylonese diplomat enjoyed good relations with Washington and London and had great ambitions for his career in the UN. Perhaps as a result of these factors, the drama did not unfold as those who planned to delay or avoid the conclusion and publication of the report had planned: after intense correspondence in the background, secret exchanges of telegrams, and interventions from the UK and developing countries, Hammarskjöld was informed in a message of June 14, 1957, that Gunewardene had accepted the report.

The publication of the report raised the issue of convening a General Assembly emergency session. This would have enabled a debate on the Hungarian question and allowed decisions to be made that many member states, particularly the Hungarians, had been expecting for months. As the Secretary-General told Mód and confirmed to Arkadyev and Ilya Chernyshev, however, he did not think the document would be debated over the summer.[23] There was relief in Budapest and Moscow, while those in the West were shocked that Hammarskjöld was so tellingly silent on convening the special session; even when quizzed by a reporter from the *Neue Züricher Zeitung*, UN leaders were not willing to comment on the issue.[24]

The publication of the report inspired an exceptionally energetic response in the press, however: radio stations, TV channels, and movie theater newsreels reported in detail on the story of the Hungarian Revolution, now seemingly complete and enjoying the seal of approval of the United Nations.[25] The document appeared in various translations and significant political leaders wrote prefaces to these various versions of the report. The UN Secretariat archived these responses as it did all relevant articles, news items, and commentaries—and thus also registered the strong resistance to the report emanating from Moscow and Budapest. The *New York Times* devoted a very long article to the report, including photographs of the Special Committee members and discussions of how the US public was anxiously awaiting a UN response on the report.[26]

When summer came, foreign service employees returned home from their missions abroad to be debriefed and given instructions and to enjoy a well-earned rest. For months, travel plans had been made, replacements arranged when vitally needed, and schedules agreed upon; travel at this time was troublesome, complex, and slow. Most European diplomats traveled back to the old continent by boat over the course of five to twelve days, whereas travel time for Asian and African colleagues was two to three times this long. However much the Hungarian question might be the scandal of the moment in central Europe, summer was summer, and, like any scandal, the intensity of interest in it inevitably faded over time.

It did not fade for everyone, however. US Ambassador to the UN Henry Cabot Lodge Jr. requested on behalf of those submitting the proposed declaration that the General Assembly be convened "as soon as possible."[27] Based on the reports of the US legation in Budapest, Lodge could clearly see that the bloody reprisals in Hungary justified placing the question on the agenda at the first possible opportunity and keeping the situation in Hungary under continued scrutiny. The UN Secretariat forwarded Lodge's request to the President of the General Assembly, Prince Wan, who by this time had arrived back home in Bangkok. Hammarskjöld had amended Lodge's demand by replacing the phrase "as soon as possible" with the words "as soon as practicable."[28] This was a substantive, not merely stylistic, alteration, and Cordier, who had composed the letter, added that there was no specific date mentioned in the US proposal.[29] This could hardly have been an accident, nor could the fact that Lodge's letter mentioned a session, not an emergency session. Cordier also wrote that the position of the other member states had solidified around the General Assembly being convened in September, though he did not cite any documents to support this claim.[30] Under-Secretary-General Cordier added that in the United Nations, it was the General Committee members who decided on the schedule, and consultation with them had determined it was not presently necessary to set a time to discuss the Special Committee's report. This meant that Waithayakon was spared the trouble of making an early return to New York. As he noted, Bangkok was hardly next door, after all.

The evident reluctance of the UN to address the Hungarian question aroused little interest or suspicion among US foreign policy or US intelligence agencies, despite Danish UN civil servant Povl Bang-Jensen providing evidence of the likely reasons for the UN's behavior. Later, many would be surprised to hear that no one had tried to contact Bang-Jensen during this time. When Lodge, head of the US delegation, together with James Barco, member of the US's UN delegation, did finally communicate with Bang-Jensen, they immediately demanded evidence for his claims, and he was not in a position to divulge such evidence. His informants, Eastern bloc diplomats at the UN, had good reason to ask him to establish high-level contact, but the conditions of their disclosures to Bang-Jensen precluded releasing the details Lodge and Barco requested. In the absence of concrete evidence, Lodge and Barco concluded that Bang-Jensen's suspicions were groundless,[31] that he was merely a lone employee who was unhappy with Hammarskjöld, and that he might be being manipulated by those opposed to Hammarskjöld's reelection.[32] The secret service agents accepted this explanation and parroted it when Bang-Jensen attempted to take action. Paradoxically that Bang-Jensen's serious claims were blocked from reaching high-level decision makers is exactly what suggests his suspicions were justified. Or was a Soviet condition for Hammarskjöld's reelection that Bang-Jensen's suspicions not see the light of day? If Soviet influence reached as far as the thirty-eighth floor of UN Headquarters, then for this influence to remain it was vital to muzzle, discredit, or displace anyone suspecting its existence.

Although there is no reply from Prince Wan to be found among the UN records, it appears he took the hint: the General Assembly President did not suggest that a session be convened in June, nor did he do so in July. And when, in early August, Cordier approached Wan, he then "did the rounds" with an informal question about the timing of the debate on the Hungarian question. There is no written record of this polling process: he quizzed the delegations verbally, and his inquiries—unusually for the UN—did not extend to every member state. According to Cordier, a "significant majority" established in this fashion together suggested September 10 as the date for the General Assembly to be convened—verbally, informally, and selectively. Prince Wan accepted the suggestion.[33] These months of delay meant that in Hungary the bloody process of what the government called consolidation would continue throughout the summer unabated.

The general assembly of the International Labor Organization (ILO), one of the UN's agencies, had previously rejected the mandate of the Hungarian delegation, thereby setting an example for its parent organization.[34] The Hungarian government speedily retracted the Hungarian ILO delegation's credentials, however, thereby precluding the public and procedural humiliation of having its mission removed.[35] That the Hungarian delegation would not have its credentials retracted at the UN General Assembly in the fall was one of the key objectives of Hungarian foreign policy. The extra months the Hungarians were granted seem to have been adequate for it to preempt this danger by influencing patterns of voting. Hungary could count on the fraternal countries whatever might happen, so the scales could be tipped in its favor if it could secure the votes of the newly liberated African and Asian countries; the Hungarians made a trip to Sri Lanka as well. Many of these countries, thanks to Hammarskjöld's important and successful efforts, had now become UN member states. These countries formed a distinctly heterogeneous bloc, and thus suitable arguments had to be found to attract their support.

Three so-called Hungarian diplomats were given the task of establishing contact with these countries: Károly Szarka, János Péter, and Pál Rácz. Of these three, at least two, Rácz and Péter, were secret service agents. The UN delegacy of Rácz was merely a cover; his role during the eventful days of the 1956 Revolution proved to be key. His real job was not a secret to the US, however, and on June 14, 1957, he was declared persona non grata and ejected from the country. Péter Mód immediately objected to what he described as a serious injustice and demanded an audience with the Secretary-General, who told him that a number of such cases were in process and that he had no jurisdiction over them.[36] Ilya Chernysev, a Soviet diplomat at the UN, informed Mód that such conflicts were more common at the UN Secretariat than at national delegations,[37] where personnel were more likely to have multiple roles. The fact that the Secretariat had been drawn into the intelligence web would later be of key significance.[38]

The other member of the delegation identified as a secret agent was János Péter, who began his career as a Calvinist pastor, then became a bishop, and was probably extorted into working for the ÁVH because of his Nazi past. Péter distinguished himself by spying on and ruining the careers of high-ranking politicians: after 1945, he worked for Zoltán Tildy and Árpád Szakasits, both briefly presidents of Hungary who were removed from power.[39] Many were disgusted by the sanctimonious way in which Péter exculpated or arrogantly acknowledged communist crimes at the pulpit of the General Assembly.

The leader of the delegation was Károly Szarka, originally trained as an iron lathe operator, who had formerly been a Hungarian ambassador to Washington.[40] No data emerged on his activity for the secret service, but he received continuous and exact information about the service's operations and cooperated on several occasions with intelligence agents. He had a reputation as a relentless and uninhibited man.

Szarka later described the preparations for the journey to the new African and Asian UN member states as "scandalous," complaining that his colleagues were incapable of completing the simplest of tasks when arranging the visit to these newly liberated countries, such as typing, copying, or making reservations. It speaks volumes about his mindset that he used the

Károly Szarka, deputy minister of foreign affairs of Hungary, visiting the UN.
Copyright: UN Photo Archive #7700716.

term "sabotage" to refer to all of these failings.[41] Nevertheless, the work of the delegation "was hugely assisted by the fact that the Soviet Union gave a volume of memoirs [. . .] to the UN member states from Asia and Africa," which was in fact a presentable form of extortion. It is worth noting that China, too, followed the journeys of the Hungarians "with interest."[42] The Hungarian government delegation was sometimes greeted by high-level officials, as they were in Ceylon, while in other places, such as Tunisia, they were not welcomed at all. Representatives from both of these countries were of course members of the Special Committee. Szarka wrote in his report that over the course of their visit, Ceylon recalled its delegation from the UN Committee; in reality, Gunewardene continued to participate in the Committee's work.

Whether these developing countries accepted or rejected the flexibly chosen arguments of the Hungarians was primarily a reflection of their interim political position. They had only recently escaped the colonial yoke of Western democracies, and they not only maintained illusions about the Soviet Union but expected real assistance from it, albeit in return for political influence. And while they could well understand the risks of a more powerful neighbor being allowed to invade a weaker one with impunity, compared to colonial aggression in the Congo or Algeria, the Hungarian case did not seem quite so outrageous. Jawaharlal Nehru and Abdel Nasser, Indian and Egyptian leaders, respectively, and the heads of what would become the nonaligned states, each welcomed the Hungarian delegation in person. The delegation was not given any concrete promises by either as to voting intentions, however, for their hosts had many other considerations to ponder: in Cairo, the Suez Crisis and in New Delhi, the situation in Kashmir.

In some places, the arrival of the Hungarian delegation enjoyed press coverage; in others, the visit of secret police officers from a puppet regime was not publicized. In certain Arab states, Hungarian delegates explained to their hosts that Imre Nagy was Jewish and that the Revolution was part of a Zionist global conspiracy. Elsewhere, the Hungarians raised the precedent set by a UN committee able to investigate the internal affairs of sovereign nation-states, something no dictator could welcome. As a sign of how much was at stake, Szarka reported directly to Hungarian prime minister János Kádár over the course of his trip.[43]

During this time, former Budapest mayor József Kővágó and many other leading Hungarian émigrés set off in similar directions, if with entirely opposing messages, to inform public opinion in developing countries about the Hungarian Revolution. They appeared at large-scale gatherings, universities, press conferences, and events hosted by nongovernmental organizations, though rarely in the political arena. Hungarian diplomats would immediately object to officially receiving these Hungarian refugee politicians. When Kővágó was welcomed by Indian prime minister Nehru,[44] the Hungarian ambassador was up in arms at once: Hungary would never allow Sheik Abdullah, who advocated for independence of Kashmir from India, onto its territory, he announced, referring to the comparable sensitivity of the Kashmir issue. The press response to visits from Kővágó and other former revolutionaries was in part the work of the Western countries that had helped organize and finance them in the first place and in part that of US intelligence, whose considerable influence extended to sponsoring these journeys.

As part of the foreign policy strategy devised in Budapest, the Hungarian chargé d'affaires in Washington, DC, Tibor Zádor, who also had a background in the secret service, was instructed to seek out those diplomats serving in the US capital whom the Kádár regime could count on during the vote at the UN. Zádor sent home extensive reports of his visits to the leaders of a long list of missions, visits where it was not enough to repeat the standard mantra but where supporting arguments were needed. He encountered Gunewardene, who proudly told him that he had accepted the post in the Special Committee to ensure that not only what he termed "enemies" would be included on it; he also bragged that he had had eighty pages removed from the report.[45] It is not known whether Gunewardene's disgraceful ostentation was the result of bitter experiences in Colombo, an attempt to position himself with a vassal of his new boss, or perhaps contained a dash of truth, but those recalling the events mention that Gunewardene's questioning of witnesses before the Special Committee was reminiscent of cross-examination by a criminal prosecutor.[46]

The Hungarian government had what they called a foreign defense attorney, Denis Pritt, British parliamentarian and winner of the Stalin Prize. It is unclear from the sources whether Pritt offered himself up for this role in the Hungarian government or was commissioned to perform it, but in his jurisprudential analysis of the report by the UN Special Committee on the Problem of Hungary he publicly sided with the Kádár regime. He objected to the fact that only capitalist countries (in his words) were represented by the members of the Special Committee, and he considered it vital for the minutes of the hearings to be made public. He contended that no court should have accepted anonymous witnesses and judged the sources of information at the Committee's disposal to be inadequate for an authoritative picture to be formed. He argued that the investigation should have been public, that witnesses on both sides should have been identified, and that the hearings should have dealt with—among other things—the lynchings of ÁVH members during the Revolution, who he claimed were innocent victims. Pritt was especially effective because he pulled a veil of British legal respectability over his twisted version of history. The Hungarian foreign ministry welcomed Pritt's work most heartily, making use of his arguments in establishing its strategy. These were arguments from an expert well versed in international law, who had served good causes, like the defense of Ho Chi Minh and cases in Africa, but also bad ones, like supporting the Soviet invasion of Finland.

Another welcome guest at the Hungarian embassy in London was Professor John Desmond Bernal, a scholar who was very much at home in politics and who made no secret of his interest in Marxism and his enthusiasm for the great Marxist historical experiment.[47] However, he used his cordial relations with the representatives of the Eastern bloc to intervene on behalf of imprisoned writers and to inform Hungarian diplomatic staff in London of the dire publicity consequences abroad of what the government called consolidation after the Revolution in Hungary. As for the Special Committee report, Bernal attempted to argue about it with his Hungarian friends with the naivete of those who knew of Marxism only from books rather than from real-life experience of Soviet methods.

Over the summer, the report not only became a media sensation—and indeed popular summer reading[48]—it was also a commercial success. Accountants at the United Nations noted that of the 30,000 published copies of the English version, 27,300 were sold, as were 11,500 of the French version; assuming copies were sold at two dollars each, the estimated sales reached close to $80,000.[49] This was no small sum, although the operation of the Special Committee cost $113,800, not including the $15,600 in per diems paid to its members.[50]

The Responses of the Hungarian Regime

After the report was published, the UN Secretariat's attention turned to monitoring its reception, which was traced and documented in New York in the greatest detail, with particular interest paid to Budapest and Moscow. On June 20 all was calm, but then the storms came, first from Moscow and followed closely by those from Budapest. These reactions came not in rhetorical form but in the form of brutal political reprisals: The day after the report was published, the Hungarian Supreme Court sentenced playwright and editor József Gáli and journalist and editor Gyula Obersovszky to death. It could be no coincidence—as Reuters put it—that from this moment the court became even more cruel with its sentences.[51] International law expert Hartley Shawcross spoke with alarm of mounting legal persecutions in Hungary, and the International Commission of Jurists collected fresh data on the exact numbers of arrests, incarcerations, and executions, based not just on the notices in the Communist Party newspaper but also on the notice boards at the courts.[52] By early September, these data, along with various statements and reports, were gathered at the secretariat of the Special Committee for use in future reports on the Hungarian question.

By the beginning of September, an extensive collection had been amassed of Hungarian and Soviet rhetorical responses to the report, with the various elements, facts, and unusual aspects of the criticism collected under different headings.[53] There was also great emphasis placed on the

Rapporteur of the Special Committee on the Problem of Hungary, Keith O. Shann, addressing the UN on its report. Copyright: UN Photo Archive #7725505.

anonymous witnesses who submitted testimony to the Special Committee; the attention they attracted in Budapest threatened that reprisals might soon follow.[54] At the same time, the UN staff noted a conspicuous absence of any potentially critical mention of the Secretary-General in the communist propaganda from Hungary.[55]

In the spring, Hungarian minister of justice Ferenc Nezvál had drawn the attention of his fellow ministers to the fact that "the international community strives at every level to besmirch our justice system and our laws," and claimed that this "has an influence on the work of the courts and the prosecutors." An appropriate response was required, and what could be more appropriate than heightened stringency?[56] This makes all the more blood-curdling a subsequent series of criticisms levied against the hanging judges and thugs-turned-prosecutors: Nezvál accused them of being soft-hearted, liberal, and weak, just as Mátyás Rákosi had done in his hard-line objections from Moscow.[57] Kádárist prosecutors responded, as if they had become fervent believers in the so-called counterrevolution, by sending many dozens of innocent people to the gallows. A marked change was that they now did so not with trumped-up charges, as in the days of the Stalinist show trials, but instead by turning the interpretation of the law upside down: it was not allegedly planned conspiracies that they punished but rather the events of the Revolution that were criminalized in retrospect.

The official anger and objections of the Soviets and Hungarians to the report was soon replaced by a remorseless hate campaign that attacked the values and achievements of 1956 and sought to sully its memory. The communist press first printed brief news stories on the report of the UN Special Committee on the Problem of Hungary, then they published distorted excerpts from it; meanwhile, loyal comrades were allowed to see an almost unadulterated version.[58] According to the foreign ministry, the "dirty document"[59] vindicated the Hungarian government's position that the Committee was illegitimate and no one affiliated with the Committee should be allowed to enter Hungary. As a result, they claimed, the Committee could not put together an authentic picture of events—the sources of their information were testimonies from fugitives, including former criminals.

At the meeting of the fraternal countries held in Prague on June 25–26, 1957, Comrade Konstantin Grepkin proposed that the Hungarian delegation follow an offensive rather than defensive strategy and strike back against the attacks of the imperialists using political rather than legal arguments.[60] In New York, the staff of the Hungarian UN Mission had been preparing their response to the report for many months now, with strict deadlines and precise coordination of duties.[61] They requested information from Budapest on economic developments, the operation of the justice system, the success of the consolidation program, and information about the members of the Special Committee that could be used to make personal attacks against them. Their attention extended to a 1951 anticommunist speech by Henry Cabot Lodge that they used as evidence of systematic efforts by US imperialists to undermine the people's democracies; in doing so, they were able to move the emphasis from internal causes of the counterrevolution to alleged external causes.[62]

In the end, the distortion of facts to this degree did not become the official position, although propaganda did play a key role in the response to the report. Meanwhile, Hungarian foreign ministry officials claimed that the Special Committee was itself creating and spreading propaganda. They argued that the report's most important source—witness statements—could not be considered representative of the population since, of two hundred thousand people who left Hungary after the Revolution, less than two hundred (0.1 percent) were allowed to give their testimony. The Hungarians' official propogandists also argued that the views of the hostile governments of the countries that received the witnesses as refugees had influenced the selection of those who appeared before the Special Committee. They claimed that the witnesses spoke "in order to provide their livelihood," because they "were paid," and because they intended to spend their lives in the West.[63] Soviet-directed Hungarian sources alleged that the witnesses could "tell lies" of any kind in their testimonies, that they took the opportunity to do so, and that the Committee accepted the statements of criminals, thieves, and murderers over those of their victims.[64] The Hungarian foreign ministry regarded the suggestion that witnesses were afraid for their families as "absurd."[65] Meanwhile, the identification of some of those providing testimony led to reports that their loved ones in Hungary were at risk: the political police were seeking opportunities for leverage over the witnesses' families. The Hungarian secret service also made plans to liquidate or kidnap some of the more important émigré leaders and force them to collaborate in undermining the credibility of the report.

Hungarian communist propaganda mentioned that Imre Nagy had condemned the October events as a "counterrevolution" and that he had ordered martial law to be declared.[66] They were aided in characterizing Nagy as totalitarian by Anna Kéthly's speech in Vienna on November 2, 1956, which mentioned the counterrevolutionary danger and revenge attacks on communists and their family members.[67] The legal staff of the Hungarian Ministry of Justice also pointed out legal errors in the Special Committee's report; arguing, for example, that the government did not have to resign in order to be dissolved and that an extension to the mandate of the Hungarian Parliament did not require an amendment to Hungary's constitution. They added that the legitimacy of the Kádár government was not in doubt, but that of the Nagy government had been, as the inaugurations had not been announced in *Magyar Közlöny*, the official bulletin of the Hungarian government. They denied that the Hungarian uprising might have been socialist, claiming that the revolutionaries had started to split up the state cooperatives, had intended to turn the Budapest central city council back into a mayoral office, had wanted to transform state firms into joint-stock companies, and so on. They sought to prove that Nagy's revolutionaries had persecuted the innocent, claiming that not only secret service agents were in peril, but also party members, directors of state cooperatives, and anyone who might be mistaken for ÁVH officers.[68] All these allegations by the Soviet-imposed Hungarian leaders were presented as evidence that the

UN had intervened on the wrong side in the events in Hungary, and as Ambassador Mód claimed, that its role "was responsible for the deaths of many young Hungarians," though how he arrived at this conclusion is unknown.[69] To rest their case, the representatives of the Soviet-imposed Hungarian government added that in the space of a few days, what they called the "counterrevolutionaries" had killed 237 people, while in the period since November 4, a total of 164 death sentences had been passed but not yet carried out by the Hungarian courts; death tolls and relative proportions of convicted and executed Hungarians during these two periods were mentioned continually and compared repeatedly. The degree of Soviet influence over Hungarian foreign policy was clearly reflected in this quote from contents of the diplomats' travel plans: "To agree with Gromov whether the UN delegation will travel on 10 September or only on 11 September." It seems that as late as August 1957, Soviet ambassador to Budapest and Soviet state security officer Gromov was the Hungarian foreign ministry's superior.[70]

The greatest supporter of the compromised but still highly active ÁVH, which had been badly weakened during the Revolution, was Soviet state security; it helped former officers regroup and rebuild their network of agents in energetic fashion, with sometimes brutal applications of pressure. In March, with the pretext of preventing the Revolution from beginning again, the political police took 250 people into so-called preventive custody, then proudly announced to the deputy minister of the interior that they had "recruited 74 agents in the last 10 days."[71] This presumably referred to weaker individuals or those more vulnerable to extortion. "The agents are recruited after suitable interviews and character checks," the political police directorate's material states, so "a number of influential former leaders and high-ranking Horthyite gendarmes and military officers" became members of the secret network. The precedents set by the arrests, internments, interrogations, and growing numbers of death sentences further boosted the number of agents, meaning that "a significant number of new comrades were granted a network of agents," as the report puts it. When the political police were entrusted with uncovering the illegal resistance network and attacking it at its roots, it became important to conduct investigations into its supposed puppet masters abroad and to start putting overseas operations into place.[72]

According to the logic of the secret service apparatus, those at the helm of the Hungarian opposition—Hungarian military officer Béla Király, Smallholder Party politician Sándor Kiss, Kéthly, and Kővágó—were the leaders of an "illegal coalition" that had fled abroad, and when they were named by the political police as witnesses for the Special Committee's investigation, the setup was complete. Their family members and friends back in Hungary were investigated and visited by the secret police.[73] The police launched investigations into the personal backgrounds of the UN witnesses, their families, and associates. They also used transcripts of interrogations of those who had been sentenced in Hungary before the Revolution—many of whom were innocent—and records taken in the process of their arrests to provide evidence for the theory that they were illegally cooperating with the UN Special Committee. This was all part of a broader plan to criminalize the UN. The UN was now presented as being in league with those supporting the counterrevolution and had become a target of the Hungarian regime; it was now targeted as one of the "Western counter-revolutionary organization centers"[74] to which Hungarian secret agents could be sent to uncover alleged anti-Hungarian activity. All this propaganda served to raise tensions and sow doubt and misinformation ahead of the upcoming UN session in which the Special Committee's report would be discussed.

The political committee of the Hungarian Socialist Workers' Party made the most important decisions on the strategy to be followed by the Hungarian foreign ministry at the discussion in front of the UN General Assembly. The elite of the party leadership put the issue on the agenda in the summer of 1957 to establish the direction for the government to follow. There was considerable overlap in personnel between the two bodies, but the hierarchy was unequivocal, as clearly shown by the fact that the political committee did not accept the foreign ministry's proposals.[75] The UN hearing was first discussed in July, when decisions were made about the speech to be given at the UN General Assembly and the planning for a "spontaneous" mass movement to be initiated and carefully organized by the communists in support of the position of the Hungarian government. Striking differences of opinion emerged among the various members of the upper echelons of the party leadership, which accurately reflected the sometimes diametrically opposed factions that determined the foreign policy of the early Kádár regime. These fractures were most keenly felt when Kádár was absent from a political committee meeting, and his comrades were able to express their opinions more freely and explicitly.[76] The language spoken at these meetings was more military than political—"rapid fire," "vulnerability," "counterattack"—in line with the wartime psychosis of the Cold War

János Kádár (*first row right*) at the session of the Hungarian Parliament in 1957. Copyright: Fortepan #117118. Donated by Ervin Szabó Library, Budapest Collection. Photographed by György Sándor.

communists. At one point Politburo member István Szirmai was concerned whether "they might be sending a UN army" to Hungary in the fall.[77] Dezső Szilágyi, in charge of the party's foreign affairs apparatus, claimed that "a few hundred million copies" of the report were being distributed,[78] which of course was more a reflection of the state of mind of the party leaders than reality. György Marosán, the most arrogant, bellicose, and vengeful member of the party leadership, claimed that the revolutionaries were fighting for the annihilation of the Treaty of Trianon, as if the "lads of Pest" might be setting in to battle to reclaim Hungary's territory lost after World War I. The perverse logic of the political committee's meetings turned history on its head: according to their arguments, on November 4, 1956, the Soviet Union acted in line with the spirit of the UN Charter in order to preserve peace in central Europe. The suppression of the Hungarian Revolution by Soviet military intervention was construed as a defense against "preplanned imperialist interference" that had led to armed unrest that had to be halted.[79] In short, the UN, instead of criticizing the Soviet Union, should express its gratitude to it.

The lackeys in Budapest had already expressed their gratitude to Moscow by this stage, and when the Hungarian minister of foreign affairs, Imre Horváth, contacted the Soviet ambassador to Budapest,[80] he called him from where Soviet deputy foreign minister Vasily Kuznetsov could issue instructions to Horváth over the telephone. After the cabinet meeting and following the political committee's resolution, Minister of the Interior Béla Biszku traveled to Moscow, while Péter Mód reported from New York that he was cooperating successfully with the representatives of the Soviet Union.

This process was personally overseen by the party's first secretary and prime minister, János Kádár: his corrections are written in red pencil on the proposed final statement.[81] The government resolutions following the sessions of the political committee established a precise division of labor: Horváth, Szilágyi, and Szirmai were entrusted with finalizing the statement, which Kádár and Gyula Kállai, a representative from party leadership, then examined and approved. They worked out a strategy in the event that Péter Mód was not given the floor at the General Assembly, knowing that the UN could employ such sanctions against member states that disregarded its resolutions. No such sanctions were issued. Kádár softened the final version of the statement slightly, achieving an almost diplomatic tone with his stylistic corrections, while approving the report's neo-Stalinist, fist-shaking substance. As a result, a consensus emerged around the need for mistakes to be "mentioned in moderation," placing the blame firmly on the West and allowing the critique of the report to express ideological continuity with Hungarian Stalinism.[82]

Legal arguments with political implications were made. Kádár accused Imre Nagy of "shov[ing] [the whole government] to one side . . . as well as the Presidential Council . . . and discard[ing] the parliament."[83] The proposed statement included other absurdities, such as the claim that Imre Nagy broke international law when "he forced the withdrawal of Soviet troops from Budapest" and violated Article 3 of 1955 (which incorporated the Warsaw Treaty into Hungarian law). This infringement of international law must have escaped the attention of both Kádár and Yuri Andropov at the time, given that the Soviets entered into negotiations about it at an official level with representatives of the Imre Nagy government and never mentioned it. Yet at that time, so the Hungarian government's statement claimed, "fascist gangs were being flung [over the border] in mass numbers," while at the imperialists' prompting, a "countergovernment" was formed in Transdanubia with the intention of splitting Hungary in two.[84] The creation of this countergovernment was alleged to be part of the United Nations' "scheming against [Hungary],"[85] which the US had begun and continued with the assistance of its "voting machines." It was again mentioned that the aid program organized by the UN served as a cover for intelligence agencies,[86] a claim that managed to pile ingratitude on top of the Hungarian government's dishonesty.

At the same time, an investigation was made into Imre Nagy, the "law-breaking prime minister," one of whose crimes was to involve the United Nations in the resolution of the conflict. This same session of the political committee determined that the criminal trial of Nagy and his associates be scheduled for late September at a closed hearing. This investigation had already led to the "implementation" of seventy-four arrests.[87] Biszku reported on all this to Andropov in Moscow, as even among "prominent trials," this would clearly be the most prominent of them all.[88] The Soviets requested that the passing of the sentence be delayed until late fall, by which time the communist world congress would have taken place in Moscow. In the meantime, the trials of writers could establish the right atmosphere of fear in Budapest, where the police were threatening opinion leaders and famous authors with harsh sentences because of their role in the Revolution.[89]

At the recommendation of the political committee and in line with the government resolution, the machinery of agitation and propaganda now leapt into action. Their plan was to work on public opinion in such a way that the campaign might reach its crescendo shortly before the UN General Assembly.[90] The size of the operation showed the significance the Hungarian authorities placed on the UN, mobilizing as it did essentially the whole of Hungarian society in opposition to its report. There had never been a campaign quite like this in Hungary before, with quite this much press coverage. The organization of the "spontaneous" protest movement was professional and efficient, and it was not lacking in theatrical set pieces—grand assemblies held on factory shop floors and cooperative farms, workers lining up to sign petitions, statements of protest handed over with celebratory fanfare, and thousands of letters and telegrams all addressed and mailed to the Secretary-General of the UN. Not only were the details unfailingly cynical but the whole affair was perfectly absurd: peasant women, miners, rabbis, academics, sportspersons, and writers all registering their protest, in a strictly supervised fashion, to a document they knew nothing about.

A clear indication of the level of the Hungarian regime's fear was that it was every bit as serious about this propaganda offensive as it had previously been about the use of armed force. The government thought of the convening of the fall General Assembly, on the eve of the Revolution's anniversary, as a continuation of the counterrevolution.[91] Officials knew that Voice of America and Radio Free Europe were presenting a series on the UN document,[92] which, the secret services estimated, was listened to by about half the Hungarian population—an act of defiance in the face of the threat of informers, direct threats, and laws pertaining to the spreading of rumors. The text of the report also found its way into Hungary, smuggled or sent by post, sometimes woven into the covers and bindings of books by communist leaders. So surveillance of the postal service was stepped up, as was the number of staff at the division for scrutinizing letters, not only to examine items arriving in Hungary but also to filter the information people wished to send to the UN during the General Assembly. The secret police considered this type of smuggling to be "disguised intelligence work," a serious category of spying.[93]

During this time, the party apparatus was working hard to poison Hungarian-American relations, publicly holding Washington responsible for the counterrevolution and then for the "illegal committee" it had forced the UN to set up.[94] Hungarian propaganda publications emphasized the role of the US in the "counterrevolution," "proving" its responsibility in picture books published in large numbers and translated into many languages, as well as at exhibitions, in newspaper stories, and in films.[95] Gusztáv Tutsek, a practicing judge considered by many to be a hanging judge, put together a document on Hungarian-American relations from 1943 onward that used what it called facts to prove the bitter enmity, which, so it claimed, the United States directed not at the socialist system but rather at the Hungarian people.

Despite these tensions and attempts to instill fear, as the UN General Assembly was convened an unexpected optimism gripped Hungarian society, however broken, desperate, and destitute it might have been. As the highest party leadership had learned from reports on the general mood of the country and confidential sources of information,[96] people began to notice the Soviets packing up to leave, while elsewhere there were rumors that the UN resolution would be binding on Hungary because of the obligatory nature of international law. Panic could be sensed within the party apparatus, and the preparedness of the central powers was concomitant with these feelings of either hope or alarm. When the General Assembly session opened on September 10, 1957, almost a week had passed since police major general Vilmos Garamvölgyi had declared "full alert," which was expanded "during the period of the discussion of the Hungarian question." Since August 8—the start of the peak of the campaign against the UN—there had been a full alert at every major police station and rapid response and policing unit, and resources had been deployed for the maintenance of public order and directing of traffic. Security had been increased at the Kistarcsa and Tököl camps and other penal and correctional facilities holding detainees who presented a public threat. In addition to the increased protection and strict control of strategic locations for travel, communication, and transportation, like railway stations, the radio building, and important traffic intersections, people were stopped more frequently for identity checks, and baggage and vehicles were examined to preempt any "hostile" activity, which had to be eliminated "with any method" needed.[97]

Part of the preventive plan was the stipulation that the secret police handlers who oversaw the network of agents should "arrange heightened meetings with operatives," particularly "in the direction of oppositional categories." By this stage, the political police had infiltrated the "criminal network" of the underworld and were trying to extract information from these sources on the assumption that the "political underworld" was connected to the criminal one and well aware of its smoothly operating system of communications.[98]

The state of emergency timed for the anniversary of the outbreak of the Revolution was a "dress rehearsal" for the level of alertness ordered for the period of the UN debate. The date of October 23 brought the memories of the previous year to life. Even the Soviet forces were put on alert for this period, the borders were closed, and at every possible location, both uniformed and plainclothes officers of the political police awaited those wishing to publicly commemorate places and events that had been emblematic of the Revolution.[99] Serious attention was paid to the potential domestic consequences for Hungary of the UN debate, so the foreign ministry was put under special protection: two squads with machine guns defended the building, thirty-two "workers' guards" were placed in strategic positions, and secret documents were removed from the archive.[100] But people had no wish to attack the building. Most were celebrating the anniversary quietly at home, some in secret, and some at public places that were emblematic for the Revolution. Many spent the anniversary in prison.

Meanwhile, at the anniversary commemorations outside Hungary—in large cities in Europe and in New York—anger and despair could be expressed in a more elemental way by émigrés and others who sympathized with the Hungarian Revolution and condemned the Soviet suppression of it. Through the Hungarian intelligence services, the Hungarian foreign ministry followed these events and reported back to Budapest. The security of diplomatic missions was boosted by the host countries, and in a number of places Hungarian diplomats were armed. Since the preceding summer, these diplomats had been obliged to report within twenty-four hours on every conversation they or any of their staff had with outside parties, whether at receptions, meetings, or just as private individuals.[101] But not even these draconian measures were enough to prevent the protests, smashed windows, and arson with which those in Western democracies expressed their disgust at the terrible crushing of the Hungarian Revolution. These acts of protest only served to prove to the political police and Hungarian party leadership that the imperialists continued with their provocations, since their earlier experiment in overthrowing people's democracy had ended in such abject failure.[102]

Even more threatening news was arriving from Moscow, where the most compromised Hungarian communists had once fled, many of whom had played a role in "convincing" Kádár in the days before November 4, 1956, with their very presence, that if he did not undertake the task of suppressing the Revolution, there would be others who would—others whose rage had been rekindled by the UN debate. Among these hardliners was Nagy's Stalinist predecessor Mátyás Rákosi, whose ambitions and desire for power were never-ending, and who was enraged not so much by the UN document—What might the working people expect of the "voting machine" of the imperialists?—as by the response of the Hungarian government, which he read "with shame and indignation," as he would inform communist leader Nikita Khrushchev and the Soviet leadership.[103] In Rákosi's extreme view only one leader of the counterrevolution—Nagy—had been pushed aside, and Kádár had been just as much to blame as his former boss Nagy had been. Rákosi did not think that the dozens of death sentences were enough, and considered that the investigations into "fascist atrocities" were being obstructed, because "the prosecutor's offices and courts are teeming with fascist, Horthyite prosecutors and judges."[104]

In his address on November 4, 1956, Kádár stated that "the government will not tolerate the workers being persecuted with any pretext just because they participated in the events of recent days," and he furthermore promised to guarantee "the democratic election of the existing administrative bodies and revolutionary councils" as well as negotiations "on the withdrawal of Soviet troops from the territory of Hungary,"[105] but these words became nothing more than a part of the historical record, not indicative of his agenda. Kádár continued to publicly subscribe to and support some of the values and achievements of the Revolution, but this messaging and all government directives had been formulated in Moscow: they had merely been tactical concessions, not promises intended to be kept. Kádár was still "perturbed" by the fate of Imre Nagy, but on November 12, Soviet communist leader and KGB officer Mikhail Suslov and Averky Aristov reassured Kádár that his actions had been legitimate. It is worth noting that Kádár even agreed with KGB general Ivan Serov that military authorities and state security organizations "should not take any more people into custody who are not enemies,"[106] so it seems they had been happy to do so up to that point.

The Hungarian authorities would of course continue to arrest and imprison people randomly, however, as would be revealed six months later in the information provided in the documents prepared for the UN debate. The documents from the Hungarian Ministry of Justice and the chief prosecutor's office would also expose the scale of this part of Kádár's regime of revenge: between November 4, 1956, and June 30, 1957, the courts passed sentence on 21,987 individuals; of these, 56 were sentenced to death, 16,427 were imprisoned, 4,098 were fined, and 820 had "other measures" imposed on them. Meanwhile, the military courts sentenced an additional 1,575 people: 62 to death, 1,183 to prison, and 350 to other punishments.[107] These summaries of sentences by the Ministry of the Interior were presumably prepared as internal material for the UN debate planned for April and covered the period from mid-February to early April, summarizing the measures that were implemented, from the retributions of the slightly more consolidated regime through the planning of the Restart in March movement to liberation celebrations recalling Hungary's freedom from the Nazi rule after World War II.[108] The arrests were in no small part the result of the "monster raids" that had been held 709 times in the spring, each involving the participation of three thousand to four thousand police officers, paramilitaries, and workers' guards. Spreading these statistics over six weeks gives an idea of the size of the operation and its intention to intimidate, which led to 12,421 arrests. Of this number of arrestees, 5,877 were accused of having committed political crimes, and 1,826 were escaped inmates who were returned to their places of detention. The rest were common (nonpolitical) criminals.[109]

In preparation for the debate at the United Nations, and in response to the international attention paid to the constant trials (including by the UN), the Hungarian foreign ministry and Ministry of Justice corresponded about how to officially represent the various modes of revenge exacted on those who had participated in the Revolution. The International Commission of Jurists (ICJ) provided detailed and current information, and many of the accredited diplomats in Hungary observed the operation of the courts with interest. In June 1957, the ICJ compiled a table of the names of the condemned, their ages and professions, the nature of their sentences, and the opportunities (if any) for appeals, publishing this as evidence of the "challenge[s]" to the rule of law.[110] In addition, under the title "Justice in Hungary," the ICJ continued to survey the workings of the courts and development of judicial abuses based on documents retrieved from numerous sources.[111]

Hartley Shawcross, who was supporting the ICJ's work, held a press conference after the report was published,[112] pointing out that the UN document tracked events up to November 4, but the reprisals had begun after this date and were still occurring. He observed that the UN's room to maneuver had narrowed, with its only option to continue to observe the situation in Hungary and measure the scale of the reprisals. A transcript of the press conference reached Jordan in his capacity at the secretariat of the Special Committee; it was not shared with the Secretary-General or even the members of the Special Committee. That it was Jordan alone who decided on the fate of the information received was, as far as protocol was concerned, worrying. So, too, was the fact that a number of documents were archived "since the Committee cannot submit this report to the G[eneral] A[ssembly] in view of resolution 1132 (XI)."[113] According to Jordan and the UN Secretariat, the decision that led to the creation of the Special Committee preempted the transfer of certain items of information and thus the possibility of taking action based on such items. This was the case even though the resolution referred to an investigation of the situation in Hungary and to further reports—that is, to continued observation of events—and not to summarily archiving information it received.

A broad range of information from Hungary flooded into the United Nations on a continuous basis through a great variety of channels. As a result, the dossiers of "Communications Received"[114] were bursting at the seams. The sources of this information could be press materials, embassy reports from the UN envoys of the countries in question, or statements made by Hungarian and Eastern European émigré organizations, but they could also take the form of private letters, summaries written by voluntary informants, or desperate calls for help. Throughout the summer of 1957, as people geared up for the General Assembly, hopes were raised that the debate on the Hungarian question would touch not just on history but also on the present horrendous situation. And there was good reason to hope, because the secretariat of the Special Committee followed domestic events in Hungary closely.[115] The UN Library put together another comprehensive reading list on the events following the Revolution, which was registered by the secretariat of the Committee in the same way as the reports of the Hungarian Revolutionary Council, the news reports on the court cases, the infringements of human rights, or "the suggestion that a witness be heard."[116] And this was the source of the problem: The reports were merely registered and filed—nothing more. They were not forwarded or disseminated among the members of the Special Committee, so they were condemned to obscurity and no actions were taken.

When questions arose later as to why the secretariat of the Special Committee had not brought often dramatic information it had received to the attention of the Committee's members, Jordan responded that the list of communications received was regularly sent to the Committee members, as were certain documents, as "the leader of the Committee's secretariat saw fit, in the light of the wishes expressed by its members."[117] In other words, the members had to actively request the documents, but all they could discern from the register of received information was when a telegram, letter, report, or other document had arrived and whom it was from; the content was only briefly mentioned. In one egregious example, a telegram sent from Brussels in August was described as suggesting the upcoming hearing of a witness, when—as would later be stated—the hearings had already ended. This telegram had been sent by György Heltai—"the deputy foreign minister," according to one UN document—and the witness was none other than the bodyguard, recently escaped from Soviet captivity, of Pál Maléter, the still imprisoned military leader of the Revolution and minister of defense under Imre Nagy. Heltai had sent the telegram from Brussels because Maléter's fate could not be a matter of indifference to the UN Secretary-General. By this time, it was also evident that arrests of lower level revolutionaries would often be followed by the arrests of more prominent figures. In other words, that the bodyguard had been arrested suggested that the leaders of the Revolution would be the next victims of reprisals.

Because the list made no mention that this cable from Brussels, item 34 on the list of materials, was about Maléter's bodyguard, no member of the Committee had or should have had any interest in it on the register of received documents, so the issue received no attention by the Committee or at the UN. The cable referred to events with enormous implications in the Fő Street Prison in Budapest, however, which concluded with the scaffold and hanging for Pál Maléter. In the meantime Jordan, given the enormous amount of material that had arrived and acknowledging its reception, would have followed standard procedure and asked Hámori to draft one of two letters. One would acknowledge with thanks the information supplied to the UN, adding that it would be circulated among the Committee members; the other would simply acknowledge receipt with thanks, and nothing else. Jordan also devised a protocol for arranging the many documents, news reports, and letters so that they could be at the Special Committee's disposal if requested.

There had been reviews on the full grisly panorama of what the Hungarian government referred to as the process of consolidation: on the cleansing of the Hungarian intellectual elite; on the reorganization of the military and the forces of law and order; on changes to the workings of the press; on the establishment of so-called people's courts, which were nothing but instruments of terror; on certain attorneys being barred from practice;[118] and so on and so forth. The UN had received Tamás Pásztor's reports from Vienna, Pásztor had also assisted the Special Committee during the hearings, and the US Department of State had also shared its information about conditions in Hungary, sometimes including erroneous material like reports of tens of thousands of teenagers being deported to China and Siberia.[119] Over the summer, the secretariat of the Special Committee also had a precise sense of the increasingly strict verdicts of the Hungarian Supreme Court. None of this would have escaped the attention of the secretariat of the Special Committee, but Committee members remained unaware of these events. They would have had to have known of their significance and requested the relevant documents by number.

Many of these documents had a direct bearing on the United Nations' investigation, like minister of state in the revolutionary government István Bibó's statement "on the fundamental values of the state, social and economic order in Hungary, and the path to political progress."[120] Bibó's statement was as good as an outstretched hand to the Soviets, offering a plan of cooperation and gentle consolidation and a proposal for Hungary's peaceful development from the political parties that reemerged in 1956. The response to Bibó would come not from the Soviets but from Budapest. That response would be a sentence of life imprisonment.

The UN Spies Meet Their End

Bibó's message and proposal for progress sent to the United Nations would appear as an "active spy connection" in the indictment of Árpád Göncz, a former revolutionary and second-order plaintiff in the trial against István Bibó, who would receive a life sentence for smuggling papers of Imre Nagy out of Hungary.[121] In other cases death sentences were passed on those charged with spying for the UN, which is a significant detail. The starting point for these tragic events was an unusual one: a UN witness named Alfonz Lengyel—described during the investigation into the "UN spies" as someone "who for a long time had been a confidant of the group associated with the counter-revolutionary committee of five"[122]—requested information through a secret courier from his former fellow prison inmates to be used during the debate at the UN General Assembly. He told Sándor Kiss, one of the 1956 Hungarian émigré leaders, that he had succeeded in establishing contacts in Hungary so his contacts could gain access to information about everything happening there.[123] There is no trace of this initiative among the UN's documents, just as there is little to be learned about Alfonz Lengyel other than that he provided testimony to the Special Committee. But he did leave letters—which in a later statement he described as fakes but which he had in fact written personally—that tell of an émigré with political ambitions who had spent time in prison and had only a partial grasp of reality.[124] Lengyel was an émigré who addressed a letter to a friend in Hungary, Csaba Füzeséry-Nagy, with the words "My dear little Csaba," asking him to take the "Imre Nagy manuscript" from László Kardos, another friend who participated in the Revolution, and smuggle it to the West. Csaba was also asked to provide a description of the political situation in Hungary every two weeks to every month, including what "the Russians" were up to, so this could be reported to the UN. Lengyel also requested that Csaba share any compromising details about Kádár that might be useful during some later change of regime, and he sent instructions about what political roles the defeated revolutionaries in Hungary should play in the future, including how potential ministerial positions should be distributed. He referred to the Bibó plan as a foundation for the withdrawal of Soviet troops but also asked for details about the activities of the army and the locations of ammunition depots, and he requested maps and observations of troop movements. All of these demands clearly went above and beyond the scope of the UN investigation. Indeed, they went in the direction of a potential armed insurrection, which at this time was not a realistic possibility, not even in the form of feeble early preparations for it. According to the investigative documents of the political police, "[Lengyel] urged the former political prisoners who had remained in Hungary to become active again. He promised every assistance for this: money, weapons."[125] In the thinking of the ex-ÁVH officers, the road from information to weapons was a short one, even if the letters had made no mention of the latter.

Lengyel's "little Csaba" was thus tasked with acquiring the reports and getting them out to the West, and to do this by—using the special terminology of the letter, which was designed to extinguish the interest of the political police—finding "Lajcsi," also known as Alajos Czermann, "to build a professional catch-all group of his former buddies."[126] In other words, he had to include his former prison mates in the work of collecting information, the results of which they would pass on to the UN. The documents show that Csaba Füzeséry-Nagy received this commission from Alfonz Lengyel in Vienna in May 1957.[127] The timing was important for the UN debate: although the Special Committee had already left the Austrian capital, at this stage it was still possible that the UN would put the Hungarian question on the agenda before the summer recess or devote a special General Assembly session to it.

As instructed by Lengyel, Füzeséry-Nagy returned to Hungary in secret and sought out László Lukács and Alajos Czermann, his friends from prison. They met at "Lajcsi's" apartment, where Füzeséry-Nagy handed the commission to Lukács, who—as informers reported on the episode—"did not show the slightest enthusiasm[. . . .] He was confronted with a commission that was disorderly and, in many ways, incomprehensible, and which did not seem very serious at all."[128] Lukács and Czermann thought it strange that Füzeséry-Nagy had crossed the border, so they asked György Cziffra, a refugee whom they thought they could rely on, to confirm whether they could trust him. Once they had this confirmation, they placed their trust in the courier, who was in fact a state security agent code-named "Szilvási." Szilvási's brother György—who was brought into the conspiracy under the guise of being a Budapest contact—was given the code name "Regős" by the political police, for which he, too, worked.

Füzeséry-Nagy and his associates were known to state security. The courier had served as a police sublieutenant in the late 1940s until he was dismissed in a disciplinary case; he was then sentenced to seven years in prison for illegal border crossing, for helping prisoners to escape, and for hiking prices and other illegal business activities.[129] Füzeséry-Nagy was soon released from prison for good behavior, as he had in the meantime been recruited as a prison informer, though his handlers had to remind him "not to take the initiative with his cell-mates."[130] He emigrated in 1956, but he retained his connections with the secret police, who made use of his services abroad.

The motivation for the conspiracy was primarily to provide information for the UN, which in another state security document was qualified as conducting "intelligence gathering."[131] It is László Lukács who would have supplied information to the UN, which the courier had to get out of the country. The commission involved a considerable fee, which Füzeséry-Nagy offered Lukács, but it is not mentioned in the documents that Alfonz Lengyel would have been the source of these funds, so it was probably "Szilvási's" real masters, the political police, who financed the clandestine activity. At least this is what is suggested by a later note in which a different division of the Ministry of the Interior asked about where the money had come from.[132] Although the source of the funds remained a mystery, the way they were spent did not: at the meetings of the conspirators, "the consumption of alcohol was at the fore,"[133] and not in small quantities. Thanks to the generous subsidy, the men would spend hours in one drinking establishment after the next. The inclusion of Alajos Czermann and then another friend, Ákos Tumbász, expanded the secret network, and, through their connections, this all appeared in the state security documents as an attempt to mobilize the counterrevolutionary capacities of other social groups and areas of the country.

Lukács was always happy to show off his network of contacts, which "Szilvási" went on to lay out, embellish, make more colorful, important, and dramatic, and pass on to his superiors. In their report of July 1957, the political police stated that "the group has extended contact with the inner districts of Budapest" (meaning that some of them lived there), "with the iron works in Csepel" (which is where Lukács lived), "within the university student population" (referring to Czermann, who was still pursuing his studies), and "to counter-revolutionary circles in Székesfehérvár, Győr and Szombathely."[134]

When "Szilvási" met Lukács again in September 1957, he not only offered money in return for the documents requested by Lengyel but also packages from the aid organization Caritas, which Lukács could pass on to the illegal resistance group.[135] To determine who was to receive aid, they made a list of those in need, which was attached to the investigation documents.[136] Because all this occurred during the period in which the UN had put the Hungarian question on the agenda, the members of the resistance considered protesting or perhaps organizing a strike to counter the state campaign established against the UN report. Füzeséry-Nagy provided material for the protest, which Lukács duplicated on the copying machine of the Catholic congregation in Budafok, Budapest. In this way, the "clerical reaction" also became a focus of the investigation.[137]

At the next meeting, Füzeséry-Nagy handed over documents to Lukács, who, according to the minutes of the investigation, agreed that he would "respond within 2–3 days to the military and UN questionnaires that had been handed over."[138] All this is curious not only because it blurred military questions with the activities of the UN but also, and most of all, because the UN did not introduce any written material into the country other than the official documents it provided to the Hungarian government.

It was of crucial importance to inform the United Nations of the key details of any reprisals, arrests, imprisonments, and other punishments. Some of the information that reached New York could have come from Lukács, just as it could have come from Tamás Pásztor, working in Vienna; from the Freedom Fighters Federation; or even from Alfonz Lengyel, although there is no evidence for this in the documents. As far as state security was concerned, however, anyone who supplied this kind of information was "undertaking clandestine activities for émigré organizations in the pay of the Western powers"[139] and was therefore to be prosecuted and punished. During the investigation, it was proved that "the theoretical basis for their clandestine work was that they hate the state and the social order prevailing in the People's Republic of Hungary";[140] in other words, they were spying out of conviction. The political police had no difficulty finding the origin of this hatred, as these men were "criminals," after all, who had previously been behind bars after being legitimately sentenced by a court. The "former buddies" had mostly been sentenced in the Grősz trial or its associated show trials;[141] it was then revealed that the ringleaders were outright fascists. Lukács and perhaps Ákos Tumbász were members of the Arrow Cross Party from 1939 to 1941, so things had come full circle: fascists were conspiring to overthrow the political system of the People's Republic of Hungary.

The conspirators had committed other crimes besides spying. Tumbász needed an identity card, so he purchased a fake document from Béla László, who had acquired it "at the behest of his handlers,"[142] as he was an agent of the political police. The other agent, Füzeséry-Nagy, supported Tumbász's aspirations as a writer by smuggling his short stories about the Revolution to the *Nemzetőr* (National guard), published in Munich—copies of which Füzeséry-Nagy handed over the political police.[143] As the ÁVH did not even trust its own agents, engineer and former revolutionary Dezső Horváth, who had been brought into the conspiracy, met its members a number of times. Horváth "offered his services" to the police "in the first minutes of his" preventive arrest and so began working in Division II/5 of the Ministry of the Interior, apparently with considerable success, as he was considered for a mission to the West. In this same "Implementation plan," Alajos Czermann was to "be kept under observation with a view to engaging him" as he had excellent connections "in the direction of illegal groups (priests)."[144] At one point in the investigation, the idea emerged of "turning" the leader of the conspiracy,[145] but nothing came of this, even though the plan made it clear just how direct a route there was between facing the gallows and joining the secret police—in one direction, at least.

Lukács, now the leader of the conspiracy and in the grip of a web of agents, was "highly on edge" by this point and feared he was under observation—so reported Füzeséry-Nagy, who was observing him and who was clearly unaware that he himself was being observed. As ordered, Füzeséry-Nagy reproached Lukács for not completing the task entrusted to him, and Lukács began to cry. He then stole the internal telephone directory of Csepel

Works from the porter's desk and handed it to Füzeséry-Nagy. Lukács, who was having financial difficulties, received a further five thousand forints in return for this—an enormous sum at the time. That this volume was "effectively a cipher"[146] was reported by agent "Laczkovics," and although an expert opinion during the investigation stated that the telephone directory was not a confidential document,[147] this would nevertheless become the corpus delicti of the Lukács trial.

According to the documents of the investigation, certain members of the "resistance group" planned to "do away with" a party functionary named Marosán, and although there is no doubt that this leading man in the reprisals was a despised figure, there was likely no opportunity for a successful attempt on his life, and nothing in the documents suggests any preparations for such an action. As the leaders of the secret police were unhappy that Laczkovics "attempted to use provocative methods to achieve results,"[148] it must be considered that this plan, too, was really just hatched in his mind. Soon after, the conspirators organized an armed gathering in a restaurant, which was intended to prove their resolve, although this might also have been a provocation. At this meeting, "Laczkovics" took out his 7.65 mm pistol and put it on the table, telling Lukács that if they were disappointed in him, they could shoot him in the head.[149] When the police learned of the intended "armed operation," civilian officers filled the room in order to keep tabs on events. These officers included the operative asset called "Kockás," whom former inmates knew well from the Budapest Central Detention Facility.[150] The conspirators became suspicious and slipped away; according to records of their recollections, they obtained a radio and spent the night living it up, surely never too far away from a source of alcohol.

The conspirators' suspicions that they were being followed and controlled continued to grow. In January 1958, Füzeséry-Nagy reported to his superiors that Lukács suspected László and Horváth,[151] and Lukács, as the "ringleader," sent a message via "Regős" to "Szilvási" that he should not come back to Hungary, as the secret police were on their tail.[152] This is when Czermann's wife received a message from an acquaintance who had just been released from prison that "everything with Csaba must be halted,"[153] meaning that the courier had also come under suspicion. Not long before this, Füzeséry-Nagy had visited Czermann's wife; together they discussed whether the session of the UN General Assembly might mean that the

Secretary-General would visit Hungary.[154] Before Füzeséry-Nagy left, the woman looked around the street to see if the coast was clear.

Csaba Füzeséry-Nagy had one last task to complete, which was not likely to have been at Alfonz Lengyel's request. He was to acquire information on the position and equipment of the divisions of the Soviet Army and the uranium mines around Pécs in southern Hungary. Lukács's brother-in-law, Ferenc Bajzik, had completed his professional work experience near Pécs, and because he spoke Russian, he would sometimes act as an interpreter for the Soviet military units stationed there.[155] Füzeséry-Nagy and Lukács commissioned Bajzik to acquire this information.[156] By this time, the political investigation division of Baranya County had established contact with the Soviet advisers. Bajzik was being followed and observed by an entire brigade of counterintelligence officers and detectives; his work phone was tapped, his colleagues were questioned, and his every step was recorded.[157] Then, as part of another "operative plan," "Regős" instructed Bajzik to buy a wooden-boxed Soviet pistol for $3,000.[158] This was a violation of military secrets and a serious crime. No one in Hungary could obtain a gun without a prior permit at that time, and Soviet weapons were considered even more sophisticated than Hungarian weapons—not even military personnel could possess those. Yet the fee was a complete fortune to Bajzik, and one that got him four years in prison

The liquidation of the conspiracy was presumably also part of the operative plan, just as its creation had been. The dramaturgy of intimidation, the preparations for the Imre Nagy trial, and the production of suitable evidence likely all played a part in its timing. László Lukács was brought before the Hungarian court in March 1958 on suspicion of illegal intelligence activity, in which the United Nations was mentioned by name.[159] Alajos Czermann was taken into custody, and the warrant for his arrest stated that "a prison agent should accompany him at all times." Czermann's father-in-law and other family members were also put under investigation, and it was ordered that any individual he had named "had to be processed."[160] At this time, Tumbász and his fiancée tried to escape the country. They set off toward the Yugoslav border, but they had been under "close surveillance" since September 1957. As it turned out, "Laczkovics," the erstwhile commander of Corvin Alley, one of the pockets of resistance after the Revolution, had informed on them.[161] Tumbász—identified under the code name "Cingár" in the case files—could hardly have known that his sweetheart

Mariann Forró had also been in the ÁVH's service. Although they were no longer in contact, one of Forró's relatives had been "one of the agents of the Soviet state security authorities" who was being considered for transfer to Hungary.[162] Tumbász and Forró left Budapest on February 21, 1958, at which time, the secret police were already tracing and documenting their every movement and questioning everyone whom they encountered. If the young couple breathed a sigh of relief as they crossed the border into Yugoslavia on February 24, it was premature. The Yugoslav authorities soon handed them over to Hungarian state security.[163]

What happened next would turn this miserable farce into real tragedy. First, there was an ill-tempered correspondence among the various divisions of the Ministry of the Interior as to where the money given to Lukács had come from, who gave the authority for the documents to be smuggled out of the country, whether they had informed the respective departments about the more important details of the operations, and so on. The corroborating report indicated that all events had occurred in accordance within the established guidelines and that Füzeséry-Nagy had not taken the initiative—suspicion that he had done so is precisely what had set the internal investigation in motion.[164] It is telling that the political police did not allow the documents to be used in the investigation; that is, the minutes, correspondence, and reports could not be handed over to the prosecutor's office or the court as the documents would refer to the role the secret services played in the "conspiracy." The ten-page indictment condemned eleven plaintiffs. On September 30, 1958, the Military Court of Budapest sentenced Lukács to death, Tumbász and Czermann to life imprisonment, Mariann Forró to two years in jail, and Ferenc Bajzik to four years in jail.[165] The court considered the crimes to be "of extraordinary danger to society," and Lukács to be "beyond rehabilitation," as an individual who had encouraged others to commit crimes.[166] Lukács was hanged on January 13, 1959, at 7:45 a.m.; the documents state that death set in eight minutes later.[167] Appeals meant that Czermann and Tumbász were also charged, and after a legal objection from Hungary's chief prosecutor, the special council of the military college of the Hungarian Supreme Court increased their sentences from life imprisonment to a death sentence. Then, acting also as an appeals court, the supreme court rejected the request for the appeal of the sentence. On the morning of March 25, 1959, between 8:40 a.m. and 9:00 a.m., Czermann and Tumbász were put to death by hanging.[168]

After their report had been completed, the UN and Special Committee members believed that they had fulfilled their task and knew roughly what to expect when the General Assembly had had the opportunity to discuss it. The Hungarian authorities remained alert to all possibilities, however, and besides preparing for the rebuttal of "unfounded charges" in the UN document, they tightened their grip on society and their citizens, and the general feeling of terror in Hungary grew significantly. There was never any reason for the Hungarian political leaders to fear, however. The UN Secretariat had worked diligently to ease tensions and avoid serious consequences for the Soviet-installed regime, regardless of all the information being sent to New York about the situation in Hungary. Although maintaining peace and commitments to human rights are central to the UN's mission, there was no response to violations of those principles in Hungary after the Revolution. In the face of Soviet aggression, these were responsibilities they did not carry out.

Notes

1. April 26, 1957. MNL XIX-J-21-a, box 33.
2. On June 20, 1957, Mód suggested that "we should criticize the chairman of the committee as being a Nazi collaborator." MNL XIX-J-1-j, box 230.
3. April 23, 1957. MNL XIX-J-24-a, box 3.
4. April 12, 1957. DHS L 179:83. Following the visit, the UK envoy to the UN stated on May 28, 1957, that Hammarskjöld "remains indifferent to the Hungarian issue and is unsympathetic towards the Special Committee." FO 371/128679.
5. DHS L 179:83.
6. April 4, 1957. MNL XIX-J-24-a, box 1.
7. Ibid.
8. April 23, 1957. MNL XIX-J-24-a, box 1.
9. Ibid.
10. Paris discussed with London on April 6, 1957: "Secretary General's inactivity as regards Hungary. French have enquired about our views." The French did not support Hammarskjöld's reelection. FO 371/128676.
11. MNL XIX-J-24-a, box 1.
12. UNARM S-0442-0139-06.
13. HCP, subject 2. "International News Service has obtained exclusively [. . .] the Report only next week distributed [. . .] most intensive and complete immediate investigation of any revolution in history."
14. MNL XIX-J-24-a, box 1.
15. UNARM S-0442-0139-06.
16. MNL XIX-J-24-a, box 1, and MNL XIX-J-1-j, box 56. According to Shann, if the text of the report were to be leaked, Gunewardene might distance himself from it. See the cable from the US delegation in Geneva on April 11, 1957, USNA

320.5764/4-1157. At the same time, and through the British delegation, Shann confidentially supplied the BBC with a copy. FO 371/128679.

17. May 31, 1957. "New developments relating to the Hungarian question." MNL XIX-J-24-a, box 1. See the telegram from the US Mission to the UN on May 22, 1957: "Shann detected lack of enthusiasm in parts of the Secretariat." NARA 310.5/5-2257.

18. Columbia University, Butler Library, Rare Books and Manuscript Collection (hereinafter ACP), box 183.

19. ACP, box 184.

20. UNARM S-0442-0139-06. Gunewardene was called back home on June 3, 1957. In over twelve pages, he listed his objections to the report, some of which the Special Committee accepted. See Shann's telegram of June 6, 1957. FO 371/128679.

21. On June 27, 1957, the Hungarian Mission to the UN sent a report on the Special Committee, saying that the Mission had established contact with Arkadyev when it learned of the differences of opinion within the Committee. The Soviet diplomat then spoke to Gunewardene, who then returned home. MNL XIX-J-24-a, box 1.

22. See the telegram of July 23, 1957, from the US Mission to the UN. USNA 310.5/7-2357. "From Cordier USUN learned Russians and Indians used considerable pressure to try to persuade Gunewardene not to sign Special Committee's report. [. . .] Menon also suggested he should append separate statement saying he agreed with much of report but not concur in all conclusions." See also Joldersma (1966), 187–90.

23. MNL XIX-J-24-a, box 1. See the information received by the US Mission to the UN (from Austrian sources): "[Hammarskjöld] [. . .] does not favor special General Assembly to consider Special Committee report." NARA 310.5/5-1457.

24. *Neue Züricher Zeitung*, June 29, 1957. "[SYG] silent on session [. . .] no comment on eventual GA special meeting." One explanation for Hammarskjöld's silence may have been the Stalinist putsch against Khrushchev that had been thwarted in the summer of 1957: he may have wanted to avoid increasing tensions.

25. Many thousand copies were sold of the UN document, which was also turned into a film. There were dissenting voices, too: on June 28, 1957, *Information* in Copenhagen called the report merely a "historical document" that was nothing other than "the old Munich spirit." NARA 759.00/6-2857.

26. June 21, 1957. The Secretariat also surveyed the *Neue Züricher Zeitung*, the *Herald Tribune*, the *Economist*, and articles in other journals, including those in Yugoslavia and Ceylon. CHP, subject area 2.

27. DHS L 179:84. June 27, 1957.

28. June 27, 1957. ACP, box 183.

29. One reason for this could have been that the US was not in favor of a special General Assembly but had to keep this a secret. See the telephone conversation between the UN secretary of state and Lodge on June 19, 1957: "On the Hungarian business, the Sec[retary of State, Dulles,] said, . . . you have to be awful careful we don't get the monkey pinned on our back that we are in the way." See Glennon, *Foreign Relations of the United States*, 638.

30. DHS L 179:84. June 27, 1957. Cordier to Prince Wan: "No reference was made to exact timing [. . .] the views of many members seem to be centering on suggestion that the Assembly might be reconvened around 10 September."

31. See the reminder of December 30, 1957. Bang-Jensen Archive (hereinafter BJI), box 33. For all this, the FBI took out the files on a few high-ranking UN officials, then determined there was no reason for suspicion.

32. On September 6, 1957, Hoover was told of a "disgruntled employee who may have a grudge against Hammarskjöld and whose charges are regarded as being without substance." BJI, box 33.

33. Waithayakon sent his telegram on August 12, 1957, about accepting the date in September. DHS L 179:84.

34. On June 21, 1957, Georges Delaney, leader of the delegation of US workers, condemned the Soviet Union. Speakers described their decision as a "lead for the UN." CHP, subject area 2.

35. On June 26, 1957. CHP, subject area 2.

36. MNL XIX-J-29 (Washington) and MNL XIX-J-1-j, box 209. Mód reported on the meeting on June 25, 1957.

37. MNL XIX-J-24-a, box 2.

38. See the recollections of Claire de Hedervary (OSZK TIT), Shevchenko, *Breaking with Moscow*; and Kalugin, *First Directorate*.

39. Radványi (1972), 90. "Undercover agent for the communist secret police." See Jordan's note on Péter in September 1957, citing his Nazi past. BJI, box 30.

40. Baráth and Gecsény-I, *Főkonzulok*, 264.

41. MNL XIX-J-24-a, box 3. Szarka put his objections on record on August 20, 1957. MNL XIX-J-1-o.

42. They strove to undermine the Special Committee's "unity of opinion," warning the governments of Ceylon and Tunisia "of the unpleasant situation [. . .] they would find themselves in were they to support the US position." See Endre Sík's notes of August 9, 1957. MNL XIX-J-1-j 00180/46/1957 and MNL XIX-J-24-a, box 3.

43. On September 20, 1957. MNL XIX-J-1-n, box 63. At the Hungarian foreign ministry, officials perused the potential lines of action against the various "capitalist" countries: in the case of Athens, they cited the fate of the Greek minority in Hungary; with Israel, they tried to gain leverage with the reuniting of families; and in the case of Iceland, they threatened to suspend the purchase of fish. Radványi (1972), 79 and MNL XIX-J-1-j, box 56.

44. MNL P 2245, box 3. On this, see Kiss (2018).

45. Zádor sent his report on September 12, 1957. MNL XIX-J-29 (Washington).

46. See the recollections of Sándor Taraszovics. OSZK TIT.

47. MNL XIX-J-41-a.

48. During this key period of the Cold War, the United Nations document played an important role in anticommunist propaganda. See Lieblich, "At Least Something."

49. CHP, subject area 2. September 12, 1957. "Publication and Distribution of Report." "Record Sale Indicated on Report on Hungary," *New York Times*, June 21, 1957.

50. September 17, 1957. Letter to the Secretary-General from B. R. Turner, an accountant. ACP, box 184.

51. See Fry's telegram of July 26, 1957. "The gap between the presentation of the Report and the debate on it has afforded the regime a breathtaking space for

incalculable repression." FO 371/128679. Reuters reported on June 21, 1957: "Budapest Courts Rulings Harsh."

52. CHP, subject area 9. In the words of Shawcross: "legal repression [. . .] increasing." On the basis of reports from the UK ambassador to Budapest, the foreign ministry in London recommended in May that the UN report on a continuous basis on the repression in Hungary, as this might act to restrain it somewhat. See Fry's report of May 24, 1957 ("current reign of terror") and Foster's analysis in London of the same day. FO 371/128679.

53. September 6, 1957. UNARM S-0188-0006-0017. "Note on the Reactions of the Soviet Union and Hungary to the UN Action in the Hungarian Question," thirty-two pages.

54. At the session of the political committee at the end of July, Márta Kolozs, director of the International Organizations Department, stated that there was "partial material" on the witnesses; they had spent weeks trying to identify them. MNL XIX-J-1-j, box 56.

55. An appendix included newspaper articles translated into English and a list of distorted quotations from the report. UNARM S-0188-0006-0017.

56. Ferenc Nezvál's letter, March 19, 1957. MNL XIX-E-1-v. In February 1957, President Dobi, Interior Minister Münnich, and Nezvál called on the leaders of the courts to be merciless in making an example of the accused. See *The Hungarian Situation and the Rule of Law*, 111–17.

57. See Szereda and Sztikalin (1993), 45.

58. MNL XIX-J-1-k 94. As a special publication of the Hungarian News Agency's Confidential Information.

59. MNL XIX-J-24-a.

60. MNL XIX-J-1-k, box 94.

61. See their report of May 30, 1957. Secret police officers were in the majority here, too (Hollai, Szabó, Rácz, Uranovicz), as suggested by their proposal that it be their responsibility to "defend the ÁVH [. . .] the organization had already confronted its crimes in 1956, punished those responsible, had been overhauled, and now only honorable workers and peasants had in its ranks." MNL XIX-J-1-k, box 94.

62. MNL XIX-J-1-k, box 55.

63. MNL XIX-J-24-a and MNL XIX-E-1-v.

64. MNL XIX-J-1-k, box 55.

65. MNL XIX-E-1-v.

66. "Basic material" for the UN General Assembly debate. MNL XIX-J-1-20-a (Brussels). Also see the "Supplement," June 24, 1957. MNL XIX-J-1-k, box 55, and MNL XIX-E-1-v.

67. Ibid.

68. Ibid.

69. MNL XIX-J-24-a.

70. This was handwritten on the proposed statement. MNL XIX-J-1-k, box 56.

71. March 27, 1957. Record of the Directorate of the Ministry of the Interior. MNL XIX-B-1-y, box 1.

72. Ibid.

73. Ibid.

74. Ibid.

75. Minutes of the political committee session on August 21, 1957. MNL M-KS 288. F. storage unit 40.

76. One such occasion was on July 30, 1957. MNL M-KS 288f. Hungarian Socialist Workers' Party (MSZMP) PB document collection, storage unit 5/37.

77. MNL M-KS 288f. MSZMP PB document collection, storage units 4, 88.

78. Ibid., storage unit 5/37.

79. MNL M-KS 288. F. MSZMP PB document collection, storage units 40–44.

80. Ibid.

81. MNL XIX-J-1-k, box 55.

82. Ibid., box 56.

83. Ibid., box 56.

84. Ibid. Károly Szarka had seen burning pyres made up of "the marvels of world literature." See his statement: MNL XIX-J-1-j, box 56. Other sources told of armed fascists flooding in, estimating that of one hundred Red Cross planes, forty carried munitions, while the UN, at Cardinal József Mindszenty's request, wanted to drop "weapons, food and medicine" to the insurgents with parachutes. Had the revolutionaries stood their ground for another three days, the US would have deployed tactical atomic weapons. See Szabó, *Foglalkozásuk emigráns*, 42–51; and Révész, *A béke volt veszélyben*.

85. MNL XIX-J-1-k, box 55.

86. Ibid., box 56.

87. Gál, A *"Jelcin–dosszié,"* 199–200.

88. See the note from Andropov, Rudenko, and Ivashutin on August 26, 1957, on the meeting held with Biszku. Gál, A *"Jelcin–dosszié,"* 199–200. At this time, Andropov was head of the division at the Communist Party of Soviet Union (CPSU) Central Committee.

89. The conference of communist and workers' parties was held November 14–18, 1957, in Moscow. Trials were held for Hungarian writers including Tibor Déry and Gyula Háy.

90. At the end of June 1957, the Secretariat of the Central Committee of the Hungarian Socialist Workers' Party (MSZMP) decided on a comprehensive campaign against the UN's report.

91. The report was a "political attack," in point of fact "the continuation of the attempt to take over power by force of arms," while Imre Nagy had been selected by the West to "usurp the worker's government." Poór and Cseh, "Az ENSZ és Magyarország, 1957," 87–88.

92. September 2, 1957. Documents of the deputy minister of the interior. MNL XIX-B-1-y.

93. MNL XIX-B-1-y, box 2.

94. November 16, 1957. Foreign ministry material for the General Assembly. MNL XIX-J-36.

95. November 1, 1957. Seventy-eight-page overview of Hungarian-American relations. MNL XIX-J-29-o. See the volume titled "The Counter-Revolution in Pictures," also here.

96. Poór and Cseh, "Az ENSZ és Magyarország, 1957," 80–90.

97. MNL XIX-B-1-a, box 31. BM order no. 43.

98. Ibid.

99. Radványi (1972), 32.

100. October 19, 1957. "Measures to secure the Foreign Ministry from 21 October to 7 November 1957." MNL XIX.-J-1-n, box 72.

101. See, for example, the instructions given to the Hungarian mission in Belgium on June 19, 1957. MNL XIX-J-20-a.

102. See the August 31, 1957, article in *Népszabadság*.

103. Gál, A *"Jelcin–dosszié,"* 170.

104. Ibid., 146–69.

105. Ibid., 90–91.

106. Ibid., 130–31.

107. MNL XX-10-k.

108. Hungary was liberated from fascism on April 4, 1945.

109. April 10, 1957. Ministry of the Interior summary report. Archive of the deputy minister of the interior. MNL XIX-B-1-y.

110. MNL XIX-J-1-j, box 82. "The Continuing Challenge of the Hungarian Situation to the Rule of Law."

111. See "Justice in Hungary. International Commission of Jurists. 3rd Report." MNL XIX-B-1-y box 82.

112. On June 27, 1957, the Hungarian ambassador to London reported what was said. MNL XIX-J-1-j, box 82.

113. CHP, subject area 9.

114. The term given by the UN to the dossiers containing all the documents it was sent.

115. CHP, subject area 11.

116. CHP, subject area 11.

117. UNARM S-0370-0041-02.

118. CHP, subject area 9. June 6, 1957. "Purge of Hungarian intellectual life," then "Julius von Mathe, major testimony about the army." March 13, 1957. "Situation and Development of Hungarian Press after the Revolution." The label on the folder reads: "Confidential: Read and Destroy. Source: Vienna."

119. The US Mission to the UN sent its report on the situation in Hungary on May 2, 1957; on May 6, Senator Hruska spoke of the deportation of 46,000 Hungarian teenagers. CHP, subject area 9.

120. Gál, A *"Jelcin–dosszié,"* 164.

121. ÁBTL 3.1.9. V-150352/2. One of the charges against Bibó was that he had requested foreign military force against his homeland. See the reports of the US embassy. NARA 764.00/6-1157. The British ambassador to Hungary learned on May 29 of Bibó's arrest. FO 371/128679.

122. ÁBTL 3.2.5. O-13111.

123. See Alfonz Lengyel's letter of July 22, 1957: "I received highly valuable information about Hungary. A smuggler I was in prison with brought it out to me. I was able to establish highly valuable contact with the resistance organization in Csepel." RL C/243.

124. The letters were handwritten and addressed to "An Herrn Csaba Füzeséry-Nagy." ÁBTL 3.2.5. O-13111.

125. Ibid.

126. Ibid.

127. ÁBTL V-146247/2. Füzeséry-Nagy is mostly mentioned in the documents as F. Nagy.

128. The report was dated June 23, 1957, and refers to the meeting of June 4, at which Czermann and the others met Füzeséry-Nagy. On June 7, 1957, "Szilvási" (the code name for Csaba Füzeséry-Nagy) claimed that he had come back from Salzburg and that he had a good relationship with the Freedom Fighters Federation. ÁBTL 3.1.5. O-12132.

129. ÁBTL 3.1.9. V-53273. According to the documents, one of his brothers was an ÁVH detective.

130. He was sentenced in 1953, and on April 10, 1954, they reported that "we have engaged him as a prison informer [. . .] he has already worked on numerous cases." ÁBTL 3.1.9. V-53273.

131. Record, April 10, 1958. "They conducted spying activities for Western powers against the Hungarian People's Republic." ÁBTL V-146247.

132. Sublieutenant József Szalma (II/2 section) requested that this be clarified. ÁBTL V-146247/2.

133. ÁBTL V-146247.

134. Ibid.

135. Ibid.

136. Ibid.

137. Ibid.

138. Ibid.

139. ÁBTL V-146247. In late July, Lukács pleaded his guilt.

140. ÁBTL V-146247.

141. A case was brought against József Grősz, archbishop of Kalocsa, based on trumped-up charges, and he was sentenced in 1951. Twenty-four associated cases were also tried, leading to more than two hundred sentences. Lukács was in prison from 1953 to 1956 for incitement. In the Grősz case, Czermann was sentenced to fifteen years in prison; indeed, he had been released "illegally" on October 27, 1956, so he was taken into custody on July 4, 1957. ÁBTL V-146247.

142. ÁBTL V-146247. Béla László fought at Corvin Alley in Budapest. While in prison, he was recruited after the detectives "had found highly compromising documents [. . .] in his case the most severe sentence was to be expected."

143. ÁBTL V-146247.

144. ÁBTL 3.1.5. O-12132.

145. Ibid.

146. "Laczkovics," who also mentions a letter written to Gergely Pongrácz, leader of the Corvin Alley resistance, reported this on December 6, 1957. ÁBTL 3.1.5. O-12132.

147. See the expert opinion of May 28, 1958, from staff at the Ministry of Smelting and Mechanical Industry. Their observations were not taken into consideration, which precisely reflects the trumped-up nature of the proceedings. ÁBTL V-146.247.

148. This note was attached to "Laczkovics's" report dated December 10, 1957. On one document is written "an agent should never initiate." ÁBTL 3.1.5. O-12132.

149. They met in a tavern in December 1957. "Péter Kovács" informed on "Laczkovics"; that is, one agent reported on the other. ÁBTL 3.1.5. O-12132.

150. Ibid.

151. Lukács's suspicions can have been raised when Béla László was let out of prison, even though the charges against him were highly serious. ÁBTL 3.1.5. O-12132.

152. Ibid.

153. The report of November 30, 1957, is from the agent "Pál Kovács." ÁBTL 3.1.5. O-12132.

154. The woman's maiden name was Mariann Forró; she was known to the ÁVH. ÁBTL 3.1.5. O-12132.

155. ÁBTL V-146247.

156. They reported on the operation on September 10, 1957, when, in addition to the data on the uranium mine, Lukács promised a description of the Budaörs and Ferihegy airports and information on "military metals." Lukács requested payment for this. ÁBTL 3.1.5. O-12132.

157. March 8, 1958. ÁBTL V-146247/1.

158. This idea was raised on January 25, 1958. This was also when they decided on the arrests, which had to be arranged without the agents' covers being revealed. ÁBTL V-146247.

159. ÁBTL V-146247.

160. ÁBTL 3.1.5. O-12132.

161. Corvin Alley (Corvin köz) was a focus of the armed resistance in Budapest in 1956. The "Summary report" created on September 21, 1957, described Tumbász's "movements," and an "operative plan" was put into place after his escape on February 11. ÁBTL 3.1.5. O-12132.

162. Ibid. Tumbász had previously married Mariann Forró at a secret church wedding. ÁBTL V-146.247.

163. Ibid.

164. On May 27, 1958, police lieutenant colonel József Szalma, director of the II/2 Division, asked about the permissions and the money, then on June 5, he received a reply: the agent did not initiate, everything took place with the knowledge of the relevant department, and everything had been agreed on with the director of the II/8 (counterintelligence) Division. ÁBTL V-146.247.

165. Ibid.

166. September 30, 1958. ÁBTL V-146.247. They added that the reason they "undertook to perform spying activities" was for the information they gleaned to be used at the UN General Assembly, which satisfies the criteria for high treason, while slander in the eyes of an inimical international power serves "drastically to increase the danger to society" of the crimes in question. HL—Military Court of Budapest 0054/1958 (d. 680).

167. See the record of the enactment of the sentence. ÁBTL 2.1.5. O-13111.

168. ÁBTL V-146.247/1.

6

THE REPORT OF THE SPECIAL
COMMITTEE ON THE UN AGENDA

Preparations for the Presentation of the
Report and Its Controversies

In September 1957 in New York, the opening of the fourteenth session of the United Nations General Assembly brought Hungary into focus, as the time had come for the report of the UN Special Committee on the Problem of Hungary to be presented—albeit an entire session later than the deadline stated in the General Assembly resolution in January of that year.[1] There were other important issues on the UN agenda, if nothing quite like the Hungarian question: the Suez Crisis had been resolved and the drama in the Congo had not yet become a tragedy. Alongside these topics for discussion were the easing of nuclear confrontation, proposals for worldwide disarmament, and the peaceful colonization of outer space.

As the summer passed, there was no special General Assembly and there were no further reports from the Special Committee, even though these were prescribed by a valid resolution of the General Assembly. What had happened, had happened and could not be changed, but in the summer of 1957, many of the horrific consequences of the Hungarian consolidation could still have been prevented: retribution, threats, reprisals, executions, broken promises, and the dismantling of the achievements of the Revolution. All of these occurred unimpeded in a fast and irreversible succession of events.

From the outset, it was part of the remit of the Special Committee to pay attention to and document the situation in Hungary. The Committee

203

compiled a list of points for consideration, which included the need "to prepare additional reports,"[2] and for this reason information needed to be gathered, so ongoing events could be made known to the General Assembly and the member states.

After the report was published, Special Committee Secretary William Jordan prepared for work of the Committee to continue, although the conditional language in one of his letters suggested he was not sure that the General Assembly's resolution would be observed. In early July, he informed UN Under-Secretary-General Dragoslav Protitch that "we need to do a certain amount of work" on the Hungarian question, but only "in the event the Committee decides to sit again."[3] And the Committee could hardly decide otherwise, so soon after the report was published, Chair of the Special Committee on the Problem of Hungary Alsing Andersen said he was "highly interested in the next step." This next step could only have been to prepare a supplementary report on recent events. Andersen knew that the UN had copious material, as the lists of documents had been circulated among the members of the Committee, so he recommended that the secretariat of the Special Committee prepare an outline by August 15 that the members of the Special Committee could accept. He also asked Jordan to contact Rapporteur Mick Shann and the other members and to get to work as quickly as they could.

Under-Secretary-General Protitch was also amassing piles of notes on the situation in Hungary, organized by date and sometimes by subject, reporting on the increasingly dramatic developments.[4] It was at this time that the International Committee of the Red Cross, always cautious and apolitical, informed the United Nations that between July 5 and July 20, the Hungarian authorities had taken three thousand people into custody and reopened an unused prison to house them. In vain, the Red Cross had requested information on the circumstances of those held, and although it assisted their families, this helped only the symptoms, not the cause of their distress. The International Committee of the Red Cross turned to the UN hoping it might help to solve the problem.[5]

Then something happened, the meaning of which was unclear, that had immediate consequences. The UN leadership contravened the resolution of the General Assembly. The ever-cautious Jordan later referred to a discussion in which he was informed of the decision that there would be no more reports. He had good reason to conjure up this memory, as the decision meant that the sabotaging of the General Assembly resolution would

Dragoslav Protitch, Under-Secretary-General of the UN, with Secretary-General Dag Hammarskjöld (*left*) and President of the General Assembly Wan Waithayakon (*middle*). Copyright: UN Photo Archive #7769339.

have to come from him. In his letter to Protitch of July 16, Jordan quoted Under-Secretary-General of the UN Andrew Cordier saying the question of the supplemental report was "pretty well out of the question," and so only the most minimal of conditions could be provided for work to continue.[6] As Andersen's position on continuing with supplemental reports was clear, Jordan contacted Shann, suggesting he disregard the Chair's instruction to prepare the outline for an additional report by August 15. In fact, Jordan wrote both Andersen and Shann a letter, the draft of which he first sent to Cordier and Protitch, emphasizing in a cover note that he was not mentioning to Andersen and Shann that it was Cordier and Protitch who did "not think it wise" to come forward with another report. So there might be no suspicion that the decision had been made at the highest level, Jordan added that, after discussions with UN Secretary-General Dag Hammarskjöld, he would present the proposal to Andersen and the other Committee members as his own, "without any indication of its being an official view of the

Secretary General or of the Secretariat."[7] It is clear that Jordan put this to paper in order to record that he was acting under orders in what was to come: it was made to be seen by those who had given him his instructions but also to make it clear that he was not going to reveal who they were.

Jordan's implementation of the requests from UN leadership on the thirty-eighth floor enabled the General Assembly resolution to be contradicted. The key figure in all this would be Shann, who had considerable prestige as the purported author of the report, even if insider gossip suggests that he played no real role in either writing or editing it and was disinterested to the point of irresponsibility throughout its preparation.[8] Hammarskjöld then wrote a letter to Shann, emphasizing in response to Andersen's suggestion that as Secretary-General he himself could not turn against the suggestion to proceed with supplemental reports.[9] From this, Shann understood that this task would fall to him. He responded immediately that he was "strongly opposed" to any steps that could lead to further reports, that further reports could hardly produce any content of value, and that he did not want to "begin to skate on the thin ice of domestic jurisdiction." He warned Jordan that the secretariat must not circulate documents related to the issuance of supplemental reports among the Committee members without the Rapporteur's agreement and that he was not willing to take part in any such operation.[10] It remained only for the Secretary-General to acknowledge that, regarding Andersen's proposal, he agreed with Shann—which is to say with himself.[11] Meanwhile, Jordan made it clear that he would not pass any documents on to the Committee members unless deliberately instructed to do so by Shann,[12] who was opposed to doing so. Things had come full circle.

Jordan replied to Andersen that he was ready to continue as he wished but added that the details of the plan were the purview of the Rapporteur—even though he knew as well as anyone that this had previously been the job of the secretariat. He expressed his concerns about changes to the domestic situation in Ceylon, saying that the head of the Ceylonese UN Mission, Sir Senerat Gunewardene, was hardly in a position to add his name to another report;[13] as it happened, however, the International News Service had at this very moment reported that the indecisive Gunewardene, the butt of domestic political attacks, considered it important to publish a further report before the General Assembly in September.[14] Tunisian UN representative Mongi Slim, meanwhile, suggested to the US State Department that the Special Committee request entry into Budapest.[15] The saboteurs had to go looking for a new excuse for putting a stop to further reports.

At the end of July, Andersen repeated his suggestion for further report-ing to Jordan, adding that if the secretariat had no new information at its disposal other than what was in the papers about incarcerations, executions, and deportations, then the evidence at hand could be used to compose the additional report. He asked the staff to put together twenty to thirty pages of material limited to a survey of the facts.[16] Jordan assured Andersen that the Special Committee secretariat was "keeping abreast with current devel-opments," but he added that the information at its disposal was "relatively slender" and that another report might deflect attention from the main re-port. He concluded his letter by saying that in the absence of guidance from the General Assembly, they were unsure what the right subject for such a document might be.[17]

This was all despite the fact that Jordan was aware of the January 1957 General Assembly resolution that established the Special Committee and that it was Jordan who received information on the devastating situation in Hungary. The member states took the resolution literally: the US an-nounced at a press conference that it would ask for the Special Committee to continue its work and requested that the UN refresh its report, with the submission of a new document if necessary. From US sources in Budapest it was learned just how much oppression in Hungary had increased, so the UN had to deal with all of this and demand an end to political persecution.[18]

When, months later, the Secretary-General was asked about possible further reports, he responded that the Special Committee would have to decide on this matter when it had adequate information at its disposal.[19] This, as if he were unaware that it was he and his inner circle, not the Special Committee, who had to decide on whether to produce further reports, and that he and his associates had more than adequate information on hand—where "adequate" meant not just the amount of evidence but also the degree to which it was shocking and devastating.

Expectations Concerning the UN's Actions
in Hungary and New York

In Budapest, the moment of truth never came: the Soviets never packed up, and UN observers were never sent to oversee a new, democratic election. Nor were the delegates of the Hungarian usurper government ejected from the UN in New York, nor were sanctions considered for those who had con-travened UN resolutions. As a result, the puppet government was effectively rendered legitimate by the silence of the United Nations. The anti–United

Nations campaign was just reaching its peak in Budapest when president of the Presidential Council István Dobi signed the credentials of the Hungarian delegation traveling to the General Assembly.[20] According to the leaders of the foreign ministry staff, there was no greater question for Hungary than the "UN affair,"[21] which official communication nevertheless tried to trivialize as a rear-guard action of the counterrevolution, an attempt at imperialist intervention, and a provocation contravening the UN Charter.

Minister of Foreign Affairs Imre Horváth would later remember this session as a time when even their friends would be cautious about being on speaking terms with him and his staff and when Deputy Foreign Minister Endre Sík would lose all his US acquaintances at once, yet the Hungarian delegation "could look anyone in the eye" at the UN, showing no remorse and no fear.[22] Hammarskjöld was present with his deputies at the reception hosted by the Hungarian delegation,[23] nine days before the first anniversary of the Revolution.

Thanks to the report of the Special Committee, UN member states were given a detailed and comprehensive picture of all that had taken place in Hungary; the General Assembly, meanwhile, drew attention to the historical outrage and the ever deepening and bloodstained process of consolidation. The floor speeches at the debate did not treat the Kádár regime with kid gloves, although there was no official UN document that described everything that had happened since the Revolution, including the ways in which Hungary had infringed basic human rights and contravened the UN Charter. The previous eleven months had effectively proven that these infringements were by no means coincidental but reflected Kádárist policy; they were not exceptions but the rule.

At the General Assembly, the Hungarian delegation presented no defense or argument against nor contradiction of the accusations of the historical outrage; instead, it went on the attack, employing angry rhetoric and claiming imperialist influence, fascist revenge, and an attempt to reconstruct the old order.[24] The so-called fraternal countries prepared for the debate in the same spirit, with a precise order of operations that involved regular consultations and requests for documents from Hungarian diplomats, who were happy to take the opportunity to share outrageous propaganda.[25] With the illogic of the Stalinist show trials, they not only constructed systems that defied common sense—like a communist-led fascist uprising—but also denied events that had been authenticated, reconstructed, and documented, as the report had painted a precise picture of the

Revolution, supported by copious evidence. Yet the Hungarian representatives of the Kádár regime and those of the fraternal countries insisted these accounts and the evidence for them were fabrications and contradicted the claims of the report with "documentation" of their own.

The work of the Special Committee came to a close with tangible achievements, but its fate and further mandate had not been settled.[26] It was not disbanded, but it did not receive support, nor was it given any assignments. The reasons for this might have been that Ceylon's participation was "unlikely," or that Tunisia's role was uncertain—as Hammarskjöld would tell Péter Mód.[27] But another consideration is more likely to have explained this impasse: the impending reelection of the Secretary-General over the course of this session, which required the unanimous support of the great powers. As Mód reported to Budapest, this was why Hammarskjöld "avoids any question he cannot solve to universal approval."[28] While this behavior was understandable, it was also at odds with Hammarskjöld's mandate, for just as the Hungarian question could not be settled "to universal approval," nor could any similar international conflict be resolved.

Later a play in Budapest theater would present the atmosphere of the UN debate on the report as a "struggle" to defend "workers' power" and portray it as a heroic battle on the part of the Hungarian delegation.[29] The truth was much more peaceful, for while some two thousand protesters stood guard outside UN Headquarters as the Hungarian question was being debated there,[30] they were kept at a careful distance from the diplomats, and the Hungarian delegation was protected by the police from any potential assaults. That Sík and Horváth considered this harassment and restrictive displayed a paranoia cloaked in the garb of ideology; yet they took it for granted that they could use all the resources provided by the institution they were slandering and battling against. They were instructed to become involved in the work of the committees of the General Assembly—the terms the Hungarian secret service used in their instructions were "infiltrate" and "penetrate"[31]—and the UN was not shy about providing equal opportunities for a member state that had ridden roughshod over its resolutions and that had had its mandate suspended.

The UN leadership sensed that the "attitude of the Hungarian government" toward the UN had "undergone a certain hardening," noting that after a brief decline in September because of the General Assembly session, in October, the number of arrests, imprisonments, and trials in Hungary began to increase again.[32] It was as if the leadership in Budapest wished to use the hostage Hungarian population to establish how the UN was not in a position to help, but could, on the other hand, cause only harm. UN analysts established that the Hungarian government had succeeded in maintaining order and calm, in some places coming to an agreement with the downtrodden and improving their circumstances. Meanwhile, Hungary's leaders blamed the events of 1956 on so-called revisionism and Western intervention rather than on the Stalinists—who also happened to make up the majority of the current Hungarian delegation in New York.

The General Assembly again condemned the Soviet Union's armed intervention and the infringement of the UN Charter with its votes and mentioned the deportations. Hungary was criticized for ignoring UN resolutions—just as had happened a year previously, with nothing in the way of consequences, either then or later. The foreign ministry in Budapest followed the vote with interest and lodged complaints in a number of cities, looking for fault in the countries that had voted for condemnation.[33] During this same session, Hammarskjöld was reelected by a large majority.

And there was another election: the selection of and mandate for the Special Representative who kept the Hungarian question on the agenda[34] and who was responsible for observing the situation that had developed—and was still developing—in Hungary and proposing solutions. The UN leadership recommended the outgoing General Assembly President Prince Wan Waithayakon of Thailand for the post. He was a well-respected intellectual from the developing countries with considerable diplomatic experience. Perhaps the leaders did not consider that his princely heritage might be a disadvantage when communicating with communists—or perhaps this was a deliberate choice, following the same strategy as with the nomination of Andersen and providing the opportunity for opponents to make future attacks on the selected candidate.

According to the General Assembly resolution of September 16, 1957, Prince Wan Waithayakon's commission was to follow and observe the developments in Hungary, take the steps deemed necessary, and report to the General Assembly.[35] The Special Representative accepted the mandate and made progress as requested, step by step, which, he announced, would take time.[36] With time, he established contact with the Soviet and Hungarian foreign ministries, neither of which had accepted the United Nations' jurisdiction on the Hungarian question, as they had repeatedly made clear. They would not even take receipt of Waithayakon's long-worded memorandum, as Endre Sík would recall with not a little perverse pleasure. The prince would have liked to have resolved the conflict using the method of quiet diplomacy, a policy Hammarskjöld also trusted, only the silence was so pervasive in Waithayakon's work that there is not a trace of it to be found in the files. According to Hungarian deputy foreign minister Sík's memoir, as soon as Sík explained to Waithayakon what had happened in Hungary in 1956, the prince gave up on his "intentions to interfere"; indeed, he became convinced of the "good intentions" of the Hungarian government, as he "was well aware of its beneficial activities."[37] According to Sík's recollections, Waithayakon ultimately wanted to travel to Hungary and report on the situation as he saw it, thereby easing "the inimical atmosphere that had developed" with regard to the Hungarians.[38] Whether this was diplomatic cunning, deceit, or simply idiocy on the part of the memoir writer we cannot know. As Sík remembers it, the prince withdrew the "submission" of his memorandum, thanking the Hungarian politicians for saving him from "making a fool of himself."[39]

At about this time, the recently reelected Secretary-General learned that Danish international civil servant Povl Bang-Jensen had suspected that the Soviets were influencing actions on the thirty-eighth floor. This did not seem to surprise Hammarskjöld, suggesting he must have heard about this before. It must have been strange for him, however, to be given this news by the leaders of the US delegation: Bang-Jensen had contacted them previously with his confidential information, and the leaders of the United States Mission to the United Nations wanted to warn Hammarskjöld of the Danish employee's accusation. For them, maintaining "cordial relations"[40] with Hammarskjöld, who had just been reaffirmed in his post for another five years, was a higher priority than protecting a diplomat who had brought security concerns to their attention. In return for sharing the information, the US asked that the UN leadership not lose sight of the Hungarian question or, at least, that an "impression" of it remain—to which Cordier nodded his approval.[41]

The first anniversary of the 1956 Revolution was a dramatic evocation of everything that had happened in Hungary, then and since. On October 24, 1957, the UN Secretariat put together a document on the Hungarian situation, which Jordan passed on to the Special Committee: "It may be useful to Prince Wan to have a copy."[42] We do not know if Prince Wan read it or not, just as we do not know whether he knew of political thinker István Bibó's proposal that he received the following day, as there is no sign of this in his record of activities. Soon Hammarskjöld would also see that the quiet diplomacy of "our prince" had had no effect at all and would state that "Under Prince Wan's benign Buddha smile Hungary is more or less forgotten."[43]

At this time, Hungary was still in a state of emergency that would only be lifted after the first anniversary of the Revolution had passed. The punishment for striking was death. The number of arrests and trials continued to grow. Many of the victims of Kádár's campaign of revenge had not yet been executed. The Hungarian government intended to raise a formal objection with the countries that played a role in "preparing the counter-revolution." Officials considered expelling British ambassador Leslie Fry and French cultural attaché Guy Turbet-Delof in the hope that the flow of news might dwindle.[44] In January 1958, Hungarian social democrat Anna Kéthly, Hungarian military officer Béla Király, and Budapest mayor József Kővágó wrote a joint letter to Prince Waithayakon, listing concrete instances of the Kádárist campaign of terror, informing the Special Representative that the workers' councils had been made illegal, and drawing attention to the fate of revolutionary leader József Dudás and Minister of Defense Pál Maléter.[45] There is no response to be found among the documents.

When Waithayakon reported to the General Assembly in early December, he was only able to list "little steps" taken, formal gestures made, and not much else.[46] This may have been the reason the Special Committee, in session again, observed that the General Assembly had not taken any action on Waithayakon's report. The Committee confirmed that, although it had not been given any official instructions, it was ready to cooperate with the prince.[47] In their own diplomatic way, both statements are significant.

The UN Secretariat, meanwhile, came to the decision that it would not publish any more General Assembly documents on the Hungarian question; letters and other materials received appeared only on the Committee list.[48] In other words, the Secretariat would not make any documents public, would not circulate them among the Committee members or UN member states, and would not even send them to the Special Representative. Hungary was not just forgotten; it was deliberately consigned to oblivion.

Behind the Scenes: The Secret Agents

All of this was on the surface, however. To this day, we can only guess as to what processes were going on below. This is true not just of the UN's procedures and unique working methods but also of the actions of the Hungarian delegation as seen through secret service documents, because they too were subject to the same universal suspicion: Stalinist methods meant that even the most loyal employees were under observation. What were they doing, what were they thinking, and what weaknesses did they have for which they could be blackmailed, discredited, or compromised? Péter Mód's chauffeur "Szalai" reported on his New York boss to his real superiors in Budapest, who gave Szalai his instructions.[49] Regular reports were sent on every employee, delegate, or interpreter, sometimes by their closest colleagues, who might be unaware they were informing on an ÁVH officer who was above them in rank.

Woven into the entirety of the system were secret missions: the wife of one secret service agent managed the telephone switchboard, while another did the cleaning, thereby preparing a distinctly intimate study of the members of the mission. Leather coats comrades took back to Hungary were documented, as was any "lack of alertness" when office assistants—themselves sometimes secret service agents—were able to look at confidential papers.[50] Reports were often requested on the behaviors, conversations, pastimes, and purchases of diplomats and their companions once they had left Hungary[51]—those still at home were at the nadir of the shortage economy, after all, with no hope for most consumer goods. In detailed reports, there is mention of Hungarian intelligence officer and UN Mission member Imre Hollai just as there is of Jenő Randé, a press attaché accused of participation in the Arrow Cross, the typist, and the accountant. Every piece of information was seen as needed and was stored, processed, and added to the documents on "personnel work," a file the foreign ministry personnel officer did not have access to.

Secret service reports included insinuations, accusations, and libelous claims, including the charge that most of the foreign ministry staff traveling to New York were of bourgeois or petit bourgeois background, something that was problematic not just in the rhetoric of the age but also in practice. The leaders of the foreign ministry's department dealing with the UN were examples of those accused of nepotism: Edit Konrád was described as a "petit bourgeois," while Márta Kolozs was a "selfish bourgeois" whose career was paved by her being the sister-in-law of Hungarian deputy foreign minister István Sebes.[52] After a secret agent submitted a report, they were reminded of their task: "The description of compromising pieces of information on well-known employees of the foreign ministry."[53]

It was in Vienna that the most successful secret service operation relating to the General Assembly debate and the report of the Special Committee was conducted. Its effect was all the more significant because the ÁVH's role in it remained a secret for so many years. The main player in the carefully planned and perfectly timed charade was a "disenchanted" Hungarian smallholder politician called Miklós Szabó, who was living as an émigré in Austria. Szabó's determination to return home to Hungary was given impetus when he realized that his homeland had simply been a tool for the US imperialism that was behind the UN's actions. This was why the UN smeared Hungary's good name, and this was why it used base manipulation, blackmail, threats, and payouts to create UN documents that its "voting machine" (a term of communist propaganda) at the UN turned into resolutions. And he would now be able to reveal the full truth. After all, he knew the circumstances that led to the report being published—for as one of the leaders of the Hungarian émigré community, he had played an active part in the preparations for it. All Szabó's actions were masterminded by the secret service leadership at the center of the political police in Budapest. Szabó pretended he was acting alone, while in fact he was executing orders from Moscow via Budapest.

Miklós Szabó took on the role of someone who broke away from the innermost circle of the émigré community to return to Hungary as a "bourgeois" politician and proud patriot, and the secret service had been willing to sacrifice one of its most successful agents for this purpose. Szabó had escaped to the West before 1956, infiltrated the leadership of the Hungarian émigré community, welcomed the 1956 refugees to Austria, been given a role in giving them aid and lodging, and had overseen and documented their affairs, including the workings of the Special Committee in Vienna.

Szabó began his political career in the coalition era as an activist for the Smallholders' Party, a conservative yet popular political group in pre- and post–World War II Hungary. This allowed him to come into contact with leading party members and earn the trust of Prime Minister Ferenc Nagy. In fact, Szabó had been on armed security duty outside the party headquarters under Nagy's leadership; after the communist takeover, Szabó was horribly broken by the ÁVH because of his military role and his stubbornness. His interrogators developed special tactics just for him[54] and as a result of this torture, he became the prison snitch and was released with an amnesty a few years later. The condition for his release was his continued work as an agent, so, after thorough training, he was posted to the West: his seeming escape from the Stalinist dictatorship appeared heroic when in fact it was just a well-prepared secret service operation.[55] His backstory and his adept political instinct won over émigré leaders, and following the Revolution, he was assigned by the UN High Commission for Refugees to welcome refugees, give them aid, and help them with their further journeys.[56] He enjoyed the trust of Anna Kéthly, Béla Király, and Sándor Kiss, and took part in the creation and then leadership of the Strasbourg Revolutionary Council, an umbrella organization for Hungarian refugees. He joined the work of the UN Special Committee in Vienna and helped in the selection and preparation of witnesses and in organizing their hearings.

A few months later, he suddenly disappeared from Vienna, causing considerable concern, as he had "been afraid" he was being watched and that he might be forcibly abducted, dragged home, and executed. Not even his closest colleagues had spotted that he had been arranging his documents for days beforehand. For he did not leave unprepared: he took almost all documentation of his activities with him. When he surfaced in Budapest, his friends put his homecoming down to his understandable bitterness and disappointment. They even saw it as a sign of his honesty that he said he had not brought his newly purchased car with him because there were still payments due on it.[57] The truth, of course, was that Szabó did not know how to drive, and though on many an occasion he had complained to émigré leaders of his trifling financial woes, he had nevertheless bought a sports car, in the interests, he stressed, of the efficient and unimpeded execution of his duties. Though the car remained in Austria, this was not true of a huge number of documents; this aroused suspicion, so Béla Király and Anna Kéthly hurried to Vienna to assess the damage.[58]

Szabó became the star of a media campaign in Budapest. His "exposé" of the Special Committee blended libel, demagoguery, and a mass of impossible constructions that combined with specific details gave a veneer of authenticity to his stories. A summary of his international press conference found its way to Hammarskjöld; in this briefing Szabó had listed the manipulations of the "imperialists," the fake nature of the Special Committee's report, the money used to prop up its lies, and the blackmail behind its findings, together with information from the innermost circles of the émigré community on its internal conflicts, intrigues, and grievances.

With more than a touch of schadenfreude, Hungarian ambassador Frigyes Puja announced from Vienna that Szabó's departure was surrounded by shock and confusion—not to mention fear, as they believed that he had in his possession the list of those who had given anonymous testimony to the Special Committee.[59] The ambassador claimed that because of this, many émigrés were afraid for their loved ones back in Hungary,[60] as news had started coming through that arrests had begun. This last claim came from former prison agent Tamás Pásztor, who had been in Szabó's apartment and had noticed that "he had taken an immense amount of documents home with him, notebooks, lists of names, whole dossiers of correspondence."[61] And his papers would not only include the names of family members still in Hungary but also the forms and channels of illegal contact—which could have consequences in criminal law.

Among the documents brought to Hungary was a "Note" on Szabó's connections with just about every significant member of the émigré community, from Béla Varga, the last speaker of the freely elected Parliament and a prominent émigré in the US; to smallholder politician János Horváth; to Király, Kővágó, and Sándor Kiss. A huge number of contacts were listed, together with their addresses, telephone numbers, and descriptions of varying lengths and levels of detail, all of which made particular mention of their potential weaknesses.[62] Another document, titled "Additional Notes by Miklós Szabó," included receipts, acknowledgments, photos, letters, and documents relating to refugee camps, schools, and students who had emigrated. These contained a wealth of confidential information.[63] The political police's greatest leverage, however, was that "it had the list of names of those interviewed" by the UN Special Committee,[64] which the Hungarian ambassador to Vienna had reported to the foreign ministry in Budapest until, in the face of growing concern over leaks and reprisals, Pásztor wrote: "I have, securely stored, the list of UN witnesses, and neither Miklós Szabó nor any other unauthorized person can have seen it."[65] Concern over the list becoming public was well-founded, but the claims about the whereabouts of the list of names were untrue. Bang-Jensen had the only copy of them.

Pásztor and Szabó may have had some kind of list, of course, as they were both involved in the work of the Special Committee in Vienna. One refugee who worked as an ÁVH agent remembered how Pásztor "brought forward the witnesses [. . .] He regularly went in to see Paul Bank Jensen [*sic*],"[66] whom the agent among the émigrés described as an administrator and prosecutor. He added that Pásztor not only produced the witnesses; he even "prepared the witness statements"[67]—a claim that was present among Szabó's aspersions.

It was at the security agencies that the strands all came together, for Tamás Pásztor had previously been a secret agent under the code name Kálmán Katona. In prison, he had begun as a simple, low-level snitch, then—as a condition for his release—he had continued his work as an informant during the Revolution. Up until October 29, he "regularly provided telephone reports."[68] If he did not do so after this time, this was because it was more expensive to call from Vienna—for he had meanwhile traveled to the Austrian capital. Before doing so, he had reorganized the Smallholder Party group in Budapest's second district, but Ministry of the Interior documents show that he had taken on a more serious project: the Hungarian secret service had placed Pásztor in internal law enforcement, which allowed him to "follow our advice and suggest Béla Kovács as minister of the interior" in Imre Nagy's reorganized cabinet.[69]

As an émigré, Pásztor tried to rid himself of his uncomfortable past, but many continued to remember him as a prison snitch. Pásztor wanted to prove that he had seen armed combat,[70] even though, as others remembered it, his only weapons were a desk, a secretary, and perhaps a cigarette or two. He had to admit to his past as an agent, however, and he later tried to prove that while working as an informant, he "had not harmed anyone, indeed was more of use to them."[71] This was a hopeless enterprise: From 1949 to 1955, Pásztor was not only a diligent prison agent but also a successful one. According to one report, "In the course of his work in building a prison network, we got about 100 years' worth of prison sentences."[72] He worked on spying operations in the West, uncovered sabotage attempts, revealed the plans of social democratic groups, and explored various other plots. It was also "on the basis of his work that József Fiala was hung."[73] The ÁVH had possession of a handwritten letter from Pásztor implicating significant smallholder politician and journalist Gyula Dessewffy, and he also "worked on József Kővágó, whom it so happens we also engaged as an unwitting accomplice."[74]

During his imprisonment, Pásztor went from cell to cell as the prison librarian. In addition to books, he shared news with his fellow inmates. To deflect the growing suspicions about him, he asked prison officers to curse him and shout at him in his cell,[75] for it was increasingly conspicuous that he had a larger ration of food, sometimes a cigarette, and that he could even send or receive the occasional letter. When he summarized his activities for his handlers, he was able to "describe every person he had worked as a prison agent" for the previous seven years, in chronological order, thanks to which "he uncovered the crime that had been kept quiet when an individual was investigated, on the basis of which they could be sentenced."[76] This sometimes meant the gallows.

Many of the refugees remembered Tamás Pásztor's inglorious efforts. One letter later recalled the encounter with him as someone who "became the Hungarian secretary of the hearings in Vienna. Many of us did not dare to give our testimony because we were afraid this well-known prison snitch and ÁVH informer would report our statements back to Hungary."[77] This, of course, meant that the political police "would learn the names and details of those interviewed relating to the Hungarian question. The consequence was that back home they implemented retributory measures against many godforsaken families among the relatives of the witnesses."[78] These words accurately expressed the witnesses' fears but did not necessarily reflect the truth, as the letter was written at the behest of the secret services with the express intention of compromising Pásztor after the agents unsuccessfully attempted, in Vienna in 1958, to persuade him to continue his services.

Shortly after Pásztor emigrated, the repeated use of agent Kálmán Katona's services seemed risky, as Pásztor "had become strongly compromised," and "his handler, Károly Müller, had also emigrated."[79] High-ranking officers would sometimes take useful documents with them, including lists of agents and other confidential information. In addition to Pásztor's confident manner, language skills, and broad network of contacts, one further consideration was pertinent to his "return to service": his love affair with Ita Glance, secretary to the UN Special Committee and William Jordan's closest colleague. The motivation for the romance between the handsome, intelligent ex-convict with impeccable manners and the mature and professionally skilled and yet romantically naive American typist was from the outset strongly overshadowed by the fact that every confidential document of the Special Committee went through Glance's hands: she not only had a full view of the workings of the Committee, but also, following Jordan's instructions, managed communication and the distribution of reports. Pásztor's influence seems to have been exceptional, as the short and busy days they spent together in Vienna not only allowed for amorous moments but led to their engagement. The dowry in this case would have been US citizenship for Pásztor, and even his emigration to the US, according to one Ministry of the Interior report, would be "in our interest."[80] And so, Pásztor's story continued in the free world.

It took some time for Pásztor's US visa to be processed, however, even though it was not only while in Vienna that he had come to the assistance of the Special Committee; he had also played an important role in informing the UN after the Special Committee's activity was over. Based on the information he received from Hungary, he collected material for additional reports, sending his summaries to New York from time to time, as he followed the structure, subjects, and style of the UN report.

The lovebirds were soon separated from one another by their work: Glance returned with the Special Committee to New York, Pásztor stayed in Vienna, and they planned their life together long-distance. "Our wedding will be before the break,"[81] Pásztor wrote in a letter to Budapest that the political police copied. The date of the letter suggests that Pásztor was referring to the Christmas break of 1957; in the same letter, he writes that "Schleswig and I were living the most beautiful weeks of our love, as her husband was staying in Germany at this time."[82] The presence of Schleswig and a love affair with a married woman makes it doubtful he married Glance for love. But there was another key factor: Glance's money, which was of quite some use to an émigré with no income. Secret service records show Glance's fiancé receiving $200 in October 1957, to be followed by further checks.[83]

Pásztor's multifaceted activities, including those facilitated by Glance, were needed in Budapest to reactivate the once-successful agent Kálmán Katona, aka Pásztor, something the Hungarian secret service officers had tried to achieve by a variety of methods: the promise of money, a car, and a job, and permission to let his elderly and much-loved mother emigrate to Austria.[84] The political police tapped the family's phone calls and made copies of their correspondence, knowing that from this moment the ex-agent could be extorted. His mother's pension was increased, and she was promised a passport for emigration purposes.[85]

In return, they asked Pásztor to "bring with him that list of the names of the witnesses interviewed by the committee of five,"[86] suggesting that Szabó had not taken this document home after all. Officers at the Vienna station, working under diplomatic cover, established contact with Pásztor, and the ex-agent gave his "theoretical approval" to cooperate.[87] Thus was new impetus given to the "repeated recruitment of traitorous agent Tamás Pásztor a.k.a. 'Kálmán Katona.'" At the meeting, set up with the appropriate conspiratorial conditions, only the final details had to be clarified. It is not yet known whether Pásztor really wanted to return home and accept the assistance of the secret services or was in fact intending to demonstrate to the Austrian police that the Hungarian agents were active in Vienna. Members of the Hungarian secret service masquerading as diplomats were surrounded by plainclothes Austrian secret police. Even if, given the Hungarian agents' diplomatic immunity, the ensuing events were not quite worthy of a scene in a Cold War movie, the standoff raised awareness of the treatment of Hungarian refugees and how they might at any time be approached by Hungarian communist officials.

This episode continued with the "diplomat" József Kertész being expelled from Austria, while Chancellor Julius Raab summoned Ambassador Puja to protest at the harassment of the Hungarian émigré.[88] The elderly Mrs. Pásztor monetized her belongings, sold her apartment, wrapped up her life in Hungary, and made all necessary preparations for leaving, but as agent Katona did not toe the line, his mother's passport was retracted twenty-four hours before her intended departure.[89] The political police's calculations were right: Tamás Pásztor "collapsed" as a result, and was shocked to find that "Vienna had become dangerous" for him, as he wrote to a friend, another letter first read by the secret service before it reached the addressee.[90] Pásztor "feared we wanted to pick him out in a violent way," the station wrote; its schedule included such a procedure. Soviet counterintelligence, which was closely following events, saw the whole affair as Pásztor's provocation, however, simply a "piece of theatre, so he [could] be taken to the US for his own safety."[91] Soviet intelligence claimed that Pásztor had been "taken under strict observation" by Austrian counterintelligence and the US embassy, which did not so much serve his defense as reveal their concerns about the truth of his identity: Who was he working for? To clarify this, the US requested an "honest opinion" of Pásztor from György Szennik, no less, the agent whom the secret service had successfully planted in Vienna.

After failing to entice agent Katona in Budapest, secret service leaders decided to discredit him, which they hoped would "result in the final despair and utter ignominy"[92] of the renegade agent, in other words, that it would dash his hopes for a US visa and disgrace him in the eyes of other Hungarian émigrés. The letter, composed on the Mercedes typewriter at the station in Vienna, was sent to forty addresses in Austrian envelopes and stamped by the post in Vienna in the name of the Archive of the Self-Defense Association of Former Political Prisoners. The addressees included leading émigrés, Hungarian-language newspapers, and former politicians.[93]

The author of the unsigned letter explained his anonymity by saying that he was "afraid of the pure-blood Hungarians"—a reference to Pásztor's Jewish origins—and intended his message as a warning because the "kike plutocrat [. . .] continues to be effective in his work, even today."[94] The letter detailed the informant's earlier activities, and the senders attached Pásztor's handwritten denunciation of Gyula Dessewffy. The generous pension paid to his mother is explained by the fact that "her son's work for us is highly effective,"[95] and the Hungarian reprisals in the wake of the Special Committee hearings are referred to as the "result" of Pásztor's endeavors.

To be on the safe side, the Hungarian secret services also placed some "compromising material" in Pásztor's flat, and they informed his aging, despondent mother of her son's work as an informer.[96] Their success was only partial, however: many spotted the hand of the political police on the whole operation—there was nowhere else the evidence could have surfaced from—while other less circumspect newspapers or those influenced directly by the secret services published the exposé,[97] which hurt not only Pásztor himself, but also served to undermine trust in the Special Committee. For it had been Pásztor who had "arranged the compilation and registration of witnesses for the UN 'Hungarian question' committee," as György Szennik, at the request of the United States, described the role of the former snitch.[98]

The service of agent Szennik ("Szeles") began well in Austria: he created a series of drawings depicting the Revolution that was published in the *Times* and was then given a Rockefeller scholarship.[99] The ÁVH used the phrase "exceptional talent" to describe his achievement both as an informant and as an artist.[100] The appearance of the painter in Vienna did not arouse suspicion; his work as a prison agent, just like his activities during the Revolution, remained unknown to the refugees, as did the sources of his prosperity: in addition to his US scholarship, the "agent with code name Szeles [Szennik] maintained by Vienna station" also received a five-thousand-schilling "provision" from his handlers.[101] The secret service wanted Szennik to penetrate right-wing émigré circles, so he was sent to West Germany.[102] Kádárist propagandists were happy to label the politically active part of the Hungarian émigré community in the West as "fascist," but agent Szeles at this point really did have former fascist buddies to reestablish contact with, many of whom lived in the Bundesrepublik.

The agent received prolonged and thorough training in Hungary before being stationed in the West; in the course of this training, he was taught how to plan and implement surveillance and trained in conspiratorial forms of making contact, setting and using drop-off locations for secret deliveries, and what to do in the event of being discovered.[103] Szennik's instructors saw him as an "active" agent "with initiative," and hoped he would find his way into "the heart of émigré circles."[104] The fact that, after the Revolution, he was arrested and beaten and his house was searched was all part of the conspiracy; no one had cause to be suspicious—not even his wife, from whom his mission was kept secret.

A few days before being put in the field, "Szeles" requested secret party membership, signing his letter "With courageous communist regards," while reassuring his superiors that "I was able to rise above the grievances I suffered." By this stage, he wrote, he intended "neither revenge, nor defection," as "I am Hungarian and feel I belong to the workers' class."[105]

After his studies and "operative" training, Szennik was "thrown over the wall," to use the secret service terminology for smuggling him into Austria. This took place at Bozsok between 10:00 p.m. and 11:00 p.m. on April 18, 1957. His wife knew nothing of all this and remained in Hungary, so the secret service developed a "legend" of his defection for her that was personal, sentimental, and authentic. It told of pain, of not being understood, and of how they would soon meet again. Mrs. Szennik had no idea that her husband had requested that his handler let his fifteen-year-old "student" Erzsébet Farkas accompany him to the West; according to ÁVH documentation, Szennik's wife did not want children, while he did.[106] Apparently he chose to have those children by a child.

Having reached the "free world," Szennik's narrative changed. He claimed: "I was one of the organizers of the uprising and one of the leaders of the siege of the Radio."[107] He also mentioned other heroic acts, such as his role in politics and in the adventurous, sometimes dangerous journey of the aid convoys. Szennik announced he had had enough of the "Bolshevik hell": he had, after all, spent "three months full of inhuman suffering" at the 60 Andrássy Avenue interrogation chambers, where "sadist scum that had emerged from the underworld tortured thousands of Hungarian patriots to death." Szennik complained that he was forced to paint enormous Kitsch canvases idealizing the three "chief rogues" responsible for the terror and suppression of Stalinist Hungary—Lenin, Stalin, and Rákosi[108]—and said that in the West he wanted to study and work, closing his explanation for the benefit of émigrés with the words: "To guarantee my life and my artistic progress, I am looking for refuge in the free world."[109]

He did indeed begin to "work," though this work involved establishing contacts, in the espionage sense, and acquiring and passing on information.

Of his targets, Károly Ney was the most important; together they had been members of the Waffen-SS, and at this time, the former Obersturmbann-führer was a leading figure in the extreme right-wing Hungarian émigré circle in Munich. According to the political police's information, Ney was an acquaintance of Lieutenant-Colonel Winkelmann, known to be a friend of NATO commander-in-chief Hans Speidel, which meant that Szennik may have come into proximity of one of Hungary's most important intelligence sources.[110]

The wife Szennik left behind in Budapest contemplated suicide, but the secret service made sure she was not without company. Police detective captain Ferenc Molnár visited Mrs. Szennik, introducing himself as "Mohácsi," claiming to be a graphic designer and offering support, just as he did for the painter's aging mother. Szennik's wife took "Mohácsi" into her confidence and told him how much she hated the socialist system, as did her husband, who had partly become "mixed up in" the Revolution because the system had not allowed him to thrive. Mrs. Szennik was first a source of information, then a hostage: Szennik's plan to make good the escape of Erzsébet Farkas got caught up in the workings of the secret service, at which point his clandestine operations became more and more erratic. He was then told that if he refused to cooperate, his wife would be put in prison and he would be charged as a traitor in absentia because he was in possession of state secrets, even the most minor compromise of which would be subject to serious sanction.[111]

Szennik failed to penetrate the inner circle of the émigrés, did not have success in West Germany, and failed to acquire significant information about key émigré figures in Austria. Most of his promises and plans remained unfulfilled, a result he put down to his limited (financial) resources. Szennik became increasingly demanding. When the secret service did not ship the young girl out to him, he requested that his wife be let out of the country instead, then repeated this demand ever more forcefully. He wanted more and more money. At covert meetings with his handler at a particular café, his tone became so loud and agitated that, on more than one occasion, he had to be hurried out of the café. Szennik's results failed to bear out the trust placed in him, but there was also the fear that with his behavior he would blow the cover of the whole station.[112] In May 1958, he was ordered home, and Hungarian secret service officers covertly "received" Szeles aka Szennik through the "Austrian border portal,"[113] a sign that the secret service could freely move in and out of Austria, taking people with them. Szennik was not of much use even after being brought home, although he did write long descriptions of his fellow émigrés, listing their addresses, professions, and character traits, with particular focus on the UN investigation and the revolutionaries who had given evidence.

Based on the activities of Szennik and other agents, the tangible fear among the witnesses before the Special Committee was justified, as their promised anonymity was no guarantee that they would not be identified and that they or their relatives in Hungary would not become targets of the ÁVH. And although the web of Hungarian agents took a pounding during the Revolution, with many having their covers blown by documents made public and others escaping abroad, the network was quickly and successfully regrouped, not in the least thanks to agents co-opted with threats or extortion. A section of the "network of individuals" who had left the country was also uncovered[114] and reactivated through either bribery or extortion.

Along with persuasion, threats, and extortion, money also played a key role in establishing and maintaining the web of agents, and the secret service was not short of material resources. According to a report from the Vienna station, Hungary's chronic hard currency deficit notwithstanding, significant sums oiled the wheels of the machinery in "rewarding our contacts": there were those given 2,500 schillings for their work, others had considerable expenses paid, and sometimes parents living in Hungary were the recipients of gifts.[115] Witnesses for the Special Committee who had been identified were held under constant observation. Thanks to their apparently generous funding, the secret services in Budapest were also able to uncover the identified UN witnesses' contacts and activities, with a particular eye on preventing sensitive information from leaving the country.

As well as acquiring information and watching "enemy" activity, the Hungarian secret service was also entrusted with going on the attack,[116] by "ravaging and crippling" émigré organizations and by preventing "attempts to establish unity." Hungarians being notoriously independent thinkers, the latter was not difficult. The political police claimed these groups "pose[d] a threat to the security of our nation,"[117] and the various divisions, arguments, and antagonisms within émigré communities provided rich pickings for the secret service center in Budapest, whether they emerged between old and new émigrés, between conservatives and liberals, or based on religious or ethnic backgrounds. Hungarians in the US wanted to root out the Marxists from their midst, even though many of the latter had escaped across the ocean. In other groups, too, it proved possible to stretch tensions to the point of rupture, as, for example, in the World Federation of Freedom Fighters or the Hungarian social democratic party in exile. Whether these disputes were the result of secret service plots or simply the product of the legendary ability of even the smallest of Hungarian groups to fall into infighting among different camps, we cannot know.

One form of attack by the Hungarian secret services was to encourage the demonization of and acts of revenge toward certain individuals in light of compromising information revealed about them. In their campaigns to discredit people, the secret services would reveal to the victim or members of their family harmful actions the targets had taken against them. Direct attacks were made as well: in a half-year secret plan for actions of the Vienna station scheduled for March 31, 1958, the "persuading of more significant figures to return home on a voluntary basis" included the possibility of their "being brought home by illegal means, or potentially their liquidation."[118] In this way, the secret services would later deploy an agent to Vienna to undertake a "special military task";[119] the training of this agent suggested that the most extreme methods could be in play. Meanwhile, another agent was working on the issue of "undercover repatriations."[120] This agent had the fullest veneer of trustworthiness: he worked for Radio Free Europe.

Many identified UN witnesses were approached via their family members;[121] some were inveigled and then sent abroad, while others were taken as hostages in Hungary and then put under strong pressure or sometimes directly coerced to work as agents. There were some, like Géza Bánkúti, a noted sportsman who had been involved in the Revolution, who volunteered for the secret service in the hope that in return their loved ones would be sent out of the country.[122] When this happened, however, the reunification of families as urged by the International Committee of the Red Cross would become another tool of the political police. In Vienna, for example, it was reported that "our intelligence officers and covert operatives occupy almost every position in the consular department."[123]

Over the course of the anti-UN operation, intercepted communications were a key source of information for the Hungarian secret service. From the messages exchanged between the French embassy in Budapest and the foreign ministry in Paris, they learned that Keith Shann, Rapporteur of the Special Committee, found it concerning that the UN Secretariat did not share the "orientation" of the Special Committee and that, in Shann's opinion, work was being negatively affected by what "in his experience was a secretariat teeming with Moscow agents."[124] They knew all this in Moscow as well, for the Soviet "comrade advisers" were present in the Hungarian Ministry of the Interior as in every other ministry. Part and parcel of secret service cooperation was the sharing of information: for example, the Soviet embassy in Budapest handed its comrades in Budapest no fewer than sixteen dossiers on "questions relating to" Hungarians who had escaped to Switzerland.[125]

One reason to identify the UN witnesses was to discredit them; to this end, their friends, colleagues, and relatives back in Hungary were sought out to help find leverage on the so-called traitors. On April 1, 1957, the agent code-named Fejér reported on Sándor Kiss, János Horváth, and Special Committee witness István B. Rácz, and added the "processing" of their contacts in Hungary: "I will look at the police records of important individuals across the country, and set up a papka," they wrote, making use of Soviet terminology for an identification card.[126] The agent code-named Ottó reported on witness György Frank[127]—unaware that his target himself worked for the political police—and the Hungarian secret services would spend many years uncovering and making use of the network of former Budapest police chief Olivér Benjámin. An investigation was conducted into individuals close to Benjámin, with questions raised about each of his relatives and many of his female acquaintances. Much of the information on Benjámin's connections in Hungary was provided by an agent with code name Muki, who had been engaged with the use of "pressure,"[128] because the secret services needed every bit of compromising material they could get. Thus they not only looked through the documents of Benjámin's show trial; they also produced records of when his house had been searched. The use of all this information allowed them to break up the unity of the Hungarian social democrats abroad. The "compromising of the leaders of fascist Hungarian émigré organizations" played a key role in provoking disunity and discord, and it was facilitated by the abundance of documents at the political police's disposal that could be used for this purpose.[129]

The Hungarian secret services organized this huge amount of information into files on Hungarian émigrés and witnesses. In Budapest, they knew to the day or even the hour where Anna Kéthly, Béla Király, Ferenc Nagy, Pál Auer, and Béla Varga were traveling, found out who paid for these journeys, and—on the basis of their Stalinist logic—surmised which secret service they were in the employ of. They considered the most dangerous enemy to be Béla Király, who, as the "most active" émigré,[130] posed a direct threat to Hungary's legal order, not least through international organizations, meaning primarily the United Nations. "Spying, subversion and acts of terror" were some of the terms used to describe his activities; to preempt these alleged actions, Division II of the Hungarian Ministry of the Interior devised a strategy of destruction, confrontation, and targeted attack. More agents were stationed around Király, allowing them to provide detailed reports on the former commander-in-chief and describe his "area of movement" and whom he met, when, and where.[131] Through telegrams, they suggested a "meeting by the border" and considered opening the border long enough to bring Király over it. They later decided to compromise him instead. The political police recalled how Király had come to the assistance of state security, and further documents proved he had worked on a network of agents in prisons.[132] They also encouraged suspicion of Király as the only person to have remained alive among many sentenced to death, especially as he had testified against the others.[133] According to the ÁVH's logic, this was all consistent with the accusations that Király was spying for the "Anglo-Saxons" again and returning to his participation in the war against the Soviet Union.[134] Király was eventually rehabilitated, and the charges against him were dropped, only for military judge Ferenc Ledényi to overturn the rehabilitation judgment: on April 26, 1957, the military court "restore[d] the validity of sentence Kb.T. 014/1952/53."[135] Restored, that is, a sentence passed on Király as the result of a show trial.

That Király would also be accused of corruption, of homosexual relationships, and of theft during the Revolution and then of betraying that Revolution, was more a reflection of the secret service leaders' vivid imaginations than of real events.[136] But the splintering of émigré groups was fueled by an inflammatory leaflet written by Király's rival and police lieutenant Gyula Szabó. Five hundred to six hundred copies were distributed "illegally," partly among military leaders who had emigrated, and partly among those political bodies where Király had a position of influence. This was all necessary if there was to be hope of discrediting the charismatic Király, principally in the eyes of the United Nations, to whose Special Committee Király's role was important and would remain so.

Unlike Király, Anna Kéthly did attempt a rapprochement with Hungary; the Hungarian and Soviet authorities learned of it, but the documents reveal that Kádár was unwilling to establish contact. Although "for tactical reasons we would take certain steps to neutralize the activities of Kéthly and her circle,"[137] they instead decided on compromising the social democratic leader, making use of her desperate letters written from prison and her confessions made under duress. All these activities were taking place only in plain view. Behind the scenes, even more dangerous and devastating processes were underway.

In summarizing the steps taken and not taken by the UN, it becomes clear that the UN resolutions were sabotaged at the highest levels, as documents prove and later events suggest. The reelection of Hammarskjöld was an obvious priority that overwrote the UN Charter. Meanwhile, the active infiltration of the Hungarian refugee community by the communist secret services proves that they could and did profit from the UN's passivity and its careless handling of sensitive data and documents.

Notes

1. *Report of the Special Committee on the Problem of Hungary. General Assembly Official Records: 11th Session Supplement No. 18. (A/3592).*

2. UNARM S-0188-0006-0018. January 17, 1957.

3. July 2, 1957. Columbia University, Butler Library, Rare Books and Manuscript Collection (hereinafter ACP), box 184.

4. UNARM S-0188-0006-0005 to -0008. Protitch Papers, "Hungarian Developments 8/26/57 [. . .] Note on Developments in Hungary since May 1957."

5. Cardia, *Magyar október,* 71–72. At the end of the summer, a "lobby group" was created to support the UN operation; the "UN committee" of the National Mission for a Free Hungary supplied delegations with news. See the letters of Sándor Kiss on August 23 and 27, 1957. Ráday Archive (Ráday Levéltár, hereinafter RL) C/243.

6. July 16, 1957. From Jordan to Protitch. ACP box 193. "After discussion with Cordier I have made what are the minimum arrangements for the continuation of work." On August 5, 1957, in his letter to Cordier, Jordan referred to this conversation: "No more Reports." ACP, box 184.

7. ACP, box 184. From Jordan to Protitch, August 1, 1957. Protitch to Jordan on August 7.

8. According to FBI documents: "Rapporteur [. . .] no part in writing or compiling the Report [. . .] totally indifferent [. . .] generally irresponsible in the matter." Bang-Jensen Archive (hereinafter BJI), box 33.

9. July 30, 1957. DHS L 179:84.

10. From Shann to Hammarskjöld on July 22, 1957. UNARM DAG 1.1.1.3. Cordier files. Jordan to Protitch, July 27, 1957. "It would be difficult to find an appropriate focus for a third report, since it would have mainly to center around the reports of trials and executions."

11. ACP, box 183. July 30, 1957.

12. ACP, box 184.

13. July 15, 1957. Jordan to Andersen. ACP, box 184.

14. ACP, box 184.

15. See the reminder of the visit on August 30, 1957: NARA 320.5764/8-3057.

16. July 31, 1957. ACP, box 183.

17. ACP, box 184. August 1, 1957. Jordan to Andersen.

18. August 26, 1957. DHS L 179:84.

19. UNARM S-0370-0041-03. See the press conference of January 21, 1958.

20. The delegation was led by Imre Horváth, who was joined by his deputies, together with ÁVH officers, a few experts, interpreters, and bureaucrats. UNARM S-0446-0116-0008-00001- UC.

21. MNL XIX-J-1-n, box 63.

22. Sík, *Bem rakparti évek*, 82–83.

23. DHS L 179:173. See the report on this among the party papers. MOL Hungarian Socialist Workers' Party (MSZMP) document collection, 288f 5/49, and MNL XIX-J-1-j, box 209.

24. This was also the subject of the Hungarian government's so-called White Book.

25. MNL XIX-J-29-0.

26. Andersen did not have a function in the UN, nor was he a member of the Danish delegation. Shann was made ambassador to Manila, to be replaced on October 2, 1957, by Ronald Walker as the "Alternate Representative of Australia." UNARM S-0442-0139-06.

27. MNL XIX-j-24-a, box 2.

28. Ibid.

29. Pálfy and Kazimir (1970).

30. MNL XIX-j-29-0.

31. In his memoirs, Endre Sík claims that they participated in the work of every committee. Sík, *Bem rakparti évek*, 83. Also see July 26, 1957. "Proposals and plans regarding the UN." MNL XIX-J-60-a.

32. November 1, 1957. "A Note on Hungary." UNARM S-0188-0006-0004.

33. MNL XIX-J-29-0.

34. On July 31, 1957, Fry suggested the nomination of a Special Representative: "Almost everyone would be more suitable, on past records, than present Secretary General." FO 371/128683.

35. UNARM S-0442-0139-06.

36. See the report of December 9, 1957. "Report of the General Assembly's Special Representative on the Hungarian Problem." NARA 764.00/12-957, and his statement. ACP, box 184.

37. Sík, *Bem rakparti évek*, 182–84.

38. Ibid. Prince Wan could have visited Hungary as the representative of his homeland, but in London, he was warned that given his mandate, he could only go as the Special Representative of the UN Special Committee. See the telegram from the UK Mission to the UN on October 17, 1957. FO 371/128688.

39. Sík, *Bem rakparti évek*, 185.

40. The same appears in the December 30, 1957, document of the FBI. BJI, box 33.

41. See the memorandum of the meeting between the US Mission to the UN and the Secretary-General. BJI, box 33.

42. "Statements Relating to Hungary." UNARM S-0188-0006-0003-0015. See also "Punitive Action Taken by the Kadar Government from November 1956 to August 1957 against Hungarian Citizens for Alleged Anti-Regime Activities during and after the October Revolution." NARA 320.5764/8-3157.

43. November 15, 1957. From Hammarskjöld to Lind. UNARM S-0009-0002-09.

44. MNL XIX-J-1-k, box 127.

45. UNARM S-0442-0139-06.

46. ACP, box 184.

47. December 17, 1957. The seventy-first session of the Special Committee. ACP, box 184.

48. January 3, 1958. From Hámori to Jordan. CHP, subject area 9.

49. ÁBTL Bt-720. "Jókai."

50. ÁBTL 3.1.9. M-20948.

51. ÁBTL Mt-20.943. "Sándor Kecskeméti."

52. ÁBTL 3.2.4. K-1925. "Hajós."

53. ÁBTL 3.2.4. K-1925. July 11, 1958. Material of the ambassadorial address. "On personnel work."

54. Agents of the US Secret Service appeared in this alongside plans for revenge on communists. Miklós Szabó's investigation dossier, ÁBTL V-111/759.

55. On the agent with code name "Kerekes," see Sz. Kovács, "A magyar hírszerzés tevékenysége Ausztriában."

56. Among the documents of the foreign ministry in Budapest, we find the mandate for Miklós Szabó to represent Hungary at the UNHCR in the name of the Strasbourg Revolutionary Council, signed by Anna Kéthly and Sándor Kiss. Here we also find a letter signed by Kéthly and Király that mentions the help given by Szabó to the Special Committee. MNL XIX-J-1-j, box 71.

57. See RL C/243.2. Also see MNL XIX-J-36 (documents of the Hungarian embassy in Vienna).

58. November 14, 1957. "The atmosphere surrounding Miklós Szabó's homecoming." MNL XIX-J-1-j (Austria).

59. October 28, 1957. MNL XIX-J-36 (documents of the Hungarian embassy in Vienna). At his press conference, Miklós Szabó claimed he knew the name of every witness. MNL XIX-J-1-k, box 127.

60. MNL XIX-J-36 (documents of the Hungarian embassy in Vienna).

61. ÁBTL 3.2.1. Bt/910/2.

62. October 12, 1957. Note on "Kerekes's" contacts. ÁBTL 3.2.5. O-8-073/7.

63. Ibid.

64. November 4, 1957. (Vienna) "The atmosphere surrounding Miklós Szabó's homecoming." MNL XIX-J-1-j (Austria).

65. Tamás Pásztor's letter of October 5, 1957. ÁBTL 3.2.1. Bt/910/2.

66. June 28, 1957. The report by "Roger." ÁBTL 3.2.1. Bt/910/2.

67. ÁBTL 3.2.1. Bt/910/2. At the interrogation of Mihály Kormány, who had returned from the West, it was said that Tamás Pásztor was "the intelligence officer of the UN." ÁBTL 3.2.1. Bt/910/3.

68. ÁBTL 3.2.1. Bt/910/2.

69. Ibid.

70. May 23, 1958. Szennik's report on Tamás Pásztor. "Szeles." ÁBTL Mt-493/1.

71. "Szeles." ÁBTL Mt-493/1.

72. ÁBTL 3.2.1. Bt/910/2.

73. October 28, 1957. Proposal. On the Fiala case: "35 reports over 218 pages." (Before the war, József Fiala was a detective; he was charged with organizing an armed conspiracy against the socialist system.) ÁBTL 3.2.1. Bt/910/2.

74. November 12, 1958. ÁBTL 3.2.1. Bt/910/2.

75. ÁBTL 3.2.1. Bt/910/3.

76. On November 4, this was attached to the documents: "The results of my work so far." ÁBTL 3.2.1. Bt/910/3.

77. October 7, 1958. ÁBTL 3.2.1. Bt/910/3.

78. Ibid.

79. Ibid.

80. Ibid. There is no evidence in the files of his activity having continued.

81. ÁBTL 3.2.1. Bt/910/2.

82. Ibid.

83. "But money came only from Ita." ÁBTL 3.2.1. Bt/910/2.

84. Ibid. "Katona."

85. ÁBTL 3.2.1. Bt/910/3.

86. March 3, 1958. Proposal for Tamás Pásztor to be "engaged." ÁBTL 3.2.1. Bt/910/2.

87. May 3, 1958. ÁBTL 3.2.1. Bt/910/2. His former cellmate, the agent with code name "Blum," also played a role in Katona being hired. ÁBTL 3.2.1. Bt/910/2. "Katona."

88. ÁBTL 3.2.1. Bt/910/2.

89. ÁBTL 3.2.1. Bt/910/3.

90. ÁBTL 3.2.1. Bt/910/2.

91. Ibid.

92. ÁBTL 3.2.1. Bt/910/3. June 12, 1958. "Subject: the discrediting of 'Kálmán Katona.'"

93. December 9, 1958. Proposal for the discrediting of Tamás Pásztor. ÁBTL 3.2.1. Bt/910/3.

94. ÁBTL 3.2.1. Bt/910/2.

95. Ibid.

96. October 13, 1960. Letter to Tamás Pásztor's mother. ÁBTL 3.2.1. Bt/910/3.

97. July 10, 1958. Klára Vass listed the charges in the journal *A Hídfő* (Bridgehead). ÁBTL 3.2.1. Bt/910/2.

98. May 23, 1958. ÁBTL Mt-493/1.

99. November 11, 1957. ÁBTL Mt-493/1.

100. ÁBTL 3.1.1. Bt 602/2.

101. ÁBTL Mt-493/1.

102. See the "Allocation plan" dated March 2, 1957. ÁBTL Bt 602/2.

103. Ibid.

104. Ibid.

105. April 8, 1957. ÁBTL 3.1.1. Bt 602/1.

106. Ibid. and ÁBTL Mt 493/1.

107. Ibid.

108. Ibid.

109. Szennik's participation in the Revolution was confirmed by Tamás Pásztor and Sándor Kiss.

110. October 7, 1957. ÁBTL Mt 493/1.

111. ÁBTL 3.1.1. Bt 602/3.

112. ÁBTL Mt 493/1.

113. ÁBTL 3.1.1. Bt 602/5. May 27, 1957.

114. ÁBTL 3.2.6. 8-034/1 (correspondence dossier from the station in Vienna).

115. ÁBTL 3.2.6. 8-073/6.

116. ÁBTL 3.2.6. 8-034/1.

117. Ibid.

118. Ibid.

119. Vienna station's plan was to deploy an agent with code name "Netter." Ibid.

120. ÁBTL 3.2.6. 8-034/1.

121. Ibid.

122. Bánkúti had already been given tasks by the ÁVH in 1957; he is mentioned as a former member of the network. In 1963, he indicated that if his family were let out of the country, "in return he would be willing to undertake certain jobs." ÁBTL 3.2.6. 8-073/3.

123. ÁBTL 3.2.6. 8-073/6.

124. ÁBTL BM6II/2. "Informational report relating to Hammarskjöld's visit to Budapest and the UN Committee of Five."

125. MNL XIX-J-1-j (Switzerland).

126. ÁBTL 3.2.5. O-8-073/4. "Prior" referred to research into an individual's past.

127. ÁBTL 3.2.5. O-8-073/7. György Frank left for France, gave evidence to the UN Special Committee, and undertook clandestine tasks for the ÁVH.

128. There were periods when three agents were working on Olivér Benjámin at the same time. ÁBTL K-1431. "The case of Olivér Benjámin." "Pressure" referred to physical abuse.

129. "László Sas," "Szepesi," and "Kálmán" all met in Vienna. As instructed, they provoked a split in the social democratic émigré community. ÁBTL K-1431.

130. July 19, 1957. "Proposal for undermining Béla Király's group." The action plan titled "The Marchers" was the work of police detective colonel Jenő Hazai. Other operations against Király were also actioned, with other code names. K-1525/1 "Radek."

131. "Paul Blum," "Roger," "Sárosi," etc. K-1525/1.

132. Király "was an ÁVH informer," they wrote, for his confession led to the arrest of his brother and that of general staff lieutenant-colonel Károly Nyitrai. Király was then "recruited for prison network operations by ÁVH major István Hevesi." K-1525/1.

133. Ibid.

134. January 26, 1957. Summary report of II/B-a group on Béla Király. K-1525/1.

135. MNL XX-5-h. "Nagy Imre *et al.* Investigation documents." Box 19, vol. 26 (V-150000/60).

136. July 30, 1958. "Proposal for the publication of an anti-Béla Király document." ÁBTL K-1525/1. "Radek."

137. May 29, 1957. Memorandum from Shepilov and Andropov. See Gál, A *"Jelcin-dosszié,"* 102. Kéthly's partial rehabilitation came only in 1961.

7

POVL BANG-JENSEN

The Concerns of the Danish UN Employee,
His Charisma, and His Conflicts

What happened on the surface and what happened behind the scenes at the UN are two quite separate stories: one written for public consumption and the other the result of raw, sometimes brutal pragmatism. How difficult it was for many to bear the UN's handling of the Hungarian question is illustrated by the story of Povl Bang-Jensen—a story that ended in tragedy and serves to reflect the gravity of these contradictions.[1]

The Danish diplomat was not willing to accept the pragmatism verging on cynicism that characterized the United Nations' treatment of the Hungarian question, both because he saw the grave contradictions from close at hand and because he believed in the institution where he worked. As Deputy Secretary of the UN Special Committee on the Problem of Hungary, he played a key role in the investigation of that question at the UN, first due to his conscientious endeavors, then because of his conflicts with the UN and a struggle that ended with his death.[2]

Bang-Jensen was an international employee of the UN Secretariat, and his official loyalty was to the UN rather than to Denmark's Mission to the UN. His background and character did not fit into the traditional idea of a foreign service official. His experiences during World War II had taught him that sometimes instructions had to be considered rather than implemented blindly and that morality trumped loyalty. Thus did the words of Heraclitus become true of him: *ethos anthropos daimon* (a man's character is his fate). From 1939, Bang-Jensen lived in the US, where, after a decade of warm relations with the American political elite, he felt at home in both a

The Bang-Jensen family. *Seated, from left to right*: Karen, Per, Helen, Povl, Nina. *Kneeling, front row*: Lise and Lars. Copyright: The Bang-Jensen family.

personal and professional sense.[3] When he became a UN officer, he joined the UN family, helped by his faith in the UN's role in international affairs and by many personal illusions that to him made the UN seem a force for good.

That the trust Bang-Jensen placed in the UN's treatment of the Hungarian question was misplaced had clear political elements to it, most notably the Soviet veto at the Security Council. But there were also increasing numbers of questions being asked about the procedures used for dealing with the Hungarian question. These included the quiet acceptance of the Kádár government's legitimacy, the unusual delays in the preparation of the UN Special Report, and the facts that the errors in the report's text were left uncorrected, that no special General Assembly session was convened, that the preparation of additional reports was obstructed, and that the nomination of an oddly unresponsive Special Representative was accepted and even appreciated. Bang-Jensen was well aware of all of these concerns and of the biggest question of all: Why had the General Assembly resolutions been sabotaged in a way that was not in the interests of the Hungarian people?

In his position as Deputy Secretary of the Special Committee, Bang-Jensen participated in finding, pre-screening, and selecting witnesses, through which he was able to observe the logistics of the operations of the Committee from the most mundane details—such as interpreters' equipment, rental of rooms, and per diems—to the broadest perspective—the evidence the witnesses gave, the arrangements for their security, and the relative importance of what they had to say. He later played a role in writing the text of the Special Committee's report and in the process of editing, standardizing, and correcting it. This was where the conflicts began.

The tensions that arose during the Special Committee's work—particularly in Vienna—could at first be explained as by-products of the difficult conditions under which the work was being conducted. These tensions were intensified by Bang-Jensen's character and mentality being so at odds with those of his direct superior, William Jordan. But the process of writing the report pitted the basic principles of the two men against each other in stark conflict, and this was where Bang-Jensen's ordeal really began. The report was the writing of history, not just in the sense that the United Nations had embarked on the work of chronicling past events but because the Special Committee had written the report with the intention of influencing future events. The task was an extraordinary one, the material vast, and the time short—all factors that led to tensions being heightened rather than eased. Any lack of clarity in the Committee's work came to the surface during the composition of the report, for while the Committee provided a framework for how the report was to be elaborated, the necessary elaborations were the details, wherein the devil lay. Meanwhile, the final decision on the chapters written by members of the secretariat no longer fell to the Rapporteur, and the documents produced had to be approved by the Committee. This meant that politics, not facts, played the key role in determining what would be included. For Bang-Jensen, however, nothing mattered more than presenting the facts, the truth, and an exact description of the situation, as it was only based on the accurate reporting of the solid evidence the witnesses gave and the facts behind their testimonies and documents that conclusions could properly be drawn.

The list of omissions and inaccuracies in the report only grew as light fell on new incidents, including deportations and atrocities enacted upon civilians, the full and factual reporting of which was a matter of principle to Bang-Jensen and theoretically, if not in practice, for the UN. Such incidents enjoyed scant attention in the report, however, so Bang-Jensen continuously drew attention to the need to correct its inadequacies. At this stage, no one doubted his "admirable work" for the Committee, as was duly noted by its Chair.[4] Thus Bang-Jensen thought it odd that his recommendations were in the main not acted on, that there was no trace of many of his suggested improvements in the version of the text to be presented to the Special Committee, and that some of the errors he had corrected later found their way back into the report. He also encountered omissions and internal contradictions and started to suspect that these were not coincidental and that the authenticity of the report was being undermined to improve its suitability as a target for communist propaganda.

Bang-Jensen first brought these inaccuracies to Committee Rapporteur Mick Shann's attention in writing, then, with no meaningful response forthcoming, tried to establish personal contact. Shann was not willing to listen to his objections[5] and instead ordered him to follow official procedure. Jordan refused to look through the list of errors. Alsing Andersen, Chair of the Special Committee and a fellow Dane, agreed with Bang-Jensen but was unable to influence his colleagues, which was unusual. As the final deadline for submitting the report loomed, it seemed likely that because of its errors, the entire report—and indeed the entire investigation, together with all the work that had been done on the Hungarian question, the UN's only serious attempt at a political resolution to the situation—would be robbed of any credibility. Jordan would later claim that time had been pressing, that fifteen hundred changes had already been made, and that Bang-Jensen was supposedly in a bad way psychologically.[6]

An episode ensued in which Bang-Jensen approached Shann in the UN delegate's lounge and a disagreement over the report and the events of that meeting followed. After this incident, the Rapporteur refused to communicate with anyone other than the Committee Secretary, thereby handing Jordan effective future control of the preparation of the report. Jordan, meanwhile, had had enough of his troublesome colleague. He barred Bang-Jensen from further participation in the project and had the most important documents removed from his office, including his notes and copies of his lists of errors.[7] The UN leadership accepted Jordan's position; at the UN, the hierarchy and official procedures mattered more than the truth. Bang-Jensen then tendered his resignation. It was not accepted, but neither was he able to conduct his work as his conscience dictated. His jurisdiction was also removed; that is, he had no official influence over that which he felt responsible for. When he turned directly to UN Secretary-General Dag Hammarskjöld, his mandate was officially suspended.[8]

Andrew Cordier, Under-Secretary-General of the UN, explained away Bang-Jensen's objections to the report by saying that he was "a very sick man"[9] because he had approached UN diplomats from the United States to arrange a meeting with the head of the CIA or with the US president. Cordier was aware that Bang-Jensen wanted to share concerns with US officials about security issues at the UN at the very highest level. Cordier was unaware, however, that in November of 1956, before Bang-Jensen had been appointed to the Special Committee, he had been approached by Eastern bloc diplomats who wanted to defect due to their disappointment in communist ideology after the Soviet invasion of Hungary. These potential defectors had security concerns about the UN but also had concerns about Soviet infiltration of the State Department and the CIA. Bang-Jensen had wanted to meet with the president of the United States or head of the CIA to relay this highly sensitive information.

The demotions and restrictions the Danish diplomat experienced at the UN meant that he was unable to follow the formation of the report of the Special Committee in its most decisive phase. He was not even given a copy of the published version.[10] His objections were brushed to the side and none were investigated: Jordan cited time pressures and the acceptance of the report by the Special Committee members.[11] In the investigation following Bang-Jensen's death under suspicious circumstances, both Jordan and Shann would recall that they had "carefully considered" the Deputy Secretary's objections.[12] In fact they had done nothing of the sort, not even when Bang-Jensen had written directly to the Secretary-General. Hammarskjöld tried to call him personally on the phone at a critical moment, but by this time Bang-Jensen had gone on holiday to Denmark with his family. Hammarskjöld had even had calls made to the port to try to catch him, but it was too late. He then asked Bang-Jensen, in a handwritten and personable letter, to meet with him once he got back from Denmark.[13]

After Bang-Jensen's return, however, Hammarskjöld could not find time for a meeting; instead, Under-Secretary-General Ralph Bunche was tasked with looking into the matter. It was clear by this time that no special session would be called, nor would there be additional reports; in short, the Hungarian question had been successfully put to bed. All of this was well known to the talented and charismatic Bunche, who must have been aware of the reasons for it; he also knew of Cordier's allegation that Bang-Jensen was mentally ill. In the Danish staff member's reservations and references to sabotage and Soviet influence, Bunche saw a return to the Cold War hysteria that had almost made a victim of Bunche himself. He approached the issue with his heart, not his head, dismissing Bang-Jensen's objections as ridiculous and avoiding any acquaintance with his evidence. Bang-Jensen stated that the Special Committee and its Rapporteur had been misled, that the mistakes in the report were not unintentional, that he had not been allowed to correct them, and that it could not be ruled out that Jordan had been "pressured."[14] He added that the Secretariat of the UN had "tried to influence" Secretary Jordan to not press for a further report. Jordan claimed there was not enough relevant material at their disposal, despite having previously complained that there was an enormous volume of documents to deal with.[15] Jordan failed to pass documentation on to members of the Special Committee, just as he had previously attempted to filter out a number of key details.[16] This could not all be a coincidence, Bang-Jensen stated—and neither could it be an accident that no one had taken seriously any of his previous objections.

Bunche later interviewed the three other members of the UN Secretariat dealing with the Hungarian question—Claire de Hedervary, Vernon Duckworth-Barker, and Marc Schreiber—in an "informal" capacity.[17] For a meeting between an Under-Secretary-General and UN employees, this informality was decidedly unusual. Bunche also consulted with Jordan, who contradicted Bang-Jensen's reservations: the Secretary of the Special Committee was authorized to present documents to the members as he saw fit, lest they be "deluged with material."[18] Additional reports sent by Hungarian émigré Tamás Pásztor were among the documents that Bang-Jensen said had not been read by the Special Committee because "no one asked to see them."[19] Things came full circle during the investigation: what the Special Committee did not know about, they had not asked for, so they did not know about it. And this was considered a satisfactory protocol for documents that people had often risked their lives to smuggle out of Hungary to the West.

Bang-Jensen's concern was evident when Jordan pinned the communication breakdown relating to deportations on the Secretary-General, just as when Jordan had failed to mention to the members that the bodyguard for the minister of defense of the revolutionary government Pál Maléter had established contact via a cable György Heltai sent from Brussels.[20] Jordan later denied the omission, instead citing the difficulties of establishing the necessary conditions for a witness interview with Maléter's close associate, who had escaped Soviet prison and might have added key details to the already-established facts in the Special Committee's report. Bunche added in confidence that "Jordan may lean over a bit too far" in that "he quite likely has expressed such views to Bang-Jensen."[21] By this stage, Bang-Jensen had written directly to Hammarskjöld of the "sabotage allegedly on your instructions," which was quite a claim to make of the leader of the UN, especially when there was only indirect evidence for it.[22] Instead of a more thorough deliberation on the issue, Bunche simply confirmed Cordier's amateur diagnosis that Bang-Jensen was mentally disturbed and might be capable of "physical violence either to himself or to others."[23] It seemed as if the plan for what would be the last two years of Bang-Jensen's life had already been established.

The Question of the Witnesses

This plan required a turning point, however, in the fate of the witnesses who had given evidence, one that seemed to press a stamp of inevitability on what had appeared to be a series of coincidences. The Special Committee heard testimony from 111 witnesses. Along with their selection, conducting interviews, and many other logistic challenges, the most important consideration was the assurance of their safety, especially among those who gave their testimony anonymously. This was a key issue from the start of the Special Committee's activity, so when Cordier wrote a letter to UN financial controller B. R. Turner regarding the costs incurred by the witness hearings, the sums in question had to be made available to Bang-Jensen based on receipts that referred simply to "Refugee 1," "Refugee 2," and so on, while Bang-Jensen maintained and guarded the accompanying list of names of the witnesses during the Special Committee's hearings.[24] The money was needed for witnesses to be able to travel to hearings, pay for visas, and cover their living expenses, sometimes for many days at a time. Of the $3,150 put in Bang-Jensen's charge, $3,099 had been spent by April 1957; that he alone was entrusted with this sum is a reflection of the trust he enjoyed.

Witnesses giving evidence anonymously on the events of the Hungarian Revolution was not unusual. At the hearings of the US Senate committee, Hungarian witnesses wore surgical masks;[25] the names of Hungarians giving testimony in Australia were withheld; and in Italy, the imperative of anonymity was put into the title of a book on refugees—Giorgio Chiesura's *Non scrivete il mio nome* (Don't write my name).[26] Many witnesses insisted on anonymity when addressing the UN: trust in that body had been greatly weakened by events during and following the Revolution. Bang-Jensen's role was crucial because many witnesses were suspicious of the UN but had faith in him.[27]

The Deputy Secretary of the Committee was aware of how enormous his responsibility was. As Bang-Jensen sought out witnesses, he offered anonymity to those who needed it, and the Chair of the Special Committee confirmed this offer before they made their statements.[28] The identities of the first three witnesses to testify were public, but after that the general rule was that sessions were closed—the members of the Committee were keenly aware of just how scared the witnesses were.[29]

The witnesses began their testimonies with a brief introduction, covering the role they had played in the Revolution, the circumstances of their escape from Hungary, and many other aspects of their personal stories that could have been used to identify them; these were not made public.[30] The risk of the records of the hearings "going astray" was not negligible—as a circular memo from Jordan illustrated.[31] At the press conference following the publication of the report of the Special Committee, Shann said that although he did not know of any witness or their family having suffered retaliation, he knew it was a possibility, and that he was not better informed was merely a function of "communication difficulties."[32] The verbatim record of one testimony, however, makes it clear that one witness wanted to testify anonymously because his wife, still at home in Hungary, had already been visited by the secret police.

Apart from the records of the sessions, the cards used to collect personal information (numbered 1 through 34) of potential witnesses were also suitable for identifying them; the correspondence of the Committee secretariat also contained identifying details of some of the witnesses. After the preliminary interviews, the Special Committee staff burned every document that might have identified witnesses, but this did not cover every item,[33] of which many nevertheless survived, providing an enormous service to historical research.[34] Other documents fell into the hands of Soviet and Hungarian state security agencies, providing an enormous service to those seeking retribution. Hungarian state security received its share of the interview records just as it turned its attention to investigating the events of the Revolution with a view toward criminal proceedings.[35]

The only full and reliable list of names was in the hands of Povl Bang-Jensen, however, which made him a central target for clandestine operatives.[36] In some documents, he was referred to as a "prosecutor," and because of the per diems he paid out, he was accused of buying the witnesses off. The communist secret services also knew of his work at the Danish consulate in Washington during World War II in cooperation with the US intelligence services and in support of occupied Denmark and the antifascist resistance. During his tenure with the Special Committee, Bang-Jensen was again trying to establish contact with Washington to assist diplomats from the Eastern bloc who had indicated an interest to defect and to share their suspicions about Soviet influence in the UN.

That the witnesses' fears of identification and repercussions were justified is borne out by documents from the Hungarian so-called justice system. A letter from István Kovács, secretary of the Hungarian Lawyers' Association, to Ferenc Nezvál, minister of justice, proves that all 111 witnesses were "by the fact of providing testimony committ[ing] the most serious crimes of treachery and spying, etc."[37] Thus they had all earned their due punishment.

The witnesses and other émigrés—now considered and characterized by the Kádár government as traitors, spies, and other criminals—were unable to feel safe even in the free world. They had good reason to be worried. According to the plan of the Hungarian station (the secret service center) in Vienna in 1960, there was an "operation relating to the coerced removal" of émigrés. An agent (a former wrestler) was stationed in Vienna to prepare for these forced repatriations to Hungary and deal with any potential resistance. Even years later, there were plans in Budapest for the liquidation of János Radványi, a Hungarian diplomat and secret service asset who defected and then applied for asylum in the United States.[38] Of the UN witnesses, a trial was brought against István Török, who was lured back to Hungary from the United States with the expectation of amnesty and was instead hanged; the groundlessness of the charges suggests that he was executed simply for his "treachery" at the Special Committee.[39] Tamás Pásztor later informed the UN that a number of the refugees tempted back to Hungary were executed: István Lenz was sentenced to death, István Loós was sent to prison, and others were recruited, extorted, and forced to cooperate with the secret services. Refugee students, meanwhile, would simply "disappear," as the UN would be informed by the Vienna envoy of the Hungarian National Revolutionary Committee.[40]

In Budapest, an expansive network of people worked to identify individual witnesses and publicize compromising details, so the crimes attributed to them could be placed within the official narrative of the so-called counterrevolution: that various fascists, Arrow Cross members, gendarmes, Horthyites, and lumpenproletariat figures were making trouble, joined by a few misled workers. Márta Kolozs, leader of the foreign ministry's International Organizations Division, complained that "we spent weeks identifying the witnesses,"[41] despite being given every requested assistance by the Ministry of the Interior. The list of documents transferred included more than one hundred items, including the "French embassy's couriered telegrams."[42]

Officials at the foreign ministry made use of everything they were able to, from horrid fantasies of bloody interrogation rooms to slanderous claims of secret agents, to thinking up new charges and to distorting facts. For example, Béla Szász (one of the defendants at the trial of László Rajk and formerly an agent of state security) was also characterized by the Kádár regime's political police as a spy, and the ex-prison snitch Tamás Pásztor, who in Vienna had refused to be amenable, was mentioned in the documents not as a witness but rather as the organizer and "instructor" of the refugees interviewed. The official Hungarian propaganda claimed that UN witness László Bereczky had killed a Soviet soldier in 1945, that György Széchenyi had been a landowner, and that Endre Szőllősy had been compromised as a military judge—they could continue the lists of accusations as long as they liked, regurgitating old claims and creating new ones.

As a result of these efforts, the families of the identified witnesses were kept under observation, reports were written on their circumstances, their letters were intercepted, their phone conversations were tapped, and agents were assigned to individual family members. It was not only the relatives of key witnesses like Béla Király, Anna Kéthly, József Kővágó, or György Heltai who became targets but also any family members of less prominent witnesses whom it was possible to identify. The task facing the network of agents in Hungary was to "find the relatives of émigrés, if still in Hungary, on a constant basis," and the material thus gathered would, in the greatest variety of combinations, be used for extortion, discrediting, and threats.

Random as the sudden need to identify the witnesses might have appeared, it was a great force in hastening the pace of events. A Hungarian refugee named Károly Szabó tried to prevent his deportation from the United States for having misled US immigration about his membership in the Communist Party by stating that he had given testimony to the United Nations, so his life could be in danger back in Hungary. On October 8, 1957, Secretary of State John Foster Dulles asked the US Mission to the UN to confirm that Szabó had been a witness,[43] only for it to transpire that there was no mention of him in the documents of the Special Committee. This was because the only existing list of names was guarded by Bang-Jensen, who by this stage had been removed from the Committee's staff. When the State Department contacted the Secretariat of the UN to ask that Jordan request the information from Bang-Jensen, he responded at once that Szabó had been a witness;[44] but his superiors then realized that something was amiss if they could have mislaid such an important document.[45] At this point, Bang-Jensen was asked to hand over the list of names,[46] but to the Dane, robbed of his post, humiliated, and never reassured about his doubts, this only reinforced his suspicions about every aspect of the UN Hungarian question and confirmed his worries about what Eastern bloc diplomats had said about Soviet influence. He refused to be amenable: for reasons of conscience, he would not hand over the list, he told Under-Secretary-General Dragoslav Protitch, who knew as well as anyone that his predecessors had been subservient to their Soviet masters (like the Soviet Under-Secretary-General who had headed the Department of Political and Security Council Affairs since 1946) and that it would be no different after him, as the Department was under Soviet directorship and where the loyalty of its employees lay was obvious. Bang-Jensen said that Protitch was naive to think that the list would be safe with his department and that he could not gamble with the trust and lives of people who had revealed their identities to him alone.[47]

Protitch informed Hammarskjöld,[48] verbally and in writing, about Bang-Jensen's reply; the Secretary-General asked Bang-Jensen for an explanation. Bang-Jensen responded that prior to the interviews he had seen the witnesses' mistrust of the UN expressed explicitly, and that many had lost heart or disappeared before their hearings. How odd, Bang-Jensen added, that Hammarskjöld had previously shown no interest in why the two eminent Hungarian communists who had given evidence in London were afraid of the Secretary-General knowing their names, although the two had justified their fears to Bang-Jensen.[49]

The Secretary-General's continued silence was every bit as awkward as the administrative to-and-froing. The list of names may have been a UN document that could not be held privately, but holding it privately was the only guarantee it would not fall into the wrong hands. Indeed, this guarantee was more important than official protocol. And it was not only the earlier episodes that highlighted Bang-Jensen's concerns but also the fact that the list, which no one had thought of for months, had suddenly become so crucial. When Bang-Jensen had previously claimed that someone had been going through his papers, no mention of the list had been made; when he was reported to his superiors, when he was dismissed, and when he was described as mentally ill, no one had asked for it.[50] Furthermore, the UN was able to give a response to the official US request—so what was the real reason? The United States Secret Service could have investigated these events, but on the orders of their superiors, they remained passive.[51]

When the issue was covered in the press, the concern among the refugees grew.[52] The Hungarian revolutionaries expressed their grave worries to the UN, while Robert Morris, legal counsel to the United States Senate, had already spoken out about the tangible panic among the Hungarian refugees after communist agent Miklós Szabó returned to Hungary from Austria.[53] News reports meant that, alongside the witnesses, public opinion would also side with Bang-Jensen, who felt that the intense and hardly comprehensible pressure from the UN leadership only proved him right. He could not risk giving in.

At his wife's request, Bang-Jensen now wrote a letter stating that "under no circumstances would I commit suicide." He then went into detail, describing the circumstances of his death two years before it happened: "If any note was found to the opposite effect with my handwriting, it would be a fake." Although he did not underestimate the forces that had understood that "it is clear that I will not retreat," he would not abandon the conflicts of his own accord.[54]

The UN leadership made the case that the other documents held by the UN, not just the list of names, could be used to identify the witnesses, but Bang-Jensen was not convinced by this.[55] He was strengthened in his resolve by the fact that no action had been taken on the suspicious activity he had reported to Jordan—that unknown individuals had opened his drawers, and others had offered him money for documents that could help identify witnesses.[56] No one else seemed to be troubled by the arrival of interpreters and security guards from the Soviet bloc joining the staff in Geneva; perhaps Bang-Jensen was bothered because of his experience with subterfuge during his time in the antifascist resistance. No one else would have thought to encrypt the list of names, to use special tools to hide it, or to leave misleading documents around his office on purpose—as Bang-Jensen would later reveal he had done. When proceedings had already started against Bang-Jensen for insubordination in the UN, the UN leadership would read Bang-Jensen's memoranda with surprise, learning that he referred to such secrets as Niels Bohr's role in the top-secret Manhattan Project, which, as the physicist's friend and an employee of the Danish consulate in exile, Bang-Jensen had once received information about.

According to Bang-Jensen, Protitch had told him that only he (Bang-Jensen) would know the names of the anonymous witnesses. A telegram from Protitch and Bang-Jensen had been sent to some witnesses confirming that they could testify "anonymously," not just secretly. Later, Protitch stated that Bang-Jensen "was not authorized to be the only one to know the witnesses' names."[57] Bang-Jensen believed that he had in fact had that authority, and in any case the witnesses had agreed to testify based on that assurance from a UN official, so the UN could not break this agreement without the consent of the witnesses.

Meanwhile, in his letter to the Secretary-General, Andersen cited the guarantee given to the witnesses as being the mutual responsibility of the Committee members and the secretariat. He argued that the records were safe inside the UN building, although he could not rule out the possibility that "spies in certain cases might be at work in the world's political headquarters in New York."[58] Shann confirmed that "the selection of witnesses [was] in most cases by Bang-Jensen," so he had the most comprehensive knowledge of this, but on the particular issue at hand, he claimed that in his home country, Australia, Bang-Jensen's handling the list would be "almost a crime."[59] The UN leadership continued to demand the list, while Bang-Jensen was firm in his belief that it did not amount to insubordination to reject an order for physical or moral reasons.[60]

Hammarskjöld was forced to act, but he called on an independent attorney to head a commission to make recommendations to him regarding the Bang-Jensen case. He appointed Ernst Gross, who had remained at the disposal of the Secretary-General during turbulent times in US domestic politics and sometimes served as Hammarskjöld's personal lawyer. He had also successfully represented Ralph Bunche when he was called to testify before the infamous Army–McCarthy security hearings. In the past, Cordier had also been a legal client of Gross. It was not only Gross's independence that was in doubt but also his inclusion in the internal affairs of the UN. Even though two high-ranking UN officials, Constantin Stavropoulos and Philippe de Seynes, were members of the Committee, the proceedings were not only unusual but at odds with the UN's personnel protocols. That Gross avoided questions at the US Senate hearing in Washington following Bang-Jensen's death is evidence that he was aware of these irregularities.

Stavropoulos, de Seynes, and Gross formed what the UN classified as an informal group that made recommendations to the Secretary-General. Gross was at once an investigator, lawyer, judge, and spokesperson. According to Hammarskjöld's calendar,[61] Gross was in frequent contact with him and with Cordier, who followed events closely. Gross and his colleagues established their positions after studying the documents and then interviewing staff. Bang-Jensen was not informed about the charges concerning his behavior, however, so he could not know what he had to defend himself against; nor was he able to access the testimony of Gross's witnesses or have his lawyer to cross-examine them. He also did not know whether his submissions were being taken into account or not. He was not given the documents he requested, and after he named his legal counsel, he was never called to give evidence. He noted that there were no fewer than 231 places in the typed version where his statement was not accurately reflected, but this objection was also ignored.[62]

At this point, Henrik von Kauffmann, Danish ambassador to the US, became involved in this increasingly awkward affair. Von Kauffmann was an excellent diplomat who had led the independent Danish mission to the US during World War II and was Bang-Jensen's friend and former superior. In December 1957, he worked out a detailed plan to establish the compromise that Bang-Jensen hand over the list of names to Andersen, who would accept responsibility for guarding it.[63] Everything was prepared for this truce, which would have enabled the UN to withdraw from the standoff with no loss of prestige, while allowing Bang-Jensen to keep his promise to the witnesses. When Andersen tried to retrieve the list from Bang-Jensen a few days later, however, his fellow Dane refused to cooperate, claiming that only the witnesses themselves could free him of his obligation to guard the list.[64]

We can only guess what might have happened in those few days. Perhaps Bang-Jensen's mind was changed by the one-sidedness of the workings of the Gross Committee: the biased nature of the hearings, or the exclusion of Bang-Jensen from the procedure that concerned him. Or perhaps there was some other, more serious reason for why the compromise did not come about. Meanwhile, highly demonstrative and humiliating steps were taken against Bang-Jensen—even before the investigation had officially concluded its work. Perhaps this was what forced him to realize that Gross's committee was not actually investigating whether security criteria were met, what promises were made, and in whom the witnesses had placed their trust. Instead, its tactics seemed to be about intimidation and humiliation—presumably to prevent the disclosure of the most important and concerning aspects of the whole affair.[65]

On December 6, 1957, Bang-Jensen was officially notified that he had been suspended from his service, only for the personnel director to add that he would be dismissed from his employment as well.[66] When Bang-Jensen asked about the reason for this decision, J. A. C. Robertson, head of personnel at the UN, would not reveal it and asked Bang-Jensen not to tell anyone about his suspension. At the door of his office, two security guards were waiting to escort Bang-Jensen from the building—an unusual measure for a purely administrative procedure like this one. This was later justified by the claim that it was necessary to be sure that he leave "empty handed"[67]— which makes the decision even more insensitive and humiliating. The scene can be reconstructed based on subsequent reports filed, precisely because of the unusual nature of the case, by its participants but not by those who were actually behind it. For on this day, the Secretary-General was not in New York; he later stated that he considered the steps taken to have been "unnecessary."[68] But it was no accident that those who considered this action not only necessary but crucial arranged for Bang-Jensen's notice to be served on this day of all days: as he left the room, they perhaps hoped that he would make a scene, that there would be noise or pushing and shoving, that this employee under investigation might angrily have demanded his papers or done anything that could have provided evidence for how unstable and even mentally ill he was. But they miscalculated. Neither Bang-Jensen nor the two "embarrassed" guards wanted any trouble. And lest there be any doubt as to their motivations, those who were behind these actions then took the opportunity to rummage through Bang-Jensen's desk and change the locks on his filing cabinet and office door. Nine days passed before Bang-Jensen was granted access to retrieve his telephone book and checkbook, at which point he was able to see how they had opened his drawers and looked through his documents.[69] When Hammarskjöld returned, everything was restored to its original place.[70]

Under-Secretaries-General Cordier and Protitch rejected calls to convene the Special Committee because they felt it "would inflate the whole issue in world public opinion wholly out of proportion to its significance," even creating the impression that certain documents were not safely stored at the United Nations. Instead, they claimed, this was a "simple and straightforward case of insubordination," for just as "all important documents over the last 12 years have been preserved in perfect safety," the same was no doubt true of the list of the witnesses' names.[71] It was as if they could not remember any of the precedents that contradicted this, as if they had not read English translations of articles in the communist press besmirching witnesses who had been named, and as if they had not noticed that UN diplomats from the Soviet bloc who had systematically been caught up in dubious affairs were expelled from the United States.

As an indication that Cordier and Protitch's statement did not satisfy everyone, a session of the Special Committee was convened on December 17, 1957, as the security problems relating to "certain documents" might be the "topic of much public controversy." Protitch and Cordier provided information on the UN's security system for managing documents,[72] which is rather revealing in itself: they clearly had to inform the Committee because its members had no idea about UN security protocols. Protitch did not know exactly what documents were in Bang-Jensen's possession, and the number of papers falling into the wrong hands was proof of the invalidity of Cordier's argument.[73] The Special Committee approved the report and threw its weight behind the UN leadership,[74] but, having declared its unswerving allegiance, even it could only wait for what Bang-Jensen would do next.

Meanwhile, many documents were studied, the hearings were finished, and the investigation was concluded—the record of the interview with Claire de Hedervary alone ran to sixty pages.[75] Gross's committee started to prepare its report, which confirmed that every document produced during its operation would become the property of the United Nations and that no one could illegally store them in private. It also stated that there was no evidence to support that the UN's security protocols were inadequate and that

Bang-Jensen's claims were therefore unfounded.[76] It ignored the numerous previous occasions on which important documents had leaked from the UN and did not think to mention the suspension and then dismissal of Ceylonese UN employee Dhanapala Samarasekara, who was accused of turning over Hungarian data to Vladimir Grusha of the Soviet delegation.[77] These omissions were as suggestive of disingenuous proceedings as the fact that Bang-Jensen was not allowed to become acquainted with the content of the report, an outline of which had been sent to Cordier. The former Deputy Secretary of the Special Committee had no chance to respond to the report's conclusions, and by the time he was finally sent a copy of them, they had also been sent to representatives of the press. The Committee investigated three specific instances out of the twenty-eight that Bang-Jensen had objected to: sabotage, the withholding of information, and security issues, but his reservations were found to be "unsubstantiated," and this was assumed to be true of all other cases as well. As during the work of the Special Committee, there had been no complaints about security procedures, so they assumed that these were adequate. Bang-Jensen, on the other hand, was characterized as slowing efforts with what were called his unfounded concerns and was said to have contravened proper protocols when he had expressed his concerns to the Chair of the Committee. Jordan was judged to have been right to filter incoming information, and it was for the Rapporteur, not the secretariat, to have an opinion on the report. The list of names of witnesses, meanwhile, had lost its credibility precisely because of the "exceptional insecurity" of its storage, and so there was no other option but to destroy it. Anthony Panuch, who provided legal assistance to Bang-Jensen, was astonished that Gross's committee had operated as examining judge, prosecutor, jury, and court simultaneously, that the internal report published during the investigation had been preordained, and that its publication meant details being leaked to the press. He considered the proceedings to be a "cowardly and ignominious attack,"[78] one that would not be allowed under US law, and therefore those devising it and implementing it were abusing their special legal status at the UN.

All of this was part of the same character assassination that led to Bang-Jensen being escorted from the UN building, aspersions being cast on his character, and his mental health being brought into doubt. It can hardly have served any other objective than of distracting attention from what really mattered: the fate of the UN witnesses. On the issue of witness confidentiality both sides had fixed themselves more and more rigidly into a strict set of basic principles that left little in the way of wiggle room. The UN's moral demand was not merely a theoretical question but also a practical one: human lives and fates depended on it, not to mention that it could become a precedent for other investigations. How could anyone dare to testify to a UN investigative committee in the future if they could not be sure that confidential information would remain confidential?[79]

In the end, Andersen recommended that the list of witnesses be destroyed. As Chair of the Special Committee, he felt a great responsibility to stand by the guarantee he had given to each anonymous witness before they testified. Destroying the list would have been not just an unusual but an extraordinary measure—but extraordinary times demand nothing less.[80] We can see what a dilemma this posed for Hammarskjöld from the notes in his diary and indeed from the profusion of newspaper articles, letters, and telegrams that reflected on the dramatic decision.

Finally, on January 24, 1958, on the roof of UN Headquarters, three envelopes were burned in the presence of Under-Secretary-General Protitch, the head of UN internal security, and Bang-Jensen and his lawyer, and a record was made of the event.[81] They watched as the sealed envelopes turned to ash—but the envelopes, as only Bang-Jensen knew, did not, in fact, contain the list of names.

After the envelopes were burned, on pain of criminal prosecution, Bang-Jensen confirmed that he did not have a copy of the list of witnesses.[82] He was telling the truth. As he clearly sensed the risk that the list of names might be taken from him by force inside UN Headquarters, in the early hours of that morning, in the fireplace in his living room, in the presence of his wife, he had burned his copy of the list of witness names.[83] The official announcements referred to what was in fact a perfectly absurd piece of political theater—the ceremonial burning of insignificant documents in sealed envelopes. But the witnesses could breathe a sigh of relief.

The UN leadership accepted this "unfortunate" precedent but was not satisfied by it. The case could have been closed, but instead it seemed like it was only just beginning. The findings of Gross's committee were overshadowed by the news value of the burning of the documents. This event was covered by the press across the globe, and Hammarskjöld had to field questions about it at numerous press conferences. The administrative and legal problems during the procedure against Bang-Jensen attracted the attention of journalists as much as the real issues of security in the UN. Samarasekara's name was mentioned—he had assisted KGB agents with decoding secret messages by turning over the codebook of the Ceylonese embassy to a Soviet agent—as were various other episodes over twelve stormy years that had confirmed the validity of Bang-Jensen's concerns about confidentiality in the UN's affairs.[84]

The political resonance of these events was significant and was exploited by the Soviet and Hungarian propagandists, often thanks to their "fellow travelers" (Soviet sympathizers) in the West.[85] As far as they were concerned, the burning of the documents invalidated the UN resolutions. And although the Gross report remained confidential—mostly because of the sensitive information it contained—quite a few copies were issued. Each was separately numbered for security and control (the UN sent Bang-Jensen copy number 25). In spite of Cordier's reassurances regarding the UN's twelve-year security record, Hungarian archives clearly indicate that Moscow had obtained a copy of the Gross report and had also sent a copy to Budapest.[86] The degree to which the UN's internal affairs were known in the Soviet Union and Hungary finally broke through the tolerance threshold of US foreign policy: Dulles wanted to know the source for the February 8, 1958, *Népszabadság* (Freedom of the people) article discussing these affairs; he also suggested the UN Secretariat be informed immediately.[87] There, however, the only question raised was the validity of the methods of the Special Committee—but "without a defense of Bang-Jensen."[88] In Budapest, meanwhile, the Bang-Jensen case joined the documents pertaining to the trial of Maléter and others in a dossier titled "Developments in the Hungarian question since the 12th session of the General Assembly."[89] This would prove prophetic.

Disciplinary Actions and Appeals

The press response to Bang-Jensen's dismissal was enthusiastic and almost uniformly on Bang-Jensen's side. To sway Danish public opinion, Andersen quoted Shann's earlier letter, in which the Rapporteur had heated words for Bang-Jensen, but this tactic backfired. The Associated Press reported that Bang-Jensen wanted to remain part of the United Nations despite having received many other offers, some of them very attractive. The expression of sympathy for his plight was exceptionally heartfelt: support came from groups as diverse as World War II veterans, Hungarian freedom fighters, and even US progressives acting in unity with anticommunist conservatives—all stressed their sympathy for and understanding of his struggle.[90]

On the recommendation of the Gross Committee, Hammarskjöld took Bang-Jensen's case to the UN Joint Disciplinary Committee, suggesting that he considered Bang-Jensen's reservations to amount to a disciplinary misdemeanor irrespective of what they referred to. The UN legal apparatus whirred into action, which would, of course, have significant consequences.[91]

On February 18, 1958, Bang-Jensen received a message that the UN had begun to hear his case: his "accusations" made against the Special Committee, his criticism of the Secretary and the Rapporteur, and his citation of the official documents in his possession.[92] The judicial committee dealt with the case from March 20 to June 5, looking through numerous documents (which would later be classified for decades), conducting interviews, requesting specialist legal opinions, and all the while remaining in close contact with Cordier. It seemed like a mere administrative issue for the UN rather than a meeting of opposing positions. The UN had established from the outset that they would not question the Special Committee's position on Bang-Jensen and that they would not investigate the "handling by the Committee of the various items of evidence and information," even though this was the key issue relating to Bang-Jensen's case.[93] According to Anthony Panuch, who gave Bang-Jensen legal assistance, if his client had sued the Gross Committee in a US court, he would have won.[94]

Bang-Jensen thought he would be able to use his legal knowledge and provide documents to give weight to his reservations and defend the truth of his position. His strategy put first and foremost the interests of the United Nations itself, in whose principles he had a steadfast belief and whose operation he sought to improve. It was in this spirit that he requested the release of important documents for his defense and put together a list of the questions to be resolved that underscored the origins of the conflicts and the development of his case. The majority of what he asked for was considered "wholly irrelevant" by the Committee, however, which did not even trouble to consider which of these could be released. The Joint Disciplinary Committee's strategy was to avoid dealing with any examination of the evidence, even when Bang-Jensen asked about the reasons behind the assumptions made about his mental health.[95] The background to Bang-Jensen's work was also considered to be beyond the remit of the investigation, while his promise to protect the anonymity of the witnesses was judged to contradict the regulations governing the actions of UN staff.[96]

Press conference given by Under-Secretary-General Andrew Cordier at the
UN. Copyright: UN Photo Archive #7724730.

In light of these restrictions in the scope of the investigation, the outcome was hardly in doubt. The decision of the Joint Disciplinary Committee was that UN staff had to "sub-ordinate their personal views to the decisions of the responsible superiors in the Secretariat" and to accept their
"over-riding authority in all matters of substance." As Povl Bang-Jensen had
not satisfied these criteria, he had proved himself unsuitable for work at
the UN Secretariat, and the Committee recommended he "be dismissed
for misconduct."[97] The Staff Council, the body for UN employees, considered the operation of the Committee to be unsound; this should have been
enough to invalidate the ruling.[98] All that Bang-Jensen had asked was for
his position be made public, as there had been no mention of the crux of the
conflict. It was not.

That the UN leadership had maneuvered itself into a morally losing
position was shown by the way it made one last attempt to smooth over the
conflict. The Danish Mission to the UN, which was loyal to the UN Secretariat, recommended, on behalf of the Danish government, that a "friendly
solution" be found to the affair, as this was also in the UN's interests.[99] The
Secretariat finally offered to accept Bang-Jensen's resignation, should he

submit it, and to express its recognition of his work—and was even ready to articulate regret over how things had developed. It was in line with this that the Secretary-General wrote a letter to Bang-Jensen, asking him to respond to the charges listed in the Committee's report.[100] Bang-Jensen was willing to comply, asking only that he receive access to documents that were necessary for him to prepare his response. He did not receive the documents, he was not able to respond, and the compromise could not be achieved.[101] On June 14, 1958, Bang-Jensen nevertheless presented his position in a twenty-nine page report, supported by evidence, touching on all significant issues, covering the critical question of the confidentiality of the list of names, and going through the proceedings initiated against him.[102] On June 16, 1958, the personnel director of the UN announced that the Secretary-General would decide about Bang-Jenson's status later that day.[103] The decision was hardly in doubt. A twelve-page letter of dismissal was formulated and was to be publicized when it was handed over.

Then it was not published after all. For it was on this same day that news reached New York of the execution of Imre Nagy and his associates, and the coincidence suggested a connection between the two events. There was indeed a connection, and on June 20, 1958, Bang-Jensen drew Hammarskjöld's attention to his responsibility—or rather his complicity—for all that had happened.[104] Bang-Jensen might have made this desperate gesture because on June 19, his two key friends, Niels Bohr and Henrik von Kauffmann, attempted in vain to stand up for him.[105] But they could not protect Bang-Jensen and his family from the ordeal of the months to come, nor could they cushion the UN from the "most adverse international press."[106]

The long letter of dismissal was finally sent to Bang-Jensen on July 3, 1958. The timing was no accident, because it was the eve of a three-day Fourth of July weekend in the United States. In the appendix to the letter of dismissal, Bang-Jensen read letters from Andersen, Shann, and Protitch, each of whom, for different reasons, uniformly condemned his work.[107] As this resolution was hardly a friendly one, Hammarskjöld wrote to the Danish prime minister on the same day, reminding him of their recent meeting and asking him to respect their agreement in his official comments.[108]

As soon as news of the twelve-page letter of dismissal spread, the press and public opinion went into an uproar: there was a constant flow of articles, telegrams, and letters expressing shock, indignation, and dismay.[109] Only Christian Winther, the New York correspondent for Danish radio, remained loyal to the UN leadership, consistently and sometimes rather arrogantly toeing the UN's official line. This line was that Bang-Jensen had once laid a hand on Shann and that Bang-Jensen was unable to find evidence for either his claim of sabotage or that information from Hungary had been silenced. Winther's writings posed the question of whether the list of witnesses was safe with Bang-Jensen if he were to change political sides—or if he were to unexpectedly die.[110]

Bang-Jensen could not accept the official statement of the UN after his dismissal and asked that his own position be published just as widely as the one that had been composed against him.[111] It was not to be. So he sought out the opportunity to acquaint others with his arguments, which ranged from sabotage to mistakes in the report. In this way, he disproved the official charges against him, one by one. He touched on the unusual legal status of the Gross Committee, adding that he had not been permitted to see the witness statements the charges were based on. He rejected the offer of a financial settlement as an attempt to buy him off, and he did not accept the reasons for his dismissal, so he did not accept the consequence that he be dismissed—at all.[112]

Feelings were riding high as a result: Andersen and Shann made public statements denouncing Bang-Jensen, while Jordan maintained that Bang-Jensen "compounded his incompetence with insubordination"—in Vienna, for example.[113] Jordan claimed that there were simply "no errors" in the report, even though he knew that the opposite was true. He stated that the issue of the mothballed telegram from Maléter's bodyguard had been "fully dealt with," and Protitch declared that "Bang-Jensen was not authorized to be the only one to know the witnesses' names."[114] That the UN leadership—primarily the Secretariat—began a whispering campaign against Bang-Jensen was proof both of the strength of their feelings and the weakness of their argument: they mentioned allegations of his alcoholism, psychopathy, and sexual problems—character assassination had taken on a new dimension. More careful observers tried to avoid being pinned down by stressing that the report had been approved by the whole Committee; indeed, the whole world had expressed its approval, even the Hungarian revolutionaries themselves.[115] As if this might redeem the irredeemable.

Bang-Jensen decided to appeal the decision of the Disciplinary Committee and also cabled the UN personnel officer, John McDiarmid, to ask that his papers be left untouched. McDiarmid responded that Bang-Jensen's office had to be emptied, and that his official documents would be stored as regulations prescribed. Bang-Jensen replied that while his appeal was still in process he was still to be considered an employee with full rights, so it was premature to make any decisions on his status. This was why he had not accepted a financial settlement of $17,416.65 and had instead returned the check.[116] That the UN had preordained the outcome of the appeal (the decision of the Administrative Court that had not yet been made) was made clear by the suspension of Bang-Jensen's medical insurance and the recall of his security pass for the UN building and the right of entry for his car—when he next visited his workplace, he had to use a day pass, as a visitor or guest might. The confidential papers concerning the Special Committee's investigation and related affairs were placed in the library under lock and key, which again did not conform to protocols for the treatment of documents.[117] As Bang-Jensen's dismissal was considered to have become official on July 3, they demanded that he empty his office. Stavropoulos read and confirmed the letters sent by the UN head of personnel, so the actions taken were given the tacit approval of the UN's chief legal counsel.[118] Bang-Jensen was accompanied on his visit to clear out the office by Robert Morris, who had been following events since November 1956 and who acted as his legal representative in this latest stage of the proceedings.[119]

At this same time, Protitch was replaced as Under-Secretary-General of the Department of Political and Security Council Affairs by Soviet diplomat Anatoly Dobrynin; with this, the Department came under Soviet control. In May, Hammarskjöld ordered that the affairs of the Special Committee be managed from June 10 by Humphrey Trevelyan, a British UN civil servant; a copy of his instructions was sent to Cordier and Dobrynin.[120] Trevelyan would later return his mandate, and first Bunche and then Cordier would be in charge of the Hungarian question.[121] This meant that almost all the documentation regarding the Special Committee came into Cordier's hands (including the contents of Bang-Jensen's desk and filing cabinet and his personal notes). All this would be protected "with a new combination lock," so only Cordier would have access.[122]

Cordier had played a key role throughout the UN's campaign against Bang-Jensen, both behind the scenes and out in the open. According to Robert Morris, the Eastern bloc diplomats who sought to defect indicated to Bang-Jensen that Cordier was Moscow's man in the UN.[123] This is what Eastern bloc diplomats must have been referring to back in November 1956, when they said that the "38th floor" (the offices of the UN leadership) was under Moscow's control at the highest level.

In the United States, anticommunist activist and chief counsel to the United States Senate Subcommittee on Internal Security Robert Morris tried to draw the Senate's attention to the Soviet influence that could be sensed at the UN, even if this took place too late—after Bang-Jensen's death. The results of the investigation by the Senate Subcommittee on Internal Security differed very little from those revealed by journalists' investigations:[124] Bang-Jensen's fate would be determined by the fact that his suspicions and struggle were music to the ears of right-wing political hawks in the United States, who had always been deeply skeptical of the workings of the UN. The implications of the actions of these hawks meant that tensions at the UN were riding high. An internal UN document referred to Morris as a Cold War veteran; it also blamed the Bang-Jensen affair for Hammarskjöld requiring round-the-clock security protection after threats made to his person and the vandalizing of his car.[125]

That the Secretary-General was the greatest "security risk" was not only suggested by the Hungarian communists giving evidence in London; it was also sensed by author DeWitt S. Copp and *New York Herald Tribune* editor Marshall Peck, investigative journalists who soon after the tragic death of Bang-Jensen turned to investigating his case. Given Hammarskjöld's unusual character, his life as a single man, his close friendships with men, and some slips of the tongue, some believed that he was gay. In Hammarskjöld's era, this was a crime, and any tangible evidence for such an allegation would have rendered him susceptible to extortion. This was the common belief, and perhaps this is what Hammarskjöld did not want to hear when Bang-Jensen offered to tell him what others had said about him and warned the Secretary-General that the vulnerability of significant individuals is significant.[126]

In the fall of 1958, officers from the FBI, personally mandated by J. Edgar Hoover, contacted Bang-Jensen and spent almost five hours interviewing him in their New York office.[127] Not even to them could Bang-Jensen reveal all that he knew, but he provided a number of indirect pieces of evidence, all of which the secret services already knew about. But none of this led to anything, only that the FBI was in a position to "protect itself," leaving the "troublemaker" to his fate. Even when a number of people suggested that Bang-Jensen's life could be threatened because of the dangerous things he knew, they did not offer him protection,[128] nor did they open an investigation. There was no suggestion of spying or other clandestine operations, so this was not within the FBI's remit,[129] nor within that of the CIA, even if both organizations watched the events with interest. On one occasion, Vice President Nixon was advised about US intelligence interviews with Bang-Jensen at a session of the National Security Council.[130]

It is hard to explain why US authorities remained so passive when Bang-Jensen asked for assistance for Eastern bloc diplomats planning to defect, raised his suspicions about the contradictions in the management of the Hungarian question, and refused to hand over the list of names, generating such heated conflicts. James Barco, a member of the US Mission to the UN, met Bang-Jensen on many occasions, but whether the messages from the Eastern bloc diplomats got stuck with him or his superiors, we cannot know.[131] Neither can we know why Barco wrote down the information Bang-Jensen shared with him, even when he had been specifically requested to not put anything in writing lest it be seen by prying eyes. Or could it have been precisely those with prying eyes who—proving his suspicions to be well-founded—managed to preempt any further steps being taken? When Barco later told his superiors that their inaction might lead Bang-Jensen to go to the press, they thought it more important to prevent him speaking out than to address the real issue.[132] And when Ambassador Kauffmann arranged a meeting between Allen Dulles, director of central intelligence, and Bang-Jensen, it seemed more like a social encounter than the confidential sharing of a serious suspicion. Dulles had by this time been successfully fed stories of Bang-Jensen's "troubled" behavior and his "contradictory" political role, which prevented him from taking the Danish diplomat very seriously.[133]

The entire US Mission to the UN turned its back on Bang-Jensen: no members would accept his phone calls or reply to his messages, even though professional etiquette would have demanded they do so.[134] That this behavior was endorsed by officials in the highest places is suggested by a meeting between Henry Cabot Lodge Jr. and Secretary of State John Foster Dulles on November 27, 1957.[135] Barco, the first person Bang-Jensen had told about his concerns, did not want to meet with him again,[136] and when Lodge wanted to know the details about what had happened, he turned not to Bang-Jensen but to Hammarskjöld. Five days after Bang-Jensen was dismissed, the Secretary-General personally informed the US delegation to the UN that the letter of dismissal would be made public at four o'clock that afternoon. Bang-Jensen's allegations—which the delegation had not thought worthy of attention—would for a later Senate investigation appear "unprecedented."[137]

The justification given to Lodge for publicizing a confidential personnel matter was that the "confusion and distortion of this case which has developed widely in this country" made this unusual action necessary.[138] After this, Lodge was somehow convinced that the Special Committee witnesses were not in danger, while his deputy, James Wadsworth, added that the Secretary-General was "fully justified dismissing Bang-Jensen."[139] To the question from Danish ambassador Aage Hessellund-Jensen to the UN as to which side it took on this issue, Lodge's surprising reply was that the US remained neutral. When Hessellund-Jensen quoted Lodge's opinion as reported in newspaper articles, which was at odds with this claim, Lodge simply denied his previous statement. At this same time, the US deputy secretary of state replied to an inquiry from the Senate Foreign Relations Committee to say that Bang-Jensen's dismissal had been processed according to the United Nations' regulations, according to procedures that were applicable to everyone and that the General Assembly had decided upon and accepted. He added that Bang-Jensen's reservations about the UN Secretariat were unfounded,[140] and it was in this light that they responded to the letters, articles, and cables expressing endless angry, shocked, and desperate messages that said effectively that the United States had abandoned someone who was a firm believer in its principles and who had consistently demonstrated this during decisive moments in history. The CIA, once an important witness for and close partner with Bang-Jensen during World War II, now merely asked State Department officials to confer with the CIA before releasing their statements.[141]

A few years later, a book would be published on the influence of the Soviet Union, which was denied or underestimated at the time, and the activities of Soviet spies, who were present during the vilification of Bang-Jensen. It made public the names of Soviets, many working at the UN, declared persona non grata from 1954 onward; Lodge himself would write the blurb for the cover.[142] This suggests that Lodge was just as aware of Soviet influence at the UN as his Danish colleague was, except that, for him, in this case, it appears, politics trumped morality. For Bang-Jensen, it was the other way around.

The press response to Bang-Jensen's dismissal was unprecedented, not just because of the Dane's personality but also the mentality and morality he represented. The Nuremberg trials, with their legal and moral precedents, were still a fresh memory, while in Eastern Europe, the Twentieth Congress of the Communist Party of the Soviet Union showed that a collective silence had been broken and the now-evident moral deficit of collective complicity was laid bare. During all this, it was primarily the media that fought for a cause that governments and diplomats did not, particularly those at the UN, suggesting that public opinion stood at odds with representatives of an institution that was hierarchical, overly ready to compromise, and sometimes even hypocritical.

It was at this same time that Bang-Jensen, while renewing his US visa, had his passport franked with the stamp reserved for diplomats from communist countries. By then, he had been living in the US for almost two decades, and his wife and children were US citizens.[143] In early 1959, to avoid the need for a visa to stay with his family, he applied for US citizenship, a process that, for unknown reasons, got held up at the Department of State.

In addition to these various episodes, the strength of feeling with which many of the participants approached the Bang-Jensen affair clearly showed that this was no longer about reasoned arguments—or these would have been enough—and more about convictions and institutionalized mentalities. Outside the UN Secretariat, the two most important members of the Special Committee, the Chair and the Rapporteur, led the way in stirring up passions. Andersen formerly shared Bang-Jensen's concerns and attempted to mediate, but by this stage, he did not want to meet with him or hear what he had to say and did not give an explanation for this change of heart. Andersen later informed Hammarskjöld that, while in Denmark, he had avoided meeting with Bang-Jensen, even though the prime minister and other ministers had met with him; the press, irrespective of political allegiance, had uniformly supported him; and Danish public opinion expressed solidarity for the Hungarians. The UN Secretary-General sent the Danish prime minister a copy of Bang-Jensen's letter of dismissal with the message that the UN had extended every consideration to Bang-Jensen and waited in the hope that its employee "might regain his emotional stability."[144]

In the United States, too, there was unanimous support for Bang-Jensen, as was accurately reflected in press coverage. It was none other than Wilder Foote—the head of the UN press office and exceptionally loyal to Hammarskjöld—who reported to the UN information center in Copenhagen that "the entire press in the US has ignored the Bang-Jensen case [. . .] with the exception of an extreme right wing publication."[145] In fact, the conflict had received thorough media coverage, which was "without exception favorable to Bang-Jensen," as the Australian foreign minister was told by US sources.

News reports claimed that "a certain Australian diplomat" had been the brains behind the campaign against Bang-Jensen, thereby assisting communists at the UN trying to discredit the report of the Special Committee on the Problem of Hungary.[146] Many were stunned that the famously anticommunist Shann—whose angry letters decrying Bang-Jensen were not just quoted in the press but were also listed by Hammarskjöld as part of the justification for the dismissal—could have come this far. The Australian foreign ministry asked for information from New York and Washington, and the country's press also threw its weight behind Bang-Jensen.[147] Meanwhile Bang-Jensen contacted Shann himself, to seek an explanation and to establish an accurate recollection of events, but he got no response, nor did he get one from Shann's successor, Ronald Walker, head of the Australian Mission to the UN. It is perhaps telling that on one letter in the UN Archives written during these events are the words "Ring Andy." This refers to Executive Assistant to the Secretary-General and Under-Secretary-General Andrew Cordier, who no doubt wished to receive information about every development—and presumably got it, not only from the staff at the Secretariat but also from the envoys of member states loyal to the UN leadership. Shann later said to Robert Morris of the conflict that if Bang-Jensen was right and of a right mind, the UN was indefensibly dishonest and even dangerous.[148]

While the world at large was almost uniformly on Bang-Jensen's side, he nevertheless found himself in a vacuum inside the United Nations; he only had recourse to public opinion and his own patience as he waited for the final decision on his appeal. He had achieved much more with his sheer stamina and resolve than the UN had with its rushed, ill-tempered campaign, and had become a moral and political symbol, principally for the Hungarian revolutionaries but also for those who cared about honoring one's word and moral imperatives. Those who resisted Bang-Jensen were—whether they liked to admit it or not—resisting these fundamental principles.

The UN leadership, preparing for the appeal proceedings, was looking for reasons to justify the final and unassailable removal of Bang-Jensen. At this point, it was suggested that "Bang-Jensen has quite a record of insubordination predating his appointment to the secretariat of the Special Committee."[149] It was as if he had a recurring habit of resisting the orders of his superiors. But those prejudging him gave little thought to the fact that Bang-Jensen's famous refusal to obey referred to orders from Copenhagen under the control of the invading Nazis. In a letter marked as read by the Secretary-General, a UN officer named Bill Kemsley also mentioned as a supposed precedent the "disquieting rumors" about the so-called Easter Crisis in Denmark and Bang-Jensen's work to influence Denmark to abandon the neutrality policy that guided Danish foreign policy during World War I and World War II.[150]

There was little doubt, based on these events, whether the United Nations wanted Bang-Jensen on its staff or not. But Bang-Jensen was no longer fighting for his job as much as for his truth, which was not only his but also that of those who had faith in him and, indeed, faith in the UN itself. For months, the institution had presented itself to him in the form of administrative procedures and various committees, at least in a formal capacity; at a personal level, meanwhile, his struggle had been accompanied by a huge amount of encouragement and sympathy. When Bang-Jensen traveled to Denmark and Prime Minister H. C. Hansen received him to gain firsthand information about the conflict with the UN, Bang-Jensen was given only modest support: Copenhagen recommended to the UN that during the proceedings, Bang-Jensen should be given access to more documents rather than fewer. And while the Danish government officially kept its distance from him, it could not remain unresponsive to public opinion, so it voted to offer a deposit of $5000 for the very considerable legal costs of his appeal, to be accounted for at a later date.[151] Danish government officials made it clear to the UN leadership that this support did not mean that they lacked trust in the organization's legal procedures nor that they took any kind of position on the case. But they knew that their compatriot's financial reserves had been depleted, that he had not accepted the financial settlement, that he had not been paid a wage since July, and that he had five children to care for. At this time, Bang-Jensen rejected the offer of a contract to write a book about his trials and tribulations—he did not want to harm the UN. He forfeited a fee of $20,000 just as he took out a mortgage on his house to avoid any financial obstacles to his continued struggle to clear his name and uncover Soviet influence at the UN.

The UN administrative proceedings[152] were based on similarly thorough and biased investigations as the two previous procedures had been, which was made abundantly clear by them being based on precisely the same documentary material. The collection of documents was immense. The index alone ran to seven volumes. The last of these documents concluded with the decision passed on December 5, 1958, with documents ordered from item 227 to item 259.[153] These documents included—rather surprisingly—such personal items as a transcript of Bang-Jensen's telephone conversations, as well as announcements, rules and regulations, letters, resolutions, and memoranda, some of which were up to fifteen pages long.[154] It might be considered procedure to contain the press coverage on the pertinent issue in such quantities, but the collection included a number of articles from the press, many of them in translation, and, alongside Bang-Jensen's statements, all the documents the appellant had requested and requested again, only to be told he was denied access to them. But they were nonetheless suitable for consideration by the administrative committee.

The committee was convened and called Under-Secretary-General Cordier as a witness, who now wanted to be directly involved in the case. He began by saying that the Special Committee was an independent body over which the UN Secretariat had no influence, so there could have been no investigation into its activities. He thus formally rejected Bang-Jensen's concerns. This was contradicted by the facts, of course: in line with the General Assembly's resolution, the Special Committee was established on the recommendations of the Secretariat, and Cordier himself had made use of the Secretariat's indirect influence on more than one occasion. The order of the Special Committee's proceedings, meanwhile, was in no small part defined by the secretariat it had appointed to it, which was in turn an important element in the larger UN administrative structure. Additionally, the five members of the Committee were only able to work on the Committee on a part-time basis; as a result, the Secretariat was able to make many direct decisions on behalf of the Committee. This administrative structure alone undermines any view that the Committee was an independent body over which the Secretariat had no influence.

Regarding Bang-Jensen's remarks on the UN leadership—and thus also on the Secretary-General—Cordier emphasized that these could be capable of undermining trust in the institution and that if the "interests of the Organization were at stake," then it was vital to take firm action against Bang-Jensen, as would indeed happen. Cordier justified the involvement of the Gross Committee by saying that, because of the public response, the affair had moved outside the UN's walls, and external assistance was now needed to resolve the issue. He dismissed Bang-Jensen's substantive reservations relating to the list of names, protection of the witnesses, and the confidential nature of the investigation, saying these related to the UN's internal security measures, of which no information could be released for fear of compromising their effectiveness.[155] This suggests that the list of witnesses' names had to be guarded, according to internal guidelines and rules for handling documents, as confidential documents from an unofficial source. It was necessary to have such items sent in a sealed envelope with a special courier, and after being used, to have them locked away. Cordier proceeded as if these procedures had been employed during or following the operation of the Special Committee. The truth, however, was that those who dealt with the documents in New York and then in Europe had no knowledge of such procedures and thus did not observe the rules Cordier referred to as generally followed guidelines. Indeed, the very fact of the affair becoming public was contradictory to rules regarding UN staff, who, according to Cordier, were not allowed to make independent statements to the press, particularly not on confidential questions. All in all, he emphasized, the record of the preceding twelve years of the UN was proof enough that confidential information could not leak out of the organization. It did not go unnoticed—by the FBI, for example—that he gave no evidence for this claim, but they did not wish to draw any conclusions from this.[156] Nor did the CIA, for that matter, which, contrary to the factual evidence, gave its full support to the official position of the United Nations.[157] The reason Cordier appeared in person in front of the committee was to avoid the fatal blow he claimed Bang-Jensen sought to inflict on the UN. Given this, the rejection of the appeal can have come as a surprise to exactly no one. The date of Cordier's testimony was November 26, 1958. Almost one year later, on November 25, 1959, Povl Bang-Jensen would be found dead of a gunshot wound to the temple.

The conflicts between Bang-Jensen and the UN present a clear example of shared principles versus the practice of the institution and the convictions of an employee in critical times. They also offer an overview of the UN's handling of the Hungarian case when confronted with empathy, solidarity, and morality that are more important principles than submission to the hierarchy of an institution. While these events were unfolding, pragmatic considerations were more important to the US and Danish Missions to the UN than holding the UN to a high standard and helping to solve internal problems, even at the cost of people's lives.

Notes

1. Povl Bang-Jensen began his career as a lawyer in his home country of Denmark, then continued his studies in the United States. After the German invasion, Bang-Jensen played a role in supporting the Danish antifascist resistance; after the war, he joined the United Nations. See Copp and Peck, *Betrayal at the UN*; Lidegaard (2000); Nagy (2005). Of the documents recently made available in the UN Archives, many thousands of pages deal with Bang-Jensen; the Federal Bureau of Investigation holds 1,300 pages of material pertaining to him, some of which I was able to access.

2. Bang-Jensen's body was found on November 25, 1959; to this day, it is not clear whether he was killed or committed suicide.

3. His wife, Helen Nolan, was American, and they had five children: Karsten, Per, Lise, Lars, and Nina. He was in contact with representatives of the US government beginning in 1940.

4. Messinesi to Stavropoulos on December 31, 1957. UNARM S-0009-0002-09. "Bang-Jensen on many occasions proved very helpful [. . .] often sent little notes. I myself benefited a number of occasions from the information he gave me." Columbia University, Butler Library, Rare Books and Manuscript Collection (hereinafter ACP), box 175. Andersen: "He had done an admirable work for the Committee."

5. May 30, 1957. Shann's note. ACP 175.

6. ACP, box 175. Also UNARM S-0009-0002-09. Jordan's note: UNARM S-370-0041-02.

7. UNARM S-370-0041-02. Jordan's note: "I arranged the removal from Bang-Jensen's possession of the surplus copies of his statement of errors [. . .] to put an end to the degree to which Bang-Jensen was undermining the work of the whole staff."

8. UNARM S-370-0041-02.

9. Cordier to Jordan, via Narayan: UNARM S-0009-0002-09. Cordier had previously described Bang-Jensen as "mad." See *The Bang-Jensen Case*, 35. Cordier's amateur diagnosis was followed by that of Jordan, in a letter of June 5, 1957: "I have no doubt that Mr. Bang-Jensen is a very sick man." Cited in Copp and Peck, *Betrayal at the UN*, 289.

10. As Jordan recalls: "I do not know whether I instructed the secretariat not to let Bang-Jensen have a copy of the final draft. Quite probably I did." On June 4, 1957, Bang-Jensen phoned Jordan, who at Shann's instruction had refused Bang-Jensen's request to see the final version of the text. UNARM S-0009-0002-09.

11. See Jordan's memo during Bang-Jensen's disciplinary investigation. ACP, box 176.

12. UNARM S-370-0041-02.

13. In his letter of June 6, 1957, to Hammarskjöld, Bang-Jensen noted the omissions and errors that had remained in the report. But in the same letter, Bang-Jensen insinuated something that might have been highly sensitive for Hammarskjöld: "My only condition is [. . .] honesty. I have seen enough to know that people can do terrible things, and still have other admirable or attractive sides to their character. [. . .] I only feel sorry for those—whoever they are—who perhaps by some mistake,

has placed themselves in a position from which they find it difficult to retrieve themselves." See Copp and Peck, *Betrayal at the UN*, 177–80. According to the FBI, the Secretary-General slipped an informal letter to Bang-Jensen at one session of the Special Committee in which he thanked him for his note and suggested they meet in person. The FBI added that the Secretary-General was presumably vulnerable to extortion, and, thus, Bang-Jensen could be in danger. Bang-Jensen Archive (hereinafter BJI), box 33.

14. August 28, 1957. UNARM S-0009-0002-09.

15. Ibid.

16. August 28, 1957. Bang-Jensen to the Secretary-General. UNARM S-0009-0002-09.

17. Ibid.

18. Ibid.

19. Ibid.

20. Ibid. According to Bang-Jensen: "Mr. Jordan did not at that time maintain that he was acting on the SYG's order but has done so later in similar cases."

21. Ibid.

22. Ibid. September 16, 1957. Bang-Jensen to Hammarskjöld.

23. August 28, 1957. UNARM S-0009-0002-09.

24. UNARM S-0009-0002-09. February 8, 1957.

25. As recalled by Béla Király (OSZK TIT).

26. April 11, 1957. "Report of Eugene Gorman, Australia." CHP, subject area 1. A series of reports on Hungarian insurgents who fled to Italy: Chiesura, *Non scrivete il mio nome*. The names of the figures depicted in *The Bridge at Andau* by J. Michener have been altered or left out.

27. Sándor Taraszovics (OSZK TIT).

28. The audiotape recorded the president's promise that anonymity would be respected. When György Heltai was approached, he was told: "You can appear anonymously in closed meeting." Heltai's response on March 4, 1957: "Stipulating full discretion because of family in Hungary." UNARM S-0442-0139-06.

29. CHP, subject area 1. "Without endangering either witnesses or other people private meeting should be the Committee's general rule." Duckworth-Barker wrote on January 3, 1958: "Fear was in many cases obvious and they made it very clear that this matter was one of utmost importance to them." UNARM S-0009-0002-09.

30. ACP, box 184. Shann's note of April 8, 1957: "To annex the testimony to the Report [. . .] there are dangers for witnesses [. . .] possible to identify."

31. BJI, box 4. Jordan: "Verbatim Records of yesterday's meeting has been distributed to members of the Committee at their hotels. [. . .] I just say this in order to make sure that none of the copies of the reports goes astray."

32. June 18, 1957. "Shann states many witnesses fearful they have been identified despite Committee's attempt at security. Believes many names may be known to Communists. Comment: this not surprising view lack real security UN HQ Geneva." NARA 320.5764/4-557. One witness claimed that the Hungarian police had visited a woman after her husband gave his testimony to the Committee. See Bang-Jensen's comment in Bogyay, *A Cry for Freedom*.

33. Schreiber to Stavropoulos on January 2, 1958. "Witnesses introduced by name [. . .] then all papers were burned." UNARM S-0009-002-09.

34. The de Hedervary collection demonstrates that confidential documents could be squirreled away from the UN, as thousands of papers found their way to the American Hungarian Foundation of New Brunswick. (Ita Pásztor phoned Ágoston Molnár, director of the foundation, to remove the documents from the UN that were about to be destroyed.) This was revealed in interviews with Ita Pásztor and Ágoston Molnár (January 2002, New York and New Brunswick).

35. For the dossiers kept at the Hungarian Information Office (formerly III/1 Division of the Ministry of the Interior), see BJI, box 35. The papers of the Chief Department of Political Investigation refer to the contents of "many records and audio recordings." See the Information report of April 6, 1957, also here.

36. See "Information on Povl Bang-Jensen." Paris, May 27, 1957. "Roger" reported to "Oszvald": "Bang-Jensen summarizes the material for the benefit of the committee." "Roger" was a witness in Geneva on April 9, 1957; by this time, the Hungarian secret services had stationed him in Paris. ÁBTL 3.2.3. Mt. 499/1-3.

37. MNL XIX-E-1-v.

38. See Szebeni, "A Radványi ügy."

39. Mink, *Tanúságtevők az ENSZ előtt*, 2. Török gave evidence in New York on February 26, 1957.

40. For Tamás Pásztor's report, see CHP, subject area 9.

41. This was said at the session of the Hungarian Socialist Workers' Party (MSZMP) political committee on July 30, 1957. MNL M- KS 288. f.

42. September 6, 1957. "The list of documents received from the interior ministry." MNL XIX-J-1-j.

43. Telegram from Dulles: NARA 320-5764/10-857. The telegram from the US Mission to the UN (J. Barco) on August 23, 1957: NARA 320.5764/8-2357.

44. After Bang-Jensen's response, Jordan informed the US Immigration and Naturalization Service (Robert Corbeales) that Szabó had given testimony on February 26 in New York and that he had been marked in the record with the letter M. Jordan to Protitch on November 19, 1957. BJI, box 4.

45. UNARM S-0009-0001-09. On October 10, 1957, from Protitch to Hammarskjöld.

46. On November 29, 1957, Protitch forwarded Hammarskjöld's instructions: "To deliver to me immediately." UNARM S-0009-0001-09.

47. Ibid. On October 10, 1957, from Bang-Jensen to Protitch. According to the FBI's reminder of December 19, 1957, this concerned "Dobrynin's pressure to turn over the names." BJI, box 33.

48. Ibid.

49. Ibid. On October 10, 1957, Hammarskjöld wrote to Bang-Jensen, who responded to the Secretary-General the following day through Protitch.

50. The diagnosis of Bang-Jensen's "illness" included a medical examination, which, following rules governing employees, he was obliged to take. The justification later given for this was that they had been looking for an explanation for his changed behavior. Later, in a note of March 16, 1960, they denied having ordered the examination. UNARM DAG 1.1.1.3. Cordier files.

51. BJI, box 33.

52. ACP, box 175. The telegram of December 12, 1957, from the "Hungarian freedom fighters": "Deeply concerned."

53. Robert Morris wrote in the *New York Times*: "panic in all refugee centers [. . .] families back in Hungary are being subjected to cruel political reprisal by the secret police." UNARM S-0009-0001-09.

54. The letter is quoted in the US Senate report. See *The Bang-Jensen Case*, 42.

55. Jordan wrote that the records of sessions, various telegrams, and lists also contained names. He later completed a nine-page questionnaire about the witnesses. UNARM S-0009-0001-09.

56. On July 16, 1958, Stavropoulos reported to Hammarskjöld that they had passed on these suspicions but nothing had been done. Later, an investigation began into the claim that unknown individuals had offered money for the session records. Stavropoulos files, UNARM S-0466-0139.

57. Ibid.

58. UNARM S-0009-0001-09. Andersen to Hammarskjöld on October 1, 1957.

59. Ibid. Shann to Hammarskjöld on October 29, 1957.

60. November 22, 1957. From Bang-Jensen to Hammarskjöld. UNARM S-0009-0001-09.

61. DHS L 179:173.

62. Bang-Jensen: "Annotations to Gross report." January 15, 1958. BJI, box 4. See also Epstein, "The Bang-Jensen Tragedy," 24.

63. From Kauffmann to Gross, on December 11, 1957. UNARM S-0466-0139 and ACP, box 175.

64. ACP, box 175.

65. The later investigation by the US Senate would be surprised to find that "tactics used in the dismissal of Bang-Jensen were vindictive and designed to damage his reputation. [. . .] UN's entire handling of the [Bang-Jensen] case was unforgivably brutal [. . .] it was somehow motivated." See the FBI's analysis of this on April 22, 1960. BJI, box 33.

66. UNARM S-0009-0001-09. See Copp and Peck, *Betrayal at the UN*, 185, and *The Bang-Jensen Case*, 2.

67. ACP, box 175. December 11, 1957. According to the Senate investigation, the use of security guards (which was unprecedented in UN history) attracted the public's attention and added weight to the charge of mental disturbance. *The Bang-Jensen Case*, 2.

68. ACP, box 175.

69. See among Cordier's documents: "Bang-Jensen's Desk." ACP, box 175. December 4, 1957. "A search of Bang-Jensen's office should be made later in the day for the missing documents." See Bang-Jensen's note on his return on December 13, 1957. BJI, box 4.

70. ACP, box 175. "06:45 Change the locks on the desk and file cabinets in Bang-Jensen's office [. . .] instruction then to reinstall the original desk lock and to install a lock on the entry door [. . .] temporary type knob lock was removed."

71. December 12, 1957. Cordier and Protitch to Meinstorp, leader of the Danish delegation. UNARM S-0009-0001-09.

72. ACP, box 175.

73. ACP, box 184.

74. DHS L 179:84.

75. CHP, subject area 1.

76. "Final Report of Committee investigating the Bang-Jensen case." DHS L 179:84. For the US delegation, the situation was clear: "No one takes important documents to the UN." See Wadsworth, *The Glass House*, 160. Between 1945 and 1965, sixteen spies were uncovered: eleven in the national delegations and six at the UN Secretariat. Between 1958 and 1966, twenty-eight Soviet diplomats were expelled from the United States. J. Edgar Hoover, director of the FBI, considered that half of the 108 Soviet employees at the UN might be agents. Wise and Ross, *The Espionage Establishment*, 19–20.

77. Samarasekara was dismissed on December 16, 1957. The Secretary-General gave the reason as his "disclosing evidence given to the committee and with providing Russia the secret Foreign Office code." "U.N. Checks on Leak; Sifts Report Ceylonese Gave Hungary Data to Russians," *New York Times*, July 4, 1957. See also *The Bang-Jensen Case*, 17. Hoover reported on the Samarasekara case to the US Congress. BJI, box 33.

78. Diary entry of Anthony Panuch concerning the Gross Committee, January 20, 1960. FDR Library, Berle files.

79. According to a later reminder from the FBI: "UN created a situation which would seriously impair if not make it impossible, to conduct another investigation of the type." BJI, box 33.

80. On December 17, 1957, Meinstorp, the deputy leader of the Danish Mission to the UN, after discussions with Andersen, described his position: "The UN must place the security of witnesses above all other considerations." ACP, box 175.

81. January 24, 1958. ACP, box 175.

82. ACP, box 175.

83. Bang-Jensen wrote a memo that the list had been burned at 1:30 a.m. on January 24, 1958; his wife signed this memo as a witness. BJI, box 5.

84. For the CIA, which was watching events with interest, it was evident that confidential documents were accessible to Soviet UN employees. BJI, box 33.

85. On February 6, 1958, British Labour MP John Baird addressed a question to Foreign Secretary Selwyn Lloyd: "If the Committee came to the conclusion that the documents are of doubtful validity, will he now withdraw the abridged report of the UN Special Committee on Hungary published by his department?" MNL XIX-J-1-n.

86. Message from the Hungarian embassy in Moscow on January 30, 1958: "The [Soviet foreign ministry] handed over the summary of this committee report for us to pass on to our organizations in Hungary, which I submit as an attachment." MNL XIX-J-1-j, box 231.

87. Dulles's telegram on February 27, 1958. NARA 764.00/2-2758.

88. See the telegram of February 11, 1958, from the US Mission to the UN, NARA 764.00/2-1158. On January 24, 1958, Péter Mód sent a report to Budapest on the international response to the Bang-Jensen affair and on the messages Hammarskjöld received (his source was Under-Secretary-General Dobrynin, who had read the Secretary-General's correspondence). MNL XIX-J-1-j, box 231.

89. Ibid.

90. ACP, box 175. All this was kept by Cordier.

91. UN Joint Disciplinary Committee was made up of high-ranking UN officers. Led by A. D. Meurig Evans from the United Kingdom, its members were C. L. Coates, J.-P. Martin, and A. Hatami, all subordinates to the members of the Gross

Committee, who had previously condemned Bang-Jensen. UNARM DAG 1.1.1.3. Cordier files.

92. UNARM S-370-0041-02. February 18, 1958. Letter from McDiarmid to Bang-Jensen: "Submission of your case to the Joint Disciplinary Committee."

93. Ibid.

94. For Panuch's letter of March 27, 1958, see BJI, box 5.

95. Despite Bang-Jensen's request, there was "no examination of evidence," while "Bang-Jensen's past records" were "outside the terms of reference." UNARM S-370-0041-02.

96. UNARM S-370-0041-02. "The Committee considered the assurances given by Mr. Bang-Jensen according to par. 44. 45. and 46. above, to have been in such contradiction with Staff Regulation 1.2."

97. UNARM S-370-0041-02.

98. Chairman K. Tsien to McDiarmid, director of the personnel division, on June 20, 1958. ACP, box 176.

99. June 13, 1958. Hessellund-Jensen to Hammarskjöld. ACP, box 176.

100. For the documents on this, see UNARM S-0466-0141. Hammarskjöld on June 13, 1958: "Answer the charges [. . .] consider a statement from you as referred in my memorandum of 6 June if it reaches me by 23 June." Here we also find the plan of April 3 for "honourable disengagement" and drafts of exchanges of letters, including the plan for a "relatively quiet solution," as well as reminders for meetings. For more on this, based on the recollections of those involved, see Copp and Peck, *Betrayal at the UN*, 226. For a study based on the documents in Danish archives, see Lidegaard, *A legmagasabb ár. Povl Bang-Jensen és az ENSZ*, 139.

101. ACP, box 176. June 13, 1958.

102. Bang-Jensen to Hammarskjöld: "You personally know that the charges against me are not true." See this, together with summaries and notes: BJI, box 5.

103. ACP, box 176.

104. Bang-Jensen's letter of June 20, 1958. "Urgent by hand" UNARM DAG 1.1.1.3. Cordier files.

105. The signatures of Hessellund-Jensen, Kauffmann, and Panuch are visible on the proposed "amicable solution." UN/DLA.

106. According to the FBI's note of April 1, 1960, "honorable resignation [would have] saved Bang-Jensen and his family of 20 months agony and saved the UN from the most adverse international press it has ever suffered on any issue." BJI, box 33.

107. UNARM S-0370-0041-03.

108. DHS L 179:84.

109. The enormous document was guarded by Cordier. ACP, box 176.

110. Ibid.

111. Ibid. "[Bang-Jensen] will fight for reinstatement and resign next day."

112. On July 18, 1957, Bang-Jensen shared his response with members of the press. ACP, box 176, and DHS L 179:84.

113. ACP, box 176. Jordan to Stavropoulos.

114. Ibid.

115. Ibid.

116. Ibid. Bang-Jensen returned the check on July 29, 1958.

117. Ibid. McDiarmid's letter of August 15, 1958.

118. Ibid. August 1, 1958. From McDiarmid to Bang-Jensen: "Termination on July 3, regardless of appeal."

119. Bang-Jensen met Morris on a total of eight occasions. BJI, box 33. See Morris's recollections of Bang-Jensen, OSZK TIT. In the words of the UN's churlish personnel officer: "Bang-Jensen came with Robert Morris [. . .] Bang-Jensen's authorized counsel at least until further notice."

120. Hammarskjöld announced the nomination of Dobrynin on May 16, 1958.

121. UNARM S-0252-0001-0018-00001.

122. ACP, box 177. January 27, 1959. Green, Chief of the Department of Staff Services, to Cordier.

123. BJI, box 34.

124. ACP, box 176. "Robert Morris' efforts to get Senate interested in the case."

125. UNARM S-1078-0064-0002-00001 UC. "[Bang-Jensen] had considerable success among the extreme right in the US to the point where threatening calls and the discovery that Hammarskjold's car had been tampered with caused the UN security office, much to Hammarskjold's distaste, to provide him special guards around the clock."

126. Copp and Peck, *Betrayal at the UN*. Notes. BJI, box 35.

127. BJI, box 34. September 2, 1958. "Bang-Jensen conversation with Simon and Danahay [. . .] Hoover's personal representatives at FBI." Copp and Peck, *Betrayal at the UN*. Notes. BJI, box 35. The motivation for the meeting was merely that the "Bureau would have to protect itself." BJI, box 33.

128. See the letter from Walter Anderson, the former director of maritime intelligence, to Hoover on January 30, 1958: "I hope he is being amply physically protected." BJI, box 34. Robert Morris quoted a Soviet counterintelligence officer who had deserted: Bang-Jensen's life, and perhaps that of his family, was in danger. See *The Bang-Jensen Case*, 51.

129. Ibid. "[Bang-Jensen's data] was not for the most part within the jurisdiction of the FBI." On November 26, 1959, following Bang-Jensen's death, they stuck to their position: "Charges involved matters of administrative nature within the UN." Procedural rules prevented them from investigating. BJI, box 33.

130. On August 18, 1958, Brig. Gen. Robert E. Cushman, on Vice President Nixon's team, prepared a report for Director of Central Intelligence Allen Dulles. The attitude of the intelligence services remained unchanged: "CIA has no internal security functions and no duties or functions related to the UN staff." BJI, box 33.

131. To protect his sources, Bang-Jensen was only willing to reveal the evidence he had to those at the highest level, as he suspected the system to be "infected" in a number of places. He did not reveal his sources even to Lodge. See the oral history concerning James Barco: *Hammarskjold, Dag as Secretary General*. BJI, box 33.

132. Barco's telegram to the State Department on November 27, 1957: "[Bang-Jensen] will reveal that, over a period of past year he has kept US government informed through US Mission of his accusations and will charge that US government has taken no action." BJI, box 33.

133. The director of central intelligence later said that the issue was not within his jurisdiction, while he had been told that Bang-Jensen was "troubled." According to his memo of January 14, 1960, their meeting had been "generally social natured," but Bang-Jensen "had clearly been a problem child." FOI Papers BJI Box 33.

134. Senator Dodd's note of January 25, 1961, states: "Bang-Jensen was well known to the State Department and to American Intelligence, had cooperated closely with our agencies arranging the Greenland base deal and in the direction of the Danish WWII underground, had been considered generally pro-American." BJI, box 33.

135. Their conversation touched on Hammarskjöld. On December 12, 1957, the Department of State sent a telegram to Hoover, copied to the CIA ESP[ionage] SEC[tion], about the Secretary-General and Bang-Jensen. A few days earlier, all of Bang-Jensen's memoranda (a total of sixty-six pages) were sent to the FBI. BJI, box 33.

136. See Bang-Jensen's notes on July 29, 1958, and the days that followed. BJI, box 4.

137. See the telegrams from the US Mission to the UN on July 8 and 9, 1958. NARA 315.3/7-858 and -958. See also *The Bang-Jensen Case*, 3.

138. ACP, box 176. July 9, 1957. Lodge to Hammarskjöld on the Bang-Jensen affair: "Proceeding confidential [. . .] has resulted in some confusion as what the truth is." Hammarskjöld replied on July 9, 1957.

139. Ibid.

140. January 2, 1959. Letter from Deputy Secretary of State W. B. Macomber to Maroy, member of the Senate Foreign Affairs Committee. BJI, box 33.

141. Note on June 23, 1958: "[Bang-Jensen] is about to be dismissed [. . .] he plans to make public his charges against Hammarskjold [. . .] State Department advised, press release [. . .] coordinate this press item with us." BJI, box 33.

142. The US diplomat publicized the names of Soviets made persona non grata from 1954 onward, and in May 1960, he handed the UN Secretary-General a new list with an additional fifteen names. See Huss and Carpozi, *Red Spies in the UN*, 110.

143. See the telegram of October 16 containing the article in *Information* and the documents of the UN proceedings: UNARM DAG 1.1.1.3. Bang-Jensen's visa application was filed among the papers of the UN legal department. UN/DLA.

144. For Hammarskjöld's letter, see RA 119. G./3/19. Pakke Nr. 1.

145. From Wilder Foote to Ivar Gundmundsson on May 9, 1958. ACP, box 175. Written on the document: "cc: Cordier."

146. Lasky's letter to Foreign Minister Casey on August 5, 1958: "Shann's campaign against Bang-Jensen [. . .] aroused considerable comment in the American press [. . .] without exception favourable to Bang-Jensen. [. . .] how you can explain Mr. Shann's peculiar conduct?" On November 7, 1958, Admiral Anderson (director of naval intelligence) wrote to the foreign minister: "My Dear Mr. Minister [. . .] a certain Australian diplomat has been prominent in defending the action adverse to Bang-Jensen." On December 2, 1958, B. C. Hill replied to the Australian UN group: "There is no factual foundation of the allegation that Mr. Shann 'engineered' Mr. Bang-Jensen's dismissal." NAAA 1838.

147. Ibid.

148. For the conversation of August 7, 1958, see Copp and Peck, *Betrayal at the UN*. Notes. BJI, box 35.

149. See the letter from William Kemsley, UN personnel officer, to his colleague Victor Reuther. "Seen by SYG." ACP, box 177.

150. The invasion seemed likely because of Soviet usurpation of power in other parts of Europe, and there was the continued occupation of the island of Bornholm,

as well as the fact that the Danish communists who had fought in the antifascist resistance had retained their weapons and were entirely obedient to Moscow.

151. On Bang-Jensen's visit to Denmark in the fall of 1958, his discussions, and the decisions made, see RA 119. G. 3/19. Pakke Nr. 2. On October 20, 1958, Hessellund-Jensen wrote to the Secretary-General: "Danish Government support legal costs." ACP, box 176. Their statement of October 23, 1958, is strictly neutral: "The Danish government has had neither the possibility nor any reason to intervene in the matter and has neither wish nor been able to express an opinion about it." ACP, box 176.

152. ACP, box 175.

153. ACP, box 176. (Vol. VII. List of Documents on Bang-Jensen's Case. UN 140 Item 227–59. Judgement December 5, 1958.)

154. ACP, box 175.

155. Ibid. The later Senate investigation denied Cordier's claims: "Lack of proper security procedures exists within the UN [. . .] no security officer [. . .] no written instructions were given to the committee staff [. . .] security policy in the UN is inadequate." See the FBI study of the outline of the Senate report. BJI, box 33.

156. According to the memorandum of the FBI on April 1, 1960: "Cordier's assurances unsupported by any details." BJI, box 33.

157. BJI, box 33.

8

THE SILENCE OF THE UN AND THE
TRAGEDY THAT BROKE IT

The Case of "Imre Nagy and His Fellow Criminals"

While the UN Secretariat appeared curiously ready to spend any amount of time, energy, and money to make an example of its previously long-trusted employee Povl Bang-Jensen, the UN leadership's silence on consequential and life-threatening proceedings taking place at the same time in Budapest was no less strange. June 16, 1958, was the date of both Bang-Jensen's letter of dismissal and of the announcement from the Hungarian Ministry of Justice of the sentencing and immediate execution of "Imre Nagy and his fellow criminals," as the verdict stated.

One reason that Bang-Jensen had to leave was because he had become acutely aware—and made others aware—of the fatal connection between the UN's failure to publish supplemental reports on the Hungarian question and the destiny of Hungary's former prime minister: Bang-Jensen felt responsible for a politician who placed his own fate and that of his country in the UN's hands. During the hours of greatest drama, it was hardly possible for the UN to offer them assistance, but twenty months had passed since the Revolution had been suppressed with no meaningful attempt to offer help.

The UN Special Committee on the Problem of Hungary repeatedly asked for information concerning Nagy and even requested a meeting with Nagy, but it did so in vain; there was little done in the way of continuing this effort after the report was submitted. And when unsettling news came from Hungary, it was Henry Cabot Lodge, the US Ambassador to the UN, who

274

asked about the revolutionary leaders, not Dag Hammarskjöld. By making these inquiries, Lodge effectively confirmed the arguments put forth by state propagandists in Hungary, namely, that the imperialists were concerned for their allies. This same slander would have been harder to cast on the Secretary-General. And although the Hungarian foreign affairs spokesman announced that Imre Nagy would not be called before a court,[1] a few weeks later, intelligence agent Sándor Rajnai moved Nagy and other members of his circle away from their families and into custody: first at a site in Snagov, Romania, then to a prison in Bucharest, and finally to Budapest.[2]

In connection with these events, a "personal and confidential" note was sent to Special Committee Secretary William Jordan by a member of the Secretariat, which drew his attention to how the Committee should deal with Imre Nagy, as "any mistake on our part may send this man to his doom."[3] Not much later, Pope Pius XII warned Hammarskjöld about the fate of Pál Maléter, as the pope had learned that he had been interrogated and tortured and would soon be tried.

The opening of the session of the Hungarian Parliament likely facilitated the onset of the formerly denied trial. In his speech, president of the Presidential Council István Dobi spoke of the need to bring the leaders of the so-called counterrevolution to account, and there had been more than enough executions to know what sentence Nagy and the others faced.[4] The United Nations had received information about the concentration camps of János Kádár's regime and about the institution of administrative custody, which suggested that, after relative stability had been established by the bloody process of consolidation, systematic reprisals would soon follow. And so, just a few months after denying it would happen, the Kádár regime's foreign affairs spokesman László Gyáros announced the start of the Maléter trial and listed the charges: Maléter had spied for the British, had planned a military dictatorship, had broken his oath, and so on.

The Hungarian party leadership wished to discuss the nascent judicial proceedings "at the highest level."[5] Minister of the Interior Béla Biszku talked to Yuri Andropov, then general secretary of the Communist Party of the Soviet Union and formerly Soviet ambassador to Budapest, who asked the comrades in Budapest to be patient.[6] As Soviet ambassador during the Revolution, Andropov had previously recommended forceful military action to end the uprising.

News of the charges reached New York from the leaders of the Revolution. From the list of names, it was clear that preparations were in place for

Nagy's trial.[7] But even so, it was only the United States that inquired as to Nagy's whereabouts and the fate of the imprisoned insurgents. When no satisfactory response was forthcoming, Lodge proposed that a special UN session be convened.[8] On December 16, 1957, Hammarskjöld sent a telegram to Minister of Foreign Affairs Imre Horváth: he was ready to travel to Budapest, but the Soviet ambassador approached Kádár to tell him to decline the visit.[9] To the Latin American diplomats, including Enrique Fabregat, who paid him a visit in person, UN representative Péter Mód described the news of the legal reprisals as "unconfirmed rumors"; with no official charges filed, the delegation was left with no one to request clemency for.

The United Nations was involved in the 1956 Revolution not only as the addressee of Imre Nagy's desperate telegrams but also because the Secretary-General had indicated that he would be personally involved in Maléter's fate. On September 10, 1957, at the start of the debate on the Hungarian question, Hammarskjöld had promised Maléter's family that he would intervene on their behalf; Mária, Pál, Mari, and Judit Maléter had even had their photographs taken with Hammarskjöld, and Mária was quoted in the *New York Times* as saying that "Mr. Hammarskjöld had told her he was hopeful of being able to do something about her plea for the thousands of imprisoned freedom fighters, including her former husband."[10] Subsequently, Hammarskjöld wrote to Foreign Minister Horváth not as the Secretary-General of the UN but simply "man to man." He did not ask for clemency by appeal to UN resolutions and international law but instead expressed his trust that the Hungarian government would keep to "the highest humanitarian standards" during the proceedings.[11] Hammarskjöld indicated that he was willing to travel to Budapest if he received a guarantee that Maléter's life would be spared. Officials in Budapest had considered inviting Hammarskjöld, only to categorically reject the opportunity for him to meddle in the proceedings against those the Kádár regime classified as counterrevolutionaries. Horváth informed the Secretary-General that this was a domestic matter that the United Nations had no say in.[12]

Among his personal papers, Hammarskjöld kept the documentation relating to the legal reprisals in Hungary and a summary, on which he had handwritten, "Prince Wan?"[13] The Secretary of the Special Committee had also sent information to Waithayakon, but there is no evidence that he replied or took any kind of action.[14] This lack of response may be the reason why the Special Committee continued to pay attention to the events in Hungary.[15]

Prince Wan Waithayakon, UN General Assembly's Special Representative on the Problem of Hungary. Copyright: UN Photo Archive #133681.

UN Under-Secretary-General for Political and Security Council Affairs Dragoslav Protitch was also observing events. In a report sent to Hammarskjöld, he confirmed that Kádár's pronouncements suggested that the revolutionaries would soon be brought to trial. He added—seeking to reassure, but it is not clear what his sources were—that "diplomatic observers" thought a compromise likely in Nagy's case.[16]

At the same time as the court case against Nagy was being prepared, an exhibition opened in Budapest on the subject of what was referred to as *the consolidation* in Hungary. And while the UN General Assembly's Special Representative on the Problem of Hungary Prince Wan Waithayakon continued to allow the Hungarian question to be forgotten, the silence was broken by the news of the executions in Hungary. So the Special Committee was convened anew, with Chair of the Special Committee on the Problem of Hungary Alsing Andersen replaced by Ronald Walker, who also took over Rapporteur Mick Shann's position.[17] Walker, who was new to the Special Committee and to the situation in Hungary, asked the UN Secretariat "to keep members fully informed" about everything that was happening in Hungary, which suggests that this had not been happening previously. He also referred to the Special Representative's heightened responsibility.[18] Jordan asked for Protitch's permission for the members of the Special Committee to form an impression of the situation in Hungary, but Shann expressly and unexpectedly interceded to oppose any continuation of their work or publication of a further report, going so far as to recommend that the Special Committee be disbanded at the next session of the General Assembly.[19] The US State Department was surprised to see the passivity of the Special Committee turn into outright resistance, so officials asked London to apply pressure on the Australians. However, even the British doubted the usefulness of a further report, so no pressure was applied.[20]

The deciding factor for this passivity was presumably the reluctance of the UN Secretariat, a reluctance that was first expressed in Manila (where Shann was ambassador), then in Canberra (where Shann's opinion mattered), and that finally came to fruition in New York. As a result, the Special Committee simply collapsed: Andersen went back to Denmark, Ratnakirti Gunewardene was replaced as head of mission, Enrique Fabregat was given a role on the UN Information Committee, and Mongi Slim prepared for his tasks at the foreign ministry of his home country of Tunisia. The Australians claimed that the Special Committee had become a propaganda tool, and that, due to his ineffectiveness, Waithayakon should be dismissed.[21] In December of 1957, Andersen was of the opinion that the Committee would have no more sessions unless there were particularly pressing circumstances—though pressing circumstances were not, of course, uncommon.[22]

At the UN Secretariat, the typed and handwritten lists pertaining to Hungary, which had become more extensive and increasingly menacing, continued to pile up.[23] Jordan asked Protitch how he should convey news items to the Committee members, suggesting that, even after summaries were prepared, this remained a task for the secretariat.[24] Through these channels UN officials learned about the government in Budapest's latest acts of reprisal and about the bloodthirsty speeches by the chief prosecutor and the president of the Hungarian Supreme Court. Following increasingly concerning news from Budapest, the US embassy in Budapest inquired about the status of a list of politicians involved in the Revolution through the Hungarian delegate. As a result of these communications officials in

New York learned about "the trial of Imre Nagy and Maléter."[25] Hungarian émigré leaders in the United States asked Hammarskjöld to meet with them to discuss the trials, but there is no evidence in the documents that such a meeting took place.

The invitation of Hammarskjöld to Budapest—as suggested by the Soviet Ambassador to the UN, Arkady Sobolev, and Under-Secretary-General Anatoly Dobrynin—helped to eradicate suspicions about the trials of Nagy and Maléter.[26] There was little chance Hammarskjöld would actually travel to Budapest, but Sobolev and Dobrynin added that it was tactically preferable that he be the one to say no. In April, Hammarskjöld sidestepped Péter Mód's invitation; Mód informed Budapest that Hammarskjöld was heading to Africa in the spring, and he would probably not have time in the summer either.[27]

Following the International Meeting of Communist and Workers Parties in Moscow,[28] the Soviet Union suddenly began a charm offensive, so Budapest had to wait before it could liquidate what it considered the chief offenders of the counterrevolution. The offensive was unsuccessful, however: neither Moscow's offers nor its subsequent actions, such as withdrawing troops from Romania and a division of troops from Hungary, resulted in a similar response from the United States.[29]

The US did not propose another debate on the Hungarian question for the agenda of the thirteenth General Assembly, even though by this time it was clear that the situation in Hungary had become more serious and the reprisals had continued.[30] Meanwhile, Mód could report with relief that the isolation of the Hungarian delegation at the UN had softened somewhat, so much so that when Soviet foreign minister Andrei Gromyko met with his Hungarian counterpart, they had even discussed the normalization of Hungarian–United States relations.[31] Gromyko was right to sense that time would be the Soviets' greatest ally and that it would allow Kádár's so-called consolidation inside Hungary to bear even more murderous fruit.[32] Meanwhile, Hungarian diplomats and secret service agents would soon be sent instructions to sound out the foreign policy implications of a possible grave decision in the offing.

Nikita Khrushchev, visiting Hungary on the thirteenth anniversary of the Soviet liberation of the country from the Nazis, stated twice, as quoted by UN reports covering the visit, that Imre Nagy was a traitor. Such statements from Khrushchev almost certainly suggest that during his time in Budapest they had come to a decision at the highest level about Nagy. The fate of those considered traitors in the history of communist parties was well known. Meanwhile developments in Moscow included Khrushchev having to squeeze his rivals out of the Politburo after successfully disarming a (neo-)Stalinist putsch attempt. The Ministry of Foreign Affairs in Budapest would soon be instructing diplomats in New York to put out feelers to determine the intentions of the Special Committee in the "most circumspect fashion,"[33] while they also elaborated the strategy for a "counterattack" should the UN go "on the attack," which it would have good reason to do. Officials of the Ministry of Foreign Affairs in Budapest looked into how many international organizations Hungary was a member of, and whether, in light of the events of November 1956, there were any it had been excluded from.[34] Perhaps even they were surprised to find that there was not a single such organization. Later, the request would come from Budapest for information about every conference Hungary had participated in, presumably as part of the same assessment of possible implications should they execute Nagy and others.[35] And while the officials of the Hungarian Ministry of Foreign Affairs began to develop the plan to "eliminate the Hungarian question," they also prepared for the expected attacks that the executions would incite.[36]

In New York, acting on instructions from the Kádár regime, Mód contacted Claude Corea, the Ceylonese Ambassador to the UN. He "gave me a warm welcome," Mód reported, and he promised "cautiously" to find out the intentions of the Special Committee. Hungarian chargé d'affaires Tibor Zádor requested a meeting with Mongi Slim in Washington; Slim told him that, two years after the events of 1956, the operation of the Special Committee was obsolete.[37] Zádor would also pay a visit to Gunewardene once he had returned to Washington. Gunewardene was apparently "tired of the whole business," and since the publication of the report, all he knew of the Hungarian situation was what he had read in the papers. At the same time, "he expressed his pleasure" to Zádor that the Hungarians "had successfully managed to climb out of such a difficult situation," adding that, "for his part, he considered the whole affair closed, and was not willing to contribute any further to the work of the committee, even though formally it had not ceased its activities."[38] Gunewardene added that, as Chair of the UN Committee on Human Rights, he had "pre-empted" US attacks on Hungary, then he admitted that his participation in the Special Committee had damaged his career, and he would not undertake any similar role in the future.[39]

Budapest had other sources of information at its disposal; for example, UN Under-Secretary-General Anatoly Dobrynin sent reports to his superiors in Moscow, and from there the news would reach Hungary. Thus Hungarian politicians were aware that reviving the Special Committee, if not out of the question, would be challenging. In April 1958, the Hungarian foreign ministry discussed the possibility that the UN was creating "a new report perhaps to be submitted," but this was not to happen.[40]

In the weeks before Imre Nagy and his associates were executed, reports coming into the UN from Hungary referred to an "intensification of pressure,"[41] listing possible trials for leaders in the Nagy government as an example. Béla Varga, a leader in the Hungarian émigré community, urgently requested that the Special Committee be immediately convened given the foreboding developments in Hungary.[42] The Committee never met, however. On May 14, 1958, the Secretariat's summaries quoted Hungarian justice minister Ferenc Nezvál as saying that the courts had on many occasions not been stringent enough and that the final "liquidation" of the antiregime forces was imminent,[43] even though the foreign affairs spokesman reported he had no information "on a trial of this kind" as late as March of that year. Kádár talked in a speech of Imre Nagy residing in a "Romanian holiday resort" he had himself chosen, even as Reuters reported, on the basis of Viennese sources, that Imre Nagy and Pál Maléter had been transported to a prison in central Budapest.[44] Officials at the US legation in Budapest felt it was "too early to say" whether this would "result in eventual trial of Imre Nagy."[45] The timing of the upcoming meeting between János Kádár and president of the Socialist Federal Republic of Yugoslavia Josip Tito could not have been an accident: Nagy had been granted asylum at the Yugoslav embassy after the Revolution, and a decision had to be made on Yugoslavia's erstwhile guest. The summit in Moscow that followed this meeting was part of a series of events during the course of which the trial of Nagy was postponed.

In a report issued May 7, 1958, Protitch emphasized that the case had been suspended, mentioning that Imre Nagy and Marxist philosopher György Lukács had been the subject of attacks in various forums but that the trial had almost certainly been postponed—to the best of his knowledge indefinitely ("sine die").[46] Lukács was released after promising not to dip into politics in the future, but the same was not true for Nagy. Once again it appeared that concerns for Nagy were assuaged, however, this time by a report to the Secretary-General from his Yugoslav Under-Secretary-General

Protitch. Protitch's report lessened the attention paid to Hungary at a time when intervention might have forestalled the execution of Nagy, Maléter, and other leaders of the Revolution. Similar motives might have been behind the preparation of a bundle of documents titled "Different Communications" that reached Hammarskjöld via Humphrey Trevelyan, an Under-Secretary in charge of Special Political Affairs working with Assistant to the Secretary-General Andrew Cordier, on June 9, 1958, exactly one week before the executions took place. A full overview of the Hungarian question had been compiled into six dossiers, but only a heartbeat before it became the Hungarian tragedy.

On June 16, 1958, Imre Nagy stood on a low stool with a noose around his neck and two officers, one on each side, restraining his already tied hands with additional ropes. On this day the assistant executioner kicked the stool from underneath him and the executioner climbed the ladder placed against the gallows tree and leaned forward slightly to break Nagy's neck. On this same day Pál Maléter and Miklós Gimes, another key participant in the Revolution, were also executed. Other participants in the Revolution accused in the trials had already been executed.

By chance, on that day Ambassadors to the UN Lodge and Sobolev had both received an official invitation to visit Hammarskjöld. According to the Secretary-General's calendar, Lodge returned to the thirty-eighth floor for another visit late the following afternoon; this can hardly have been unconnected to what had happened at dawn the previous morning in the courtyard of the Central Detention Facility in Budapest.[47] At the same time, among the entries in Hammarskjöld's diary for that day, the name Fabian was crossed out, indicating that the leading Hungarian émigré politician Béla Fábián had a scheduled appointment with him, but it did not take place. Nagy's execution prompted Anna Kéthly to send a telegram to Lodge asking for an audience with him, but he refused to meet her on the grounds that she was not an official representative of the government.

Under the circumstances, Imre Nagy's execution was as inevitable as it was unexpected. The year 1956 came not long after the so-called iron age of communism, during which differences of opinion inside the party were more often resolved with hangings than with open debate, where the primary way to voice criticism was through the prosecutor's office, and where judges announced sentences rather than considering evidence. What was shocking was the timing, which intimidated a country just as it had become almost completely pacified, and while the written guarantee given to Nagy

Burial place of executed revolutionaries in the far end of the Budapest Public Cemetery with unmarked graves and handmade crosses and signs that were regularly destroyed by the police. Copyright: Fortepan #163273. Donated by Rózsa Hodosán.

when he was in the Yugoslav embassy confirming he would not be harmed was still fresh in the country's memory. The charges against Nagy included inciting a fascist insurrection and appealing to the UN, which was considered tantamount to treason. The Hungarian public only learned that there had been a trial of Imre Nagy, of the charges against him, and of the verdict after his death.

The Nagy trial was connected to the Special Committee in important ways. As the collection of evidential material would later be remembered in a letter from a member of the Committee's secretariat, "At the trial of Imre Nagy and his associates, the most serious and most decisive charges were surely provided by the confidential confessions made by people in good faith, trusting in the greatest secrecy."[48] Foreign policy had played an important role in the UN investigation, just as the demands of the Revolution had referred to foreign policy: neutrality, withdrawal from the Warsaw Pact, and the rethinking of Hungary's relationship with the Soviet Union. These were reconstructed with the greatest authenticity by the UN investigation, so secret service agents "were in a position to gain access to material that could be of crucial significance in the sentencing of Imre Nagy and his circle."[49] Some of the witness statements did indeed make their way from the United Nations' Special Committee investigation to the prosecutor's office in Budapest as among the witnesses as well as among the refugees there were agents of the Hungarian secret services. These were used in the trials of the leaders of the Hungarian Revolution by those who had exploited one of the UN's most critical failures: its relaxed attitude toward the management of confidential documents.[50] Here Bang-Jensen's story intersects with that of Imre Nagy. Some believed that if the UN continued issuing reports after June 1957 focusing on arrests, trials, imprisonments, and executions, there would have been a greater chance that the execution of Imre Nagy and his associates would not have occurred. As of early July 1957, the issuance of supplemental reports had been supported by a majority of members of the Special Committee and by Bang-Jensen both before and after that time. Unfortunately, the UN Secretariat had different priorities.

The UN and the Execution of the Hungarian Prime Minister

Shock, dismay, and outrage spread throughout the UN leadership after the executions—if there was guilt it was not as openly expressed, at least not in a tangible way. Hammarskjöld and his colleagues were faced with a serious dilemma as to how the United Nations should respond to the news. By this time, the Special Committee had for all intents and purposes disintegrated: Special Representative Waithayakon was busy with Thailand's foreign affairs, and it was hard to tell whether Prince Wan learned of the executions from the UN's telegrams or from the international press. It was not from reports reaching the UN, as he was not being sent any of them.

The day after the executions, Anna Kéthly demanded that the UN "exclude the delegation of the illegitimate Kádár government,"[51] which did not happen, not then nor later. When the UN wrote a letter to the Hungarian Ambassador asking for an explanation and registering its objections, Major Imre Hollai, deputy to Ambassador Mód, sent it back, and sarcastically mocked the letter's legitimacy, by noting that someone was abusing the insignia of the UN. The Secretary-General was in Jerusalem at the time and remained silent. The United Nations had to make a statement, however, so the Special Committee as a whole and Special Representative Waithayakon separately published communiqués condemning the executions. Prince Wan called them an "inhuman act,"[52] while the Committee recalled the guarantees that the victims—whom it called "symbols of hope"—had received from those who would become their executioners.[53]

But what should happen next was a different question. Trevelyan informed the Secretary-General that some of the Special Committee members would meet in the next few days and decide on what action should be taken, at least during the "remaining existence" of the Committee—suggesting its days were already numbered.[54] The secretariat of the Special Committee compiled an extensive dossier on the trials and executions from Hungarian and international sources and prepared a program of operations, which included the participation of Andersen, who rushed back from Denmark to New York.[55]

Walker, now the Chair and Rapporteur of the Special Committee, waited for guidance from Canberra, concerned that the US would pressure the Committee members before instructions arrived.[56] Shann, when asked for his advice, merely responded that they had been a fact-finding committee, the function of which had "evaporated."[57] Orders did finally arrive for the Special Committee to be convened at the earliest possible opportunity, which was presumably preceded by a telephone conversation between New York and Canberra, the conclusion of which was that if they did not take the initiative, they would be dragged along by the heels.[58]

As the Committee members read through the documentation, it became clear that news reports received from Hungary had given fair warning of what eventually took place on June 16, 1958, although Hungarian state propaganda had placed everything that occurred in its version of context. After the Special Committee made its statement, Jordan sent a letter to Special Representative Waithayakon saying that they were ready for consultation and cooperation should he wish it.[59] This response seems rather belated and suggests that it had not originally been part of the plan. A few days later—perhaps after having received a response or perhaps in the absence of one—Jordan offered to provide a list of news reports that had been sent to the UN on the Hungarian question and that could be of interest to Waithayakon. There is no sign that these reports were ever sent, however, except for one telegram in which Waithayakon states that the Special Committee was right to continue to collect information to report to the General Assembly. That was, of course, his job—or at least it should have been.[60]

The separate statements from Special Representative Waithayakon and the Special Committee and the telling silence of the Secretary-General following the executions clearly displayed the success with which the matter had been put to bed and the effectiveness of the disinformation used. For those who had been killed this mattered little, but it did matter to those still alive: the broken promises, the betrayal of international law, and the open and systematic disregard of the UN Charter overstepped a threshold that had apparently been minimal. Telegrams, letters, protests, and calls for the convocation of a special session came in great numbers. Attention was focused on those still alive in Hungary but whose trial cases had entered a new phase: more than a hundred were waiting for their cases to be reviewed. The innovation brought by the Kádárist judicial system, however, was that court sentences were subject to judicial review that could result in harsher sentences. Even more troubling was that a defendant's appeal could also result in increasing the severity of sentences: if a defendant appealed a life sentence, their sentence could be changed to a death. The lives of many in Hungary at that time were under direct threat.[61]

As well as a quick, if rather uncoordinated, condemnation of the executions, the UN Special Committee decided to compile and publish a new report, which it had the authority to do under its General Assembly mandate. The preparation of this report was challenging, as later described by Andersen in a letter: "You can hardly imagine how difficult it was to write our tiny report on Imre Nagy—with Fabregat's temperament on the one side and the reluctant Sir Claude Corea on the other, intimidated as he was by the brave Gunewardene's experience." Surprisingly, Andersen anticipated the imminent end to the Special Committee's activities,[62] an eventuality that could not at this point be made public, particularly not before the publication of the planned supplemental report and in an atmosphere of fresh and elemental international outrage. The Special Committee's report was not just "tiny" but also awkward, as it primarily contained a list of the steps that the UN had taken in its interactions with Hungary but no indication that it had any, even small, responsibility for not doing more to help prevent the executions. Apart from publishing letters and telegrams, the new report documented how the countries most affected—Hungary, the Soviet Union, and Romania—rejected these efforts at diplomacy or failed to reply to them. Alongside this, all the report consisted of was official news reports that had been received and opinions of the executions based on international law and UN resolutions, all of which pointed to the UN as being, because of its passivity, partially responsible.[63] Jordan did his best to preclude the creation of an additional report, for though Walker, who led the

Special Committee, began to put together a new text, Jordan said he was "a little disturbed by the project" because he was "by no means convinced that a satisfactory document can be assembled on this subject."[64] Later, Jordan expressed the view that "there does not exist sufficient additional material for any report comparable with the main Report."[65] Yet if there was anyone who knew just how much material had reached the United Nations, it was Jordan, who had acknowledged, registered, and passed on the alarming reports from Hungary. To be exact, Jordan had passed them on to the secretariat, and to be even more exact, to the filing cabinets in the secretariat. Jordan knew well that these documents recorded the brutal consolidation in Hungary that reached its climax in the execution of the Revolution's leaders. If a report did have to be written, he added, then it should be a "formal" document—one that covered the trials, the executions, and the steps taken by the Special Committee.[66] This, and no more than this, should be the swan song of a committee that only had two more sessions left in the course of its activity.[67] Yet the conflicts within the Special Committee made even a unanimous condemnation of the executions a challenge. What Fabregat considered a problem, Corea thought a success, while Slim compared Hungary's tragedies to those of his homeland, and the Australian was unable to resolve the disagreements. Chair Andersen did not even consider the shocking news continuously arriving from Hungary worthy of mention at his press conference on the topic; he merely gave formulaic responses before traveling home to Copenhagen.

At the same time, the Secretary-General received a plan for the "remaining existence" of the Special Committee, which suggests there had been some discussion of the possibility. This plan tells us that the reports coming from Hungary had been passed on to the Human Rights Committee, that the most important documents had been sent directly to the Special Committee members, and that lists of less crucial sources of information were circulated among them.[68] Presumably, this was done so there would be no misunderstandings regarding the sharing of news reports and so there could be a process of selection before they were distributed.

This again speaks volumes about the workings of the UN. Ceylonese diplomat Gunewardene had previously stated that he followed events only in the press, as had Andersen. When, a week after the executions, Hungary's interim chargé d'affaires János Bartha paid a visit to Gunewardene, he did so because during the investigation Gunewardene had already been in contact with Hungarian diplomats and had been present at a screening at the Hungarian embassy of a film designed to present Kádárist propaganda to foreigners. Gunewardene "spoke respectfully of Hungary's solid position,"[69] which sounded decidedly tone-deaf just a day or two after the death sentences were carried out. He added that he had received no kind of summons from the Special Committee or any instructions from his own government. In a strange coincidence, during Chargé d'affaires Bartha's visit with Gunewardene, Gunewardene took a call from Rapporteur of the Special Committee Shann and agreed to be present at the next meeting of the newly re-assembled Special Committee, even though he had previously stressed that not only Ceylon but also Denmark and Tunisia now considered the Hungarian issue to be closed. In his report on the visit and the call, Bartha characterized Gunewardene's willingness to participate as simply a "manifestation of careerism," adding that he was vain and liked to be the center of attention—his official office was, after all, decorated with portraits of himself.

That the members of the Special Committee would soon be replaced was both a cause and a consequence of these events and developments. Walker would represent Australia, Raúl Montero-Bustamante would represent Uruguay, and Ernst Meinstorp, the deputy leader of his nation's UN delegation, would represent Denmark. Ceylon's delegate would now be Claude Corea, and Slim's successor on the part of Tunisia would be Moncef Kedadi. The members were all newcomers who had not been part of the first stage of the Committee's work; the same was true of Trevelyan, who now represented the UN Secretariat.[70] This was how the Committee that had been thrown to the winds the previous June now returned to work, and it did not hold just one meeting, as Jordan had envisaged, but at least seven between June 26 and July 17, 1958. Walker was unsure whether they could manage the task of working together and producing a report at all, given Fabregat's passion for human rights and Corea's unwillingness "to accept anything critical to the Soviets." When Ceylon replaced Corea with Gunewardene, they instructed him to abstain.[71] On clarifying the Committee's purpose, it became clear that they could only be responsible for the investigation and producing a report, and that they had no authority to convene the General Assembly.[72] Regarding their responsibilities and those of the UN, however, they stressed that Imre Nagy had once turned to the UN for assistance, which had implications in international law concerning the guarantees applicable to a number of UN member states and the person of the executed prime minister. By this time, Australia had shrugged off its "reluctance" toward the operation of the Special Committee, perhaps sensing that it could have played a part in the tragedy that had occurred.[73] Arriving in the US for the session of the Special Committee, Andersen nevertheless "congratulated the principal secretary and his staff on the excellent monthly summaries,"[74] which, considering the circumstances, must have sounded somewhat strange. When the Committee did begin work, it soon became clear that one or two sessions would not suffice: the production of a new Special Report was the subject of considerable debate, both on the role and capacities of the Committee and on the extent of its mandate. During this debate, there was mention of the fact that Kádár had been part of the government that had approached the United Nations for help and that it could be important to stress this. There was general shock at the brutal way the international conventions on the right to asylum for Nagy and his associates at the Yugoslav embassy in Budapest had been breached by the Soviets.[75] One of the cruxes of the Committee's debate was the idea that the UN had been passive. Fabregat and Slim stressed that "the special representative [. . .] had not communicated with the Committee and had taken no action on behalf [of the] accused."[76] This was in part the passing of blame and in part the expression of justified anger after the tragedy, which should be written into the upcoming report. Andersen, as Chair, thought it would be "very unfortunate to give the impression that there were conflicts between the Special Representative and the Committee."[77] At the session on the following day, Marc Schreiber, representing the UN Secretariat, read out a telegram from Prince Wan in which he expressed his appreciation for the work of the Special Committee; it would have been awkward to respond to this with a criticism.[78]

Slim was keenly aware that the renewed interest of the Committee could save lives—the lives of those who were waiting for their fates to be determined. As he put it (referring specifically to Júlia Rajk, the politically active widow of the executed minister during the Stalinist purges in 1949), an "expression of concern [. . .] might help save her life."[79] Between 1956 and 1958, it was not just in Hungary that historic changes resulted in tragedies, so Slim added that it was not just the executions per se but their "how and why" that made a further statement necessary; the Soviets' handling of the Hungarian case could hardly be compared to the actions of the French in Algeria.[80]

After further meetings of the Committee and work sessions, the report was completed. It included the background, official requests, and rejections leading up to the executions. The Committee members attached a polished description of the Special Committee's activities and quoted Kádár's earlier statement that "neither Imre Nagy nor his political group wished knowingly to assist the counterrevolutionary system."[81] They condemned the executions and expressed their shock. The appendix contained documents including letters, press releases, and court sentences.[82]

On July 17, 1958, at the eightieth session of the Special Committee, the diplomats were packing up to leave. Slim left New York the next day, Andersen was making travel preparations, and Walker was dragged away by other obligations. The remaining members returned to their previous appointments. The minutes of the session record their concern about the increasing numbers of arrests in Hungary, the growing activity of the secret police, and the weakening of the judicial system, but this was the extent of their response.[83] And with this, the work of the Special Committee was ended, once and for all. On the same date, according to the schedule posted on the door of the courtrooms of the Hungarian Supreme Court in Budapest, the case review of 105 cases had been initiated. This information was also sent to New York.[84]

The International Responses to the Reprisals of the Kádár Regime

In Budapest, government officials had a clear idea of how shocking[85] the news of the executions was for the West. They continued to instruct Hungarian diplomatic missions abroad, drawing their attention to the "provocation" that had followed the executions. At the same time, they banned the missions from making any statements of their own; they were only permitted to repeat the announcement of the Hungarian Ministry of Justice.[86] They received instructions to be on heightened alert and to increase security precautions; they had a good sense of how they were testing the threshold of what international public opinion could tolerate. The strict guidelines were not followed by meaningful information, however; Hungarian diplomats were forced to provide only very concise communications and, even if they wanted to, they could not share further announcements with their foreign colleagues or journalists. That this alertness extended to observing the diplomatic employees was obvious from the fact that during this period, leading Foreign Affairs officials Frigyes Puja and János Péter communicated with the foreign minister using the usual channels but in handwritten letters marked "for your eyes only."

The political committee of the Hungarian Socialist Workers' Party (MSZMP) considered the world response to the executions. Country by country, it produced proposals for how to lessen the effect of the most damaging consequences.[87] These decisions were followed by instructions; the "foreign policy" methods outlined in these ranged from blackmail to persuasion and the offering of favors.[88] A number of developing countries were given information by Hungarian diplomats suggesting that the counterrevolution had been timed to occur on the most eventful days of the Suez Crisis so that events in Hungary would distract attention from the imperialists' bloodstained exploits. Hungary warned of the "immediate danger of fascist restoration" and told of the "death lists" that the "counterrevolutionaries" had kept, on the basis of which they would have killed tens of thousands of people. This bold variety of arguments and "facts" made full use of the imagination of the interrogators and prosecutors of the Stalinist show trials.[89]

While they were pursuing these efforts, officials in Budapest also prepared a balance sheet of the expected losses. One of the most important of these was the mass resignation of numerous Communist Party members in the West. Also on the deficit side of the balance sheet was the dramatic worsening of relations with Yugoslavia, whose objection had been expected. Even though Hungary had previously enjoyed Yugoslavia's assistance, Budapest now began a serious smear campaign against the government and political system of Yugoslavia. The source of greatest anxiety, however, was the United Nations. There was fear that it might withdraw Hungary's suspended mandate and exclude it altogether. Budapest laid out plans for the Hungarian delegation in this eventuality: before it was robbed of its accreditation, the delegation was to hurry out of the Hall, and Hungary's Presidential Council was to send a telegram to Hammarskjöld withdrawing the Hungarian delegation's mandate.

From the report of its chargé d'affaires in Washington, Budapest learned that the Special Committee had been called into session again, and although officials there were informed that "there is not the adequate moral energy in the world for the UN action required" to withdraw Hungary's mandate, as Hungarian US émigré Ferenc Nagy put it, they could not be entirely certain of this.[90] On June 20, 1958, a "plan of action" was devised in the event that a special session of the General Assembly be convened. That did not happen, so preparations were made in advance of the General Assembly in the fall.[91] This delay occurred despite the fact that Hammarskjöld already had an urgent initiative of France and the US on his desk regarding the investigation of the executions in Hungary that seemed to threaten the lives of dozens more revolutionaries, for which only the timing had to be clarified. On June 19, Marc Schreiber, one of the UN's leading lawyers, asked Jordan to investigate the necessary conditions and make a suggestion for action on behalf on the accused Hungarians. The initiators later revoked their plan for the UN to take further steps, however; this seemed as much due to resignation as it did to pragmatism.[92] In Budapest, it seemed an inauspicious sign that the Hungarian mandate had been rejected at the conference of the UN International Labor Organization, and the delegation's isolation was proving a strain on its members, who were understandably concerned that the question of the Hungarian mandate would be "be raised in the most pronounced form" at the General Assembly in the fall. The Hungarian authorities were not afraid of being stigmatized; they wrote that this "meant next to nothing in practice."[93] Nevertheless, if Hungary was chastised for contravening the UN Charter, for ignoring UN resolutions, and for its government's dubious legitimacy, it might face a level of international isolation so great as to have dire consequences.

The wave of international protest was enormous: demonstrations were held outside Hungarian and Soviet embassies, while huge numbers of telegrams, memoranda, and letters reached the Hungarian foreign ministry; even India, a friend of Hungary, "requested explanations" about the trials. The Hungarian government tried to convince the world that its position remained unchanged but that, since it had announced its amnesty, an investigation into events had brought new information into its possession. This meant that it had to face an "attempted putsch," and it was stressed that "political trials are not a Hungarian specialty." At this time, people were imprisoned for their beliefs in a variety of places, but here, the issue involved an attempt to usurp power. A whole volume's worth of evidential material was compiled on "the conspiracy of Imre Nagy and his associates" and was published, in four languages, in time for the fall session of the General Assembly, as a five-volume part of the White Book, as such government-issued official publications are called. Plentiful copies of the tome were supplied to diplomatic missions and to parties in fraternal and socialist countries. Copies were also sent to the pope, and, of course, to the United Nations.[94]

Among the great powers in the West, the idea of isolating the wrong-doer—of breaking off diplomatic relations with Hungary—was again mooted but came to nothing. The US Department of State recommended that the issue be resolved by the UN.[95] After his discussions with Moscow, Péter Kós announced in late July 1958 that there would not be a special session of the General Assembly and that, while the Hungarian authorities had observed the preparations and publication of a further report with concern, having read it, they felt there was little to be worried about. But they left nothing to chance: four working groups put together rebuttals to the anticipated "attacks" that had been instigated against the People's Republic of Hungary "because of a few condemned traitors."[96] The propaganda machinery was at work. In the story it told, the United Nations was "the patron of criminals," and the newer report of the Special Committee was judged "a disgrace for the UN."[97]

In addition to provoking strong feelings, Hungary's propagandists also breathed new life into the use of the "anti-fascist" arguments, which were considered useful vis-à-vis the UN, although the 1957 report had already been full of "the lies of fascists who had fled abroad."[98] They conjured visions of battles with SS divisions, military supplies carried on Red Cross airplanes, newly freed war criminals and fully-armed terrorists, not to mention Gehlen (West German secret service) agents, whom they considered to be synonymous with fascism. They produced one document of over fifteen typed pages listing the previous crimes of prisoners who had been freed. Alleging that robberies and murders "had become usual" during the "counter-revolution" became part of the logic of the propagandists; they also experimented with raising the specter of fascist "revenge."[99] Propaganda for the event of a special UN General Assembly was completed in Budapest by June 20; among its arguments were that those executed "were punished in line with the weight of their crimes" and that the previous "position of tolerance" had become unsustainable, as "highly condemning items of evidence" had come to light: "With their official sanction, 234 defenseless citizens were slain, and a further 3,000 put in prison; they also drew up a death list with more than 10,000 names on it."[100]

The justification for the Imre Nagy trial emerged not only from this absurd line of reasoning—accusing communists, antifascists, and those of

Jewish origin of being Nazis—but also from the results of a so-called investigation, during which the government alleged that Nagy had "prepared the illegal murder of Hungarian citizens,"[101] although they had difficulty producing evidence that such crimes were planned to be committed. Hungarian propagandists also took pains to emphasize that the laws on the basis of which the judgments were brought were not passed after the communist takeover of power and certainly not after November 4, 1956; these statutes had already been on the books in the 1930s and in the penal codes of 1934 and 1946.[102] In a similarly complete departure from reality, they stated that the arrest of Maléter "was performed by the police divisions of the Revolutionary Worker-Peasant Government"[103]—suggesting an unusual identity for General Ivan Serov of the KGB, as Soviet troops were throughout this time pursuing their operations at the request of the Hungarian government and "always on the basis of its instructions."[104] By this logic, it could only have been inferred that the Nagy government must have actively requested its own liquidation.

It would have been more difficult to include Yugoslavia, headed by Tito, an antifascist partisan leader, in this proposed great fascist conspiracy, so a Hungarian diplomatic memo was left to preempt and defuse the objections to the executions expected to come from Belgrade. In this memo, Belgrade was accused of helping to prepare the Revolution, and while the Hungarian authorities warmly acknowledged the "significant selfless efforts" made to "consolidate the situation in Hungary," they asserted that those responsible "were claiming asylum in the country that had offered them support in the past."[105] Indeed, the "Nagy group" was responsible, with Yugoslav assistance, for the armed resistance, the organization of the strike, maintaining communication with Radio Free Europe, and for illegal publications—at least, this is what are told of the days during which in fact Soviet tanks held the Yugoslav embassy in Budapest, with Nagy and the others inside it, in their tight embrace.

If the propaganda is to be believed, the counterrevolutionaries were attempting to make Sopron, at the western edge of Hungary, secede from the country, so it could act as a kind of alternate European government to represent Hungary at the United Nations, like Taiwan for mainland China, even forcing international intervention, an eventuality the selfless Soviet comrades were kind enough to prevent. Regarding the Kádár government's legitimacy, meanwhile, the Hungarian communist politicians claimed that the majority of votes at the UN was not equivalent to the majority of the world's people, for the "people's China" was on Hungary's side, with its many hundreds of millions of communists.[106]

Based on these questionable arguments, Budapest informed the UN that enough was enough—though not quite enough for them to have instructed the Hungarian Ambassador to demand that the issue be taken off the agenda.[107] Such an attempt would have been overwhelmingly voted down, and the preceding debate would do nothing to improve the Hungarian foreign ministry's position. For similar reasons, Hungary did not want the examination of one of its key claims, that of US "sabotage," on the agenda, as the US would surely agree to this being investigated in the field, which Hungary would have had to refuse.[108]

The Bang-Jensen affair, which attracted public attention at exactly this same time, was a great boon to the Hungarian propaganda machine. The dismissal of the Danish UN official allowed it to revive its arguments concerning the destruction of "evidence"—which it claimed was true not just of the list of names of witnesses but also of minutes of meetings—that Budapest used to cast doubt on the veracity of the entire investigation.[109] According to their argument, the reason that the list of witnesses' names had to be burned was that its destruction compromised the UN less than publishing the list would have done.[110]

Despite all these efforts, however, Hungarian diplomacy became ever more isolated, something the Hungarian chargé d'affaires in Washington could sense from his dealings not just with Western countries but also certain "fraternal" ones.[111] Bartha's job, just like that of the Hungarian UN Mission in New York, was made more difficult because he received so little information from Budapest; he mostly gleaned reports from the press or sometimes from Soviet comrades. The latter would reassure the Hungarian diplomats that not only was there no risk of a special General Assembly session, but that the Special Committee had also "finally ended its activity."[112] In September, Special Representative Waithayakon requested that he not be kept up to speed on the Hungarian question, and the Australians proposed that Prince Wan's mandate be revoked, bringing the Committee's work to an end. This was an unexpected move, even for their allies: Washington noted that Australia's reasoning was "not entirely clear."[113]

None of these changes regarding the Special Committee freed Hungary's diplomatic staff from the shadow cast by the martyred prime minister. The sudden appearance in the United States of what the Hungarians called an "Imre Nagy cult"[114] was understandably unsavory for them, and all the more so because they could remember the Americans' ambivalence toward Imre Nagy, whom they called the Revolution's "Muscovite" leader. At about this time, László Varga, a lawyer living in the US, wanted to provide an explicit legal framework for the elemental outrage that followed the executions. This had not been included in the UN report, and the omission had caught the eye of certain American lawyers.[115]

The Hungarian government had a stroke of luck when it was offered assistance by British politician and jurist Denis Pritt. Pritt had been invited to the Hungarian embassy in London, prior to the executions, in January 1958.[116] This visit must have laid the foundation for the offer he made in early July to write a study of the Imre Nagy trial. Perhaps it was no coincidence that the UK ambassador in Budapest was the first to inform his home country of the possibility of such a trial.[117] Pritt requested that the Hungarian Ministry of Justice invite him to Budapest, together with his wife, so he could have access to the trial documents, just as he had been invited to Moscow in the 1930s at the time of Stalin's show trials.[118] The embassy provided a "free visa" for Pritt and his wife.[119] In Budapest, Pritt met the chief prosecutor, judges, and attorneys, and was able to study the evidence from the Nagy trial. He would later recollect that there were whole rooms stacked high with evidence against Nagy.[120] Pritt considered the trial to have been necessary, "regular," and governed by "regular procedures." To Mohamed Rahman, the Indian chargé d'affaires, who was hosting him for dinner, Pritt said of Nagy that "almost every country would have sentenced him to death."[121] His words shocked Rahman and the other dinner guests, as did his acceptance of the arguments of the "hanging court" that the revolutionaries had planned mass murders. Pritt also entertained a vision of a civil war being prepared by the US Congress with the support of the resistance in Eastern Europe.[122] Pritt collated his opinions in a study for the *New World Review*. One copy of the typewritten text underwent a number of amendments at the Hungarian foreign ministry; to this revised document the Hungarians added a description of the "kidnapping" of Imre Nagy and his relocation to Romania, followed by the reasons for his extradition to Hungary, as justified by information the Hungarian authorities had acquired in the meantime.[123]

Pritt's statements, as a former Labour MP, provided serious ammunition for the Hungarians in the UN debate in the fall of 1958; in December, to express its gratitude, the Hungarian mission in London held a dinner in honor of "our friend Pritt."[124] Previously, the Hungarian ambassador to the

UK had dined with British Communist Party leaders who considered the execution of Nagy a political mistake, as their organization was now in an even worse position than it had found itself in after the counterrevolution. The executions followed their delegation to Budapest having been told by Kádár in March that there was no prospect of Imre Nagy being tried.[125]

Two months after the publication of the summer 1958 report, Hammarskjöld extended a dinner invitation to the Hungarian foreign minister, who was visiting New York, together with the leader of his delegation.[126] For all their rhetorical shaking of fists, the Hungarian communists accepted. During the meeting, Foreign Minister Endre Sík understood Hammarskjöld as saying that the Hungarian question would almost certainly not be added to the agenda of the General Assembly.[127] Given the international outrage that ensued, the Secretary-General had to correct this "misunderstanding,"[128] claiming that he could only remember saying that the debate on Hungary would be shorter than it had been in the past.

Even as attention to events in Hungary was faltering, documents on the Hungarian question continued to accumulate,[129] and the situation in Hungary continued to worsen. Although Jordan mentioned to his colleagues that news reports were being received, these were immediately archived, despite the fact that quite a number of them demanded immediate action.[130] As a result, from that point on, not even the Special Committee members would receive reports arriving from Hungary, as even the Special Representative had presumably not been granted access.

The barely concealed apathy of the United Nations may also have paved the way for retributions in Hungary to continue, as observed, for example, by the *Glasgow Herald*: "Hungary is effectively beyond effective help."[131] In his speech to the General Assembly, Hungarian deputy foreign minister János Péter stated that, as a former bishop, he would prefer to rescind all the death sentences, but this was not yet possible, especially in the case of capital crimes.[132] As he said this, there were about one hundred people who were still alive who would soon succumb to these reprisals, a fate they had no hope of escaping.[133] The willful silence from Hungary had been broken, only to be replaced with a muteness that was even more deafening.

The tragic trials, condemnations, and executions of Imre Nagy and the other leaders of the Revolution demonstrated with tragic clarity that the UN's approach toward the Hungarian "problem" was totally inadequate. Even though more than sufficient information was available to UN officials—those in the best position to help those facing serious punishment and death in Hungary—the lack of help and protest by the international community encouraged the Hungarian leadership to continue their brutal reprisals with no fear of consequences whatsoever.

Notes

1. February 27, 1957. Press conference held by László Gyáros. Columbia University, Butler Library, Rare Books and Manuscript Collection (hereinafter ACP), box 182.

2. Imre Nagy and his closest associates were kept in Snagov, Romania, from November 1956 until their arrest. Rainer (1996). The story of the arrest of the Imre Nagy circle, and its possible consequences, was written up and sent to Washington on February 20, 1958. NARA 764.00/2-2058.

3. CHP, subject area 8. March 22, 1957.

4. CHP, subject area 8. May 9, 1957. In describing the parliamentary session, a document referred to Dobi's speech: "Prepare trials against Imre Nagy and Maléter."

5. On August 26, the political committee asked the Ministry of the Interior for the prosecutor's office to prepare the indictment by the fall. At the same time, the committee prepared the Déry-Háy trial, which was intended to test the water for public opinion abroad. The Imre Nagy trial was scheduled to take place after the UN debate. Stikalin (1993), 264–66.

6. They suggested the trial be delayed until December 1957 or January 1958. Gál, *A "Jelcin–dosszié,"* 203. According to Kádár, "The key strategic question for the enemy is the amnesty [. . .] the more influence they bring to bear on us, the later the amnesty will be [. . .] legal procedure must be given free rein." Kádár considered that the trials could only be delayed if this would disturb the Soviet peace offensive, but they should return to this later rather than accept weaker sentences. See Kiss, Ripp, and Vida, eds., *Top Secret*, 258–62.

7. On December 12, 1957, a list was made of the secret trials. ACP, box 184. The list of the names of the accused was in an appendix to the report. ACP, box 182.

8. December 17, 1957. Radványi (1972), 45.

9. MNL XIX-J-1-k, box 70.

10. Kathleen McClaughlin, "Divorced Wife Asks U.N. to Intercede for Arrested Chief of Hungarian Rebels," *New York Times*, September 11, 1957.

11. ACP, box 183. Hammarskjöld's letter of December 15, 1957.

12. The Secretary-General's telegram was taken to mean that he wished "to petition the Hungarian government in person to end the proceedings against the persons who played an active part in the counter-revolution." MNL XIX-J-1-k, box 55. Horváth's letter of December 25, 1957. DHS L 179:84.

13. December 13, 1957. ACP, box 183.

14. December 20, 1957. DHS L 179:84. "[Wan] be informed of this action."

15. Ibid. "The Committee will continue to watch the situation in Hungary under its mandate from the General Assembly."

16. Kádár saw a number of options for the progression of the Imre Nagy trial: "1. We postpone it. 2. We conclude it, but influence the procedure of the trial, so that a sentence is passed that does not exacerbate the international situation. This

option would be a very bad one, however." Cited in Kiss, Ripp, and Vida, eds., *Top Secret*, 281.

17. The session of the Special Committee was held on December 20, 1957. ACP, box 184.

18. ACP, box 184.

19. For the Australian position, see the telegram from the US Mission to the UN on January 20, 1958. NARA 764.00/1-2058. The British Ambassador to the UN claimed that the instructions to the Australian delegation were "to oppose vigorously any proposals for a further report." This instruction came from Mr. Casey, who "has apparently been much influenced by Mr Shann." In line with the instructions, Walker did not convene the Special Committee, as British delegate Pierson Dixon reported on January 21, 1958, but the issue was not taken off the agenda. FO 371/134853.

20. See the US State Department memo of March 19, 1958: "[Australia] [. . .] prevented from taking any public action." This despite Australia receiving reports.

21. May 2, 1958. From Canberra, they wrote to London that the Special Committee was only of the "R[adio] F[ree] E[urope]-variety." FO 371/134855. The French foreign ministry cites the Australian proposal of May 14, 1958—thirty-three days before the executions—that the Special Committee be disbanded. AD NUOI 244 C2.

22. See Andersen's telegram of December 18, 1957, to Copenhagen. RA 119. G. 3/19. Pakke Nr. 1.

23. From January to April 1958, information was received on a constant basis, from Béla Fábián and Béla Varga, among others. ("List of Communications.") CHP, subject area 9.

24. ACP, box 184. January 7, 1958. From Jordan to Protitch: "How to proceed?" See "Summaries."

25. Statements from Szénási and Domokos can be found in the document "Note on the Measures Taken by the Hungarian Workers-Peasants Government," UN-ARM S-0188-0006-0012.

26. February 1, 1958. Note. MNL XIX-J-1-k, box 55.

27. Ibid. April 20, 1958. This is where the letter from Lodge and Wadsworth to Mód about the trials can be found. See also MNL XIX-J-1-j, box 209.

28. From November 14 to 16, 1957, Communist Party leaders from various countries gathered in the Soviet capital.

29. Radványi (1972), 36.

30. The US embassy in Budapest reported on the sentences on successive days: March 11, 12, and 13, 1958. USNA 764.00/3-1158, -1258, -1358.

31. February 20, 1958. "Outline for the summary of the 12th General Assembly." MNL XIX-J-1-k, box 55.

32. April 7, 1958. MNL XIX-J-1-n, box 53.

33. April 21, 1958. MNL XIX-J-24-a, box 2.

34. March 25, 1958. Note to the Foreign Ministry. MNL XIX-J-1-k, box 55. In the preceding years, the ILO, the PEN Club, and the International Atomic Energy Authority had all considered ostracizing their respective Hungarian delegations.

35. April 21, 1958. Hungarian foreign ministry working material on "eliminating" the Hungarian question. MNL XIX-J-24-a, box 2.

36. In Budapest, they were aware that in technical terms it would be difficult to convene the Special Committee with its members being away. April 21, 1958. MNL XIX-J-24-a, box 3, and MNL XIX-J-1-o, box 6.

37. May 22, 1958. MNL XIX-J-1-o, box 6.

38. Tibor Zádor's report of May 28, 1958. MNL XIX-J-1-j, box 231.

39. May 28, 1958. MNL XIX-J-29-a (Washington), box 15.

40. April 24, 1958. Submission from the foreign policy staff. MNL XIX-J-1-o, box 6.

41. UNARM S-0188-0006-0007. May 7, 1958. The staff of the US embassy in Budapest learned of the planned trials from the noticeboard of the Hungarian Supreme Court.

42. May 14, 1958. CHP, subject area 9.

43. UNARM S-0188-0006-0008. Protitch's report of May 7, 1958. According to an exchange of letters in March 1958 between Boris Ponomarev (then chief of the international department of the CPSU Central Committee) and Gyula Kállai, Hungarian minister of state, interior affairs officers traveled to Bucharest to prepare the trials as planned. Sereda and Stikalin (1993), 260–61.

44. Fry wrote about this on May 17, 1957, adding that they might well be sentenced to death. FO 371/128678.

45. See the May 23, 1958, telegram from the US embassy in Budapest. NARA 764.00/5-2358.

46. UNARM S-0188-0006-0008. May 7, 1958. "Protitch Report."

47. DHS L 179:174.

48. October 10, 1958. ÁBTL 3.2.1. Bt-910/3.

49. ÁBTL 3.2.1. Bt-910/2 and 3. All this is in the document "Proposed letter to compromise Tamás Pásztor." It was created as a provocation, but it must have been true, as the folder states "We have documents of this nature."

50. ÁBTL 3.2.1. BT 910/3.

51. June 17, 1957. DHS L 179:84.

52. June 20, 1958. Waithayakon's telegram from Bangkok. UNARM S-0441-0192-0008-00001.

53. CHP, subject area 8. June 21, 1958.

54. ACP, box 182. June 21, 1958. Trevelyan to the Secretary-General (in Jerusalem): "Special Committee [. . .] deploring executions [. . .] No other decision was taken [. . .] meet again to consider whether they should take any further action."

55. Ibid. June 21, 1958. "Material Related to the Trial and Execution of Imre Nagy, General Maléter and Their Two Companions."

56. NAA A 1838 33/1/5/1.

57. AUS NAA A 1838 33/1/5/1 Part 4. Shann: "We would not contemplate any action other than issuing the statement." He added that it was the job of the General Assembly, not the Special Committee, to take any direct action.

58. Ibid. The instruction for the urgent arrangement of a meeting came on June 19, 1958, when Walker reported that pressure was growing: "The pressure on him and on the Mission had been very substantial."

59. June 21, 1958. Jordan to Wan. ACP, box 182.

60. ACP, box 182. On the tasks of the Special Representative, see the resolution of the General Assembly and the previous report by Waithayakon. Bang-Jensen Archive (hereinafter BJI), box 25.

61. CHP, subject area 9. June 27, 1958: "List of Communications." This mentions "public personalities" whose lives were in danger, secret trials, and death sentences.

62. NAA A 183833/1/5/1. Part 4. From Andersen to Shann. On June 27, 1958.

63. On June 20, 1958, Jordan informed Trevelyan about the material that had been prepared. ACP, box 182.

64. ACP, box 182. June 20, 1958. Jordan to Trevelyan.

65. June 24, 1958. Jordan's note. Ibid.

66. Ibid.

67. Ibid. "The Committee would complete its business at two meetings this week."

68. ACP, box 184. June 24, 1958.

69. MNL XIX-J-29-a (Washington), box 14.

70. For the documentation on this, see CHP, subject area 8.

71. See the July 11, 1958, telegram of the US Mission to the UN: NARA 320.5764/7-1158.

72. June 26, 1958. 73rd session. CHP, subject area 8. See Schreiber's letter to Jordan of June 19, 1958. ACP, box 184.

73. According to a report from the US embassy in Canberra: "Reevaluation previous Australian reluctance let UN Committee on Hungary continue to function." NARA 764.00/6-1958.

74. CHP, subject area 8. July 2, 1958.

75. Ibid. July 16, 1957. Seventy-eighth session.

76. Ibid.

77. Ibid.

78. Ibid. July 17, 1958. Eightieth session.

79. Ibid.

80. Ibid. The Algerian War of Independence lasted from 1954 until 1962, during which time a multitude of mass murders, acts of torture, and war crimes took place. There are only estimates as to the number of victims, ranging from four hundred thousand to one million. In the course of the war, nine hundred thousand people fled the country.

81. Kádár's speech on November 11, 1956. CHP, subject area 8.

82. UNARM S-0442-0140-0001-00001.

83. CHP, subject area 8.

84. In Washington, it was realized that international attention could prevent executions, as had been shown in the cases of József Gáli and Gyula Obersovszky: "Dramatic action by the Special Committee could have similar results." See Dulles's instructions on June 27, 1958. NARA 764.00/6-2758. In Budapest, after the "reviews of cases" announced at this time, they planned an additional 130 for July. See the telegrams from the US embassy in Budapest on June 23 and July 5, 9, and 10, 1958. The last of these refers to the fate of Obersovszky and Gáli. NARA 764.00/6-2358, /7-958, /7-1058.

85. July 1, 1958. Note on the judgment passed down on Imre Nagy and his "accomplices." MNL XIX-J-1-k, box 55.

86. June 20, 1958. "Tasks relating to the Imre Nagy case." (From Károly Szigeti) MNL XIX-J-29-a (Washington), box 15.

87. On June 7, 1958, a series of proposals was elaborated for the tasks necessitated by the Nagy trial. MNL XIX-J-1-n, box 53. July 28, 1958.

88. MNL XIX-J-1-n, box 53.

89. Radványi (1972), 38, 50–57. See also MNL XIX-J-1-j, boxes 55, 56. July 15, 1958. Submission to the Political Committee. August 5, 1958. Hungarian government statement. MNL XIX-J-1-n, box 53.

90. Bartha reported on June 25, 1958. MNL XIX-J-29-a (Washington), box 15.

91. June 20, 1958. MNL XIX-J-1-k, box 55.

92. See the French position: NUOI 244/F. See also Schreiber's letter to Jordan on June 19, 1958. UNARN DAG 1.1.1.3. Protitch files. All this can be found in the French diplomatic papers: AD NUOI 244/C2.

93. MNL XIX-J-1-k, box 55.

94. August 13, 1958. MNL XIX-J-1-j 82. See also MNL XIX-j-1-n, box 66, and MNL XIX-J-1-k, box 55.

95. See the memorandum from the State Department in Washington dated June 17, 1958, on the suggestion from the Italian ambassador that diplomatic relations be discontinued. NARA 764.00/6-1758.

96. July 14, 1957. "Our position." MNL, MSZMP documents, 288 f. storage unit 1958/11. The political committee proposal for the UN General Assembly was ready for August 28, 1958.

97. August 6, 1958. MNL XIX-J-1-k, box 55.

98. Ibid.

99. On August 7, 1958, they put together a collection of documents on the crimes committed during the so-called counterrevolution. According to this, 9,952 common criminals were freed as well as 3,524 political captives, including some charged with war crimes. MNL XIX-J-1-j, box 82.

100. MNL XIX-J-1-j, box 82, and MNL XIX-J-1-k, box 55.

101. June 23, 1958. "Plan." MNL XIX-J-1-j, box 82.

102. July 14, 1958. "Our position." MNL, MSZMP documents, 288 f. Storage unit 1958/11.

103. MNL XIX-J-1-k, box 55.

104. MNL, MSZMP documents, 288 f. Storage unit 1958/11.

105. June 23, 1958. Proposed government statement in response to the Yugoslav memorandum. Gál, *A "Jelcin–dosszié,"* 210–11.

106. MNL XIX-J-1-k, box 55.

107. Ibid.

108. November 23, 1958. János Péter's (handwritten) letter to Endre Sík. MNL XIX-J-1-n, box 66.

109. MNL XIX-J-1-k, box 55.

110. MNL, MSZMP documents 288 f. Storage unit 1958/11.

111. August 26, 1958. János Bartha's report. MNL XIX-J-29-a (Washington), box 14.

112. Soviet councilor Striganov told Bartha this on August 26, 1958. MNL XIX-J-29-a (Washington), box 14. Walker conveyed Hammarskjöld's position to Lodge: the Special Committee had "outlived [its] usefulness." NARA 320.11/12-458.

113. The US Mission to the UN reported on this on September 26, 1958. NARA 310.5/9-2658. On Australia's intentions, see NARA 320.5764/9-858. When Slim contacted the US Mission asking that the UN exert whatever political pressure it had to prevent further tragedies, he learned that Canberra was "opposed in principle

to continuing UN machinery on Hungary." See the report of the US Mission to the UN on October 23, 1958. NARA 320.5764/10-2358.

114. MNL XIX-J-29-a (Washington), box 14.

115. CHP, subject area July 8, 1958. László Varga: "Legal Aspects of the Imre Nagy Case." July 17, 1958. According to US attorney John Keisder: "[Attorney of Law, Greensburg, PA.] [. . .] the recent documentation by your Committee of the executions in Hungary [. . .] several earmarks and hasty and prefixed bias and few of such a juridicial approach as would be expected of a UN Committee."

116. January 2, 1958. MNL XIX-J-41-a (London).

117. See the British diplomatic report of January 27, 1958, FO 371/134853, and the telegram from the US embassy of January 31, 1958, NARA 764.00/1-3158.

118. July 1, 1957. MNL XIX-J-41-a (London). According to Australian diplomatic records, the Special Committee also requested the documents of the trial: "Committee asks for records of trials [. . .] This would not be handed over but such a step has propaganda value." NAA A 1838 33/1/5/1. Part 4.

119. August 30, 1958. MNL XIX-J-41-a (London).

120. Rahman, *Magyarország, 1959–1959*, 6.

121. Ibid. MNL XIX-J-41-a (London).

122. Ibid. "Murdering indiscriminately thousands of people who were suspected of being supporters of the Soviet state [. . .] US Congress voted 125.000.000 USD."

123. Ibid. "The Trial of Imre Nagy," *New World Review*. "Addendum: Kidnapping [. . .] safety in Rumania."

124. December 9, 1958. MNL XIX-J-41-a.

125. The trial had already been recommenced from February onward. MNL XIX-J-41-a.

126. September 26, 1958. According to the calendar of events of the delegation to the General Assembly. MNL XIX-J-24-b (New York).

127. November 19, 1958. CHP, subject area 8. On October 9, 1958, in *Népszabadság*: "Sík said he had been unofficially told by the UN SYG Dag Hammarskjöld that the Question of Hungary would not come up for debate."

128. Ibid. November 19, 1958.

129. August 3, 1958. Tamás Pásztor: "Report about the present situation and latest events in Hungary based on documents and testimonies of witnesses." CHP, subject area 3.

130. Ibid. See Jordan's instructions to Hámori on August 25, 1958.

131. September 22, 1958. MNL XIX-J-1-j (Great Britain), box 14.

132. MNL XIX-J-1-o, box 6.

133. In total, the reprisals involved the deportation of 13,000 people, the imprisonment of 20,000, and the execution of 231 individuals as sentenced by a court. One source of documentation for this is Berle, Cherne, and Luce, eds., *Hungary under Soviet Rule. A Survey of Developments from September 1957 to August 1958.*

9

EPILOGUE

The Solution of the Hungarian Problem

The Special Representative and His Controversial Activity

In May 1958, Under-Secretary-General Dragoslav Protitch was replaced by Anatoly Dobrynin, who used the power of his new office to obtain copies of numerous documents relating to the Hungarian question. This probably did little to change events in Hungary, but it did make the position of the UN clearer to the Soviet Union—the country that made the Hungarian question a question in the first place.

The UN leadership was well aware of the controversies surrounding Dobrynin's appointment, and although Humphrey Trevelyan briefly took over the case from Protitch at one point, five months later, it would be handed back to Protitch.[1] As leadership migrated between the officials, so did the accompanying documentation, and in ways that could not guarantee its security. Povl Bang-Jensen's story suggested that, for UN leaders, it was not just the security risk that was the problem; the greater danger was in that security risk being made public.

Late in the summer of 1958, the Hungarian foreign ministry was considering all possible scenarios and responses to them. Although there was no indication in the United Nations that the report it published in July might have any consequences, in Budapest there was concern that this would not be the last word on the issue of the executions. Meanwhile, those "of like mind" made up a majority of the Committee reviewing the Hungarian UN mandate, so the Hungarian delegation was able to remain in post not only because of the rather paradoxical legal continuity but also because the Committee judged its accreditation to be in order.[2]

Because the UN had been so passive in the face of the repression and retributions following the Hungarian Revolution, in November 1958, the Emergency Committee for UN Action on Hungary was established. Its members included US senators, politicians, intellectuals, and financiers—from David Rockefeller to FBI director J. Edgar Hoover.[3] For some the formation of the committee merely served to confirm communist propaganda that US imperialists, spies, and capitalists were behind the UN's condemnation of Hungary; for many others, it showed that the UN's passivity was beyond the pale. The committee recommended that what they called the Hungarian puppet delegation be removed and Hungary's membership be suspended. If, during the Suez Crisis, France and the UK had adhered to the resolutions of the international community, the Soviet-installed Hungarian government should have done the same.

The fall 1958 session put the Hungarian question on the agenda, but not as an urgent matter. Based on the latest report, the General Assembly condemned the executions, ruled against Hungary for ignoring its resolutions, decried the persecution throughout the country, and made significant demands on Hungary[4]—all as if these demands had not been included in every single previous resolution and report. Clear evidence of the inactivity of the UN's leaders was given by the telling silence that crowned the formal role played by Prince Wan. The UN leadership thanked him for the work he had done, even though the report was a testament to his tragic ineffectiveness. In the diplomatic language of the UN, as its leading legal counsel Constantin Stavropoulos explained, this expression of appreciation meant the end of Waithayakon's mandate, without the need for this to be made explicit. The same was true for the UN Special Committee on the Problem of Hungary itself. But for the Hungarian question to remain on the agenda, a new Special Representative was appointed: New Zealand politician Sir Leslie Munro, former President of the General Assembly. At the suggestion of the UN leadership, his jurisdiction would be reduced in scope, but he retained the right to submit reports and display "useful initiative."[5]

Hungarian foreign minister Endre Sík noted with satisfaction that after the failures of the Secretary-General and then Prince Wan to secure official visits, Munro "did not even attempt to visit Hungary."[6] Munro approached Péter Mód about doing so a number of times, but he was told that while he could come to Hungary as a private citizen, the Hungarian government did not acknowledge his mandate, claiming it "contravened the UN Charter."

Sík referred to the $10,000 over and above his expenses that Munro was given by the UN to investigate the Hungarian question as "a wage earned with no labor" with the implication that the New Zealander should able to spend that on his "European jaunts" while pretending to investigate the Hungarian question.[7]

By this time, Ceylon's envoy Gunewardene, at the instructions of his government, had left the Special Committee and indeed argued for it to be disbanded.[8] Budapest was later informed that the Ceylonese Ambassador to the UN would not vote for any resolution condemning Hungary, a reassurance of the greatest importance from one of the Special Committee's member states, and one that came in the same year that Imre Nagy and his associates had been executed.[9] For his part, Sík stressed that "he had been mandated to announce that the trial proceedings had closed and been completed." This was not true.[10] In the weeks preceding the General Assembly session, news reached the UN from Budapest of a Stalinist counteroffensive: many members of the "old guard" returning from Moscow had apparently turned against János Kádár.[11]

There was a surge in further retributions, including the arrest and prosecution of many leaders of the Hungarian Red Cross. The aid effort had been brought to an end in 1958, power had been consolidated, and any additional aid could be sent to Hungary only indirectly. News of trials of Hungarian aid workers reached New York, but there is no indication that the United Nations responded to it. The Red Cross headquarters in Geneva offered to pay the lawyers who defended the workers; their legal fees were enormous and, given the nature of the proceedings, would be only good money thrown after bad.[12]

At about this time, the Hungarian Mission to the UN started to be considered more presentable in UN circles. Not half a year had passed since the executions, but dinner invitations started to arrive, and, despite the resolution condemning Hungary, the isolation of the Hungarian diplomats was softening, and reports from New York now detailed a variety of contacts being established.[13] However strongly-worded US rhetoric had been, it did not prevent the operations of the Special Committee from being shut down.[14] Early in the following year Ceylon established diplomatic relations with Hungary, and in 1959 Indian diplomat Arthur Lall would even pay a visit to Budapest.[15]

In March 1959, Péter Mód must have been reassured to see that William Jordan, Munro's key adviser, "conducts his other secretariat-related work in Comrade Dobrynin's department quite normally"[16] and to learn from Under-Secretary-General Andrew Cordier that "it cannot even be said of [Munro] that he has a permanent office." These circumstances made it clear that the General Assembly resolution on establishing the right working conditions for the Special Representative was not being implemented. Meanwhile, Munro's party was defeated in the New Zealand general election, so he had only as much political room to maneuver as the UN job gave him, even though, as early as May, it had been noticed in Washington that Munro was already "doing nothing as a UN rapporteur."[17] When Jordan passed the correspondence between Munro and Mód to Washington, perhaps he intended to prove just how much passivity had become institutionalized.

During this period Mód met with Cordier a number of times. It was in Cordier's office that Mód was able to read the submission of the International League of Human Rights and the documents of Tamás Pásztor concerning the situation in Hungary, which he had sent from Vienna. As a result, Mód was able to send a detailed report to Budapest with all the names mentioned in both these sources. The authors of the International League of Human Rights report wished to draw the UN's attention to the fact that many émigrés returning to Hungary with the promise of amnesty had been arrested, and others had simply disappeared after entering the country. Later, a number of émigrés who had returned would be executed.

At the end of the summer of 1959, there was no indication that Munro might wish to produce a report, for the reason, as Mód saw it, that "the only employee who up till now was nominally entrusted with the Hungarian question, was for a prolonged period called to a different area."[18] Despite her other duties, UN civil servant Klára Héderváry completed her administrative tasks conscientiously, and waited for the documentation she had compiled and kept constantly updated to be requested. On one occasion, Cordier told Mód that the two UN members of staff entrusted with the Hungarian question were working on other affairs "95% of the time."[19] Apart from the fact that Munro had no mandate to investigate or to make proposals,[20] his unpopularity might have influenced the issue it was his job to represent. United States representative to the UN Henry Cabot Lodge Jr. said of Munro that he was "thoroughly disliked by virtually all members."[21] Mód reported to Budapest that the Secretary-General had "emphatically" informed him "that the secretariat does not ascribe much significance to Munro's appointment, so if for this reason alone does not provide him with much assistance."[22] When Dag Hammarskjöld was preparing for the next session of the General Assembly at the end of the summer of 1959, a US Mission report indicates that the Secretary-General pondered the fate of the Hungarian question and considered it time for it to "peter out."[23]

At the foreign ministry in Budapest, the "tabling of the Hungarian question" was cause for concern, so officials requested that "the fraternal countries support Hungary at the UN Secretariat," saying that this "had proved extremely useful in the past."[24] It was, it seems, possible to influence the thirty-eighth floor, even on such important issues. This was when Soviet deputy minister of foreign affairs Vasily Kuznetsov pointed out to UN member states that bringing Hungary back to the agenda would "seriously interfere with the relaxation of international tension."[25] To this Lodge replied that ignoring UN resolutions was also less than helpful for this relaxation. The Soviet threat did not fall on deaf ears: Australia did not wish to evoke Moscow's ire, lest it scupper Canberra's plans in New Guinea or for the Antarctic.[26]

The UK used harsher words: if Munro had nothing significant to report—since he was unable to visit Hungary—then his activity was limited to conversations in New York and looking over the material collected by the Secretariat, and it would be better if the question were not raised at all.[27] As the third anniversary of the Revolution approached, Munro had not yet submitted his report, even though he knew it could not be included on the agenda once the schedule of the General Assembly had been agreed on.

During his time in London, Munro paid a visit to Mick Shann, who had been stationed there. Describing their meeting, Shann wrote, without an ounce of malice, that while Munro was surely well suited to the task, "he is furious with the English press for not noticing him." Munro was resentful of both this lack of interest and what he perceived to be his overly modest fee. In Shann's opinion, it was the latter that interested Munro more.[28] Munro did not want to give up the position, Shann continued, even though his meeting with the British foreign minister had come to so little. As a result, Shann wrote, Munro wanted to handle relations with the press himself and was planning to write his own article. He traveled to Austria to visit a refugee camp, even though it was hard to evaluate the relevance of such an effort three years after the events in question.[29]

The editors of the *New York Times* were happy to accept Munro's offer to write an article, and its publication during the course of the UN debate was well timed.[30] At Munro's request, the office of the UN High Commissioner for Refugees (UNHCR) officially arranged for him to visit the refugee camp, where he met and talked with Hungarians and learned of their circumstances, their pasts, and their perspectives on their status as refugees.[31] The Special Representative dedicated just one morning to this, during which he met with some of the women residing in the camp, looked around their living quarters, and listened to what they had to say. By this time, the majority of refugees had already left Austria, and those who had stayed had integrated into Austrian society. Munro nevertheless wrote seven pages about this visit and sent it to the *New York Times* as promised, but upon reading it, the newspaper declined to print his uninteresting yet bombastic article. The paper seemed to find it preferable to save both themselves and a diplomat working on such an important issue from public scorn.[32]

Munro also visited the foreign ministry in Vienna. After his meetings there, Austrian foreign minister Bruno Kreisky contacted his Hungarian colleagues and suggested that the Special Representative be allowed into Hungary and that he stay in a hotel on the Danube and write a report, after which the whole affair could be closed. Munro, it was claimed, would not want to undertake any kind of investigation but would merely talk to a few leaders[33]—which was, of course, an odd interpretation of his mandate as UN Special Representative. This unusual communication was later confirmed by the director of the political department in the Austrian Foreign Office, Heinrich Haymerle. Despite Munro's official role, in Budapest he could be treated as a private individual, and his visit would enable the whole Hungarian question to be settled quietly and peacefully.[34] This visit did not occur.

At this time the authorities in Budapest wanted to settle quite different scores, news of which would reach New York in a report titled "Trials and Sentences."[35] The US assistant secretary of state spoke in critical terms of the UN's lost opportunities and was joined by Lyndon B. Johnson, then leader of the Democratic Party in the US Senate: while the UN had remained silent, over one hundred enemies of the regime had been executed in Hungary.[36] This number would soon be doubled.

Although in his role as chief adviser to the Special Representative Jordan assisted Munro in his work, he questioned the authenticity of the news reports coming from Hungary.[37] In the submission to the UN General Assembly, Jordan failed to see the need to include the list of reports of oppression, even as an appendix.[38] In the end, thanks to US intervention, the Hungarian question was put on the agenda, three years after the Revolution broke out and one year after the Revolution's leader was executed. It was placed as item seventy-four on the schedule of the General Assembly.[39]

One reason for the lengthy delay may have been that Munro did not want to submit his report in advance: he insisted that it be distributed to the representatives of member states as he was giving his speech. It caused displeasure among many that a year after his appointment, Munro was still "hanging on" to the report,[40] and the President of the General Assembly was reluctant for them to debate a document that had not been read in advance.[41] The Hungarian question was, however, finally put on the agenda. In the end, Munro's report did accurately describe the reprisals, contravened UN resolutions, and constant violations of the law in Hungary following the Revolution. But because three years had passed and the intensity of the repression had not abated, these violations had now become normalized. The debate was followed by a press release, the publication of the record, and diplomats stating their positions. Then the General Assembly passed a resolution that Munro should "continue his efforts."[42]

The live TV coverage on CBS on November 25, 1959, provides an overview of these events.[43] For a fee of $150, Munro sent a number of letters to the program's producer. The "unofficial transcript" of this overview is kept not in Munro's folder relating to the Hungarian question but rather in the "Speaking Engagements" dossier titled "The UN in Action." When the interviewer asked what this "action" was, Munro responded that he had asked the Hungarian delegation to the UN to make representations to its government that the secret trials should end and that an amnesty be announced. "I do not think anything substantial has been done in this matter," he added, saying that he had compiled his report based on news reports and official Hungarian announcements.[44] He did not respond as to whether he had used any other sources or, if his "actions" had not had significant consequences, whether perhaps he should see to it that something did happen. "People in Hungary should know they are not forgotten," Munro concluded, a statement that offered precious little comfort as the terror in Hungary continued. It is not only in retrospect that this attitude appears strange: on this same TV program, a journalist mentions how disappointing the Special Representative's report was "because it does not contain much information."[45] This was not because the UN had any shortage of it.

The Twenty-Fifth of November, 1959

It was on the same day that the Hungarian question was put on the agenda, the same day that the Special Representative for this issue was giving a lecture hundreds of miles from Manhattan, that Povl Bang-Jensen's body was found, in the early hours of the morning in an area close to where he had lived. The relationship between the United Nations and its employee entrusted with the Hungarian question had ended in July of 1958, but considering his removal to be illegitimate, Bang-Jensen had not accepted an offered financial settlement and had not given up on his struggle for justice. His disciplinary case had nothing to do with the real conflict behind his dismissal; it was in the UN's interests that he wished to vindicate himself and those who believed in him. In the meantime, he had been employed on a temporary basis by the aid organization CARE (Cooperative for Assistance and Relief Everywhere), where his salary was much lower than that at the UN.[46]

The way Bang-Jensen had been removed from the UN and the way the UN had handled the proceedings brought against him only served to confirm his doubts about the integrity of the organization. If he had previously only suspected it, by July 1958, he could be certain that something was amiss in the skyscraper in Turtle Bay that housed the UN. By this time, he was not constricted by the internal regulations of the UN, but neither did he want to harm the institution in whose mission he still had so much faith. His lawyers attended to the possibility of his legal rehabilitation. Many both inside and outside the UN came to his assistance, but others rejected his reservations. Meanwhile, many were concerned for his welfare—and some for his life.[47] In a hand-written, personal letter, Walter Anderson, a retired admiral, brought Bang-Jensen's vulnerability, his situation, and the unusual aspects of the proceedings against him to the attention of J. Edgar Hoover, adding that over the course of a transatlantic sea voyage, he had seen for himself that the Dane was in excellent emotional and intellectual health.[48] Anderson received a reply informing him that the FBI had no right to undertake an investigation until it was instructed to do so by the attorney general.[49] The CIA, meanwhile, conducted a "discreet inquiry" into Bang-Jensen's current job and income and investigated his relationships with the Danish foreign service and other diplomatic bodies as if he were the one under suspicion.[50]

It is not really possible to know what happened after the proceedings were closed at the UN. At the end of the summer of 1959, at a meeting with people he did not know, Bang-Jensen was offered pieces of evidence that confirmed his suspicions. Further meetings took place, during which, as his friends recalled it, Bang-Jensen said he had "stumbled onto something very big."[51] One evening in late October Bang-Jensen was out all night. By this time, he had cleaned the pistol he had bought during the war and was carrying it on his person. His children recollected how at night they would place a metal baking sheet behind the front door of the house so that it would rattle should anyone enter. Bang-Jensen knew that what he had gotten himself into was dangerous, and he wanted to protect himself and his family.

Documents from his last days suggested inauspicious developments—ones the US authorities did not investigate at the time and have not investigated to this day.[52] A warning Bang-Jensen had received would later be evoked: he "should not underestimate" the power of the forces opposed to him. He responded to this in his farewell note: "I underestimated the forces I was up against." Supposedly, Bang-Jensen had been promised sound recordings by an unknown individual, who then "slammed the door in his face"—which must have been a preplanned strategy. In September, Bang-Jensen warned Hungarian émigré politician János Horváth that "they should not give up on him," but added that he was now in contact with people who were "not friendly."[53]

By November 25, the morning on which the United Nations prepared to debate the Hungarian question, Bang-Jensen had been missing and his whereabouts unknown for three days. Before, he had left home as on other mornings, and there was nothing unusual at his office either: his raincoat, hat, and papers were all there.[54] It was the day before Thanksgiving Day, which he always spent with his family. When his wife reported that he was missing, his personal details and details of his appearance were circulated to twenty-four thousand police officers, and the news was immediately cabled to FBI director J. Edgar Hoover. Hoover instructed his colleagues at the FBI not to investigate;[55] nevertheless the following morning's newspapers reported that a search of the nearby forested areas had begun.[56] The fact that Bang-Jensen's body would not be found until three days after his disappearance by locals walking their dogs in Alley Pond Park in Queens—despite newspaper headlines reporting that he had gone missing and publishing his description—only thickened the plot of the mystery,[57] as did the facts that he was found lying by the road with his face clean-shaven and that his farewell note seemed to include secret messages.[58] The New York Police Department immediately began an investigation, during which it would commit a number of grave errors.[59] Interestingly, as soon as Bang-Jensen went missing, his attorney, Clifford Forster, began to prepare his wife "for the worst." The New York FBI had joined the investigation, only to be called off from Washington.[60] This was decidedly unusual. Also unusual was a reference in the police communications during the search to Bang-Jensen's "dark" mental state, as if they intended to foreshadow the possibility of suicide.[61] Of course, he had reasons to be in a dark mood, but also some cause to be in a bright one, not just because of his positive nature but because he had real plans for the coming fall: people in high places had shown interest in him, new horizons beckoned, and expressions of solidarity continued to flood in.[62] Many supported him in his struggle, but that came to an end on this fateful day in late fall.

The UN Archives reveal that UN leaders gathered every piece of information, newspaper article, and official document on Bang-Jensen's disappearance and the circumstances of and investigations into his tragic death. Among these were police reports and a request for a search among Cordier's papers, along with descriptions of Bang-Jensen's last days, including his wife's mention of his possible "amnesia." It is hard to find an explanation for why all this documentation had to be kept on a staff member who by this stage had not been an active employee of the UN for a full sixteen months.[63]

The UN Archives preserved the telegrams sent by Hammarskjöld and Mr. and Mrs. Cordier conveying their sympathy to the grieving widow. Even Ernst Gross, the prosecutor in the case against Bang-Jensen, which was reminiscent of a show trial, expressed his "deep sympathy" to the victim and his family. This same Gross would later write in confidence that the examination of the circumstances surrounding the death was wholly inadequate, and that the police investigation was slap-dash in its handling of the affair. The police did not question local residents, did not establish a precise time of death, did not look for the truck that drove up to the site, and did not investigate the documents that Bang-Jensen left behind.[64] In light of these numerous oversights, it is even more strange that the body was so quickly cremated, as if to avoid it becoming the subject of any further examination, even though two existing autopsy reports came to different conclusions.[65]

It was not only the police whose work was inadequate, as US officials would later conclude; they had been assisted in their work by the United States Secret Service. While the latter sensed irregularities in the police investigation, they stopped short of uncovering further evidence that would establish responsibility for these failures to follow procedure. When the Secret Service's own failures to properly investigate were later revealed, they simply repeated the charges that the UN itself had formulated against Bang-Jensen: "grave misconduct," "dislike for Hammarskjöld," and "troubled behavior," and suggested suicide as the cause of death. During the Senate investigation, one FBI leader announced that there was no factual basis for the claim that "the Soviets killed Bang-Jensen," even though the FBI had documented faults in the investigation and sensed contradictions behind it.[66] The Assembly of Captive European Nations asked for the circumstances of the tragedy to be examined, and CIA documents suggest that such an investigation would have enjoyed the confidential approval of CIA director Allen Dulles. But this did not take place.

The great number of suspicious circumstances encouraged many to consider that nothing in this case could have been unintentional, and that UN leaders must have had reasons to be frightened of something that had ended in Bang-Jensen's death. Some said that one day the UN would have to pay for their inaction. For the time being, however, it was only Bang-Jensen who paid—with his life. His funeral in Copenhagen was quiet but upsetting. His five children gathered around the urn. Niels Bohr, Henrik von Kauffmann, and other heroes of the Danish resistance were among the mourners. The Danish foreign minister appeared in a private capacity, and the US embassy was also represented.

Almost without exception, press coverage of the case condemned the United Nations, seeing as it did a series of causal connections among Bang-Jensen's doubts and reservations, the disciplinary procedure instigated against him, the accompanying character assassination, and finally his dismissal and death. Rather than putting an end to the story, the tragedy of the Dane's death meant that it was no longer possible to keep what had happened to him a secret.

After the funeral the whole story was revealed to Hammarskjöld, who said many events had unfolded in his absence or without his knowledge. For example, he said at the time that he had not been informed about the so-called medical examination into Bang-Jensen's mental state; it was described as "a friendly initiative on Bang-Jensen's behalf" that had been kept confidential.[67] The Secretary-General sent newly revealed documentation to Gross, indicating that legally speaking he did not consider the matter to be closed. Hammarskjöld's concern was that Bang-Jensen's death might encourage "McCarthyish hysteria." Many former critics of the UN were now siding with Bang-Jensen, although it was clear to Hammarskjöld that Bang-Jensen had previously had little time for these critics and that his doubts had been independent of any political motivation.[68]

In contrast, Cordier described Bang-Jensen's doubts about security as "corridor gossip" and dismissed claims about the Eastern bloc diplomats wanting to defect as mere rumormongering; everything Bang-Jensen was trying to prove was, as he saw it, "wholly without foundation."[69] The path from condolence to sacrilege was a short one: on December 22, 1959, a "chronological reminder" repeated the UN's arguments regarding the Bang-Jensen issue, stressing that there had never been a problem in the UN with the management of confidential information.[70] Early the following year, another memorandum was published, in which, as part of the now-posthumous campaign against Bang-Jensen, the so-called facts were laid out. One hundred copies were made, and the Secretary-General himself determined those to whom it should be distributed. One member of staff at the FBI drew a large question mark over the claim in a circulated UN document that information had never been leaked from the UN.[71] Just how dangerous the knowledge at Bang-Jensen's disposal was is made evident by the suggestion from those working on the Senate investigation, a year and a half after his death, that his widow hand over his journals to the Senate for "reasons of personal security."[72] Previously, attorney Clifford Forster had recommended the investigation be halted "to protect the family."[73]

The press in the United States, Denmark, and nations as far away as Australia had a clear understanding of the scale of the problem in the United Nations and beyond, even if no police, secret service agents, or politicians sought to get to the bottom of whatever Bang-Jensen had been unable to get to the bottom of. Two journalists, DeWitt Copp and Marshall Peck, attempted to finish what had been left unfinished by seeking out the most important individuals and locations, getting all those who could have played a role in the events to talk, reading all of the available documents— a helpful member of staff at the UN leaked information and papers to them[74]—and talking to Bang-Jensen's widow. That their book investigating the story provoked the ire of both the Soviets and UN leaders is a testament to the success of their efforts. Ultimately, US political leaders had no choice but to make a statement.[75] Bang-Jensen had been an important ally during the war, and over the course of his conflicts, he had on numerous occasions sought to force relationships with figures in US politics. A year or so after the tragedy, the Senate Subcommittee on Internal Security undertook an investigation during which it heard testimony from forty witnesses, requested and analyzed five thousand pages of documents, and ultimately published a report. However, they were unable to determine the level of Soviet influence at the United Nations, made no mention of the contradictions in the work of the Special Committee, and were merciful in their portrayal of Hammarskjöld. Secrets remained secret, not only about the UN in general but also about the precise cause of Bang-Jensen's death. Those who had worked to achieve this vague outcome had done a good job.[76] Many would conclude from Washington's passivity that Soviet agents had achieved influence at key points in the US administration. It was to this danger that Bang-Jensen had wanted to draw the world's attention.

The Australian foreign ministry stated almost as a matter of record that the UN Secretariat was being used by the communists to spy and gain influence.[77] Canberra was implicated in the Hungarian question and Bang-Jensen's fate because of its involvement in the Special Committee and paid careful attention to the comments and statements relating to Shann. For it had been Shann who had refused to look at Bang-Jensen's list of errors, only to deny doing so. It had been Shann whom Bang-Jensen had passionately tried to convince of the report's problems to no avail, and it had been Shann's letter the Secretary-General had cited when he dismissed Bang-Jensen. These events had to be revisited in what had since become a tragic context, and Shann knew very well that the UN Secretariat was buzzing with Moscow's agents. The Australian foreign minister published "guidance" for members of the press,[78] but he could not control the content of Copp and Peck's book. Shann, meanwhile, described the whole thing as "fiction," thereby saving himself from having to confront his own role in Bang-Jensen's fate.[79]

Shann wanted to share responsibility with those who had used him as a pawn, so he cited the letters he had exchanged on the subject of Bang-Jensen with Hammarskjöld, Cordier, and Gross. Shann had, after all, willingly listened to both Cordier and Hammarskjöld, whether on the subject of sabotaging future reports or brushing aside Bang-Jensen's well-founded accusations. As such, even if indirectly, he had harmed the cause he was working toward and unwittingly assisted the "Kadir régime,"[80] as it was misspelled in Canberra. The Australian foreign ministry objected to this claim, calling it nonsense and calling Copp and Peck's work rubbish,[81] but it revealed its sense of political realism by noting that, based on the US Senate investigation's report, Bang-Jensen's death was "murder rather than suicide."[82] But that was as far as they would go in their interpretation of the matter.

János "Kadir" and the United Nations

William Jordan, not free of responsibility in these matters himself, noted that at the start of the year he had looked at the chances of keeping the Hungarian question and Bang-Jensen's concerns on the agenda, but discussion of both issues had died at the UN. The latest General Assembly resolution did require Munro to report on all "special developments" in Hungary, but the chief adviser doubted whether any kind of thorough or sound document would now be forthcoming.[83] He also presumed that there would hardly be justification for the publication of a further report, with Claire de Hedervary, the only staffer working on events occurring in Hungary, continuing to work only part-time. He did add, "If, however, the question of Hungary should not be regarded as in effect a dead question [. . .] the present arrangements are, in my opinion, inadequate."[84] The experienced bureaucrat again reflected not on the real issues of importance—the contravention of UN resolutions, the apathy of the Special Representative, and the passivity of the UN despite continuing terror in Hungary—but rather on procedures and protocol, wishing to put into writing that the present system was not suited to do the job satisfactorily. In doing so, he was really only seeking to protect himself.

At the same time, UN officials were compiling a list of the more important US organizations that had taken an interest in the Hungarian question and thoroughly describing their operations and influence, presumably in order to gauge their lobbying potential.[85] The partial amnesty announced in Hungary in 1960 may have played a role in these developments. The amnesty meant that, among others, the writers Tibor Déry and Gyula Háy were freed, as were loyal Stalinists Mihály Farkas and Vladimir Farkas, leaders of the Stalinist military and the secret police.[86] The internment camps were abolished at this time, and although the majority of the 1956 Revolution's convicts were still behind bars, the strained mercy of the People's Republic of Hungary had expanded to include certain World War II war criminals.

The Hungarian secret services also sought to establish contacts with Hungarian organizations operating in the US, attempting to infiltrate some of these, like the Hungarian Committee, which had been most actively involved in UN affairs. The attorney for the Hungarian Committee, László Varga, appeared in various contexts as a "counterintelligence object": the Hungarian secret services tried to find leverage on his parents, secretly kept his New York office under observation, studied his movements and circle of acquaintances, and even persuaded an old friend of his, who was employed as an asset, to try to recruit him. They used various pretexts to be in contact with Varga, and offered him generous sums of money through official channels for meaningless tasks.

During this time period, in January 1960, UN Special Representative Munro traveled to the Middle East. Munro was accompanied by his wife on this trip, which was arranged by a US bank whose goal was to establish business relationships in Saudi Arabia and Kuwait. The Special Representative on the Hungarian Question was, with the full knowledge and approval of the UN, acting as an agent and lobbyist for US companies in the Middle East. In this capacity the Munros visited Libya, Egypt, Lebanon, Saudi Arabia, and Kuwait.

US representative to the UN Lodge told the General Assembly of Munro's "admirable qualifications,"[87] but the Hungarian question appeared in the press less and less, as the cruel consolidation process in Hungary was now receiving less media attention, and its news value continued to decline. In the summer of 1960, the *Albany Times* published an article calling Munro the "Top Red target," that is, Moscow's public enemy number one. The article stated that the "200 pounder" and "six foot two" Munro was a "watchdog who bites the Kremlin oppressors of Hungary at every opportunity."[88] The author of the piece, Pierre J. Huss, was by this time collecting material for his book on the many communist agents who had infiltrated the UN—exactly the subject Bang-Jensen had drawn attention to but that the UN did not wish to acknowledge.

Munro recognized the "deficit" in the performance of his duties, so he held a press conference in Geneva on the Hungarian question, which was prepared by László Hámori.[89] A second program—setting up meetings in Munro's official capacity—was facilitated by Sir Leslie and Lady Munro in Geneva but was also organized primarily by Hámori: the Munros met representatives of the World Council of Churches, the leader of the UNHCR, and the president of the International Committee of the Red Cross, Léopold

Boissier.[90] At the press conference, there was mention of Hungary's failure to comply with UN resolutions, its amnesty that only partially covered the 1956 insurgents, its unjustifiably high levels of criminal prosecutions, its use of legal procedure as a political instrument, and its obstruction of international inspections at first hand. The only innovation was the "repatriation program" organized in cooperation with the UN, of which there had been reports of people being "taken to other places," perhaps not of their own volition, while others simply disappeared. The UN even heard stories of "re-indoctrinations" and "executions."[91]

Thanks to a Hungarian diplomat placed in Geneva, all this information came back to Budapest and assisted the Kádár regime in their preparations for rebuttals during the UN fall session.[92] Meanwhile, Hungarian state security dealt with sensitive internal news reports—and how they were passed on to the West. As an indication of the real objective of the press conference, Munro hurriedly sent full documentation of the event to Washington—to Secretary of State Christian Herter in person[93]—and Hámori was entrusted with compiling the press response and sending this to New York. These actions served as evidence that Munro's efforts on behalf of investigation of abuses in Hungary were not declining.[94]

The increasingly evident failure of Munro's efforts to adequately address political persecution and espionage by the Kádár regime had long been apparent to seasoned diplomats, especially given the high profile executions in Hungary.[95] Munro successfully lobbied to stay at his post; Italy would have considered his resignation to be "the official burial of the Hungarian Question."[96] Lodge asked Munro for his suggestions about matters in Hungary being put on the agenda, though one document suggests that a decision on whether to include a discussion at all was very slow to emerge, as was a decision on whether to continue with Munro or to appoint someone else to his position at the UN.[97]

By early August, the UN had elaborated a thorough expression of gratitude to Munro, which was its way of making it "clear that his services are no longer required."[98] But if Munro was not going to deal with the Hungarian question any longer, what would follow? Australia, which played a key role in the Special Committee, learned from London—at least as Shann reported the British position—that the Hungary debate was "likely, to say the least, to be less than productive."[99] The Australians now also sensed that they could lose the goodwill of the UN's new member states, primarily developing countries, if they forced the Hungarian question onto the agenda.

The foreign ministry in Canberra instructed its UN envoy not to support the debate on the issue if this would only serve to prove the "ultimate powerlessness" of the UN.[100] The UK would also have convinced the US to take the matter off the agenda, claiming that the world had moved on from this problem, and that the US position was "quite unrealistic."[101]

The Hungarian government was circumspect in its preparations for the UN session, as the leaders of the socialist countries, led by Nikita Khrushchev, would be there in person.[102] Thus "His Excellency" János Kádár himself, a preeminent denigrator of the UN, requested permission to enter the United States to speak at the General Assembly, the authority of which was constantly being undermined in Budapest. In New York, however, it was US policy that was the main target of his criticism; he denigrated the UN primarily for acting only as a "voting machine" in implementing the orders of the imperialists. But noticeable in its absence was any criticism of Hammarskjöld. Budapest officials were well aware that the Secretary-General "does not support Munro's Cold War activities," and Hammarskjöld's failure to visit Hungary, four years overdue, was interpreted to mean that "Hungary does not present any kind of problem."[103]

The leadership of the UN made significant overtures to the socialist heads of state and party secretaries-general during these negotiations. Cordier himself notified them that the debate on the Hungarian question had been postponed until those most affected by it had left New York, which enabled their colleagues in Budapest to breathe a sigh of relief: "The period in which the UN will bury 'the Hungarian question' has begun."[104] Socialist leaders then launched an ideological offensive from the pulpit of the UN in a densely packed political arena, which pushed the Hungarian question further into the background. On the question of putting it on the agenda, a good number of the UN's new member states abstained.[105] Meanwhile, more than half of the delegates left the Assembly Hall before Kádár's speech to show that they did not accept the "legal succession" of the usurpatory regime that had taken power by violent means.[106]

The Hungarian government's "legal succession" was primarily debatable only because for two years it had not paid its annual contributions to the United Nations. This failure to meet its financial obligations could have led to sanctions and Hungary having its right to vote withdrawn.[107] Of the socialist countries, the People's Republic of Hungary was the only one to have run up such a debt: in 1958, it failed to send $163,667 to the organization it had much maligned, and in 1959, the figure was $231,558.

Whether this was an oversight, the consequence of a chronic shortage of foreign exchange, or a considered strategy, we do not know. After Kádár's visit, Hungary settled its bill, suggesting that its mandate would not be suspended for long.

Even if belatedly, Munro's report raised the hope that it would be worth presenting evidence from the terrible process of consolidation in Hungary to the UN, which had received more messages relating to the hunger strike of 1956 prisoners and news that some of these—including István Bibó, Árpád Göncz, and László Kardos—were being transported to Budapest to face a military court that might sentence them to death.[108] Smallholder politician Sándor Kiss telephoned the secretariat of the Special Representative with this dramatic news, but Munro merely dismissed the information, although it had in fact come in the same form from three separate sources, as impossible to verify. Not only did he take no action on it; he did not even trouble to check its veracity.[109]

On November 29, 1960, Munro gave an informal lunch for a number of important diplomats and their colleagues to help consolidate his position. Present at the lunch were Burmese delegate U Thant and William Jordan, but James Wadsworth, the new US Ambassador to the UN, did not join them, and neither did Indian head of mission Krishna Menon or Mongi Slim.[110] It cannot be mere coincidence that a few days earlier, the Secretary-General had invited three former Presidents of the General Assembly for a consultation and Munro was left out. The Special Representative wrote a rueful letter to Hammarskjöld stating that he could guess the reason for his being kept at bay, but noting that he could at least have been told that reason.[111] The message did not go into details, so we can only guess why Hammarskjöld did not wish to see him, but there can be little question that this cast a shadow over Munro's prestige as a Special Representative.

Munro submitted his report to the General Assembly on December 1, 1960, summarizing in eighteen pages all that had taken place in Hungary, as well as what had not—namely, the implementation of the UN's resolutions.[112] Deputy Foreign Minister János Péter sent a letter of objection to the Secretary-General, which—at his request—the UN made public as an official document, just as Munro's report had been.[113] According to the resolution passed by the General Assembly after a brief debate, Munro could retain his position, thereby prolonging a program of minimal "life support" for the Hungarian question. Alongside his other offers and commissions, Munro was also invited by Károly Nagy, representing Hungarian students at Rutgers University, to attend their Hungarian Week events, but this letter joined those on the pile of refused invitations. Munro handwrote "Unable to accept" on the letter, meaning that the students did not get a direct reply from him, only a standard response from his secretary.[114] On the fourth anniversary of the Revolution, it seems the Special Representative simply could not find the time in his schedule to travel to nearby New Brunswick, where a considerable Hungarian community had settled.

Meanwhile, the International Commission of Jurists sent its overview of the situation in Hungary to the United Nations: Hungary's new laws, rules, bills, and trials all pointed to "legal repression" becoming more radical. The commission wrote, inter alia, that defendants were not being defended in court, that the legal position of those previously deported to the Soviet Union was still "unresolved," and that the institution of police oversight was being extended.[115] Hammarskjöld thanked the Committee in a letter, but he was aware that the person who could bring the institutionalized contravention of the rule of law to the attention of the member states—Munro—was not, as far as he was concerned, an acceptable negotiating partner for him. A partner who would, in fact, and all too regrettably, soon be appointed by Hammarskjöld to become secretary-general of the International Commission of Jurists.

By this stage, Munro was aware that he could not represent the Hungarian question for much longer, and so he put himself forward for a role in his party in New Zealand. The country's domestic developments did not favor his ambitions, however, so for the time being, he had no alternative but to continue working on the Hungarian question, a job that became increasingly anachronistic, not least because of his contribution to it.

The Hungarian Secret Services in the UN and the Removal of the "Hungarian Problem" from the Agenda

While during the days of the 1956 Hungarian Revolution many of the intelligence stations functioning at Hungarian diplomatic missions abroad were publicly exposed, one of the key clandestine Hungarian agencies had survived the ups and downs of this period in New York and indeed even managed to perform some successful operations. The station did lose one of its secret service officers, Pál Rácz, who was ordered home after being exposed; in Hungary, he was promoted and given a role in heading the secret services. Rácz was to be replaced by another officer sent from Budapest, who was to be trained for "smaller operative actions," but it transpired that the diplomat under consideration was already working as "the military's agent," so the Hungarian secret services had to find a different candidate.[116]

The role of the Hungarian secret services in the New York station was of key significance for the entire period that the Hungarian question was on the UN's agenda; its top task was to survey and influence upcoming developments. Access to the UN's documents was not difficult to obtain, and as the UN leadership had repeatedly stressed that confidential papers could not possibly fall into the wrong hands, suspicions had been allayed at the highest possible level. Today, it is clear that a number of such documents reached Budapest, and from there, Moscow; these included documents that had been sent to New York via Western diplomatic channels.[117] Claire de Hedervary, as Assistant for the Special Representative Klára Héderváry was called in the UN, had preserved more than eight thousand documents over the years, documents she spirited away from the UN building, retaining them for historical research and, without intent, demonstrating the gaps in UN security.[118]

One important task for the Hungarian secret services was to discredit the three witnesses who had publicly given evidence to the Special Committee. This mission was one the political police conducted with aplomb. Béla Király, commander of the National Guard during the Hungarian Revolution, remained in contact with the UN throughout this process, and, as a leading émigré figure, attempted to unite the distinctly loose and haphazard Hungarian émigré community. More than one asset was positioned around Király; they were to participate in the organization or rather—in line with their instructions—the disruption[119] of the Hungarian émigré community. This led to a division in the Hungarian Freedom Fighters Federation. At a case brought against Béla Király in a New York court, the judge must have had no notion that in passing judgment he might be implementing a secret service master plan.

As László Varga was the "editor, and a leading, substantive author of submissions" to the UN, in the early 1960s, the "gradual preparation of his recruitment" was again under consideration.[120] The staff of the center in Budapest thus first visited Varga's parents in Hungary to offer the elderly couple consular passports.[121] They then commissioned Varga's childhood friend, Dr. Béla Bollobás, to arrange a meeting with Varga in person at a European location to attempt to persuade him to cooperate.[122] They knew Varga was homesick, that he would be willing to make a sacrifice in return for his parents leaving the country, and that he was suffering from depression: it seemed reasonable to think he could be turned.

The recruitment of the Hungarian experts sent to work for the United Nations was an easier task; despite Hungary's mandate being suspended, its arrears with the payment of its dues, and its contravention of the UN's resolutions, the UN was still accepting Hungarian members of staff. In 1961, Edit Gömöri, a highly educated lawyer who spoke three languages, arrived from Budapest to join the Human Rights Committee. She was a survivor of Auschwitz, and perhaps it was precisely her horrendous experiences there that had pushed her into a career in international law. Her UN colleagues gave her a warm welcome as the first member of a committee to come from a "people's democracy."[123] The young Gömöri was known by the Hungarian secret services under the code name "Sásdi," and, after she arrived in New York, she established contact with her handler, "Róna." According to the plan, she was to establish contacts with the UN Secretariat. To this end, she attempted to earn the trust of Claire de Hedervary, who at the time was Munro's closest colleague.[124]

The UN Secretariat was one of the most important "objects" for the Hungarian secret services, which sent out more agents.[125] After the Hungarian service of UN radio was abolished, editor Emery (Imre) Kelen applied to the Hungarian Mission, but his work was instead needed by the intelligence station.[126] In another notable case, the UN's librarian, who was of Hungarian extraction, was chosen as a "go-between" with the code name "Petit" and was pressured to cooperate because, for Hungarian intelligence, the UN's administrative center was the place where "our task is to build an agency."[127] The administrative center was a place where many were busily at work and which would soon be ready to normalize relations with Hungary, one of its member states, even though that state had done everything in its power to undermine the UN's investigation of its internal affairs.

Five years after the Hungarian Revolution, the United Nations' room to maneuver continued to diminish, and the international events of 1961 distracted attention from Hungary: The annexation of Tibet, the splitting of the Congo, the crisis in Cyprus, the drama in Lebanon, and the shooting down of a US spy plane over the USSR all presented a series of constant challenges that were more pressing than the still-unresolved Hungarian question.

On hearing the news of negotiations between Moscow and Washington concerning a moderate détente, Munro asked Jordan to write a proposal against taking the Hungarian question off the agenda, and a resolution was prepared for the fall session of the General Assembly,[128] which the Hungarian authorities also learned of.[129] And although it had already been decided that Munro would take over the presidency of the International Commission of Jurists in Geneva, his position as Special Representative, and his semblance of activity in this regard, remained.

In late April, a press conference detailed the qualities of Munro, and the New Zealand diplomat began to prepare for his move.[130] State security in Budapest knew that Munro had essentially lost all credibility at the United Nations, and his alcohol problem may have contributed to his being sent away from New York.[131] It was at this time that three members of the 1956 Baross Square uprising in Budapest were executed. Major newspapers across the world reported that land was again being taken from peasants in Hungary and described the difficult circumstances of the workers, the strengthening of the Stalinist opposition, and the total state control of cultural life. This information was passed on to Munro by his colleagues, but there is no indication that he took any action in response, despite the hundreds of pages of material that had accumulated on the situation in Hungary.

A UN Senate subcommittee asked why the UN failed categorically to condemn "Soviet colonialization," given that it had up-to-date information about the situation in Hungary, the scandal of which was only made all the more glaring by the UN's silence on it.[132] At the same time, UN records show that for the years through May 1961, the Special Representative spent a total of twenty-eight days on the Hungarian question, that is, at least one day, sometimes two days, per week. This was evident not from Munro's achievements, however, but rather from his expenses: on May 22, 1961, he accepted a payment of $1,400 for per diems at $50 a day, and, as a sign that his work would continue to be required, on September 5, 1961, the UN also wired him a further sum of more than $2,000, which included his travel expenses.[133] Receipts for airplane tickets and railroad journeys and the costs of taxis and phone calls made up the remaining sum. However, not everything could be reimbursed; the UN financial controller did not accept one of his lunch receipts, which must have been beyond even the institution's generous tolerance level.[134] As to how much Munro's attention was focused on Hungary over and beyond his expense account, this is revealed in the book he published at this time. In the 180 pages of *United Nations—Hope for a Divided World*, a total of three pages mention Hungary, the country the UN had appointed him to work on for a period of three years. A similar story is told by the subjects Munro offered to NBC for a television appearance: these included discussions of the UN's peacekeeping forces and the Turkish-Syrian conflict but nothing about Hungary. He took a real interest in the reception of his book: UN documents suggest that he was in negotiations over its rights and on his lecture trips he would try to sell copies of it. He commissioned a company to keep track of reviews; in publicity photographs for the book, Munro sometimes appeared alongside Hammarskjöld and sometimes alongside Dulles. These were old photographs, as he was no longer particularly welcome either in New York or Washington.[135]

The opening of the General Assembly was approaching, but it was doubtful whether the Hungarian question would appear on its agenda. Munro's approximately thirty-page report on the issue was compiled by his subordinates.[136] The documents concerning the organization of Munro's lectures and the collection of his fees ended up filling up more space than the papers about the Hungarian question.

In the end, the Hungarian question became item 81 on the agenda of the UN General Assembly.[137] Although the US sensed that Munro was of no significance because he "could not accomplish anything," he was nevertheless received in November, probably by Charles Bohlen, special assistant to Secretary of State Christian Herter. This was followed by the debate at the General Assembly, then by his mandate being extended by another year. A number of member states were now urging that something finally be done on the Hungarian issue, but when there was talk of Frederick Boland, the Irish President of the Security Council, being sent to Hungary, Munro successfully preempted any such move, further preserving his exclusive role and his institutionalized passivity.[138] As the fifth anniversary of the outbreak of the Revolution was approached, attention was again paid to downtrodden Hungary. In preparation for the General Assembly debate, Hungarian social democrat politician and minister of the revolutionary government Anna Kéthly requested an audience with Munro, as did Hungarian émigré politicians Béla Varga and Pál Auer.[139] According to his diary, in October, Munro talked with József Kővágó, mayor of revolutionary Budapest, Dind Tamás Pásztor, and in November, with another expatriate Hungarian politician, László Bartók. Meanwhile, he also met Hámori and Jordan, but none of this was reflected in his activity as a Special Representative.[140] And although Valerian Zorin, Soviet Ambassador to the UN, objected to the Hungarian question being put on the agenda,[141] it did remain on the program, even with a dwindling majority voting for the inclusion of the question, an ineffectual Special Representative, and, for all the resolutions that had been passed, the same powerlessness to take concrete action that had characterized the UN in the preceding few years.

The tragic pretext for a shift from this impasse would be the death of Secretary-General Hammarskjöld,[142] which ushered in a new era of relations between the UN and Hungary. Just how important the Hungarian question was for U Thant—who took over Hammarskjöld's position—can be seen in the documents, although there were those who surmised that the price of Soviet approval for his election came at the cost of the problem being shoved under the carpet rather than being solved.[143]

The Burmese delegation led by U Thant had at one time condemned Soviet interference in Hungary and, in a circumspect fashion, continued to hold a consistent line on this later, too, all while paying attention to the global response to the suppression of the Revolution, though more to that of the nonaligned states than of the Western ones.[144] Documents reveal that the new Secretary-General was fully informed about previous diplomatic efforts, Hammarskjöld's experiments and failures, and the role of the UN in the assistance offered to refugees, while making himself aware of the path that countries in the Soviet bloc had no choice but to follow.[145]

The new Secretary-General gained information on the Hungarian question not from the Special Representative but from the latter's chief adviser, William Jordan, who wrote a memorandum stating that he did not consider the publication of another report to be realistic and noting that Munro had only a "defined and limited mandate."[146] That drastic changes were taking place at the UN Secretariat was clear from Jordan's following memorandum, in which he made clear that he considered Munro to be the obstacle to progress, not the mandate.[147] Munro had thwarted Boland's visit to Hungary with his claim that he had an exclusive mandate from the General Assembly to represent the Hungarian question, while, five years after the Revolution was crushed, a demand for complete and unconditional compliance with UN resolutions was rather hard to contemplate. A Soviet withdrawal, the holding of free elections, and neutrality could not be a realistic program proposal in 1961; the only feasible demand to remain on the list was that for full amnesty. Why, during their years of working together, Jordan did not mention any of this to Munro remains a mystery, just as it is unknown whether Munro's insistence on a strict interpretation of the regulations was principle, cynicism, or selfishness.

France Soir was the first to publish the news that the UN Secretary-General was considering the possibility of visiting Budapest, although this claim coincided with the announcement that the UN General Assembly had again condemned Hungary for ignoring its resolutions.[148] Munro immediately responded to the story by saying that it had not been approved by him, indeed had not even been mentioned to him, that he had heard of the planned visit with "surprise and concern," and that he had turned to the Secretary-General for advice on its veracity.[149] In a press release, the Secretary-General's office confirmed the acceptance of Hungary's invitation and, looking for legal arguments to placate the Special Representative, turned to UN legal counsel Constantin Stavropoulos. The attorney made a precise description of the Secretary-General's areas of responsibility as compared to that of the Special Representative, and also cited the General Assembly resolution of December 1956, according to which the Secretary-General was authorized for "any initiative" that he "deems helpful."[150] Jordan, who was perhaps the most knowledgeable on this issue, described Munro's activity as "abortive"—a term he had previously applied to the Special Committee and the erstwhile Secretary-General. And, having devoted hundreds of pages to an overview of the efforts of the Special Committee, and its ineffectiveness, Jordan concluded that "the dignity of the UN will not be served if the question drags on."[151]

There was one point on which Jordan could see room to maneuver: the amnesty. In his opinion, the United States would not raise any objections to the Secretary-General's visit to Budapest if Hungary were to accept certain conditions.[152] And while on the one hand, the visit would be a de facto acceptance of the regime that had never for one moment accepted the authority of the UN, on the other hand, it meant that discussions could begin that could lead to the question being resolved, even if on the terms determined by the UN Charter. In 1963, Budapest was home to fifty-nine diplomatic missions, compared to forty in 1957; following the Soviet intervention, Hungary had not lost its diplomatic relations with any country. That is, its series of conflicts with the UN and the suspension of its UN mandate did not bring Hungary into isolation in its foreign affairs.

By the early 1960s, Péter Mód had been recalled to Budapest to take up a post as deputy foreign minister, and the new Hungarian delegate to the UN, Károly Csatorday,[153] would be able to use his position to compensate for his wavering positions in 1956 with outrageous propaganda battle cries. Even though Hungary's UN mandate had still not been restored, the news of Csatorday receiving his credentials hit the headlines. In the name of the Hungarian government, Csatorday confirmed the invitation for U Thant to come to Budapest, and the Secretary-General signaled his willingness to accept.[154]

After all this, there could be little doubt that the issue of the UN and the Hungarian question would soon be permanently shelved. If the Secretary-General really were to visit Budapest, that would represent absolute capitulation of the UN, for Hungary did not regard any aspect of the UN resolutions as valid, and the visit would do nothing to force any change to this position. A movement began to "defend the Hungarian nation at the UN"; its participants looked for supporters, attempted to find ways to gain influence, acquired political partners, kept pressure on Hungary, and tried to keep their hopes alive for as long as they could. Yet the number of member states at the UN recommending that the Hungarian question be put on the agenda continued to dwindle, while the number of states abstaining on votes to condemn Hungary continued to grow.[155] The US effort mentioned by Jordan soon became a mere act of putting out feelers behind the scenes; the US entered into secret negotiations with Hungary, a sign that there was political will on both sides for "normalization."[156] When news of this leaked, one US senator called on the government to urgently refute the rumors lest the Soviets try to negotiate for the Hungarian question to be dropped behind the backs of UN member states and the country affected.[157] By 1962, neither the US secretary of state nor his deputy would receive Munro, which the Special Representative acknowledged in a self-pitying letter, noting that the Hungarian question had been pushed to the very last place on the agenda. He was not alone, he wrote, in having "much anxiety" about US government policy "on this important matter."[158]

In 1962, despite his concerns—or perhaps to relieve himself of them—Special Representative Munro made a trip around the world. It is not clear from the documents just what his mission was, but the fact that the papers relating to it can be found in the UN Archives suggests that the arrangements and perhaps even the financing of the journey were the organization's job.[159] During the fall session of the General Assembly, U Thant consulted Jordan, not Munro,[160] so Munro gave an "informal reception" to only his closest colleagues in an effort to lobby for his position. The invitees included Jordan, Protitch, secretary Nora Fuchs, Myer Cohen, who had previously organized aid operations, Claire de Hedervary, and Tamás Pásztor and his wife—a properly intimate affair.[161] Despite the small number of guests, Munro ordered three crates of alcoholic beverages, all of which, according to the documents in the UN Archives, he had taken to his office "unopened." This would have meant that each of his former colleagues consumed two bottles of spirits to celebrate the Hungarian question being removed from the UN's order of business—or perhaps the rumors of the Special Representative's alcoholism were not unfounded.[162]

On the fifth anniversary of the 1956 Revolution, the United Nations received numerous petitions from numerous sources representing a great variety of intentions, proposals, and expectations, all of which were passed on to Munro. The Special Representative sent seven filing boxes of documents to Jordan, noting that these were "very confidential" and that they should be retained until June 30, 1963.[163] The UN's protocol for managing documents might have been the explanation for this date. Munro had a standard response composed to be sent to the petitioners. This was sent to fifty addressees, together with a copy of the Special Representative's report.[164]

It was not only these petitions that suggested that public opinion had not abandoned hope of the UN resolving the Hungarian question; so, too, did the information coming out of Hungary. As well as these letters, Munro's colleagues also compiled press reports and translated into English the more important statements of the Hungarian Parliament and the Hungarian Socialist Workers' Party, as well as the proceedings of the Hungarian courts and the sentences they passed.[165] All of these documents painted a picture of the results of the consolidation, with the slow regeneration of the Hungarian economy, the gradual strengthening of its industry, and the recovery of its agriculture. There were even signs of the repression of the private sector being eased, the embryonic beginnings of what would later become a characteristic of the Kádár system. In the summer of 1962, Kádár succeeded in disposing of certain secret service leaders who posed a threat to him, thereby potentially avoiding an internal putsch. And, in a feat that was not unrelated to changes in Soviet domestic politics, Kádár then managed to consolidate his grip on power, displacing vengeful and zealous Stalinists from the corridors of power and from the path to consolidation, once and for all.

As the date of the 1962 session of the UN General Assembly approached, it became ever less certain that the Hungarian question, as item eighty-five on a list of ninety-two subjects, would remain on the order paper.[166] This uncertainty could be attributed in part to recent changes in the global situation, with the UN General Assembly having to deal with many imminent international crises: in addition to political instability developing into a civil war in the Congo, these included nuclear threats or disarmament, the liberation struggles of former colonies, and the establishment of a committee to investigate Hammarskjöld's death. The outrage over the Hungarian question, unresolved for six years, had waned, and when it was voted on, those who did not wish to indict Kádár and his comrades or who preferred to abstain outnumbered those who wanted him called to order. Meanwhile, with the help of the socialist countries, Csatorday began to develop an administrative obstacle that would end consideration of the Hungarian question for good. And during the general debate, Lisbon's envoy to the UN proposed that the issue of Portugal's colonies was a domestic matter, and former colonialist countries also firmly objected to putting the South African crisis on the agenda. The Special Representative's latest report, this time a mere twelve pages and revealed by the documents to be the work of Hámori, Jordan, and de Hedervary,[167] was nevertheless an important text, as it provided both wide-reaching portrayals and specific examples of the contradictions of the situation in Hungary, the enormous sacrifices the emerging consolidation required, and the ambivalent "successes" it brought. Munro's critics raised the issue of his hefty fees, presumably aware that this could have been a sensitive issue within the UN.

What many in the Assembly Hall felt—that the Hungarian question should be relegated to the past and Munro's mandate be brought to an end—would by December 1962 similarly cross the minds of the UN leadership. The intention was for this act to be "implied rather than explicitly stated" to Munro and the rest of the world. So even though his dismissal was mentioned in internal documents, Munro himself only received thanks for the work he had done.[168] With considerable irony, the General Assembly's resolution of December 1956 was cited, which stated that the Secretary-General should "take any initiative" and that the work of the Special Representative "need no longer be continued."[169]

The endgame was not dramatic; if anything it was pathetic, even if it did create a catharsis of sorts. This was in part because the only concession that it was possible to extract from the usurpers was amnesty for those participating in the Revolution, which was little more than a call for restraint on the unrestrained punishments the Hungarian authorities had already enacted. But not even this could be stated directly and unequivocally, let alone demanded: Kádár had made it very clear to János Radványi, Hungary's chargé d'affaires in Washington, who was conducting secret negotiations with the

Americans, that the stronger the clamor from the other side of the Atlantic for amnesty, the less Budapest would be likely to grant it.[170] Later, desperate to introduce economic reforms, the Hungarian regime eased its grip on the population, as demanded by US diplomats in secret talks with Radványi. As the Soviets also agreed to certain concessions, a general amnesty became an increasingly likely notion. Meanwhile, Kádár was aware that the internal opposition in the party would attack him as a former accessory to crimes in 1956 if he were to liberate the imprisoned revolutionaries from the legal consequences of their actions.[171] Thus the UN demand for amnesty, stipulated as the condition for Hungary's UN mandate to be restored, planted in the minds of the Hungarian leadership, as if it were their own initiative, to consider April 4, 1963, the eighteenth anniversary of Hungary's liberation from Nazism, the appropriate date on which to show mercy to those prisoners who had survived—some of them, at least. And this was observed by the UN, where the announced amnesty was thoroughly scrutinized, not by Munro or by Jordan but by the organization's lawyers. In an accurate English translation, paragraph by paragraph, they inspected the various legal categories and exceptions, comparing the new law with the amnesties of 1959 and 1960, studying the relevant statutes, and considering judicial customs. The lawyers concluded that this was a comprehensive pardon, which covered a wide variety of "crimes," but there were a surprising number of exceptions to the pardons, the majority of which happened to specifically exempt the 1956 revolutionaries.[172]

Slowly but surely, it became clear to both the UN leadership and the General Assembly that relations between the UN and the People's Republic of Hungary were turning a new page. The return of full membership, that is, the restoration of the Hungarian UN mandate—coming as it did after Hungary had ignored the UN's resolutions and slandered the UN as an enemy power, all without facing any consequences—was a devastating precedent, one that shook for many the very foundations of the UN's moral order. The US nevertheless decided in June of 1963 to settle the issue of the Hungarian UN mandate; further, should the amnesty be forthcoming, it would also support the Secretary-General's visit to Budapest. All this happened behind the scenes, as the tradition of putting the right values on display was more important than what might amount to an embarrassing level of pragmatism. In 1963, even the Soviets only protested against the UN "interfering in domestic affairs" of Hungary out of habit, though they did so not in the name of Leonid Shatov, the Soviet Ambassador to the UN, but rather in that of the late Eugeny Kiselev, UN Under-Secretary-General appointed by Moscow.

How to lay the Hungarian question to rest in practice presented quite a challenge to U Thant. The memorandum surveying the issue confirmed the Secretary-General's room to maneuver, but at the same time listed the UN resolutions Hungary had contravened, thereby seriously violating the principles laid down in the UN Charter.[173] In U Thant's notes and in the memos written for him the dilemma is laid out clearly: Which was more important? Improving the situation in Hungary? Or adhering to the fundamental principles of the UN? And if U Thant chose to restore Hungary's UN mandate, did this not mean that he risked incurring the wrath of the great powers who had once laid down those principles, and who were also the UN's key sponsors?[174] Yet if he did not restore the mandate and thus kept the Hungarian question on the agenda, did he not risk an uncomfortable, even humiliating defeat at the next General Assembly vote?

Following Radványi's talks with the US, he reported back to Budapest that, given the normalization of relations and the amnesty, the Secretary-General's visit was to be expected.[175] With this, the path opened out from a hopeless impasse toward a more hopeful direction. Of course, the secret services were present here too. Radványi had himself been an agent of the ÁVH in 1950 under the code name "Pál Tinta," working under diplomatic cover in Switzerland with Pál Rácz and József Száll. He was later given a commission at the secret service station in Paris.[176] He must have played a successful part in the workings of the intelligence services as he went on to be appointed chargé d'affaires in Washington and then entrusted with secret Hungarian–American negotiations. Radványi later applied for political asylum in the United States, and the former chief negotiator, Kádár's emissary, and one of the heroes of the restoration of Hungary's UN mandate was sentenced to death in Hungary for treason in absentia. His execution could only take place overseas, however, so once his whereabouts in the US were known, a special feasibility study was undertaken for his liquidation, and an assassin was selected. The "special events dossier" comprised a number of alternative means to murder the renegade Hungarian agent, from cutting tools to poisoning, but in the end none of these plans were implemented.[177]

The restoration of the Hungarian mandate gave the Kádárist foreign ministry enough perspective to see that political successes lessened the need to make an example of people. The government in Budapest was aware that leading Hungarian political émigrés had suffered a serious defeat, as their

U Thant, Secretary-General of the UN, visiting Hungary and being greeted by István Dobi, president of the Presidential Council of Hungary. Copyright: UN Photo Archive #7438580.

last hope to retain international attention was keeping the Hungarian question on the UN agenda. Béla Király compared the loss of this last hope to the Hungarian surrender at Világos in 1849, and émigré politician Sándor Eckhart claimed that, with the restoration of the UN mandate, the Hungarian nation had suffered a "greater tragedy than Mohács or Trianon."[178]

Memorabilia from the Secretary-General's visit to Hungary are kept in the UN Archives: in high-quality photographs, we see U Thant clinking glasses with the murderers, giving speeches at Budapest airport and the Hungarian Academy of Sciences, smiling, shaking hands, and paying attention. There is much to be learned from the drafts of speeches and handwritten notes in the dossier[179]—everything but the point. If the whole affair was so very simple, why had there been any need for all the effort that had previously been made?

For Hungarians, what remained was survival and self-pity. Mohács. Világos. Trianon. New York. Hope dies last. But die it did.

Notes

1. The letter of transfer dated May 29, 1958, was copied to Dobrynin and Cordier. CHP, subject area 6.

2. MNL XIX-J-1-k, box 55.

3. And from Albert Szent-Györgyi to Bruno Walter. November 4, 1958. MNL XIX-J-1-k, box 55.

4. December 13, 1958. UNARM S-0442-0139-06.

5. UNARM S-0501-0008-0022-00001 UC. Regarding his appointment, Munro approached the UK Foreign Office, which, highlighting the UN's powerlessness, warned him against following Waithayakon's approach. It offered him its assistance on the condition that confidential information not be passed onto the UN Secretariat. FO 371/134863.

6. Sík, *Bem rakparti évek*, 188. Mód met Munro on a number of occasions, but the delegate was not willing to discuss the situation in Hungary. See Mód's report of April 25, 1959. MNL XIX-J-1-j, box 231.

7. Sík, *Bem rakparti évek*, 188.

8. October 27, 1958. Dinner with the leader of the Ceylonese Mission to the UN. MNL XIX-J-1-j, box 209.

9. December 8, 1958. They cite Ceylonese diplomat Subasinge. MNL XIX-J-1-j, box 209.

10. Cited in Radványi (1995), 49.

11. See the Australian documents: "Stalinists returning from the USSR and taking leading positions." NAA A 1209 1958/5436.

12. Cardia (2006), 115.

13. January 19, 1959. "The difficulties caused by the Hungarian question are constantly diminishing [. . .] the Mission has emerged from what its isolation of a kind." MNL XIX-J-1-j, box 210.

14. January 26, 1959. Hungarian government submission [on the US]: "Although its tone continues to be strong, it quietly accepts that the operation of the committee of five has ended." MNL XIX-J-1-o, box 6.

15. MNL XIX-J-1-j (Ceylon), box 1. August 12, 1958. The invitation to Hungary of Lall, Indian ambassador to Vienna. MNL XIX-J-1-j, box 210.

16. February 24, 1959. MNL XIX-J-24-a, box 5.

17. Ibid. See the memorandum of May 5, 1959, on the meeting with Secretary of State Dulles. NARA 764.00/5-559. Munro was the Special Representative, not the Rapporteur.

18. May 20, 1959. XIX-J-24-a, box 5.

19. For Mód's report of March 3, 1959, see MNL XIX-J-1-j, box 231.

20. See Glennon, ed., *Foreign Relations of the United States*, vol. 2, 103.

21. See the telegram from the US Mission to the UN on November 26, 1959. NARA 764.00/11-2659.

22. Mód reported on April 24, 1959, on his visit to Hammarskjöld. See MOL XIX-J-1-j, box 231.

23. See the report of the US Mission to the UN on August 13, 1959. USNA 764.00/8-1359. By the fall, a number of countries wished to avoid a debate on Hungary. See the telegrams of October 23, 25, and 26 from the US Mission to the UN relating to putting the Hungarian question on the agenda: USNA 764.00/10-2359, -2559, -2659.

24. July 31, 1959. MNL XIX-J-1-k, box 55.

25. Radványi (1995), 83.

26. July 15, 1959. NAA A 1209 1959/661.

27. Ibid.

28. July 18, 1959. NAA A 1209 1959/661.

29. Ibid.

30. UNARM S-0927-0002-0013-00001 UC.

31. Ibid. September 25, 1959. Munro's letter to McCoy (UNHCR Resettlement Office, Austria).

32. Ibid. October 10, 1959.

33. September 12, 1959. Kreisky's letter to Ambassador István Sebes. MNL XIX-J-1-k, box 55.

34. October 10, 1959. MNL XIX-J-1-k, box 55.

35. The document from the Assembly of Captive Nations lists the judgments brought relating to 1956. UNARM S-0890-0008-0001-00001 UC. For the report of the US embassy, see "Trials and sentences of officials held prisoner by the Hungarian government." UNARM S-0442-0140-0001-00001.

36. On September 15, 1959, Héderváry passed on the Senate's criticism of the UN, together with the speech by the assistant secretary of state. UNARM S-0890-0008-0001-00001.

37. UNARM S-0927-0001-0001-00001 UC. November 3, 1959. From Jordan to Cordier, on the credibility of news reports. Columbia University, Butler Library, Rare Books and Manuscript Collection (hereinafter ACP), box 182.

38. September 24, 1959. CHP, subject area 3. "List of Communications." At Héderváry's request, Jordan wrote on the document: "I do not think a list is necessary."

39. November 25, 1959. UNARM S-0442-0140-0004-00001. The Assembly Hall was busy, so hall number 4 was allocated for the debate. Washington considered the change of venue "to play down the importance of the Hungarian debate." It added: "The [United Nations] Secretariat was distinctly unhelpful in the inscription and handling of the Hungarian item on the agenda this year." NARA 320/12-1859.

40. NAA A 1209 1959/661.

41. UNARM S-0927-0001-0006-0014-00001 UC.

42. December 8 and 9, 1959. UNARM S-0927-0001-0001-00001 UC.

43. It was on this day that Bang-Jensen's body was found, with a gunshot wound to his temple.

44. November 25, 1959. UNARM S-0927-0008-0010-00001 UC.

45. Ibid. Joseph Lask, UN reporter.

46. He worked as a legal adviser; he was recommended for this by Bohr, Kauff-mann, and US attorney Burling. Lidegaard, *A legmagasabb ár. Povl Bang-Jensen és az ENSZ*, 160.

47. See the interviews held with the Bang-Jensen family, OSZK TIT. See also *The Bang-Jensen Case* and Copp and Peck, *Betrayal at the UN*, 272.

48. Bang-Jensen Archive (hereinafter BJI), box 33.

49. BJI, box 33. The FBI had not begun an inquiry on a previous occasion. On August 29, 1958, it drew the attention of the Domestic Intelligence Division of the State Department to Bang-Jensen's claims about the loyalties of certain UN employees. In line with Executive Order 10422, they found everything to be in order.

50. January 5, 1959. BJI, box 33.

51. Lasky is cited in Carpozi, "Mysterious Death of the Danish Diplomat." See also Copp and Peck, *Betrayal at the UN*, 268–70, and *The Bang-Jensen Case*, 46. Robert Morris talked to Bang-Jensen three weeks before his death: "He had new information." BJI, box 33.

52. According to a source of information on December 11, 1959, there was talk before Bang-Jensen's death of outside influence and various kinds of intrigue; the source (a woman) was able to supply two examples from the day before the tragedy. (Only part of the document is accessible for research.) BJI, box 33.

53. This has all survived among the FBI's documents, from the time of the US Senate investigation. BJI, box 33.

54. All of these were placed in a box; after Bang-Jensen's death, the investigators did not even look inside it, something that caused dismay during the Senate investigation. See *The Bang-Jensen Case*, 5.

55. Hoover received the cable of November 24, 1959, at 2:55 p.m. "Captioned individual disappeared on 11-23-59." His response: "Conduct no investigation in this matter." BJI, box 33.

56. Bang-Jensen's disappearance was reported by his wife to Nassau County Police at 12:30 p.m. the following day. See Copp and Peck, *Betrayal at the UN*, 7, and Carpozi, "Mysterious Death of the Danish Diplomat." See also the November 25, 1959, article in the *New York Herald*.

57. "Official Fired after Hungary Revolt Probe/Refused to Name Witnesses, Left L.I. Home Monday," *Sun*, November 25, 1959. "Ousted UN Aide Missing, Wide Search Launched," *Journal American*, November 25, 1959. "Ex-UN Probe, Enemy of Reds, Feared Slain," cited in Carpozi, "Mysterious Death of the Danish Diplomat."

58. Many people observed that covering up political murders as suicide was a favorite method of the KGB. The paper on which Bang-Jensen wrote his suicide note was of unknown origin, and his message had no date (even though he always dated his notes), the only markings being "Nov." and "6A," which may have been a reference to the address of the hearings in Vienna (Wallnerstrasse 6/a) but may have been "GA," the abbreviation for the General Assembly. There was oily rust on the hand of the dead body from a weapon that had not been used for a time but was regularly cleaned. The injury to the right index finger as described in the autopsy report could have been the wound of an inexperienced user of a weapon, from the fastener slamming back in place. The investigation did not cover the question of whether the shot was "absolutely close" (within half an inch) or merely "close" (within a foot or a foot and a half), though this would have clarified whether it was

done by Bang-Jensen's or someone else's hand. See Dr. Lajos Kovács, *Elemzés*. BJI, box 35. When his body was found, he had already been dead for a day, yet he could hardly have been lying for twenty-four hours on the path because dogs would have noticed him. See Copp and Peck, *Betrayal at the UN*, 23–27.

59. Such as the body being turned over, a failure to secure evidence, and the acceptance of mutually incompatible postmortem reports. See Copp and Peck, *Betrayal at the UN*, 20–32.

60. At 11:00 a.m. on November 25, 1959, the Espionage Section of the FBI learned of Bang-Jensen's disappearance, but handwritten on the paper was the note: "New York instructed to conduct no investigation." BJI, box 34, and *The Bang-Jensen Case*, 53. At 1:30 a.m. on November 26, 1959, the FBI announced that it had found Bang-Jensen's body and the cause of death was suicide. (A document dated the previous day had described Bang-Jensen as unsuicidal.) BJI, box 33.

61. Cited in Carpozi, "Mysterious Death of the Danish Diplomat." This was mentioned on a number of occasions: "Bang-Jensen, apparently without the knowledge of his wife, consulted three psychiatrists prior to his death [. . .] talked of self-destruction." See the text by the *True Detective* in the February 9, 1960, memorandum from the FBI. Of the three psychiatrists mentioned, one was the family doctor, the second assisted Bang-Jensen with his change of career, and the third unambiguously described him as unsuicidal. Copp and Peck, *Betrayal at the UN*. The FBI announced on November 25, 1959, that according to its sources, Bang-Jensen's emotional state had been stable and he lived happily with his family. BJI, box 33.

62. On November 26, 1959, according to a close friend, E. Christiansen: "One month ago I had a long conversation with him about his possibilities for embarking a new career [. . .] the conversation which he had with the Danish FM had given hope for future possibilities." ACP, box 177.

63. The police reports carried by UPI and AP are among the Cordier documents, as are documents relating to Bang-Jensen's last days. ACP, box 177.

64. BJI, box 33.

65. ACP, box 176. The February 2, 1960, FBI report states that "[XXX] also feels that criticism of the NYPD will impair our current relations with Steve Kennedy." BJI, box 34. The conclusion of the US Senate investigation is also damning, as is that of investigative journalists studying the case. Copp and Peck, *Betrayal at the UN*, 47–49. The autopsy established that 30 milliliters of a brownish liquid had been in the stomach, but no attempt was made to identify this. (See Dr. Grimes, Autopsy Report.) Copp and Peck, *Betrayal at the UN*. M. Notes. BJI, box 35. After Bang-Jensen's death, an unknown caller informed the FBI New York office of the name of the chemical compound that could have come from the laboratories of communist secret service agencies: a depressant with self-destructive potential. All this was documented, but nothing was done. On December 10, 1959, Hoover wrote: "FBI laboratories are constantly available [. . .] Jensen's body was cremated in less than two days which destroys the identity of chemicals." BJI, box 34. The Danish consul was informed that the police would not release the files but would respond to questions. The toxicological examination, which ruled out the presence of such chemical materials, was concluded on December 15. See the correspondence of the Danish high consul in New York on the death of Bang-Jensen in December 1959. RA 119. G. 3/19. Pakke Nr. 3.

66. BJI, box 33. On May 31, 1960, De Loach to Hoover.

67. ACP, box 177. March 16, 1960.

68. UNARM S-1078-0064-0002-00001 UC. Hammarskjöld to Stig Sahlin. It is telling that the Secretary-General unambiguously referred to his death as a suicide.

69. ACP, box 177. See Cordier's statement to the AP on January 13, 1960. A few days previously, a member of staff at the UN Secretariat, Vadim Aleksandrovich Kiriliuk, had been dismissed for activities "incompatible with diplomatic status." See Huss and Carpozi, *Red Spies in the UN*, 136–40.

70. December 22, 1959. BJI, box 53. The CIA noted only that the chronology was an "accurate account" of events. BJI, box 33.

71. See among the FBI files. BJI, box 33.

72. According to the FBI note of May 8, 1961. BJI, box 33.

73. Undated memo: "Drop the investigation—to protect the family." BJI, box 33.

74. Claire de Hedervary was the source with whom they had secret meetings.

75. For the interview with the two authors, see OSZK TIT. Their correspondence with a Soviet diplomat alludes to the reaction in Moscow (BJI, box 35), while for UN leaders their claims were nothing but libel. UNARM S-1078-0064-0002-00001 UC.

76. Regarding the suspicion of murder, the FBI on February 17, 1964, mentioned "unconfirmed allegations," referring to the role played by Hungarian diplomats. BJI, box 33.

77. NAA A 1838.

78. Ibid. January 23, 1961. "Guidance to Australian press [. . .] off the record or background."

79. Ibid. January 25, 1961. Shann to the Australian Mission to the UN: "so-called facts [. . .] reconstructed conversations are largely fictional."

80. Ibid. On February 10, 1961. Publicity officer Ian Hamilton writes: "Any suggestion that Mr. Shann had helped the Kadir [*sic*] regime was nonsensical."

81. Ibid. January 23, 1961.

82. Ibid. January 13, 1961. Australian embassy in Washington.

83. January 4, 1960. Jordan to Cordier. ACP, box 182. A key memo from the State Department in Washington on Munro's visit of September 25, 1959, reads: "Some delegations were getting bored with the Hungarian issue. [. . .] no progress was being made." USNA 764.00/9-2559.

84. January 4, 1960. Jordan's letter to Cordier. ACP, box 182.

85. In ten parts: "List of Hungarian organizations in the US" UNARM S-0927-0001-0001-00001 UC.

86. Déry and Háy were sentenced as part of the "writers' trials," while the latter were tried and tested Stalinists. The UN also collected information on the amnesty. UNARM S-0927-0001-0003-00001 UC.

87. Munro was mentioned on September 21, 1960, because Frederick Boland, President of the General Assembly, was planning a visit to Hungary. UNARM S-0927-0008-0003-00001 UC.

88. May 5, 1960. *Albany Times*. UNARM S-0927-0008-0009-00001 UC.

89. László Hámori joined the Narcotic Drugs Division in Geneva in 1960. CHP, subject area 6.

90. UNARM S-0927-0006-0008-00001 UC.

91. Ibid.

92. April 8, 1960. MNL XIX-J-1-k, box 55.

93. UNARM S-0927-0006-0008-00001 UC.

94. April 12, 1960. UN 274 UNARM S-0927-0006-0009-00001 UC.

95. UNARM S-0890-0008-0001-00001 UC. See, for example, "Survey of Hungarian developments. 1 April–15 June, 1960." Twenty-four pages and an appendix.

96. Ibid.

97. NAA A 1209 1960/5279.

98. Ibid. September 1960.

99. Ibid. August 4, 1960.

100. Ibid. September 13, 1960.

101. Ibid. November 11, 1960.

102. June 4, 1960. "Plan of preparation for the 15th General Assembly of the UN." MNL XIX-J-1-n, box 53.

103. June 4, 1960. MNL XIX-J-1-n, box 53.

104. "Deputy secretary-general Cordier informed our delegation that at present they do not intend to debate the report." MNL XIX-J-1-o, box 6, and Radványi (1995), 89.

105. Radványi (1995), 89.

106. Kádár "especially sensitive about the walkout of more than half the delegates present." Radványi (1995), 93.

107. December 9, 1960. Note on the contribution arrears. MNL XIX-J-24-b.

108. In addition to the messages mentioned (November 30, 1960), the documents included *Hungary under Soviet Rule*, vol. 4, as well as papers relating to the failure to reunite families. UNARM S-0921-0001-0005-00001 UC. The hunger strikers were given disciplinary punishments. (In his message to Jordan, Hámori included telegrams.) ACP, box 182.

109. October 27, 1960. De Hedervary to Jordan: "S. Kiss phoned, Bibó, Kardos, Göncz trials reopened at military court." CHP, subject area 6. Munro: "Could not verify." UNARM S-0921-0001-0005-00001 UC.

110. November 29, 1960. 1:00 p.m. "Luncheon by Munro." UNARM S-0921-0001-0005-00001 UC. Wadsworth followed Lodge at the helm of the US Mission to the UN, after Lodge became the vice presidential candidate alongside Nixon in the US presidential election.

111. UNARM S-0927-0008-0006-00001 UC. November 25, 1960.

112. December 1, 1960. UN GA Special Representative Report. UNARM S-0884-0009-0011-00001 UC.

113. December 8, 1960. "Letter of Protest against Munro's Report." UNARM S-0442-0140-0002-00001 UC.

114. October 11, 1960. UNARM S-0927-0008-0010-00001 UC. "Munro: Speaking invitations—not accepted, 1959–1962."

115. December 22, 1960. UNARM S-0921-0001-0005-00001 UC.

116. June 6, 1958. Agent with code name "Tardos" (József Triebwasser). ÁBTL 3.2.5. O-8-079.

117. For example, the memoirs of journalist Péter Földes, who gave his testimony at the French embassy in Budapest, which was then sent by diplomatic post to Paris, then to New York. Földes would be reunited with his witness statement at a

Hungarian police station after being arrested. See Interview with Péter Földes, Oral History Archive, 150.

118. He also mentions this in his interview. See OSZK TIT.

119. Alongside his aide, code-named "Virág," they also introduced agent "Erdős." "Kátay" participated in the UN General Assembly in 1960 as European president of the Hungarian Freedom Fighters Federation, having passed on to the Hungarian authorities the UN's records, together with Király's notes. ÁBTL K-1525/2.

120. Political police lieutenant Pál Csincsik: "I copied out the compromising information from the archive." ÁBTL K-1799/2.

121. ÁBTL K-1799/1. "Mickey B." The document states that "the possibility of his later recruitment seems a realistic one."

122. Bollobás had worked since spring 1956 under code name "Roberto" for Subdivision 3-B of state security group Directorate III/II. ÁBTL K-1799/1.

123. According to a report of February 14, 1961. ÁBTL 3.1.9. V-146247 MT-14/1.

124. According to dossier number ÁBTL 3.2.5 0-8-079, the "operative detection" of Claire de Hedervary continued over many years, and she was processed under code names "Titkár" ("Secretary") and then "Alary," but she was not recruited.

125. Among others, József Révész. ÁBTL 3.2.1. Bt-122. "Róna affair dossier."

126. ÁBTL Kt-451/52 K-770/T. "Zordid." The once-successful caricaturist moved to the US before the war and later joined the UN.

127. ÁBTL 3.1.9. V-146247 MT-14/1.

128. March 8, 1961, UNARM S-0927-0001-0001-00001 UC, then April 15, 1961, UNARM S-0884-0009-0011-00001 UC.

129. MNL XIX-J-1-k, box 55.

130. April 26, 1961. "Press Release ICJ Munro's nomination." UNARM S-0927-0006-0001-00001 UC.

131. May 9, 1961. ÁBTL 3.2.5. O-8-79. "The UN's various committees." The Hungarian secret services noted that Munro "could only find drinking buddies among the security guards."

132. UNARM S-0927-0001-0001-00001 UC.

133. May 22, 1961. "28 days = 1,400 USD," then, on September 5, 1961, "UN cheque: 3,426.05 USD Sir Leslie Munro [. . .] honorarium and travel expenses." Also "Voucher for Reimbursement of Expenses, Special Representative of Hungary, 48 days, 50 USD/day." His receipts can also be found here. UNARM S-0927-0008-0001-00001 UC.

134. May 22, 1961. The "Luncheon" receipt crossed out. UNARM S-0927-0001-0001-00001 UC.

135. For the reviews and the correspondence regarding rights and distribution, see UNARM S-0927-0006-0016-00001 UC.

136. UNARM S-0442-0140-0003-00001.

137. MNL XIX-J-1-n, box 53.

138. Boland's visit was considered in May 1961: "Getting something moving." NAA A 1209 1957/5279.

139. UNARM S-0927-0001-0001-00001 UC and UNARM S-0927-0006-0012-00001 UC.

140. UNARM S-0927-0008-0001-00001 UC. József Kővágó and Béla Király held commemorations of the Revolution, in Latin America in 1959 and in Asia in 1961,

hoping to influence the vote at the fall General Assembly. In Chile and Argentina, Kővágó was received by heads of state. See Kiss, "Emigrációba kényszerülve."

141. UNARM S-0800-0008-0001-00001 UC.

142. The airplane carrying the Secretary-General and his colleagues crashed in the Congo on September 18, 1961, presumably the result of foul play.

143. Documents relating to the Hungarian question hint at U Thant's interest: "Private Papers of the SYG U Thant prior to November 1961." UNARM S-0890-0008-0001-00001 UC and "Burmese Report to the UN on Hungary." UNARM S-0800-0008-0001-00001 UC.

144. In 1957, U Thant told *Pravda* that the Hungarian question was distracting the General Assembly from more important questions, like Algeria. *Pravda*, September 14, 1957.

145. Among U Thant's personal documents are reports on the situation in Hungary, on the Twenty-Second Congress of the Soviet Communist Party, and an overview of the socialist countries, detailing the circumstances in Hungary and Poland. We also find documents on diplomatic efforts. UNARM S-0890-0008-0001-00001 UC.

146. December 7, 1961. Jordan to the Secretary-General. ACP, box 183.

147. Jordan to Narasimhan (Under-Secretary for Special Political Affairs, Chef de Cabinet). February 8, 1962. "Attitude of Sir Leslie Munro is itself a factor in the situation. His opposition to the visit by Mr. Boland was a considerable factor in the failure to arrange it." UNARM S-0884-0009-0011-00001 UC.

148. The news appeared on December 7, 1961. The General Assembly passed its resolution on December 20, which was announced on December 21. "Note to correspondents: SYG's invitation to Hungary and his willingness to accept." UNARM S-0884-0009-0011-00001 UC.

149. December 7, 1961. Munro to U Thant. UNARM S-0884-0009-0011-00001 UC.

150. December 11, 1956. Stavropoulos to U Thant. UNARM S-0884-0009-0011-00001 UC 1961. U Thant replied to Munro on December 22, citing Stavropoulos's arguments. UNARM S-0884-0009-0011-00001 UC.

151. UNARM S-0890-0008-0011-00001.

152. The US kept the issue of the amnesty on the agenda, repeatedly applying pressure on the Hungarian government in this regard. See: Borhi, *Magyarország a hidegháborúban*.

153. UNARM S-0884-0009-0011-00001 UC. See also MNL XIX-J-1-k, box 127.

154. January 25, 1962. UNARM S-0927-0002-0003-00001 UC.

155. At the Sixteenth General Assembly, the vote on the Hungarian question saw 49 votes for, 17 against, and 32 abstentions.

156. János Radványi recalls these negotiations from his own experience. For a historical overview, see Borhi (2014), 43–110.

157. September 10, 1962. Senator Keating spoke of this on a TV program on Hungary. UNARM S-0927-0002-0007-00001 UC.

158. November 26, 1962. Munro to Dean Rusk (secretary of state): "I regret very much that you are unable to see me this week." UNARM S-0927-0008-0003-00001 UC.

159. UNARM S-0927-0002-0007-00001 UC.

160. September 26, 1962. U Thant: "Lunch and discussion with Jordan." UNARM S-0927-0008-0003-00001 UC.

161. September 13, 1962. UNARM S-0927-0002-0007-00001 UC.

162. Ibid.

163. March 22, 1962. A. Greenwood to Jordan: "7 boxes of petitions sent to Munro are being sent to your office for retirement. They are very confidential . . . kept until June 30, 1963." Handwritten: "Copy in Hungarian file in Mrs. Pasztor's office." UNARM S-0927-0001-0012-00001 UC.

164. UNARM S-0927-0001-0012-00001 UC.

165. Hámori sent Munro the outline of the report on September 11, 1962. UNARM S-0927-0001-0001-00001 UC and UNARM S-0927-0002-0007-00001 UC.

166. September 17, 1962. UNARM S-0927-0002-0004-00001 UC.

167. UNARM S-0884-0009-0011-00001 UC.

168. December 5, 1962. A two-page document titled "The Question of Hungary" says of Munro: "Termination of the tasks entrusted to him may be implied rather than explicitly stated." January 7, 1963. "Discharging Munro." UNARM S-0884-0009-0011-00001 UC.

169. January 7, 1963. UNARM S-0884-0009-0011-00001 UC.

170. "Until the State Department officials stopped insisting on an amnesty as a precondition for improvement, no amnesty will be granted." Radványi (1995), 92.

171. Ibid., 109.

172. April 11, 1963. See the letter from Oscar Schachter, Director of Legal Division, to Omar Lotfi, Under-Secretary for Special Political Affairs: "There are number of exceptions in the amnesty, some of which apply particularly to the insurrection of 1956." UNARM S-0884-0009-0011-00001 UC.

173. May 22, 1963. The document listed the previous six General Assembly resolutions. UNARM S-0884-0009-0011-00001 UC.

174. "Evolving situation in Hungary relaxation of political atmosphere even Munro reported about certain amelioration." UNARM S-0884-0009-011-00001 UC.

175. June 24, 1963. According to Radványi's report, the US Mission to the UN considered the question of the Hungarian mandate to be closed. MNL XIX-J-1-j, box 86.

176. Szebeni, "A Radványi ügy," 8.

177. "Roland" was sentenced to death on February 22, 1968, then group 2 of III/I Division of the Hungarian Ministry of the Interior planned his liquidation. Szebeni, "A Radványi ügy," 12–13.

178. Világos (today Șiria, Romania) was the location of the surrender that ended the Hungarian Revolution of 1848–1849. Mohács was the scene of the Hungarian rout in 1526 at the hands of the Ottomans. The Treaty of Trianon in 1920 saw Hungary lose the majority of its historical territory.

179. "Free, Frank and Useful Discussion with Prime Minister." UNARM S-0883-0004-0010-00001 UC. A few weeks later, in the Note for File of July 19, 1963, we find that, following the restoration of the Hungarian UN mandate, the various letters and petitions, as a matter of protocol, had to be passed on to the Hungarian authorities. UNARM S-0884-0009-0011-00001 UC. Here, too, it was the end of the road.

CONCLUSION

TWO GENERATIONS HAVE GROWN UP since the events recounted in this book occurred, yet some of the fundamental problems described here remain unsolved, continuing to frustrate those who were and still are hopeful that the United Nations—the organization that was created for the purpose—might be effective in global crisis management. As I write these lines, Ukraine is being attacked and systematically destroyed by the Russian Army, vividly recalling memories of the Syrian war and many other armed conflicts. In all of these cases, the United Nations has remained paralyzed due to the veto system of the Security Council, and those suffering have been trapped in a machinery created nearly three generations ago, during the Second World War, when the allies—then called the United Nations—were first, even if forcibly, united against a common enemy.

The 1956 Hungarian Revolution was and remains important as a case study in the global context, and the need to fully explore its international effects and outcomes with a special focus on the UN is still crucial. This is especially true because many important details of the events have been unknown for six decades. During this time, speculation, misunderstandings, and misinterpretations have taken the place of concrete knowledge of such crucial issues as, for example, the changes of policy of the Imre Nagy government, questions about the validity of accrediting enemies of the Revolution in the Hungarian UN Mission, and the whole truth about humanitarian crises and their solutions, both inside and outside the borders of Hungary. While the UN has worked successfully to provide humanitarian aid in accordance with its Charter, it has failed to act effectively in matters conflicting with the interests of great powers.

Besides the conflicts and compromises that shaped Hungary's history until 1989, the controversies inside the United Nations after the 1956 Revolution must be presented and addressed. As the story of Povl Bang-Jensen shows, the influence of certain countries on the UN Secretariat may have had fatal consequences. As the handling of the Hungarian problem demonstrated, the Secretariat is in a strategic position to inform the Secretary-General, to prepare actions, and to facilitate the workings of the General Assembly and other bodies of the organization, and yet it did and still does operate primarily behind the scenes. The issue of handling sensitive information in the UN is just as significant today as it has always been, and the effective management of conflict and readiness to correct failures inside the organization are crucial for the UN to work successfully. These are important lessons learned from the years following the brutal suppression of the Hungarian Revolution when these systems failed catastrophically. It may be hard or impossible to eliminate or even limit the activities of secret services in the UN, but it is still alarming that communist agents worked there successfully in prominent positions both during and after the 1956 Revolution. The structures that prevented prompt action on behalf of the Hungarian revolutionary government and in other international conflicts need to be wholly revealed and laid out in detail in the hope that better solutions may be found one day.

Finally, the actions and inactions of the UN clearly demonstrate the limited room for movement within an international organization established during a Cold War, dominated by great powers, and governed by the lethal logic of mutually assured destruction by nuclear weapons. Hungary was a minor player; it attracted international solidarity and assistance that was unparalleled before 1956, yet the country could not and did not change either the post–Second World War global political landscape or its own fate. The Soviet Union made no further concessions after leaving eastern Austria in 1955, particularly in facing the consequences of the Suez Crisis. The case study of Hungary also illustrates the role of developing countries, which became more and more determinant; for example, formerly colonized countries like Tunisia and Ceylon (now Sri Lanka) were represented in the UN Special Committee on the Problem of Hungary, although the Soviets successfully applied pressure or extortion to the representatives from those member states. In the meantime, the United States had to realize that none of the promises to liberate the countries under the Soviet yoke could be achieved. Any encouragement for self-liberation, often heavily propagated by Washington, could lead to a bloodbath instead of liberty, and the "free world" would bear collective responsibility for that suffering. The research has also revealed the global resonance of the Hungarian crises as a new phenomenon; for example, the role India played in the crisis was caused by the same determinant as Australia's reluctance to risk its country's interests on the opposite end of the globe to support legality and justice in a small central European country. The frailty of "the non-aligned nations" could be seen in the role Yugoslavia played in assisting in the suppression of the Hungarian Revolution, both in the open and behind the scenes, by Josip Tito giving his consent to Khrushchev for the Soviet invasion and by Dragoslav Protitch manipulating Dag Hammarskjöld seemingly for Soviet interests, claiming their share of blame in the execution of Imre Nagy, which they otherwise harshly yet hypocritically condemned.

All this may explain why the "solution" to the Hungarian problem came not from New York or Moscow, once Budapest was not in a position to contribute to shaping the country's fate, but from Washington. The final bargain was struck between Hungarian communist agents acting as diplomats and State Department bureaucrats for a double rehabilitation: on the one side, that a regime that refused to observe nearly all the resolutions from the organization it was a member of could gain back its UN mandate, and on the other side, that people who wanted to live in a free and independent country could receive amnesty—accept the compromise offered and leave prison—both on a national and global level. A bitter cup to consume, and its aftertaste stayed and continues to stay with us.

BIOGRAPHIES OF THE MORE
IMPORTANT PERSONALITIES

Andersen, Alsing (1883–1962) Danish social democrat politician, Chair of the UN Special Committee on the Problem of Hungary, president of the Socialist International (1957–1962).

Andropov, Yuri Vladimirovich (1914–1984) Ambassador of the Soviet Union to Hungary (1954–1957), officer and later chair (1967–1982) of the KGB, first general secretary of the Communist Party of the Soviet Union (1982–1984).

Bang-Jensen, Povl (1909–1959) Danish lawyer, politician, and diplomat; senior international civil servant at the UN Secretariat; Deputy Secretary of the Special Committee on the Problem of Hungary.

Cordier, Andrew W. (1901–1975) Political scientist, Under-Secretary-General of the UN (1946–1961), president of Columbia University.

Eörsi, Gyula (1931–1992) Hungarian legal expert on international law, consul in Washington, adviser to the Stalinist government and Kádár regarding international legal matters.

Fabregat, Enrique R. (1895–1976) Journalist, diplomat from Uruguay, member of the Special Committee on the Problem of Hungary.

Gunewardene, Ratnakirti S. (1899–1981) Sri Lankan politician and diplomat, head of the Ceylonese UN Mission, member of the Special Committee on the Problem of Hungary.

Hammarskjöld, Dag (1905–1961) Swedish economist and politician, second Secretary-General of the UN.

Héderváry, Klára / Claire de Hedervary (1920–2020) Hungarian-born Belgian economist and international civil servant at the UN, Assistant to the Special Committee on the Problem of Hungary.

Hollai, Imre (1925–2017) Hungarian intelligence officer under diplomatic cover, President of the UN General Assembly.

Horváth, Imre (1901–1958) Hungarian communist politician, minister of foreign affairs (1956–1958, with the exception of November 3–12, 1956).

Jordan, William (1910–1966) British expert on foreign affairs, international civil servant of the UN, Secretary of the Special Committee on the Problem of Hungary.

Kádár, János (1912–1989) Hungarian communist politician, member of the Stalinist and then Imre Nagy government, joined the Soviets and suppressed the 1956 Revolution.

Kéthly, Anna (1889–1976) Hungarian social democrat politician, imprisoned both by Nazis and communists, member of the Imre Nagy government.

Király, Béla (1912–2009) Hungarian military officer serving under all regimes (1935–1956), leader of the National Guard established during the 1956 Revolution.

Kós, Péter (1921–1994) Hungarian diplomat serving as the first delegate to the UN until recalled during the 1956 Revolution.

Lodge, Henry Cabot (1902–1985) American diplomat, United States representative at the UN (1953–1960), politician, and United States senator.

Mód, Péter (1911–1996) Hungarian communist diplomat and representative at the UN (1957–1961).

Munro, Leslie (1901–1974) Politician and journalist from New Zealand, President of the UN General Assembly (1957–1958), Special Representative on the Problem of Hungary (1958–1962).

Nagy, Ferenc (1903–1979) Hungarian politician and prime minister (1946–1947), forced to emigrate and settle in the United States.

Nagy, Imre (1896–1958) Hungarian communist politician and prime minister (1953–1955 and again during the Revolution), executed 1958.

Protitch, Dragoslav (1902–1972) International civil servant of the UN from Yugoslavia (of Croatian origin), Under-Secretary-General between 1954 and 1958.

Rácz, Pál (1928–1986) Hungarian intelligence officer, member of the Hungarian UN delegation, expelled from the United States (1957) but later returned as the head of the Hungarian UN delegation (1980–1986).

Radványi, János (1922–2016) Hungarian intelligence officer and diplomat, chargé d'affaires in Washington from 1962 until 1967 when he defected to the United States.

de Seynes, Philippe (1910–2003) French diplomat, UN Under-Secretary-General responsible for humanitarian issues (1956–1957).

Shann, Keith Charles Owen "Mick" (1917–1988) Australian diplomat, Rapporteur of the Special Committee on the Problem of Hungary.

Slim, Mongi (1908–1969) Tunisian diplomat and politician, representative of his country at the UN, President of the UN General Assembly (1960–1961), member of the Special Committee on the Problem of Hungary.

Szarka, Károly (1923–2005) Hungarian politician, ambassador to the United States (1953–1956), observer at the UN (prior to 1955), deputy minister of foreign affairs (1956–1968).

U Thant (1909–1974) Burmese politician, head of the UN delegation of Burma, Secretary-General of the UN (1961–1971).

Waithayakon, Wan (1891–1976) Thai prince, politician, and diplomat; President of the UN General Assembly (1956–1957); UN General Assembly's Special Representative to the Special Committee on the Problem of Hungary (1957–1958).

BIBLIOGRAPHY

Activities of United States Citizens Employed by the United Nations. Hearings before the Subcommittee to Investigate the Administration of the Internal Security Act and Other Internal Security Laws. Committee of the Judiciary: Washington, DC: United States Senate, 1952.

Ailinger, Jospeh F. "Cold War Policy under Fire: The United States' Response to Revolution in Hungary." PhD diss., Boston College, 1990.

Arendt, Hannah. *Die ungarische Revolution und der totalitare Imperialismus*. Munich: Piper, 1958.

The Bang-Jensen Case. Report to the Subcommittee to Investigate the Administration of the Internal Security Act and Other Internal Security Laws of the Committee on the Judiciary. United States Senate, 87th Congress, 1st Session, September 14, 1961. Washington, DC: United States Senate, 1961.

Baráth, Magdolna, and Lajos Gecsényi, eds. *Főkonzulok, követek és nagykövetek, 1945–1990*. Budapest: MTA Bölcsészettudományi Kutatóközpont, 2015.

Békés, Csaba. *Az 1956-os magyar forradalom a világpolitikában*. Budapest: 1956-os Intézet, 1996.

———. *Európából Európába—Magyarország konfliktusok kereszttüzében, 1945–1990*. Budapest: Gondolat, 2004.

Békés, Csaba, and D. Gusztáv Kecskés, eds. *A forradalom és a magyar kérdés az ENSZ-ben, 1956–1963. Tanulmányok, dokumentumok és kronológia*. Budapest: Magyar ENSZ Társaság, 2006.

Berggren, Henrik. *Dag Hammarskjöld—Markings of His Life*. Stockholm: Max Ström, 2016.

Berkesi, András. *Októberi vihar*. Budapest: Magvető, 1970.

Berle, Adolf A. *Navigating the Rapids 1918–1971. From the Papers of Adolf A. Berle.* Edited by Beatrice B. Berle and Travis B. Jacobs. New York: Harcourt Brace Jovanovich, 1973.

Berle, Adolf A., Leo Cherne, and Clara Boothe Luce, eds. *Hungary under Soviet Rule II. Survey of Developments from September 1957 to August 1958.* New York: American Friends of Captive Nations, 1958.

Bethlenfalvy, Géza, ed. *India és a magyar forradalom 1956. Dokumentumok az Indiai Köztársaság Külügyminisztériumának archívumából.* Budapest: Argumentum Kiadó, 2006.

Bindoffer, Györgyi, Pál Gyenes, and Gyula Kozák, eds. *Pesti utca—1956.* Budapest: Századvég-1956-os Intézet, 1994.

Bogyay, Katalin, ed. *A Cry for Freedom. Reflections on the 1956 Hungarian Revolution at the UN and Beyond.* Kőszeg: Permanent Mission of Hungary to the United Nations, in Collaboration with the Institute of Advanced Studies, 2017.

Bohlen, Charles E. *Witness to History.* New York: Norton, 1973.

Borbándi, Gyula. *Magyarok az Angol Kertben: A Szabad Európa Rádió Története.* Budapest: Európa, 1993.

Borhi, László. "Az Egyesült Államok Kelet-Európa politikájának néhány kérdése 1948–1956." *Történelmi Szemle* 37, no. 8 (1995): 277–300.

———. *Magyarország a hidegháborúban—a Szovjetunió és az Egyesült Államok között, 1945–1956.* Budapest: Corvina, 2005.

———. "Rollback, Liberation, Containment or Inaction?" *Journal of Cold War Studies* 1, no. 2 (1999): 67–108.

———. *A vasfüggöny mögött—Magyarország nagyhatalmi erőtérben 1945–1968.* Budapest: Ister, 2000.

Broadwater, Jeff. *Eisenhower and the Anti-Communist Crusade.* Chapel Hill: University of North Carolina Press, 1992.

Bujdosó, Alpár. *299 nap.* Budapest: Magyar Műhely Kiadó-1956-os Intézet, 2003.

Calhoun, F. Daniel. *Hungary and Suez, 1956.* Lanham, MD: University Press of America, 1991.

Campbell, John C. "Az Egyesült Államok kormánya és a magyar forradalom." *Világosság* 32, no. 10 (1994): 739–749.

Cardia, Isabelle-Vonéche. *Magyar október, vörös zászló és vörös kereszt között. A Nemzetközi Vöröskereszt Magyarországon 1956-ban.* Budapest: Socio-typo, 2006.

Carpozi, George, Jr. "Mysterious Death of the Danish Diplomat." *Newsweek*, 1960.

———. *Red Spies in the US.* New Rochelle, NY: Arlington House, 1973.

Chiesura, Giorgio. *Non scrivete il mio nome.* Turin: Einaudi, 1957.

Copp, DeWitt, and Marshall Peck. *Betrayal at the UN.* New York: Devin-Adair, 1961.

Dag Hammarskjold as Secretary General. Oral History Recollections by Sven Ayman, Andrew W. Cordier, Ernest Gross, C.V. Narasimhan, Oscar Schachter, Brian E. Urquhart. New York: Research Office, Columbia University, 1962–1964.

Decsy, János, Ferenc Fejtő, István Kemény, and Mihály Sozan, eds. *A forradalom előzményei, alakulása és utóélete.* Paris: Magyar Füzetek, 1987.

Dodd, Thomas J. *Freedom and Foreign Policy.* New York: Bookmailer, 1962.

Dugan, James. *American Viking.* New York: Harper & Row, 1963.

Eörsi László. "Budapest ostroma." *Budapesti Negyed* 8, nos. 3–4 (2000): 256–310.

Epstein, Julius. "The Bang-Jensen Tragedy: A Review Based on the Official Records." *American Opinion: An Informal Review* 3, no. 5 (May 1960): 1–46.

Finger, Seymour M. *Your Man at the UN.* New York: New York University Press, 1980.

Foss, Nils. *Global Business and Leadership—Through Danish Eyes.* Copenhagen: Lindhardt og Ringhof, 2014.

Fry, Leslie. *As Luck Would Have It. A Memoir.* London: Phillimore, 1978.

Gál, Éva, ed. *A "Jelcin–dosszié." Szovjet dokumentumok 1956-ról.* Budapest: Századvég-1956-os Intézet, 1993.

Garthoff, Raymond L. "A magyar forradalom és Washington." In *'56 Évkönyv V 1996/1997,* edited by András B. Hegedűs, Péter Kende, Gyula Kozák, György Litván, and János M. Rainer, 214–227. Budapest: 1956-os Intézet, 1997.

Gáti, Charles. *Hungary and the Soviet Bloc.* Durham, NC: Duke University Press, 1986.

Gerbet, Pierre, Marie-Renée Mouton, and Victor-Yves Ghébali. *Le reve d'un ordre mondial.* Paris: Imprimerie Nationale Éditions, 1966.

Gereben, István. "Adalék 1956 történetéhez. Varga Béla tanúvallomása az Egyesült Államok képviselőházában." *Élet és Irodalom* 44, no. 44 (November 2000): 13.

Géza, M. Szebeni. "A Radványi ügy." *Grotius* (2011): 1–13. http://www.grotius .hu/doc/pub/DBTRNE/2011_115_m.%20szebeni%20geza_a%20oradvanyi -%C3%BCgy.pdf.

Gibianski, Leonid. "Soviet-Yugoslav Relations and the Hungarian Revolution of 1956." *Cold War International History Project Bulletin* 10 (March 1998): 139–148.

Glaster, Jon. *Jeg anklager Buhl og Alsing Andersen for højforraederi (I accuse Bruhl and Alsing Andersen of treachery).* Self-published, 1954.

Glennon, John P., ed. *Foreign Relations of the United States, 1955–1957.* Vol. XI. *United Nations and General International Matters.* Washington, DC: United States Government Printing Office, 1990.

———. *Foreign Relations of the United States, 1958–1960.* Vol. II. *United Nations and General International Matters.* Washington, DC: United States Government Printing Office, 1990.

Grose, Peter. *The Gentleman Spy: The Life of Allen Dulles.* Boston: Houghton Mifflin, 1994.

Gross, Ernest A. *The United Nations: Structure for Peace.* New York: Harper & Brothers, 1962.

Hajdú, Tibor. *Magyar-jugoszláv kapcsolatok 1956. Dokumentumok.* Budapest: MTA Jelenkorkutató Bizottság, 1995.

Hammarskjold, Dag as Secretary General. Oral History Recollections by Sven Ayman, Andrew W. Cordier, Ernest Gross, C.V. Narasimhan, Oscar Schachter, James Barco, Brian E. Urquhart. New York: Research Office, Columbia University, 1964.

Haraszti-Taylor, Éva. *The Hungarian Revolution of 1956. A Collection of Documents from the British Foreign Office.* Nottingham: Astra, 1995.

Haynes, John E., and Harvey Klehr. *In Denial. Historians, Communism & Espionage.* San Francisco: Encounter Books, 2003.

Hazzard, Shirley. *Defeat of an Ideal. A Study of Self-Destruction of the United Nations.* Boston: Little, Brown, 1973.

Hegedűs, András B., ed. *1956 Kézikönyve I. kötet: Kronológia, II. kötet: Bibliográfia, III. kötet: Megtorlás és emlékezés.* Budapest: 1956-os Intézet, 1996.

Hollós, Ervin. *Kik voltak, mit akartak?* Budapest: Kossuth, 1976.

Hollós, Ervin, and Vera Lajtai. *Drámai napok.* Budapest: Kossuth, 1986.

The Hungarian Situation and the Rule of Law. The Hague: International Commission of Jurists, 1957.

Huss, Pierre J., and George Carpozi. *Red Spies in the UN.* New York: Coward-McCann, 1965.

International Communism (Revolt in the Satellites). Staff Consultations with János Horváth, Sándor Kiss. Washington, DC: Committee of Un-American Activities, House of Representatives, 1957.

Izsák, Lajos, József Szabó, and Róbert Szabó, eds. *1956 plakátjai és röplapjai.* Budapest: Zrínyi Kiadó, 1991.

Joldersma, Jerry. *Ceylon and the United Nations.* PhD Diss., University of Kentucky, 1966.

Kádár Zsuzsa, B. "A szociáldemokraták fürkészése itthon és külföldön." *Rubicon* 13 (2002): 6–7.

Kajári, Erzsébet, ed. *Rendőrségi napi jelentések.* Budapest: Belügyminisztérium- 1956-os Intézet, 1996.

Kalugin, Oleg. *The First Directorate. My 32 Years in Intelligence and Espionage against the West.* New York: St. Martin's, 1994.

Kecskés, Gusztáv D. *Humanitárius akció globális méretekben—A Nemzetközi Vöröskereszt és az 1956-os magyar menekültek.* Budapest: MTA Bölcsészettu- dományi Kutatóközpont, 2020.

———. "Humanitárius segítségnyújtás globális méretekben. A Vöröskereszt Tár- saságok Ligája és az 1956-os magyar menekültek." *Múltunk* 63, no. 4 (2018): 75–119.

———. "Menekültszállítás *és* hidegháború. Az Európai Migráció Kormányközi Bi- zottsága (ICEM) *és* az 1956-os magyar menekültek." *Századok* 152, no. 1 (2018): 145–170.

———. "A NATO *és* az 1956-os magyar forradalom." In *A magyar forradalom eszméi,* edited by Béla Király and Lee W. Congdon, 106–129. Budapest: Atlanti Kutató és Kiadó Társulat-Alapítvány, 2001.

———. "A példa nélküli lehetőség. Bizalmas CIA-cikk az 1956-os magyar menekül- tek titkosszolgálati felhasználásáról." *Betekintő* 9, no. 2 (2016): 1–10. https:// www.betekinto.hu/sites/default/files/betekinto-szamok/2016_2_kecskes.pdf.

———. "Pénzgyűjtés *és* propaganda: Az ENSZ-intézmények információs tevékeny- sége az 1956-os magyar menekültválság megoldása *érdekében.*" *Századok* 146, no. 1 (2012): 109–145.

Kéthly, Anna. *Szabadságot Magyarországnak!* Budapest: Kéthly Anna Alapítvány, 1994.

———. *Száműzve, de le nem győzve. Kéthly Anna emigrációs levelezése, 1957–1976.* Budapest: Országos Széchenyi Könyvtár- Széphalom Könyvműhely, 2007.

Király, Béla. "A Magyar Forradalmi Tanács 1957. Január 5–7-én tartott *ülésének* határozatai." In *'56 Évkönyv III 1994,* edited by János Bak, András B. Hegedűs, György Litván, János M. Rainer, Katalin S. Varga, 35–46. Budapest: 1956-os Intézet, 1994.

———. "A magyar kérdés az ENSZ-ben." In *ENSZ-Akadémia.* Budapest: Magyar ENSZ Társaság, 1993.

———. "Az ENSZ *és* a magyar forradalom." In *A magyar forradalom eszméi,* edited by Béla Király and Lee W. Congdon, 130–144. Budapest: Atlanti Kutató és Kiadó Társulat-Alapítvány, 2001.

———. "Military Aspects." In *The Hungarian Revolution of 1956 in Retrospect,* edited by Béla K. Király and Pál Jónás, 57–71. New York: Columbia University Press, 1978.

Kirov, Alekszandr. "A szovjet hadsereg és a magyar forradalom." In *'56 Évkönyv V, 1996–1997,* edited by András B. Hegedűs, Péter Kende, Gyula Kozák, György Litván, and János M. Rainer, 67–72. Budapest: 1956-os Intézet, 1997.

Kis, János. "Az 1956–57-es restauráció." In *A forradalom előzményei, alakulása és utóélete,* edited by János Decsy, Ferenc Fejtő, István Kemény, Mihály Sozan, 120–154. Az 1986-os budapesti konferencia előadásai. Paris: Magyar Füzetek, 1987.

Kiss, András. "Emigrációba kényszerülve. Kővágó József 1956 utáni szerepvállalásai." *Múltunk* 63, no. 4 (2018): 120–158.

Kiss, József, Zoltán Ripp, and István Vida, eds. *Top Secret—Iratok a magyar-jugoszláv kapcsolatok történetéhez.* Budapest: MTA Jelenkor-kutató Bizottság, 1995.

Kissinger, Henry. *Diplomacy.* New York: Simon & Schuster, 1994.

Kő, András, and Lambert J. Nagy. *Tököl, 1956.* Budapest: Publica, 1992.

Koh, Byung C. *The United Nations Administrative Tribunal.* Baton Rouge: Louisiana State University Press, 1966.

Korányi, Tamás G., ed. *Egy népfelkelés dokumentumai.* Budapest: Tudósítások Kiadó, 1989.

Kőrösi, Zsuzsanna, Éva és Rainer Standeisky, and M. János, eds. "Az olvadás Kelet-Európában a Nyugat szemével. A NATO Nemzetközi Titkárságának belső dokumentuma." Edited and translated by Kecskés, D. Gusztáv. *Az 1956-os Intézet évkönyve.* Budapest: 1956-os Intézet, 2000.

Kecskés, D. Gusztáv. *Az 1956-os Intézet évkönyve.* Budapest: 1956-os Intézet, 2000.

Kovács, Lajos, *Elemzés.* BJI, box 35.

Kramer, Mark. "New Evidence on Soviet Decision-Making and the 1956 Polish and Hungarian Crises." *Cold War International History Project Bulletin* 8 (Winter 1996/1997): 358–384.

———. "The Soviet Union and the 1956 Crises in Hungary and Poland: Reassessments and New Findings." *Journal of Contemporary History* 33, no. 2 (1998): 163–214

———. "A Szovjetunió válasza az 1956-os eseményekre." In *'56 Évkönyv V 1996/1997,* edited by András B. Hegedűs, Péter Kende, Gyula Kozák, György Litván, and János M. Rainer, 73–92. Budapest: 1956-os Intézet, 1997.

Lash, Joseph, P. *Dag Hammarskjold. Custodian of the Bushfire Peace.* New York: Doubleday, 1961.

Lasky, Melvin J., ed. *The Hungarian Revolution.* New York: Praeger, 1957.

Lefebvre, Danis. *A szuezi ügy.* Budapest: Osiris, 1999.

Lidegaard, Bo. *Defiant Diplomacy. Henrik Kauffmann, Denmark and the United States in World War II and the Cold War, 1939–1958.* New York: Peter Lang, 2003.

———. *A legmagasabb ár. Povl Bang-Jensen és az ENSZ. 1955–1959.* Budapest: Magyar Könyvklub, 2000.

Lie, Trygve. *In the Cause of Peace.* New York: Macmillan, 1954.

Lieblich, Eliav. "At Least Something: The UN Special Committee on the Problem of Hungary, 1957–1958." *European Journal of International Law* 30, no. 3 (August 2019): 843–876.

Litván, György. "A Nagy Imre-per politikai háttere." *Világosság* 10 (1992): 743–757.

———. *The Hungarian Revolution. Reform, Revolt and Repression 1953–1963.* London and New York: Longman, 1996.

Lodge, Henry Cabot. *As It Was.* New York: Norton, 1976.

Løkkegaard, Finn. *Det danske Gesandtksab i Washington 1940–1942.* Copenhagen: Gylendal, 1968.

Luard, Evan. *A History of the United Nations.* London: Macmillan, 1989.

Machcewicz, Pawel. "Lengyelország az Egyesült Államok külpolitikájában, 1956." In '56 *Évkönyv V 1996/1997*, edited by András B. Hegedűs, Péter Kende, Gyula Kozák, György Litván, and János M. Rainer, 95–104. Budapest: 1956-os Intézet, 1997.

Manly, Chesly. *The UN Record. Ten Fateful Years for America*. Chicago: Henry Regnery, 1955.

Markó, György. *A pesti Rambo*. Budapest: KKETTK Közalapítvány, 2018.

Marton, Endre. *The Forbidden Sky*. Boston: Little, Brown, 1971.

McCargar, James C. "A Szabad Európa Bizottság és a magyar emigránsok 1956-ban." In '56: *Évkönyv V 1996/1997*, edited by András B. Hegedűs, Péter Kende, Gyula Kozák, György Litván, and János M. Rainer, 272–280. Budapest: 1956-os Intézet, 1997.

Menon, Kumara P. S. *Journey Round the World*. Bombay: Bharatiya Vidya Bhavan, 1965.

Méray, Tibor. *Thirteen Days That Shook the Kremlin*. London: Thames & Hudson, 1959.

Michener, James A. *The Bridge at Andau*. London: Bantam Books, 1957.

Micunovic, Veljko. *Tito követe voltam*. Budapest: Interart, 1990.

Miller, Richard I. *Dag Hammarskjold and Crisis Diplomacy*. New York: Oceana, 1961.

Mindszenty, József. *Memoirs*. New York: Macmillan, 1974.

Mink, András, ed. *Tanúságtevők az ENSZ előtt–1957*. Budapest: Nagy Imre Alapítvány, 2010.

Morris, Robert. *Self Destruct: Dismantling America's Internal Security*. New Rochelle, NY: Arlington House, 1979.

Mosley, Leonard. *Dulles*. New York: Dial Press, 1978.

Munro, Leslie. *United Nations—Hope for a Divided World*. New York: Henry Holt, 1961.

Murányi, Gábor. *Az átkos múlt hetek*. Budapest: Szerzői Kiadás, 1996.

Nagy, András. *A Bang-Jensen ügy – '56 nyugati ellENSZélben*. Budapest: Magvető, 2005.

Nagy, Kázmér. *Australia and the Hungarian Question in the United Nations*. Canberra: FMPress, 1966.

Nagy, László J. "La Hongrie et les relations entre la Tunisie et la France (de 1952 a 1962)." In *La Méditerranée vue de l'Europe Centrale*. Szeged: Université de Szeged Press, 2000.

Olgyay, George. *The Hungarian Revolution and the United Nations. Limitations of Parliamentary Democracy*. PhD diss., University of Notre Dame, 1971.

Pálfy, József, and Kazimir, Károly. *A magyar kérdés*. Dokumentum-dráma két részben. (The play was performed at Thália Színház on February 12, 1970). In *Rivalda 1969–70*. Budapest: Magvető, 1971.

Pálóczi-Horváth, György. *Khruschev*. Boston: Little, Brown, 1960.

Poór, Edit, and Gergő Bendegúz Cseh. "Az ENSZ és Magyarország, 1957." *Társadalmi Szemle* 50, no. 5 (1995): 80–92.

Radványi, János. *Hungary and the Superpowers, the 1956 Revolution and Realpolitik*. Stanford, CA: Hoover Institution Press, Stanford University, 1972.

Rahman, Mohamed Attaur. *Magyarország, 1959–1959. Egy indiai diplomata emlékei*. Budapest: Hamvas Béla Kultúrakutató Intézet, 2006.

Rainer, János M. *Nagy Imre. Politikai életrajz.* Vol. 1. Budapest: Századvég, 1996.
———. *Nagy Imre. Politikai életrajz.* Vol. 2. Budapest: 1956-os Intézet, 1999.
Report of the Special Committee on the Problem of Hungary. General Assembly Official Records: 11th Session Supplement No. 18. (A/3592). New York: United Nations, 1957.
Révész, István Gy. *A béke volt veszélyben.* Budapest: Kossuth, 1957.
Ripp, Zoltán. *Ötvenhat és a hatalom.* Budapest: Napvilág Kiadó, 1997.
Shevchenko, Arkady N. *Breaking with Moscow.* New York: Knopf, 1985.
Sík, Endre. *Bem rakparti évek.* Budapest: Kossuth Kiadó, 1970.
Sólyom-Fekete, William. *The Legal Effects of a Revolution.* Washington, DC: Library of Congress/Law Library, 1982.
Soós, Katalin. *1956 és Ausztria.* Szeged: JATE BTK, 1999.
Standeisky, Éva. *Antiszemitizmusok.* Budapest: Argumentum, 2007.
———. *Az írók és a hatalom.* Budapest: 1956-os Intézet, 1996.
Swartz, Martin B. *A New Look at the 1956 Revolution: Soviet Opportunism, American Acquiescence.* PhD diss., Taft University, 1988.
Sz. Kovács, Éva. "A magyar hírszerzés tevékenysége Ausztriában (1945–1965)." *Betekintő* 2 (2013): 1–15.
Szabó, Miklós. *Foglalkozásuk: emigráns.* Budapest: Kossuth, 1958.
———. *Home Again.* Budapest: Pannonia, 1960.
Szász, Béla. *Volunteers for the Gallows.* London: Chatto & Windus, 1971.
Szenes, Imre. *Az utolsó napjuk.* Budapest: Kossuth, 1957.
Szereda, Vjacseszlav, and János Rainer, eds. *Döntés a Kremlben, 1956—a szovjet pártelnökség vitái Magyarországról.* Budapest: 1956-os Intézet, 1996.
Szereda, Vjacseszlav, and Alekszandr Sztikalin, eds. *Hiányzó lapok 1956 történetéből. Dokumentumok a volt SZK KB levéltárából.* Budapest: Móra Ferenc Ifjúsági Könvkiadó, 1993.
Townley, Ralph. *The United Nations.* New York: Charles Scribner's Sons, 1968.
Urquhart, Brian. *Hammarskjold.* New York: Harper & Row, 1984.
———. *Ralph Bunche. An American Life.* New York: Norton, 1993.
Uruguayan Institute of International Law. *Uruguay and the United Nations.* New York: Carnegie Endowment for International Peace, 1958.
Van den Haag, Ernest, and John P. Conrad. *The U.N.: In or Out?* New York: Plenum, 1987.
Váradi, Natália. "56-os magyar forradalmárok az ungvári börtönben." *Acta Academiae Beregsasiensis* 15, no. 2 (2013): 13–20.
———. "1956-os deportálások a Szovjetunióba." *Acta Academiae Beregsasiensis* 12, no. 2 (2010): 39–55.
Wadsworth, James J. *The Glass House.* New York: Praeger, 1966.
Weiner, Tim. *Legacy of Ashes. The History of the CIA.* New York: Random House, 2008.
Wise, David, and Thomas B. Ross. *The Espionage Establishment.* New York: Random House, 1967.
Yeselson, Abraham, and Anthony Galgione. *A Dangerous Place. The United Nations as a Weapon in World Politics.* New York: Grossmann, 1974.
Zacher, Mark W. *Dag Hammarskjold's United Nations.* New York: Columbia University Press, 1970.

ANDRÁS NAGY is Professor Emeritus in the Faculty of Humanities at the University of Pannonia.